Essays in Economic Sociology

MAX WEBER

Essays in Economic Sociology

EDITED BY RICHARD SWEDBERG

PRINCETON UNIVERSITY PRESS

PRINCETON, NEW JERSEY

Library of Congress Cataloging-in-Publication Data
Weber, Max, 1864–1920.
Essays in economic sociology / Max Weber ; edited by Richard
Swedberg.
p.   cm.
Includes bibliographical references and index.
ISBN 0-691-00906-6 (cloth : alk. paper)
1. Sociology—Economic aspects.   2. Economics—Sociological
aspects.   I. Swedberg, Richard.   II. Title.
HM35.W42   1999
306.3—dc21   99-17413

This book has been composed in New Caledonia

All figures in the Introduction are from Richard Swedberg, *Max Weber and the Idea of
Economic Sociology*, copyright © 1998 by Princeton University Press.

The paper used in this publication meets the minimum requirements of
ANSI/NISO Z39.48-1992 (R1997) (*Permanence of Paper*)
http://pup.princeton.edu

Printed in the United States of America

1 2 3 4 5 6 7 8 9 10

CONTENTS

NOTE ON THE TEXTS
OF THE READINGS

THE READINGS in this anthology have been excerpted from authoritative English translations of the most important works of Max Weber pertaining to economic sociology. The texts are reprinted as they appear in the original English versions, which sometimes vary in spelling, punctuation, and citation conventions. Occasional typographical errors and translation slips have been silently corrected, and cross-references to material that does not appear in the excerpts have been deleted. Although no systematic attempt has been made to standardize varying translations of Weberian terminology, a few especially important terms have been silently made consistent, and of course, the footnotes have been renumbered to run continuously within each excerpt.

Editorial interpolations in the text, mostly of an explanatory nature, are contained in brackets. Those ending in the initials "RS" are the work of the present editor; otherwise, they are the work of the original editors or translators of the English versions. Explanatory footnotes added by the present editor likewise end in "RS," while those inserted by the original editors or translators are identified accordingly. All other footnotes are Weber's.

Essays in Economic Sociology

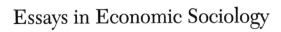

Introduction

RICHARD SWEDBERG

ONE OF THE MOST fascinating and sophisticated attempts to create an economic sociology can be found in the work of Max Weber (1864–1920), and this anthology contains a selection of some of his most important writings on this topic. Though written nearly a century ago, Weber's work has the quality of a true classic, and the reader will find many ideas in his writings on economics that are applicable to current conditions. These include, for example, his discussion of what we now would call social capital, his analysis of which institutions are needed for a well-functioning capitalist economy, and his more general attempt to introduce social structure into economic analysis. Indeed, what basically motivated Weber to pursue economic sociology was the realization, shared by many economists and sociologists today, that it is absolutely imperative to take the social dimension into account when one analyzes economic phenomena.[1]

In the rest of this introduction—which has as its main purpose to present and discuss Weber's contribution to economic sociology—I will first give a brief overview of Weber's life and his work in economics. I will then take a close look at the different stages in Weber's thinking and try especially to show how he attempted to develop his economic sociology as part of a broader vision of economics, what he himself called "social economics," or *Sozialökonomik*. To complete the picture, I will also comment on his contributions to economic theory

---

[1] The major economic sociologists include, for example, Ronald Burt, Nicole Woolsey Biggart, Neil Fligstein, Mark Granovetter, Harrison White, and Viviana Zelizer. For references to their major works, as well as to many other interesting studies, see the overview of economic sociology during the period 1985–95 in Richard Swedberg, "New Economic Sociology: What Has Been Accomplished, What Is Ahead?" *Acta Sociologica* 40 (1997): 161–82. For the literature on separate topics in economic sociology, see especially Neil Smelser and Richard Swedberg, eds., *The Handbook of Economic Sociology* (Princeton, N.J.: Princeton University Press, and New York: Russell Sage Foundation, 1994). For general overviews of new institutional economics, see Thráinn Eggertsson, *Economic Behavior and Organizations* (Cambridge: Cambridge University Press, 1990); Eirik G. Furubotn and Rudolf Richter, eds., *The New Institutional Economics* (Tübingen: J. C. B. Mohr, 1991); Terry Moe, "The New Economics of Organization," *American Journal of Political Science* 28 (1984): 739–77; and Louis Putterman, "The Economics of the Firm: Overview," pp. 1–29 in Putterman, ed., *The Economic Nature of the Firm* (New York: Cambridge University Press, 1986). For a critique of new institutional economics from a sociological viewpoint, see Mark Granovetter, "Economic Action and Social Structure: The Problem of Embeddedness," *American Journal of Sociology* 91 (1985): 481–510; and Anthony Oberschall and Eric Leifer, "Efficiency and Social Institutions: Uses and Misuses of Economic Reasoning in Sociology," *Annual Review of Sociology* 12 (1986): 233–53. See also in this context Robert Bates, "Contra Contractarianism: Some Reflections on the New Institutionalism," *Politics and Society* 16 (1988): 387–401; and Steven N. S. Cheung, "On the New Institutional Economics (Comments by Gary Becker and R. H. Coase)," pp. 48–75 in Lars Werin and Hans Wijkander, eds., *Contract Economics* (Cambridge: Blackwell, 1992).

and economic history as well as to economic sociology. Weber, it may be added, was interested in all of these areas and often worked in them simultaneously. These three perspectives are clearly linked in his writings—indeed, this is one of the reasons for the richness of Weber's work—but it is also helpful to make distinctions between them. The last and final section of the introduction contains a reader's guide to the texts included in this volume.

WEBER'S LIFE AND HIS WORK IN ECONOMICS

Max Weber was born on April 21, 1864, in Erfurt, Germany, and both of his parents belonged to the bourgeoisie.[2] His father, also Max Weber, was a magistrate and would later become a deputy in the German parliament, the Reichstag, which led the family to move to Berlin in 1869. Weber's mother, Helene Fallenstein-Weber, was intensely religious and came from a wealthy Huguenot background. The two parents were opposite characters: the father was nonreligious, somewhat superficial, and in general a secular kind of person; the mother, on the other hand, detested frivolity and devoted herself wholeheartedly to her family, her religious duties, and to helping the poor.

As a boy, Weber was precocious in many ways. He read avidly in literature, history, and philosophy at an age when most children would rather be playing. In school, for example, while pretending to follow what the teacher said, he secretly read Goethe's collected works in forty volumes. And in preparation for his confirmation, he taught himself Hebrew in order to read the Old Testament in the original. He also liked to present his parents with historical essays as gifts: one that he gave them when he was fifteen years old was entitled "Observations on the Ethnic Character, Development, and History of the Indo-European Nations." The essay argued, among other things, that nations follow certain historical laws, which cannot be abandoned at will. Early on Weber also began to take notes on his reading and to accumulate knowledge in a truly encyclopaedic manner.

In 1882 Weber began his university studies, first in Heidelberg, and later also in Göttingen, Strasbourg, and Berlin. The topic he chose was law, even though he also read widely in philosophy, religion, and history. Like all law students, Weber was required to do some minor work in economics, a subject in which he at first does not seem to have been very interested. His teacher was Karl Knies (1821–1898), one of the founders of the historical school of economics, and Weber initially found his lectures rather boring. Soon, however, he warmed to the subject and began to enjoy Knies's lectures, as well as works in economics more generally. But this was the only course in economics that Weber took during his university years.

[2] For this brief introduction on Weber's life, I have mainly relied on the biography by his wife and the helpful volume by Dirk Käsler. See Marianne Weber, *Max Weber: A Biography* (New York: John Wiley & Sons, 1975); and Dirk Käsler, *Max Weber: An Introduction to His Life and Work* (Cambridge: Polity Press, 1988).

Law remained the focus of his studies, and his first dissertation was in legal history. Weber chose to examine medieval trading corporations, and his adviser was Levin Goldschmidt, the foremost expert in commercial law in Germany and probably also in the world. In 1891 Weber presented his dissertation, which was part of a larger work entitled *On the History of Trading Companies in the Middle Ages, According to Southern European Sources.*[3] What especially interested Weber about these trading companies was the role they had played in the evolution of the modern corporation. More precisely, what Weber studied—drawing on medieval legal sources—was the emerging separation between the family and the economic enterprise, and the role that the notion of limited liability played in this. On a more general level, one can say that Weber had focused on one aspect of the rise of Western capitalism. This is also true for his second dissertation (a necessary qualification in Germany for teaching at the university level), *Roman Agrarian History and Its Importance to Public and Civil Law.*[4] The topic this time was the emergence of private property in land in Rome, and as with the first dissertation, the scholarship was of high quality. In 1892 Weber was judged qualified to teach Roman and commercial law at the university level.

Even though Weber had worked very hard and methodically on his studies in law, by the time he had finished his dissertations and passed his examinations, he was not sure what profession to choose. He taught law for a while at the University of Berlin, as a replacement for Levin Goldschmidt who had fallen ill. While he was a student he had also become involved in a political organization that carried out social science research and to which many prominent economists belonged, the *Verein für Sozialpolitik* (Association for Social Policy). In 1892 Weber published a study, commissioned by the *Verein,* of *The Conditions of the Agricultural Workers in the Areas East of the River Elbe,* which received much praise from economists and agrarian historians.

With this study, Weber showed that he could produce works in economics (as the discipline was conceived in Germany at the time), and in 1893 he received a call from the University of Freiburg to become a professor of economics (*Nationalökonomie und Finanzwissenschaft*). Weber accepted, even though he had not been trained as an economist. One reason for this, Marianne Weber (his wife and biographer) tells us, was that in Weber's view,

As a science, economics was still elastic and "young" in comparison with law. Besides, it was on the borderline of a number of scholarly fields: it led directly to the history of culture and the history of ideas as well as to philosophical problems. Finally, it was

---

[3] The title of the dissertation itself (Part III of the larger work) was "The Principle of Joint Liability and the Separate Fund in Business Partnerships: Their Development out of the Household and Trade Communities in the Italian Cities." See Weber, "Zur Geschichte der Handelsgesellschaften im Mittelalter," pp. 312–443 in *Gesammelte Aufsätze zur Sozial- und Wirtschaftsgeschichte* (Tübingen: J. C. B. Mohr, 1988).

[4] Max Weber, *Die römische Agrargeschichte in ihrer Bedeutung für das Staats- und Privatrecht (1891), Max Weber Gesamtausgabe I/2* (Tübingen: J. C. B. Mohr, 1986).

more fruitful for a political and sociopolitical orientation than the mere formal problems of legal thought.[5]

At Freiburg Weber worked even harder than usual since he knew so little economics.[6] The first course that he took in economic theory, he would later jokingly tell his friends, was the one that he himself gave in Freiburg. Weber delivered a famous inaugural lecture in May 1895 and was extremely busy as a teacher, a public speaker, and a researcher. He wrote an educational pamphlet for workers, *The Stock Exchange* (1894–96), as part of the debate on this subject, which was very lively in Germany at the time. He also continued to do work on the agricultural workers, this time as part of his activities on behalf of a reform-oriented Protestant organization. The new study, like the first one, was based on a huge survey; and it is clear that Weber had by now developed good quantitative research skills.[7]

In 1896 Weber was appointed professor of economics (*Nationalökonomie und Finanzwissenschaft*) in Heidelberg, to replace his old teacher Karl Knies. This was a step up in the academic world since Knies was a famous and respected economist in Germany. Weber continued to work punishingly hard, for one thing to improve the teaching of economics, which the aged Knies had let slip. He also lectured widely and conducted all kinds of research, just as he had done in Freiburg.

If we stop for a moment and contemplate Weber in the mid-1890s, it is clear that he was the picture of success. He was only in his early thirties but had already written several impressive works; he held a prestigious teaching position; and he was highly respected in academic circles. His future, in brief, looked very bright. But there was more to Weber's life than this, and in 1898 he suffered a severe nervous breakdown. For several years, he was fully or partially incapacitated and could not adequately perform even the most rudimentary academic duties. Sometimes Weber felt better, but then there was another relapse, and he finally felt compelled to resign from his position in Heidelberg. It was not until 1903 that he could resume some of his scholarly activities, notably writing. Since both Weber and his wife had some money of their own, it was possible for Weber to live as a private scholar. It was not until 1918 that he began teaching again, first in Vienna and later in Munich.

---

[5] Weber, *Max Weber*, p. 200. The translation has been altered by myself. The areas to which economics led directly, according to Weber, were "Kultur- und Ideengeschichte [und] philosophische Probleme."

[6] Mises's caustic comment on Weber's appointment to a chair in economics without any real background in the field is worth citing: "He was appointed professor of economics without having dealt with this science before, which was a customary procedure at the time." See Ludwig von Mises, *A Critique of Interventionism* (1929) (New Rochelle: Arlington House, 1977), p. 103.

[7] The reason for emphasizing this is that Weber is often perceived as only having done qualitative, historical work. For Weber as a sophisticated empirical sociologist, see especially Paul Lazarsfeld and Anthony Oberschall, "Max Weber and Empirical Social Research," *American Sociological Review* 30 (1965): 185–99; Anthony Oberschall, *Empirical Social Research in Germany 1848–1914* (New York: Basic Books, 1965), pp. 111–36; and Gert Schmidt, "Max Webers Beitrag zur empirischen Industrieforschung," *Kölner Zeitschrift für Soziologie und Sozialpsychologie* 32 (1980): 76–92.

The reasons for Weber's breakdown have been much discussed. It is clear that he had worked excessively hard, possibly to exhaustion, at Freiburg and Heidelberg. Economics was not, after all, a topic that he knew when he was appointed to a professorship in this subject. It has also been speculated that there might have been a propensity to nervous illness in the Weber family. An important and possibly decisive event was a terrible quarrel that Weber had with his father in July 1897. Weber had for a long time resented the way that his father treated his mother, and he now told him so in no uncertain terms. The result was a serious split between Weber and his father—who then died a few weeks later, before any reconciliation had taken place. Weber, who earlier had been able to rely on his seemingly inexhaustible energy and on his capacity to rise to any occasion, be it an important debate with his academic peers or hours of public lecturing, now began to suffer from insomnia and nervous ailments of various kinds. He could not lecture in public, nor carry out his scholarly work; at best he could read literature in other fields than economics. Weber was tormented as well as humiliated by his illness. One of the worst things, he said, was the feeling that everybody thought he should be able to overcome it by a sheer act of will.

In 1903 Weber started to improve so much that he could work a few hours a day, and the next year he and his wife made a trip to the United States. Weber was highly invigorated by this visit and received many new ideas for his scholarship. It was also during the next few years that Weber produced his first truly great works. These include a series of brilliant methodological writings, some of which are available in English as *The Methodology of the Social Sciences,* and which mainly deal with economics and social science in general.[8] One of the most important of these, from the viewpoint of economics, is an essay of 1908 on marginal utility theory. Another is "'Objectivity' in Social Science and Social Policy" (1904), a programmatic article for a social science journal of which Weber was one of the editors. The journal, the *Archiv für Sozialwissenschaft und Sozialpolitik,* was to be interdisciplinary in nature, and to focus on "the general cultural significance of capitalist development."[9] In 1904 and 1905 Weber published two articles in the *Archiv* that would eventually make him famous in the scholarly world: *The Protestant Ethic and the Spirit of Capitalism* (the two articles were revised in 1920 and translated into English by Talcott Parsons in 1930). A few years later Weber conducted research on workers and their productivity at a textile factory belonging to one of his relatives. And in 1909 he published a book-length study, *The Agrarian Sociology of Ancient Civilizations,* which can be characterized as a social and economic history of antiquity.

Around the time when Weber was working on his history of antiquity, he also helped to found the *Deutsche Gesellschaft für Soziologie* (German Society for Sociology), and it seems that it was around this point in time that Weber decided to get serious about sociology and try to set it on a sound scientific foundation.

---

[8] Max Weber, *The Methodology of the Social Sciences* (New York: The Free Press, 1949).

[9] Edgar Jaffé, Werner Sombart, and Max Weber, "Geleitwort," *Archiv für Sozialwissenschaft und Sozialpolitik* 19 (1904): v. Emphasis in the original.

"At the turn of the century, sociology meant for Weber an inflated approach, vainly claiming the status of a master science," Guenther Roth has noted, "yet by 1910 Weber accepted the term 'sociology' for his interpretive study of social action as well as his comparative approach."[10] Around this time Weber also laid the theoretical foundation for his sociology in his article "Some Categories of Interpretive Sociology" (1913).[11] It was here, for the first time, that Weber presented a program for what a rigorous sociology should be like. Sociology, he suggested, should be a science of *social action*. By this latter term he meant actions by individuals which are invested with meaning and which are oriented to the behavior of others.

In 1908 Weber accepted an offer to edit a handbook in economics, which the publisher hoped would replace Gustav Schönberg's well-known but outdated *Handbuch der politischen Oekonomie (Handbook of Political Economy)* (1st ed. 1882; 4th ed. 1896–98). The project entailed a huge investment of work from Weber's side, and he hesitated for a long time before he accepted. Once Weber had said yes, however, he threw himself wholeheartedly into the work, and the giant book that is today known as *Economy and Society* constitutes Weber's own contribution to the handbook. By the time of his death in 1920 Weber had completed only Part I of *Economy and Society*, consisting of four chapters including a key text on economic sociology, "Sociological Categories of Economic Action" (chapter 2). (The remaining text in the English version of *Economy and Society* consists mainly of unrevised material.)

The handbook of economics, which began to be published in 1914 under the title *Grundriss der Sozialökonomik (Outline of Social Economics)*, took up much of Weber's energy in the 1910s. But he was also engaged in a series of other enterprises, and in 1911 he started to work on another giant project, entitled *The Economic Ethics of the World Religions*. The main idea was to further explore the kind of problem he had started to investigate a few years earlier in *The Protestant Ethic*, namely how religion and economic life affect each other, with special emphasis on economic rationality. Weber completed three volumes before his death: *The Religion of China* (1915, revised 1920), *The Religion of India* (1916–17), and *Ancient Judaism* (1917–20). Several other volumes were planned but never written.[12]

During the periods when Weber felt better he also led an active social life, meeting and discussing with a wide variety of academics and intellectuals.

---

[10] Guenther Roth, "'Value-Neutrality' in Germany and the United States," p. 37 in Reinhard Bendix and Guenther Roth, *Scholarship and Partisanship: Essays on Max Weber* (Berkeley: University of California Press, 1971).

[11] Max Weber, "Some Categories of Interpretive Sociology," trans. Edith Graber, *Sociological Quarterly* 22 (Spring 1981): 151–80. An excerpt from this essay can be found in Max Weber, *Economy and Society: An Outline of Interpretive Sociology*, trans. Guenther Roth and Claus Wittich, 2 vols. (Berkeley: University of California Press, 1978); see "Types of Social Action and Groups," pp. 1375–80.

[12] For the full project, see Weber's description of 1919 as reproduced in Wolfgang Schluchter, *Rationalism, Religion, and Domination: A Weberian Perspective* (Berkeley: University of California Press, 1989), p. 425.

Among his closest friends were Ernst Troeltsch (religion), Robert Michels (political science) and Georg Jellinek (law). Weber also knew a number of economists, including Werner Sombart and Joseph Schumpeter, but was on less intimate terms with them; Gustav von Schmoller was only a distant acquaintance, as was Friedrich von Wieser. Weber took an active part in politics, especially during World War I and the years immediately afterward. At one point he nearly got appointed envoy of the new German republic to Vienna, and later on he almost became secretary of state for the interior. In 1919 he also took part in the German delegation to Versailles as an expert adviser.

Weber was intensely patriotic, and this sentiment is present in many of his political writings. But he was also a first-class political theorist and has left behind a number of important writings on the nature of the modern state, democracy, and German political life in general.[13] Among his most penetrating works in this respect are "Parliament and Government in A Reconstructed Germany," which appeared in a series of articles in the *Frankfurter Zeitung* in 1917, and "Politics as a Vocation," first presented as a lecture in 1919. Some interesting political reflections can also be found in Weber's inaugural lecture at Freiburg.

World War I led to a change in financial circumstances for Weber and his wife, and in 1918 he accepted a position in economics at the University of Vienna, where he replaced Eugen von Philippovich. His lectures were very popular and he became friends with Ludwig von Mises, among others. Weber, however, wanted to be in Germany and not in Austria, and in 1919 he was appointed to Lujo Brentano's chair at the University of Munich. In Munich Weber seems to have worked nearly as hard as in the days of his youth, even though he was now able to choose his own courses. His chair was formally in "social science, economic history, and economics" (*Gesellschaftswissenschaft, Wirtschaftsgeschichte und Nationalökonomie*), eliminating finance, in which Weber was no longer interested: Brentano's chair had been in *Nationalökonomie, Finanzwissenschaft und Wirtschaftsgeschichte*. One of the lecture series that he gave, while in Munich, is especially famous since it was later published as a book, under the title *General Economic History*.[14] Teaching and writing at full speed, Weber caught pneumonia in the early summer of 1920. On June 14, 1920, he died, only fifty-six years old. Among his last words, according to his wife, were: "The true is the truth" ("Das Wahre ist die Wahrheit").[15]

After this brief account of Weber's life, it is necessary to take a look at his contribution to economics in order to show how he came to develop his economic sociology. It is important to stress at the outset that Germany had developed its own version of economics in the nineteenth century, and that Weber's work in this area grew out of this tradition but also constituted a reaction against it.[16]

---

[13] See especially Max Weber, *Political Writings* (Cambridge: Cambridge University Press, 1994).

[14] Max Weber, *General Economic History* (New Brunswick, N.J.: Transaction Books, 1981).

[15] Weber, *Max Weber,* p. 698.

[16] For a good introduction to nineteenth-century German economics, see Harald Winkel, *Die deutsche Nationalökonomie im 19. Jahrhundert* (Darmstadt: Wissenschaftliche Buchgesellschaft, 1977). See also Keith Tribe's fine study, *Governing the Economy: The Reformation of German Economic Discourse 1750–1840* (Cambridge: Cambridge University Press, 1988).

Even though Adam Smith and the British economists had quickly been translated into German, from the mid-nineteenth century onward German economics was dominated by a very different approach, known as the historical school. This type of economics was part of a larger intellectual movement, historicism, which was to influence German culture very deeply.[17] In 1843 Wilhelm Roscher published what is usually seen as the manifesto of the historical school of economics, a short work entitled *Outline of Lectures on Political Economy Using the Historical Method*.[18] Roscher attacked the view that economics was only about egoism and making profits, and he recommended, in its stead, a type of historical-empirical economics. "Our aim," he stated, "is purely to describe man's economic nature and wants"; and economics was defined as "the doctrine of the laws of a national economy."[19] With the help of Bruno Hildebrand and Karl Knies the historical approach grew into a distinct type of economics, and by the second half of the nineteenth century it dominated the field in Germany.

By the time that Weber began his university studies in the early 1880s, a new generation of historical economists had grown up, led by Gustav von Schmoller (1838–1917). This generation was much more advanced in doing historical research than the founders had been. Its members also insisted that economics was an ethical discipline, and in particular that it should assist the young German state in its economic and social policy. Furthermore, they took a militant stance against the analytical type of economics that in the meantime had developed outside of Germany, not only in England but also in the Austro–Hungarian Empire, through the work of Carl Menger. In 1883–84—in other words during Weber's second and third years as a university student—the famous "Battle of Methods" (*Methodenstreit*) broke out between Menger and Schmoller, and quickly spread throughout German-speaking Europe as well as to many other countries, including England and the United States. At the beginning of this acrimonious academic dispute, which was set off by a dismissive review by Schmoller of one of Menger's books, the issue was whether analytical economic theory or a historical approach should constitute the center of economics. Soon, however, the debate turned into a heated quarral, and the question now became whether economics as a whole should be analytical or historical in character. Economics had split into "*two* sciences," as Weber put it in 1904.[20]

Much of Weber's work in economics can be seen as an attempt to mediate be-

[17] See, e.g., Georg G. Iggers, *The German Conception of History: The National Tradition of Historical Thought from Herder to the Present* (Middletown, Conn.: Wesleyan University Press, 1983), and "Historicism: The History and Meaning of the Term," *Journal of the History of Ideas* 56 (1995): 129–52.

[18] Wilhelm Roscher, *Grundriss zu Vorlesungen über die Staatswirtschaft: Nach geschichtlicher Methode* (Göttingen: Verlag der Dieterischen Buchhandlung, 1843). The preface has been translated into English by W. J. Ashley as "Roscher's Programme of 1843," *Quarterly Journal of Economics* 9 (1894–95): 99–105.

[19] Wilhelm Roscher, *Principles of Political Economy*, vol. 1 (New York: Henry Holt & Co., 1878), p. 111; *Grundriss*, pp. iv, 3.

[20] Weber, "'Objectivity' in Social Science and Social Policy," p. 63 in *The Methodology of the Social Sciences*. Emphasis in the original. Weber here cites a Viennese economist.

tween the positions associated with Menger and Schmoller in the Battle of Methods. Weber also reacted very strongly against the argument of the historical school that economics should be an ethical science, and he played an active role in the attempts to refute it. Weber's activities on this score were part of a debate known as the "Battle of Value Judgments" (*Werturteilsstreit*). Weber's famous doctrine of objectivity did not exclusively grow out of his attempt to distance himself from Schmoller et al., but their works definitely constituted one of his major targets.

Weber gradually developed his own vision of what economics should be like. His preferred term for this type of economics was *Sozialökonomik* or "social economics" rather than the ones that were popular around the turn of the century in Germany, such as *Volkswirtschaftslehre* and "*Nationalökonomie*."[21] The term "social economics" is usually traced back to the 1820s, more precisely to a work dating from 1828 by Jean-Baptiste Say in which the expression *économie sociale* is used, and from there it soon entered the terminology of European economics.[22] John Stuart Mill, for example, discussed Say's term (which he translated as "social economy") in one of his essays of the 1830s.[23] Some well-known economists also adopted it for their own purposes, such as Alfred Marshall and Adolph Wagner.[24] The term, however, never really caught on, and after having reached a peak of popularity between 1890 and 1920, it vanished from the discourse of economics in most countries.

To those who used it, however, the term "social economics" had the virtue of clearly indicating that economics was a *social* science and that economic phenomena were *social* phenomena. Like most terms, however, "social economics" was used in a variety of meanings,[25] and Weber, as always, had his own definition. More precisely, to Weber *Sozialökonomik* meant primarily two things: (1) that economics should be broad in scope and include a historical as well as a social dimension; and (2) that economics should draw on several distinct social sci-

---

[21] *Sozialökonomik* is also known as *Sozialökonomie;* and it can be translated as "social economy" or "social economics." In translating it as the latter, I am following Schumpeter. See Joseph A. Schumpeter, *History of Economic Analysis* (London: George Allen & Unwin, 1954), p. 21.

[22] The history of the term "social economics" is traced in the author's *Max Weber and the Idea of Economic Sociology* (Princeton, N.J.: Princeton University Press, 1998), pp. 177–80.

[23] John Stuart Mill, "On the Definition of Political Economy; and on the Method of Investigation Proper to It (1838)," p. 136 in *Essays on Some Unsettled Questions of Political Economy* (London: John W. Parker, 1844).

[24] Alfred Marshall, who helped to replace "political economy" with "economics" through his work *Principles of Economics*, used the term "social economics" as synonymous with "economics" in the 1890s. More precisely, he did so in the third (1895) and fourth (1898) editions of *Principles of Economics*, but not in the fifth edition (1907). See Alfred Marshall, *Principles of Economics*, 2 vols. (London: Macmillan, 1961), 1:43, 2:159. For Adolph Wagner, see, e.g., *Theoretische Sozialökonomik oder allgemeine und theoretische Volkswirtschaftslehre* (Leipzig: C. F. Winter'sche Verlagshandlung, 1907).

[25] To Walras (and following him, Knut Wicksell), for example, "économie sociale" meant "the science of distribution and social wealth." See Léon Walras, *Elements of Pure Economics or the Theory of Social Wealth* (1874) (London: George Allen and Unwin, 1954), p. 79, and Knut Wicksell, *Föreläsningar i nationalekonomi*, vol. 1 (1901; repr. Lund: Gleerups, 1966), p. 79.

ence disciplines in its analyses. Not only economic theory should be used in economic analysis, Weber argued, but—depending on the problem at hand—also economic history and what he called "economic sociology" (*Wirtschaftssoziologie*). The main idea, in other words, was not to produce a new interdisciplinary type of economics but to use several different disciplines in analyzing economic phenomena.

Weber's ideas on economic sociology undoubtedly represent his most innovative contribution to economics, but he also did some very important work in economic history. He had less talent for economic theory, even though it is of interest to follow his development in this field as well. Weber's writings on economics, broadly conceived, include several monographs as well as a considerable number of articles, and it is a challenging task to present all of this material in a few pages. I will nonetheless try to do so, and especially to highlight the theme of social economics or *Sozialökonomik* in Weber's work. I will show how Weber's vision of a broad economics slowly emerged, and also discuss his contributions to each of the three constitutive fields of *Sozialökonomik*: economic theory, economic history, and economic sociology. Special attention will naturally be paid to Weber's view of economic sociology.

THE DEVELOPMENT OF WEBER'S WORK IN ECONOMICS: ECONOMIC THEORY, ECONOMIC HISTORY, AND ECONOMIC SOCIOLOGY

Early Works (late 1880s to late 1890s)

The first period in Weber's work in economics begins in the late 1880s, when his first dissertation was published, and ends in the late 1890s, when he fell ill and had to stop teaching and writing. These ten years were very productive for Weber, so far as economics was concerned, and resulted in several books as well as a number of minor writings. He was also very active as a lecturer in economics and in this role produced two works intended for students, which were unpublished at the time: a guide to the literature of economics, and lecture notes introducing basic economic concepts. Together, these works are today known as the *Outline of Lectures in General ("Theoretical") Economics (1898)*.[26] As to Weber's published works, there are first of all his two dissertations in legal history and the study for the *Verein für Sozialpolitik* on the agricultural workers. He also wrote a number of important articles on economic history, some of which are still of general interest. There is, for example, a famous article on the decline of Rome and another on the social and economic history of antiquity (which

---

[26] Max Weber, *Grundriss zu den Vorlesungen über allgemeine ("theoretische") Nationalökonomie (1898)* (Tübingen: J. C. B. Mohr, 1990). The reading guide and the notes on economic concepts were originally printed separately and only put together in 1990 when they were officially published. The title that was given to the two items in 1990 was that of the reading guide, while the title of the notes is *Erstes Buch: Die begrifflichen Grundlagen der Volkswirtschaftslehre*.

Weber turned into a book-length study a decade later).[27] The most outstanding of Weber's articles from these years, however, is probably his inaugural lecture as professor of economics at Freiburg University, "The National State and Economic Policy."

Was it already during this first period, when Weber was in his mid-twenties and mid-thirties, that he got the idea of *Sozialökonomik?* According to Schumpeter, all great discoveries are made between twenty and thirty years of age or during "the decade of sacred fertility." This, however, does not seem to have been the case with Weber, at least when it comes to his theory of social economics. If we start with the term itself, it is clear that it can be found in many of the works that Weber had studied in the 1880s and later also lectured from, such as those of Carl Menger (1883) or Karl Knies (1883).[28] There is also the fact that Weber, while in Heidelberg, had participated in, and perhaps even initiated, an academic association, the *Sozialökonomische Vereinigung* (Social Economic Association), which had as its purpose to bring together students from noneconomic fields with teachers of economics. Nonetheless, if we look at Weber's *Outline* of 1898, we find that he did not use the term *Sozialökonomik* but preferred more conventional German terms for economics, such as *Volkswirtschaftslehre* and *Nationalökonomie.*

But even if Weber did not use the term *Sozialökonomik,* how about the *concept* of social economics—especially the idea that economics is a very broad subject and needs to draw on several distinct social sciences, such as economic theory, economic history, and economic sociology? That Weber already in the 1890s saw economics as encompassing a wide area is clear, for example, from his earlier cited statement that he chose to accept the offer from the University of Freiburg to become an economist because economics appeared to him, in contrast to law, as a young and flexible science, with direct links to philosophy, the history of ideas, and the history of culture. At one point in his study of agricultural workers for the *Verein für Sozialpolitik* Weber also points out that "a purely economic standpoint" is "unrealistic" and should be complemented by other approaches.[29] Most importantly, however, Weber's guide to economics of 1898 allows us to state with confidence that Weber already in the early part of his career viewed economics as being a very broad field, and believed that the economist must draw not only on economic theory but also on economic history, depending on the problem at hand. According to the same source, the student of economics

[27] Max Weber, "The Social Causes of the Decay of Ancient Civilization," *Journal of General Education* 5 (1949–51): 75–88 (reproduced in this volume as reading 10); *The Agrarian Sociology of Ancient Civilizations* (London: New Left Books, 1976). The latter work is a much-expanded version of two articles of 1897 and 1898.

[28] See, e.g., Carl Menger, *Untersuchungen über die Methode der Socialwissenschaften und der politischen Oekonomie* (Leipzig: Duncker & Humblot, 1883), p. 251 ("sociale Oekonomie," with citation of Say); Karl Knies, *Die politische Oekonomie vom geschichtlichen Standpunkte* (1883) (Leipzig: Hans Buske, 1930), p. 3 ("sociale Oekonomie").

[29] Max Weber, *Die Lage der Landarbeiter im ostelbischen Deutschland* (1892), *Max Weber Gesamtausgabe* I/3 (Tübingen: J. C. B. Mohr, 1984), pp. 920–21.

should also use sociology to understand "the relationship of the economy to other cultural phenomena, especially to law and the state."[30] The idea of applying sociology to economic phenomena themselves—that is, economic sociology in a more strict sense—is, however, absent at this point from Weber's thought; and so is his notion that what is distinctive about sociology is the idea of *social action*, that is, action to which a meaning is attached and which is oriented to the behavior of others.

Regarding Weber's contribution to economic theory from the late 1880s to the late 1890s, it should first of all be noted that he would never again be so active as a teacher of economics. From 1894 to the time he stopped teaching at Heidelberg Weber taught about twenty-five courses and seminars in economics.[31] Still—and this is worth noting—he did not produce one single article in economic theory during these years. If we want to get a sense for how Weber viewed economic theory during this period we again have to look at his 1898 *Outline*. From the guide to economic literature, which lists close to six hundred works, it is clear that Weber was familiar with both the historical tradition (e.g., Knies, Roscher, and Schmoller) as well as the analytical tradition (e.g., Menger, Marshall, and Walras). Likewise, the lecture notes, which introduce the reader to such basic concepts as "goods," "production," and "income," show that Weber saw both the historical and the analytical traditions essential for an understanding of economic phenomena. At one point, for example, Weber says that the historical tradition can help to explain the evolution of economic institutions. At another, however, he refers approvingly to the notion of *homo economicus* and argues that under certain circumstances it is helpful to make the assumptions

---

[30] Weber, *Grundriss zu den Vorlesungen über allgemeine ("theoretische") Nationalökonomie (1898)*, p. 10. By "cultural phenomena" (*Kulturerscheinungen*) Weber roughly means what we today would call social phenomena.

[31] Weber taught the following courses and seminars while at Freiburg: winter semester, 1894–95: "General Theoretical Economics" and "Finance"; summer semester, 1895: "Practical Economics (Economic Policy)", "The German Labor Question in the City and in the Countryside" and a seminar or a course in "Agrarian Policy"; winter semester, 1895–96: "General Theoretical Economics" and "Money, Banking, and the Stock Market"; summer semester, 1896: "General Theoretical Economics" and "History of Economics"; winter semester, 1896–97: "Finance" and "The Stock Market and Its Legal Regulation." Together with his colleague Schulze-Gaevernitz Weber also co-taught each term a "cameralistic seminar" (on state economic policy). At the University of Heidelberg Weber taught the following courses: summer semester, 1897: "General ('Theoretical') Economics" and "Seminar in Economics"; winter semester, 1897–98: "Practical Economics: Trade Policy, Industrial Policy, and Infrastructure Policy" and "Agrarian Policy"; summer semester, 1898: "General ('Theoretical') Economics, excluding History of Economics" and "The Social Question and the Labor Movement"; winter semester, 1898–99: "Seminar in Economics" and "Practical Economics (excluding Money and Banking), General Part: Population Policy, Trade Policy, Industrial Policy, Infrastructure Policy, and Agrarian Policy"; and winter semester, 1899–1900: "Agrarian Policy" (not completed). See Wolfgang Mommsen and Rita Aldenhoff, "Einleitung," pp. 41–42 in *Landarbeiterfrage, Nationalstaat und Volkswirtschaftspolitik, Max Weber Gesamtausgabe I/4* (Tübingen: J. C. B. Mohr, 1993). For some additional information, see also Keith Tribe, *Strategies of Economic Order: German Economic Discourse, 1750–1950* (Cambridge: Cambridge University Press, 1995), pp. 83–86.

that the economic actor has complete knowledge, is totally rational, and has only economic goals.[32]

The *Outline* furthermore gives the impression that Weber at times was trying to unite as well as to mediate between the perspectives of historical and analytical economics. Thus, in Weber's discussion of price formation, he starts out with the idea of marginal utility but then argues that when you go from "the theoretical price" to "the empirical price," you have to take a number of other factors into account. These latter include imperfections in the market, the historical formation of needs, and the "struggle" (*Kampf*) among economic actors.[33] In the *Outline* Weber also uses many of the concepts that were later to become central to his economic sociology of 1919–1920, such as "economic action" (*Wirtschaften*), "power of control and disposal" (*Verfügungsgewalt*), and "opportunity" (*Chance*). At this stage, however, these concepts were not very much developed; they were also defined exclusively in economic terms, as opposed to later, when Weber transformed them into sociological concepts.[34]

Weber's work in economic history during the period from the late 1880s to the late 1890s was quite extensive. There are, first of all, his two dissertations which both draw on legal and economic history. To the earlier mentioned articles on antiquity should also be added a lecture series that Weber gave in 1897 in Mannheim, entitled "The Course of Economic Development."[35] What is most remarkable about this course—which is structured rather like the *General Economic History* (1919–20)—is that it testifies to Weber's ambition to cover the economic evolution of humanity in a truly encyclopedic manner. But even if Weber was extremely knowledgeable in economic history already in his early thirties, he also had his favorite topics, and this is as evident from the lecture series in Mannheim as it is from his two dissertations. What especially fascinated

---

[32] Weber, *Grundriss zu den Vorlesungen über allgemeine ("theoretische") Nationalökonomie (1898)*, p. 30. See in this context also Joseph Persky, "Perspectives: The Ethology of *Homo Economicus*," *Journal of Economic Perspectives* 9 (1995): 221–31.

[33] Weber, following the Austrian economists, thought that the price of the means of production could be determined and derived from consumer needs ("goods of higher order," in Menger's terminology). See Weber, *Grundriss zu den Vorlesungen über allgemeine ("theoretische") Nationalökonomie (1898)*, pp. 47, 51–53. For Austrian price theory, see, e.g., Schumpeter, *History of Economic Analysis*, pp. 909–24.

[34] Weber defined "economic action" (*Wirtschaften*) in the following manner: "By 'economic action' we understand a specific kind of *external and purposive aspiration*—i.e., conscious, well-planned behavior with respect to nature and humans—that is *compelled* by those needs, which require *external means* for their satisfaction, regardless of whether they are 'material' or 'ideal' in kind, and which serve the purpose of *providing for the future*." Weber, *Grundriss zu den Vorlesungen über allgemeine ("theoretische") Nationalökonomie (1898)*, p. 29.

[35] No manuscript record of this lecture series survives, and our knowledge of it comes from newspaper reports. The lectures were entitled "The Emergence of Private Property and the Agrarian Foundation of the European Economy," "Feudalism and the City Economy in the Middle Ages," "The Development of the National Economy and the Mercantilist System," and "The Social Situation of Modern Capitalism." See Weber, "Der Gang der wirtschaftlichen Entwicklung," pp. 842–52 in *Landarbeiterfrage, Nationalstaat und Volkswirtschaftspolitik*.

Weber, from the very beginning of his academic career, was *the origin and evolution of capitalism*. At this stage of his thinking, Weber was looking at capitalism in its earliest form, especially in antiquity, and also how it evolved in the Mediterranean during the Middle Ages. That Protestantism had played an important role in the evolution of modern capitalism was also clear to him, and he lectured on this theme as early as 1898.[36]

Regarding Weber's contribution to economic sociology during these years, it has already been mentioned that he had not yet realized that one could apply the sociological perspective with full force to economic phenomena; and that rather, he saw sociology as being of help in tracing the links between the economy and noneconomic phenomena, such as the state and law. Nor had he developed his own version of sociology, as he would do in the 1910s. Nonetheless, if we use economic sociology in a broad and less precise sense, it is obvious that several of Weber's writings from these years constitute interesting contributions to the field. In particular, the study on agricultural workers, a few articles on German agriculture, and some of Weber's writings on the stock exchange contain discussions of contemporary economic problems from a social, as opposed to an economic theory perspective. It is not possible to summarize the content of all these works here, but some of the general ideas that can be found in them deserve nonetheless to be mentioned. There is, for example, Weber's insight that what drives people in their economic behavior is not only their *material interests* but also their *ideal interests*. In his work on the German agricultural workers, Weber speaks, for example, of the role that "the *magic* of freedom" plays in making them give up a safe economic situation for one that is more insecure but where there is no need for personal submission.[37] In the *Outline* he also says that people's needs are "ideal" as well as "material."[38]

In addition, Weber emphasizes the role that *tradition* plays in economic behavior. The reason why the Polish agricultural workers in Germany, for example, could live on so much less than their German counterparts had to do with the fact that they had become accustomed to a different and cheaper diet over the centuries. And, finally, there is the role that *struggle* (*Kampf*) plays in the economy. Here, too, Weber uses the example of German agricultural workers versus Polish workers, with the latter winning out because of their capacity to survive on a more primitive diet. But the notion of struggle among economic actors can

[36] That Weber lectured on the basic theme of *The Protestant Ethic* already in 1898 is important in that it shows that his ideas on this score were not decisively influenced by Werner Sombart's *Der moderne Kapitalismus* (1902), as is sometimes argued. Some of Weber's inspiration came instead, according to himself, from Georg Jellinek's suggestion that the modern notion of human rights had come into being as a result of seventeenth-century religious ideas. See Georg Jellinek, *The Declaration of the Rights of Man and of Citizens: A Contribution to Modern Constitutional History* (1895) (Westport: Hyperion Press, 1979).

[37] Max Weber, "The National State and Economic Policy (Freiburg Address)," *Economy and Society* 9 (1980): 433. Weber also refers to the famous Bible text, "Man shall not live by bread alone" (Mt. 4:4). See Weber, *Die Lage der Landarbeiter im ostelbischen Deutschland*, p. 920.

[38] Weber, *Grundriss zu den Vorlesungen über allgemeine ("theoretische") Nationalökonomie (1898)*, p. 29.

also be found in some of Weber's work on the stock exchange. In his pamphlet on the subject of 1894–96 Weber concludes, for example, that just as "rifles and canons" are needed in war, a "strong stock exchange" is needed in peace, "as long as nations carry on their inexorable and inevitable struggle for national existence and economic power."[39]

The most important results from Weber's empirical research on German agriculture in the 1890s are summarized in his inaugural address at the University of Freiburg, "The National State and Economic Policy."[40] But the lecture also contains a number of other ideas, and it is rather these that make it into such an interesting document that it is still worth reading today. The lecture is not mentioned in the standard histories of economic thought, which is a pity since it discusses the situation of economics in modern society with great clarity and force. To Weber, writing in the 1890s, it was obvious that economics had become *the* way of looking at reality in modern society, especially in political discourse and in the social sciences. While legal science had earlier held this strategic role, this was no longer the case. What was problematic, however, with economics becoming the master science of modern society, to Weber's mind, was that so many economists believed that economics could also provide a direction for which actions should be taken in society. To Weber, this was nothing but an "optical illusion" since he believed, like Hume, that an "ought" can never be derived from an "is."[41] What economists have to realize, he argued, is that science in itself is neutral, and that when social scientists take a political stance—as they should, in their capacity as citizens—it can only be based on personal values.

In his inaugural address Weber proudly proclaimed that he was an "economic nationalist" and that he wanted to serve the German nation. In particular, he said, there must be a "stemming [of] the Slav flood" into Germany.[42] To modern ears, this may sound chauvinistic and narrow-minded, and many years later Weber would express regret over what he had said.[43] But there were also parts of Weber's lecture that have a more universal and lasting appeal, such as the fol-

---

[39] Max Weber, "Die Börse," p. 321 in *Gesammelte Aufsätze zur Soziologie und Sozialpolitik.*

[40] The original title of the Freiburg lecture was "Nationality in Economic Life." For the Freiburg address, see especially the introduction by Wolfgang Mommsen and Rita Aldenhoff to the volume of the *Gesamtausgabe* containing the address: *Landarbeiterfrage, Nationalstaat und Volkswirtschaftspolitik: Schriften und Reden 1892–1899, Max Weber Gesamtausgabe I/4* (Tübingen: J. C. B. Mohr, 1993). See also Arnold Bergstraesser, "Max Webers Antrittsvorlesung in zeitgeschichtlicher Perspektive," *Vierteljahrshefte für Zeitgeschichte* 5 (1957): 209–19; Wilhelm Hennis, "Max Weber in Freiburg," *Freiburger Universitätsblätter* 86 (1984): 33–45; Keith Tribe, ed., *Reading Weber* (London: Routledge, 1989); and Max Weber, *Political Writings* (Cambridge: Cambridge University Press, 1994).

[41] Weber, "The National State and Economic Policy (Freiburg Address)," p. 440; "Der Nationalstaat und die Volkswirtschaftspolitik," *Max Weber Gesamtausgabe I/4,* p. 563.

[42] Weber, "The National State and Economic Policy (Freiburg Address)," p. 440; "Der Nationalstaat und die Volkswirtschaftspolitik," p. 556.

[43] In 1913 Weber said that he did not any longer "identify" with what he had said in his inaugural speech on "many important points." See Weber, "Gutachten zur Werturteilsdiskussion im Ausschuss des Vereins für Sozialpolitik," p. 127 in Eduard Baumgarten, *Max Weber: Werk und Person* (Tübingen: J. C. B. Mohr, 1964).

lowing: "The question which leads us beyond the grave of our own generation is not 'how will human beings *feel* in the future' but 'how they will *be*'. In fact this question underlies all work in political economy. We do not want to train up feelings of well-being in people, but rather those characteristics we think constitute the greatness and nobility of our human nature."[44]

Weber's Work in Economics after His Illness (1903–1909)

The second period in Weber's work in economics starts in 1903, when he had recovered enough that he could begin to write academic articles again. There is no natural end to this second period, as there is to the first one which came to a conclusion when Weber fell ill; and to some extent the reason for seeing the years 1903–9 as a unit is simply heuristic. But it is also a fact that something important happened to Weber's ideas on sociology around 1910. Before this date, as we know, Weber had shown little interest in sociology and rather looked upon it with a certain disdain; in the 1910s, on the other hand, he devoted a great part of his energy to creating a scientific sociology. It is true that some of Weber's most famous writings from 1903 to 1909—such as his essays in methodology and *The Protestant Ethic and the Spirit of Capitalism*—are today regarded as works in sociology, but they were not intended as such when they were produced. The same is true of Weber's studies of the psychophysics of industrial labor and *The Agrarian Sociology of Ancient Civilizations*, the original title of which, *Agrarverhältnisse im Altertum* (*Agrarian Conditions in Antiquity*), does not in fact refer to sociology.

It was also during the 1903–9 period that Weber for the first time used the term "social economics" or *Sozialökonomik* to characterize his own type of economics. He furthermore attempted to define exactly what he meant by this term and what topics it was supposed to cover. All of this is done in his famous essay entitled "'Objectivity' in Social Science and Social Policy," which appeared in the *Archiv für Sozialwissenschaft und Sozialpolitik* in 1904. What is important about this essay, so far as Weber's ideas on social economics are concerned, is primarily two things. First of all, Weber here anchors his theory of social economics in a philosophy of cultural (or social) science. And second, instead of simply stating that economics has a very broad subject area, he attempts to theorize about this area and suggests a way of conceptualizing its different parts.

During the years 1903–9 Weber was preoccupied with the distinction between the natural sciences and the cultural or social sciences, and his theory of social economics reflects this. While the meanings that people attach to various phenomena play no role in the natural sciences, they are absolutely crucial to the social sciences, including economics. Like most economists, Weber regarded scarcity as central to the constitution of economic phenomena, but he also emphasized that what ultimately matters is *the meaning* that people attach to real-

[44] Weber, "The National State and Economic Policy (Freiburg Address)," p. 437; "Der Nationalstaat und die Volkswirtschaftspolitik," p. 559.

ity: "The quality of an event as a 'social-economic' event is not something which it possesses 'objectively.' It is rather conditioned by the orientation of our cognitive interest, as it arises from the specific cultural significance which we attribute to the particular event in a given case."[45]

Even though Weber, from early on, felt that economics should cover a broad range of phenomena, he had made little effort to explain which phenomena it should include, and on what grounds. Such an attempt, however, is made in the essay on objectivity, where Weber introduces the following three categories: *economic phenomena, economically relevant phenomena,* and *economically conditioned phenomena* (see fig. 1). The first of these categories covers economic phenomena in a strict sense, such as economic events and economic institutions; and Weber has little to say about this category except that it includes phenomena "the economic aspects of which constitute their primary cultural significance for us."[46] Economically relevant phenomena, on the other hand, are phenomena that are not economic in themselves, but which "have consequences which are of interest from the economic point of view."[47] If a certain aspect of religious behavior affects economic behavior, for example, it constitutes an economically relevant phenomenon. The third category—economically conditioned phenomena—denotes phenomena that are not economic in themselves, but which are influenced by economic phenomena. This type of phenomena, Weber notes, includes "behavior in 'non-economic' affairs [which] is partly influenced by economic motives."[48] One example of this, which is taken from Weber's later work, would be how religious behavior is influenced by an economic factor, for example by the economic class to which a believer belongs.

As to economic theory, Weber made two contributions during this period that are still of some interest: he clarified the role that abstractions play in economic theory through his well-known notion of *ideal types,* and he wrote an article explaining why marginal utility theory does not rest on a psychological foundation. Ideal types, according to Weber, represent an important tool in all the social sciences and are produced through an "analytical accentuation of certain elements of reality."[49] Modern economic theory, for example, "offers us an ideal picture of events on the commodity market under conditions of society organized on the principles of an exchange economy, free competition and rigorously rational conduct."[50] Viewing the world in these terms entails a picture of the world as "a cosmos without contradictions," Weber notes, but that does not lessen its usefulness as an analytical tool.

[45] Weber, "'Objectivity' in Social Science and Social Policy," p. 64 in *The Methodology of the Social Sciences;* "Die 'Objektivität' sozialwissenschaftlicher und sozialpolitischer Erkenntnis," p. 161 in *Gesammelte Aufsätze zur Wissenschaftslehre* (Tübingen: J.C.B. Mohr, 1988).

[46] Weber, "Objectivity,'" p. 64; "'Objektivität,'" p. 162.

[47] Weber, "Objectivity,'" p. 64; "'Objektivität,'" p. 162.

[48] Weber, "Objectivity,'" p. 65; "'Objektivität,'" p. 162.

[49] Weber, "Objectivity,'" p. 90; "'Objektivität,'" p. 190.

[50] Weber, "Objectivity,'" pp. 89–90; "'Objektivität,'" p. 190.

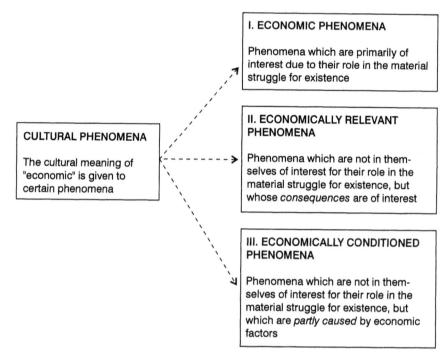

Figure 1. The Constitution and Scope of Social Economic Phenomena, according to Weber's Essay on "Objectivity" (1904)

Source: Max Weber, "'Objectivity' in Social Science and Social Policy," pp. 64–65 in *The Methodology of the Social Sciences* (New York: The Free Press, 1949).

Comment: According to Weber, people attach the cultural meaning of "economic" to phenomena that they view as central in the material struggle for existence and which are characterized by scarcity. The science of economics covers a very broad area; it includes not only "economic phenomena," but also "economically relevant phenomena" and "economically conditioned phenomena."

In 1908 Weber published an essay, "Marginal Utility Theory and 'The Fundamental Law of Psychophysics,'" which is interesting in that it is the only work by Weber that economists view as a distinct contribution to economic theory.[51] George Stigler, for example, refers approvingly to "Max Weber's famous essay," and other economists, such as Lionel Robbins, Friedrich von Hayek, and Paul

---

[51] The economists who participated in the so-called Mises Seminar (1920–34) were rather interested in Weber's methodology, especially in his ideas on ideal types and *Verstehen*. The most important contribution to come out of this circle was *The Phenomenology of the Social World* (1932) by Alfred Schutz, but there also exist a few interesting articles especially by Fritz Machlup. See Robert Holton and Bryan Turner, "Max Weber, Austrian Economics, and the New Right," pp. 30–67 in *Max Weber on Economy and Society* (London: Routledge, 1989); Christopher Prendergast, "Alfred Schutz and the Austrian School of Economics," *American Journal of Sociology* 92 (1986): pp. 1–26; and Mie Augier, "The Interpretive Sociology of Alfred Schütz and the Austrian School of Economics: Some Addenda" (unpublished paper, Copenhagen Business School, 1997).

Rosenstein-Rodan, have expressed similar positive opinions.[52] What these economists like about Weber's essay is that he firmly rejects the idea that psychology represents the foundation for economic theory. The notion of marginal utility rests instead, according to Weber, on three perfectly common experiences of people in their everyday lives: (1) that human beings are motivated by needs that can be satisfied through scarce material means; (2) that the more of something that is consumed, the more a need is usually fulfilled; and (3) that people allocate scarce goods in accordance with the importance they attach to different needs.

It may be added that one part of Weber's argument in the article on marginal utility has not been noted by the economists, even though it has interesting implications for economic theory. This is the suggestion that marginal utility works so well as an analytical tool because we live in a capitalist society. The "historical peculiarity of the capitalist epoch," Weber says, is that there exists an increasing "approximation of reality to the theoretical propositions of economic theory."[53] "The heuristic significance of marginal utility theory," Weber concludes, "rests on this *cultural-historical* fact, not on its supposed foundation in [psychology]."[54] One consequence of this argument is that contemporary economic theory is not applicable to preindustrial societies; another is that economic theory will fit less well in those parts of the world where capitalism is less developed (say contemporary Russia). It also throws an interesting light on why we today see ideas such as social capital, public choice, and so on becoming ever more popular.

Weber also made some important contributions to economic history during the 1903–9 period. One is of a methodological nature, and consists of Weber's argument that historians use ideal types in their analyses, whether they know it or not. Historians may think that they simply depict reality, Weber says, but just like all other social scientists they have to exclude much more than they include, and they also have to accentuate certain aspects of reality in order to make an analysis. Another important contribution to economic history from these years is to be found in *The Agrarian Sociology of Ancient Civilizations*. In his usual encyclopaedic style Weber covers the economic and social structure of ancient Mesopotamia, Israel, Egypt, Greece, and Rome. Of special interest in this work

[52] George Stigler, "The Development of Utility Theory II," *Journal of Political Economy* 58 (1950): 377; Friedrich von Hayek, *The Trend of Economic Thinking* (London: Routledge, 1991), p. 360; Paul Rosenstein-Rodan, "Marginal Utility (1927)," p. 204 in Israel M. Kirzner, ed., *Classics in Austrian Economics* (London: William Pickering, 1994); and Lionel Robbins, *An Essay on the Nature and Significance of Economic Science* (London: Macmillan, 1984), p. 85. Böhm-Bawerk also mentions Weber's article, but mixes praise with criticism and says that "certain statements of Weber's [about the opposition of economic theory and psychology] may definitely be said to overshoot the mark." See Eugen von Böhm-Bawerk, *Capital and Interest, Vol. 2. Positive Theory of Capital* (1912) (South Holland, Ill.: Libertarian Press, 1959), pp. 430–31, n. 81.

[53] Weber, "Marginal Utility Theory and 'The Fundamental Law of Psychophysics,'" p. 33; "Die Grenznutzenlehre und das 'psychophysiche Grundgesetz,'" p. 395 in *Gesammelte Aufsätze zur Wissenschaftslehre*.

[54] Ibid.

is Weber's analysis of capitalism. In contrast to Marx and many contemporary historians, Weber did not view capitalism as existing only in modern times but argued that it also could be found much earlier, especially in antiquity. In those early days, however, a different kind of capitalism existed, more precisely one that was centered on politics rather than the market: "Ancient capitalism was shaped by political forces. It was, one might say, only indirectly economic in character, for the critical factors were the political fortunes of the *polis* and the opportunities it provided for profit through contacts for tax farming and wars for human and (especially in Rome) territorial booty."[55]

In light of the fact that Weber himself did not view his own work as "sociology" till around 1910, one might ask whether it is appropriate to regard some of his writings from the period 1903–9—such as the essay on the psychophysics of industrial labor and *The Protestant Ethic*—as sociological, and possibly even as exercises in economic sociology. The answer, again, is yes—as long as we keep in mind that Weber had not yet hit upon the idea of a distinct *Wirtschaftssoziologie*.[56] It should also be noted that the main thrust of the analysis in *The Protestant Ethic*, as well as in the essay on the psychophysics of industrial labor, is directed toward an "economically relevant phenomenon" rather than an "economic phenomenon." In *The Protestant Ethic* Weber was analyzing the impact of religion on the economy; and in the essay on the psychophysics of industrial labor he was trying to establish what role people's biological constitution may have on their work behavior, especially as this relates to productivity.

The Protestant Ethic (1904–5, revised 1920) is Weber's most famous work and has resulted in an enormous literature over the years.[57] Weber's basic argument is that up till the late 1500s and the 1600s capitalism was of a traditional character (see fig. 2). By "traditional," Weber means in this context that capitalism was not very systematic and also that the goal for the individual merchant, as well as the individual laborer, was primarily to satisfy one's needs rather than to always gain more and work more. What prevented traditional capitalism from becoming more rational and systematic in character was not so much that it lacked the organizational know-how or that people did not want to make money—there obviously existed sophisticated trading and banking corporations as well as ambi-

---

[55] Weber, *The Agrarian Sociology of Ancient Civilizations*, p. 358; "Agrarverhältnisse im Altertum," p. 271 in *Gesammelte Aufsätze zur Sozial- und Wirtschaftsgeschichte*.

[56] It may also be mentioned that Weber was later to include *The Protestant Ethic* in a volume entitled *Collected Essays in the Sociology of Religion*. See Weber, "Die protestantische Ethik und der Geist des Kapitalismus," pp. 17–206 in vol. 1 of *Gesammelte Aufsätze zur Religionssoziologie* (Tübingen: J. C. B. Mohr, 1988).

[57] To get a picture of the debate, the reader may consult the following two works: Hartmut Lehmann and Guenther Roth, eds., *Weber's Protestant Ethic: Origins, Evidence, Contexts* (Cambridge: Cambridge University Press, 1993); and Richard Hamilton, "Max Weber and the Protestant Ethic," pp. 32–106 in *The Social Misconstruction of Reality* (New Haven, Conn.: Yale University Press, 1996). One of the most solid discussions of *The Protestant Ethic* is, in my opinion, to be found in Gordon Marshall's *In Search of the Spirit of Capitalism: An Essay on Max Weber's Protestant Ethic Thesis* (London: Hutchinson, 1982). Marshall is particularly interested in the question whether we have the empirical evidence that is needed to check Weber's arguments.

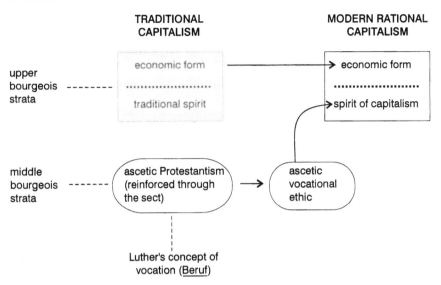

Figure 2. The Contribution of Ascetic Protestantism to the Qualitative Formation of the Modern Capitalist Spirit in the Late Sixteenth and Seventeenth Centuries, according to *The Protestant Ethic*

Source: Max Weber, *The Protestant Ethic and the Spirit of Capitalism* (London: Allen & Unwin, 1930), pp. 75, 91, 220, 159, 273.

Comment: Weber's goal in *The Protestant Ethic* (1904–5) was to outline and explain the contribution made by ascetic Protestantism to "the qualitative formation and the quantitative expansion" of the capitalist spirit. The shaded area in the figure represents economic activity which was considered "ethically unjustifiable or at best to be tolerated," according to the prevalent religious view. The argument about the sect reinforcing ascetic Protestantism was added by Weber in an article of 1906.

tious merchants in, say, the fifteenth century—but rather the fact that religion still had a firm grip on people's minds. In Christianity, as well as in other religions, the making of money was looked upon with considerable suspicion, Weber points out, and this is what kept capitalism back.

In the West, however, there emerged in the late 1500s and the 1600s a novel interpretation of Christianity, and according to its teachings it was possible to serve God by working hard and methodically, and also to make a profit this way. This is what Weber called "ascetic Protestantism," which was to be found in Calvinism, Baptism, and Pietism (and later also Methodism). This type of religion helped to break the hold on society of the traditional type of religion, and it also encouraged a new and much more methodical attitude to economic affairs, albeit in an indirect and unintended manner. The individual believer felt compelled to change his or her behavior in a radical direction, and this spilled over into the economic sphere. Weber emphasizes that ascetic Protestantism had such a strong impact on people because it supplied both a motive and also—

in contrast to, say Catholicism—an effective sanction for a change of behavior.[58] Another social mechanism through which the ideas of ascetic Protestantism were translated from the realm of conviction into actual behavior, Weber was later to add, was the sect.[59] When people daily supervise one another's behavior, as they do in a sect, the pressure on the individual to live up to the common ideology becomes exceptionally strong. Once the hold of religion had been broken in the West, Weber adds, the new attitude to economic affairs soon took on a life of its own and left religion behind.

Weber's Work in Economics during His Last Decade (1910–1920)

During the last ten years of his life Weber was very active as a scholar, and it was in this period that he made his definitive turn toward sociology. Likewise, when he resumed teaching he concentrated on economic sociology and other sociological topics, rather than on economic theory.[60]

Weber's great accomplishment during this period, so far as social economics is concerned, is definitely the *Grundriss der Sozialökonomik*, which was eventually to result in a set of more than a dozen huge volumes (1914–30). The original title had been *Handbook of Political Economy*, but the publisher wanted a different title to distinguish Weber's handbook from that of Schönberg, and Weber suggested something with *Sozialökonomik* in the title since this was "the best name for the discipline [of economics]."[61] He also made clear that he did not attach much importance to whatever term was used. The *Grundriss der Sozialökonomik* has a fairly complicated structure, but it can be briefly described as an attempt on Weber's part to produce a guide to the different aspects of economics as well as modern capitalism (see fig. 3). Weber's understanding of social economics comes out most clearly in the first of the book's five major parts,

---

[58] According to Weber, most religions demand a certain type of behavior from the believer but lack effective sanctions to alter behavioral patterns. In Catholicism, for example, a believer who has sinned can confess and be forgiven by the priest—and then sin again. In ascetic Protestantism, on the other hand, the believer cannot be forgiven in this manner but has to accept the consequences of his or her actions, and it is this, Weber argues, that makes the believer change his or her ways. See, e.g., Weber, *Economy and Society*, pp. 518–76.

[59] Weber, "'Churches' and 'Sects' in North America: An Ecclesiastical Sociopolitical Sketch," *Sociological Theory* 3 (1985): pp. 7–13. This article was revised in 1920; see "The Protestant Sects and the Spirit of Capitalism," pp. 302–22 in Hans Gerth and C. Wright Mills, eds., *From Max Weber* (New York: Oxford University Press, 1946).

[60] At the University of Vienna Weber taught "Economy and Society: A Positive Critique of the Materialistic Conception of History" (summer term, 1918); and at the University of Munich he taught "The General Categories of Social Science" (summer term, 1919), "Outline of Universal Social and Economic History" (winter term, 1919–20), "Socialism" (summer term, 1920) and "General Theory of the State and Politics: Sociology of the State" (summer term, 1920—not completed, due to Weber's death). See Wolfgang Mommsen and Wolfgang Schluchter, "Einleitung," p. 21, n. 82, in *Wissenschaft als Beruf, 1917/1919; Politik als Beruf, 1919, Max Weber Gesamtausgabe I/17* (Tübingen: J. C. B. Mohr, 1992).

[61] Max Weber in a letter to Paul Siebeck, March 22, 1912, in Johannes Winkelmann, *Max Webers hinterlassenes Hauptwerk* (Tübingen: J. C. B. Mohr, 1986), pp. 12, 25.

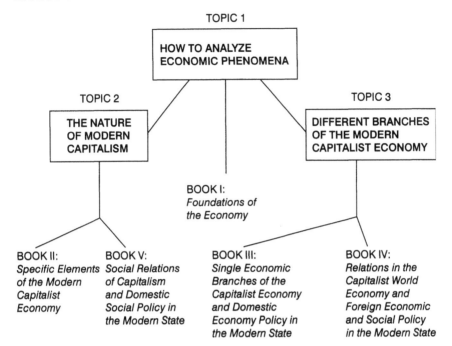

TOPIC 1

HOW TO ANALYZE
ECONOMIC PHENOMENA

TOPIC 2

THE NATURE
OF MODERN
CAPITALISM

TOPIC 3

DIFFERENT BRANCHES
OF THE MODERN
CAPITALIST ECONOMY

BOOK I:
*Foundations of
the Economy*

BOOK II:
*Specific Elements
of the Modern
Capitalist
Economy*

BOOK V:
*Social Relations
of Capitalism
and Domestic
Social Policy in
the Modern State*

BOOK III:
*Single Economic
Branches of the
Capitalist Economy
and Domestic
Economy Policy in
the Modern State*

BOOK IV:
*Relations in the
Capitalist World
Economy and
Foreign Economic
and Social Policy
in the Modern State*

Figure 3. The Structure of *Grundriss der Sozialökonomik,* on Which Weber Worked 1908–1920

Source: "Grundriss der Sozialökonomik: Einteilung des Gesamtwerkes," pp. x–xiii in *Grundriss der Sozialökonomik, I. Abteilung: Wirtschaft und Wirtschaftswissenschaft* (Tübingen: J. C. B. Mohr, 1914).

Comment: The *Grundriss der Sozialökonomik* was published during 1914–30 in more than a dozen physical volumes. It has a complicated structure, and this figure represents an attempt to give a simplified picture of it. The *Grundriss* is centered around three major topics, which are analyzed in five major "books." These books are divided into a number of further subdivisions.

"Foundations of the Economy." This part includes sections on economic theory and economic history, and Weber had commissioned articles from representatives of analytical economics (Friedrich von Wieser and Joseph Schumpeter) as well as the historical school (Karl Bücher).[62] Weber himself was to cover a huge part of the section on "Economy and Society," including population and economy, geography and economy, and technology and economy. In brief, Part I of the *Grundriss der Sozialökonomik* shows that Weber at this stage of his life conceived of economics as a very broad and interdisciplinary enterprise.

[62] Weber did not want to include a full economic history in the handbook since its focus was to be on contemporary events. Nonetheless, Book I contains an essay on the economic stages throughout history by Karl Bücher. See Karl Bücher, "Volkswirtschaftliche Entwicklungsstufen," pp. 1–18 in *Grundriss der Sozialökonomik, I. Abteilung: Wirtschaft und Wirtschaftswissenschaft* (Tübingen: J. C. B. Mohr, 1914).

Weber did not do any work whatsoever in economic theory during these last years, and some of his colleagues even felt that he had become hostile to theoretical economics. Weber, in response, said publicly as well as privately that this was not at all the case; he both respected economic theory, he said, and wished that he had made some contributions to it.[63] Throughout his life, it can be added, Weber held economic theory in very high regard, and this included the 1910s.

But even if Weber did not write anything in economic theory during his last years one can perhaps say that he made an indirect contribution to this field in another way. In his capacity as editor of the *Grundriss*, Weber was concerned with the way that economic theory was presented in the handbook, and he especially wanted it to be very clear how the transition from theoretical economics to a more social and empirical form of economic analysis could be made. "The *key* question is how *theory* is introduced," Weber wrote to his publisher, "and once this is properly done, everything else will fall into place."[64] Consequently, he was very pleased when he succeeded in getting Friedrich von Wieser, one of the great Austrian economists, to write the section on economic theory. Von Wieser's contribution, *Theorie der gesellschaftlichen Wirtschaft* (*Theory of the Social Economy*), consists of a methodical attempt to go from theorizing about simple and unconnected economic units ("the simple economy") to a more complex economy that consists of interacting units ("the social economy").[65]

Certain parts of *Economy and Society* also deal with economic history—for example, the analysis of feudalism and patrimonialism, as well as the book's general comparative method and its attempt to clarify the differences between a historical and a sociological approach. But Weber's single most important work in economic history during the period 1910–20 was the *General Economic History*.

---

[63] When Edgar Jaffé and Robert Liefmann argued that Weber was hostile to economic theory, he vehemently denied this. According to Schumpeter's more ironic formulation, Weber "saw no objection of principle to what economic theorists actually did, though he disagreed with them on what they thought they were doing." See Edgar Jaffé, "Das theoretische System der kapitalistischen Wirtschaftsordnung," *Archiv für Sozialwissenschaft und Sozialpolitik* 44 (1917): 1–2 (and the answer by Sombart and Weber in the same volume on page 348); Robert Liefmann, *Grundsätze der Volkswirtschaftslehre*, vol. 1 (Stuttgart: Deutsche Verlags-Anstalt, 1917), p. 15; Weber's letter to Robert Liefmann, dated March 9, 1920, in William Hennis, "The Pitiless 'Sobriety of Judgment': Max Weber between Carl Menger and Gustav von Schmoller—the Academic Politics of Value Freedom," *History of the Human Sciences* 4 (1991): 29; and Schumpeter, *History of Economic Analysis*, p. 819. It may also be mentioned that when Weber in the 1910s was involved with the German Historical Society, he suggested the creation of a section for theoretical economics, so that there would be a closer link between sociology and economics.

[64] Weber in a letter to Paul Siebeck, December 26, 1908, in Weber, *Briefe 1906–1908, Max Weber Gesamtausgabe II/5* (Tübingen: J. C. B. Mohr, 1990), p. 705. Weber repeats this statement nearly verbatim in a letter to Siebeck of mid-April 1909; see Weber, *Briefe 1909–1910, Max Weber Gesamtausgabe II/6* (Tübingen: J. C. B. Mohr, 1994), p. 106. The theory section, according to the 1910 plan for the *Grundriss*, was by means of "decreasing abstraction [to] be directed toward empirical reality." Ibid., p. 767.

[65] When von Wieser's work was translated in 1927 it was simply called *Social Economics*. See Friedrich von Wieser, *Social Economics* (New York: Augustus M. Kelley, 1967). The preface is by Wesley Clair Mitchell.

It should be noted that this work should be treated with a certain caution since the text was not written by Weber but consists of notes taken by students during one of his lecture courses. Nonetheless, the *General Economic History* is a very rich work, and it has been given high marks by such first-class economic historians as A. P. Usher and Eli Heckscher.[66] According to Usher, writing in 1928, this work "is the most important single contribution that has been made in economic history for more than fifty years," and according to Heckscher, writing at about the same time, the *General Economic History* is "invaluable through its richness of ideas."[67] A complete reading of the work gives a very good sense of how Weber viewed the development of economic history and especially the emergence of modern capitalism in the West. Weber firmly rejects technological determinism, and he views what is today known as the Industrial Revolution only as an important link in a very long chain. He also views ascetic Protestantism in a similar light: this type of religion was very important to the birth of rational capitalism but did not create it on its own. Finally, the *General Economic History* is also a very good complement to Weber's theoretical writings in economic sociology, such as "Sociological Categories of Economic Action," since the reader gets to see how Weber applies his concepts to historical material. Many of the concepts that Weber uses in the *General Economic History*, it may be pointed out, come directly from his sociology.

Weber's most important contribution to economics during the years 1910–20 falls, however, in the field of economic sociology, and here two different achievements should be distinguished. First of all, Weber now worked out a new and much more stringent approach to sociology itself. Already during 1903–9 he had decided that the notion of *meaning* was central to all of the cultural and social sciences; he now added that what characterizes sociology as a distinct science is that it deals with behavior to which the individual attaches meaning *and* which is also oriented to the behavior of others. Secondly, Weber applied this perspective to economic phenomena and thereby created a truly economic sociology. This application grew more radical during the 1910s and two distinct stages can be discerned in Weber's attitude to economic sociology as well.

During the first of these stages, which began in 1910 and lasted till the end of World War I, Weber was primarily concerned with analyzing the relationship between the economy and certain parts of society. During the second stage, on the other hand, he applied the perspective of sociology directly to economic phenomena. The *Economic Ethics of the World Religions* project was conceived during the first of these two stages, and it makes contributions to the sociology of

---

[66] Eli Heckscher, "Den ekonomiska historiens aspekter," *Historisk tidskrift* 50 (1930): 1–85; A. P. Usher, review of Weber, *General Economic History, American Economic Review* 18 (1928): 104–5. See also the positive review of von Below; Georg von Below, "Review of Max Weber, *Wirtschaftsgeschichte,*" *Weltwirtschaftliches Archiv* 20 (1924): 487–89.

[67] Usher, review of Weber, *General Economic History*, p. 105; Eli Heckscher, *Industrialismen: Den ekonomiska utvecklingen sedan 1750* (Stockholm: Kooperativa förbundets bokförlag, 1938), p. 346.

religion as well as to economic sociology. In the three monographs that Weber produced as part of this project, he traced the impact of economy on religious beliefs and vice versa in a number of major religions. He also introduced the concept of "economic ethic" into his analysis. By this term Weber means evaluative attitudes toward economic phenomena, such as work, profit-making, trade, and the like. If, for example, methodical work and profit-making are looked down upon in a society, he notes, its economic ethic is such that rational capitalism is unlikely to emerge. These attitudes are, on the other hand, compatible with political capitalism, as examples from antiquity show.

Weber's most sustained contribution to economic sociology during this period, however, is to be found in his contribution to the *Grundriss der Sozialökonomie,* and it was as part of this work that he developed his economic sociology in a more strict sense. In 1909–10 Weber produced the first plan for the handbook, according to which he was supposed to write a section entitled "Economy and Society." This section was to include three topics: "Economy and Law (1. Fundamental Relationship, 2. Epochs in the Development of Present Conditions)," "Economy and Social Groups (Family and Community Associations, Status Groups and Classes, State)," and "Economy and Culture (Critique of Historical Materialism)." Weber had also assigned to himself a number of other topics, presumably to fill in where he could not find a suitable writer.[68]

By 1914, when Weber produced a second plan for the handbook, his own major contribution had changed its name to "The Economy and the Social Orders and Powers," although it still was to be part of an overall section on "Economy and Society."[69] The contribution had also grown considerably in size, and the original three sections had now become eight. The section on economy and law was still there (but in a novel form), while that on economy and culture had been eliminated. The section on the economy and social groups had been expanded into three sections, and a few new ones had been added as well.[70] Weber

---

[68] These additional sections were: "Economy and Race," "The Object and the Logical Nature of the Central Questions [in Economics]," "The Modern State and Capitalism," "The General Importance of Modern Transportation Links and Communication Services for the Capitalist Economy," "The Limits to Capitalism in the Agrarian Economy," "Types and Scope of the Restraints, Reactions, and Setbacks of the Capitalist Economy," "Agrarian Capitalism and Population Groups," (together with Schwiedland) "Policy Measures to Protect the Middle Class (Industrial Corporate Policy in the Widest Sense of the Term; Retailer Policy; Farmers' Corporate Policy: Policy for Incorporation and Limits to Debts; Farmers' Estates)," "Positive Middle Class Policy Measures: (a) Domestic Colonization Policy," "The So-Called New Middle Class [Mittelstand]," "The Nature and Social Position of the Working Class (a. The Concept of Workers' Material Class Position and Material Class Interests. b. The Social Position of the Proletariat)," and (possibly together with Alfred Weber) "The Tendencies toward Internal Reorganization in Capitalism (Monopolistic, Collectivistic, and Bureaucratic Tendencies in the Context of Their Social Effects; Rents [das Rentnertum]; Tendencies toward Internal Regrouping)." See, e.g., Winkelmann, *Max Webers hinterlassenes Hauptwerk,* pp. 150–55.

[69] "Die Wirtschaft und die gesellschaftlichen Ordnungen und Mächte" and "Wirtschaft und Gesellschaft," respectively.

[70] According to the 1914 plan, Weber's section ("The Economy and the Societal Orders and Powers" or Part I of "Economy and Society" in Book I in the *Grundriss*) was to include the following

was also forced to make some further additions to his contribution when Karl Bücher's article turned out to be of low quality. After Weber had made these last changes, he wrote to his publisher:

> Since Bücher's treatment of the "developmental stages" is totally inadequate, I have worked out a complete theory and exposition that relates the major social groups to the economy: from the family and household to the enterprise, the kin group, ethnic community, religion (comprising all religions of the world: a sociology of salvation doctrines and of religious ethics—what Troeltsch did, but now for all religions, if much briefer). I can claim that nothing of the kind has ever been written, not even as a precursor.[71]

By the summer of 1914 Weber felt that his contribution was more or less finished and could soon be sent off to the printer. World War I, however, broke out in August 1914, and from then until the end of the war, Weber did practically no work on the handbook. Once the war was over, Weber resumed work on his contribution with great energy, though he now wanted it to become *"shorter"* as well as *"more textbook*-like."[72] It was at this point that the second stage of Weber's economic sociology began, and he now decided to apply his ideas on sociology directly to economic phenomena, rather than to the links between the economy and other parts of society. In 1918–20 he produced a totally new manuscript, which he labeled "Part I" and which consisted of four chapters. It is in chapter 2, "Sociological Categories of Economic Action," that Weber analyzes economic phenomena with the help of sociology.

Weber did not have the time to rewrite the rest of his contribution, but it would in all likelihood have been devoted to an analysis of the relationship between the economy and selected aspects of society, along the lines of his earlier writings for the *Grundriss*. It is generally assumed that Weber would have added sections on the sociology of law, the sociology of the state, and the sociology of religion. In the current U.S. edition of *Economy and Society*, the four first chapters or Part I can be found on pages 3–307, and many of the early, unrevised

---

sections: "1. Categories of the Societal Orders; The Fundamental Relationship Between Economy and Law; The Economic Relations of the Associations in General," "2. The Household, Oikos, and Enterprise," "3. The Neighborhood Association, Sib, and Community," "4. Ethnic Community Relations," "5. Religious Communities: The Conditioning of Religion by Class Constellations; Cultural Religions and Economic Attitudes," "6. Market Relationships [Marktvergemeinschaftung]," "7. The Political Association: The Developmental Conditions of Law; Status Groups, Classes, Parties, The Nation," "8. Domination [Die Herrschaft]: a) The Three Types of Legitimate Domination; b) Political and Hierocratic Domination; c) Nonlegitimate Domination: The Typology of Cities; d) The Development of the Modern State; e) Modern Political Parties." See the 1914 outline as translated in Schluchter, *Rationalism, Religion, Domination: A Weberian Perspective*, p. 467.

[71] Weber in a letter to Paul Siebeck, December 30, 1913, translated by Guenther Roth, "Introduction," pp. xxv–xxvi in Wolfgang Schluchter, *The Rise of Western Rationalism: Max Weber's Developmental History* (Berkeley: University of California Press, 1981). Weber was also discontented with von Wieser's contribution but did not undertake any changes in it before World War I (personal communication from Wolfgang Schluchter).

[72] Letter from Weber to Paul Siebeck, October 27, 1919, in Winkelmann, *Max Webers hinterlassenes Hauptwerk*, p. 46.

manuscripts on pages 309–1372. While it is definitely good to have both the finished and the unfinished parts of *Economy and Society* easily available in one work, it is also somewhat confusing to the reader, who gets the impression that all of this material constitutes one single work.

As to "Sociological Categories of Economic Action"—the most important theoretical text on economic sociology that can be found in Weber's work—it deserves to be noted that this text has largely been ignored in the enormous secondary literature.[73] A few exceptions naturally exist; however, the authors of most of these works have not been interested in what Weber has to say on economic sociology but rather have looked at this text with other purposes in mind.[74] The best commentary is still that produced by Talcott Parsons in 1947, as part of his introduction to *The Theory of Social and Economic Organization*

---

[73] A few commentators have not only ignored the chapter but argued that it is of little interest or, alternatively, written in such a difficult way that it deserves to be ignored. Alan Sica, for example, has decried the "almost unreadable accretion of definition piled upon definition" in the chapter; and Guenther Roth has said that it "proved a waste of effort" and that "economists and sociologists [with minor exceptions] have ignored it." See Alan Sica, *Weber, Irrationality, and Social Order* (Berkeley: University of California Press, 1988), pp. 146, 208; Guenther Roth, "Weber's Political Failure," *Telos* (Winter 1988–89): 149.

[74] See Veith Michael Bader, Johannes Berger, Heiner Gassmann, and Jost v. d. Knesebeck, "Max Weber: Soziologische Grundbegriffe des Wirtschaftens," pp. 193–320 in *Einführung in die Gesellschaftstheorie: Gesellschaft, Wirtschaft und Staat bei Marx und Weber* (1976) (Frankfurt: Campus Verlag, 1987); Julien Freund, "The Sociology of Economics," pp. 149–75 in *The Sociology of Max Weber* (1966) (Harmondsworth: Penguin Books, 1972); Bryn Jones, "Economic Action and Rational Organization in the Sociology of Weber," pp. 28–65 in Barry Hindess, ed., *Sociological Theories of the Economy* (London: Macmillan, 1977); Stephen Kalberg, "Max Weber's Universal-Historical Architectonic of Economically Oriented Action: A Preliminary Reconstruction," *Current Perspectives in Social Theory* 4 (1983): 253–88; Talcott Parsons, "Weber's 'Economic Sociology,'" pp. 30–55 in "Introduction" to Max Weber, *The Theory of Social and Economic Organization* (New York: Oxford University Press, 1947); Gianfranco Poggi, "The Conceptual Context," pp. 13–26 in *Calvinism and the Capitalist Spirit: Max Weber's Protestant Ethic* (Amherst, Mass.: University of Amherst Press, 1983); and Johannes Winkelmann, *Wirtschaft und Gesellschaft: Erläuterungsband* (Tübingen: J. C. B. Mohr, 1976), pp. 35–43. Many of these interpretations do not look at the second chapter from the viewpoint of economic sociology, however. Kalberg, for example, is mainly interested in the chapter so that he can develop a universal-historical typology for civilizational analysis; Poggi argues that the chapter supplements the analysis in *The Protestant Ethic* through its focus on the way that capitalism operates; and so on. To what extent the chapter has been taught and lectured from is, of course, impossible to say. Three cases in the United States may nonetheless be mentioned. The first involves Frank Knight and Edward Shils, and is described by the latter as follows: "In the middle 1930s, [Frank] Knight conducted a seminar [at the University of Chicago] on the first chapters of *Wirtschaft und Gesellschaft*, in which I participated, where we studied the text line by line." According to Daniel Bell, Alexander von Schelting taught a course in 1939 at Columbia University that was exclusively devoted to the two first chapters of *Economy and Society*: "we spent the entire term . . . mostly on definitions of economic and rational actions." Finally, Karl Polanyi discusses the chapter in the mimeographed notes that he distributed to his students at Columbia University in 1947. See Edward Shils, "Tradition, Ecology, and Institution in the History of Sociology," *Daedalus* 99 (Fall 1970): 823, n. 21; Bell in Swedberg, *Economics and Sociology*, p. 217; Karl Polanyi, "Appendix," pp. 120–38 in *Primitive, Archaic and Modern Economies* (Boston: Beacon Press, 1971). As far as I know, no economist has ever commented on the chapter, including the Austrian economists who were very interested in Weber's work.

(Part I of *Economy and Society*).[75] Parsons's text is still worth reading, but it has also aged on a few points and is perhaps not as thorough as one might have wished.

A READER'S GUIDE TO THIS VOLUME

The texts in this volume have been arranged in such an order that they can be read straight through; they can also be used for teaching in the same order as they now stand. A glossary of Weber's key terms in economic sociology has been included, as well as a bibliographical guide to Weber's economic sociology. The readings in Part I (Modern Capitalism) introduce the reader to Weber's general view of modern capitalism and its origin; they also present the basic economic institutions of capitalism. Part II (Capitalism, Law, and Politics) adds to the material in Part I by focusing on the relationship between the economy and politics (including law) in modern capitalism. Part III (Capitalism, Culture, and Religion) continues along the same route, by taking cultural phenomena, especially religious ones, into account. Part IV (Theoretical Aspects of Economic Sociology) is more abstract in nature and also contains more difficult texts; it has therefore been placed at the end of the volume. For those readers who already know some aspects of Weber's work or who are interested in getting a theoretically precise understanding of Weber's economic sociology from the beginning, a study of reading 16 is highly recommended. This reading consists of an excerpt from Weber's attempt to lay a theoretical foundation for economic sociology in the second chapter of *Economy and Society* ("Sociological Categories of Economic Action"), and it is absolutely essential for those who want to get a deeper understanding of what Weber was trying to accomplish with his economic sociology.

Throughout his life Weber's main interest as a scholar was to study modern or rational capitalism—to establish its character as well as its historical origin. The two first readings in the anthology are examples of Weber's efforts to determine what modern capitalism is like (for its origin, see especially chapter 11). The very first reading comes from the *General Economic History* and is as easy as it is interesting to read. Weber primarily discusses what characterizes modern capitalism, mentioning in particular the following features: rational capital accounting, freedom of the market, rational technology, calculable law, and commercialization. He also touches on a few other topics, such as the emergence of the shareholding corporation.

Reading 2 ("The Spirit of Capitalism") comes from *The Protestant Ethic and the Spirit of Capitalism,* and its emphasis is on the cultural dimension of modern capitalism. While *The Protestant Ethic* contains a very complex argument as well as much religious material that is difficult for today's reader, this excerpt is straightforward and deals mainly with economic matters. Weber first of all outlines the spirit of modern capitalism and contrasts it to the spirit of traditional

[75] See Parsons, "Weber's 'Economic Sociology.'"

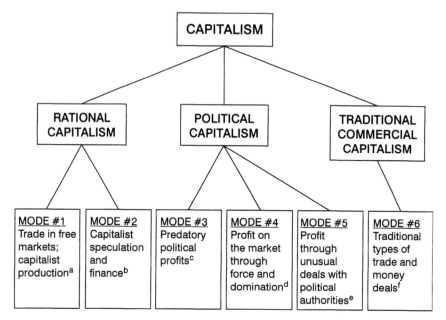

Figure 4. The Main Types of Capitalism and the Principal Modes of Capitalist Orientation of Profit-Making, according to *Economy and Society*

Source: Max Weber, *Economy and Society* (1922) (Berkeley: University of California Press, 1978), pp. 164–66.

Comment: Weber does not give a general definition of capitalism in the crucial chapter 2 of *Economy and Society* on economic sociology, but talks instead of six "principal modes of capitalist orientation of profit-making" (section 31, pp. 236–38 below). These are then divided into rational capitalism (numbers 1–2), political capitalism (numbers 3–5), and what can be called traditional commercial capitalism (number 6). Different types of capitalism typically coexist and do so, for example, in modern capitalism, which is predominantly of a rational character.

[a]Continuous buying and selling in free markets; continuous production of goods in capitalist enterprises.

[b]Speculation in standardized commodities or securities; continuous financial operations of political organizations; promotional financing of new enterprises by selling securities; speculative financing of new enterprises and other economic organizations to gain power or a profitable regulation of the market.

[c]Predatory profit can come, e.g., from the financing of wars, revolutions, and party leaders.

[d]Continuous business activity thanks to force or domination, e.g., tax and office farming, colonial profits (plantations, monopolistic and compulsory trade).

[e]No more information on this type of political capitalism is to be found in section 31.

[f]Trade and speculation in currencies, professional credit extension, creation of means of payment, the taking over of payment functions.

capitalism. But he also discusses other types of capitalism, and the reader may want to compare this typology of capitalism with the final one that can be found in "Sociological Categories of Economic Action" (see reading 16 and fig. 4).

After these initial readings on the general character of modern capitalism there follows some material on two of its most important institutions: the market (reading 3) and the firm (reading 4). Weber does not attempt to develop a theory of how prices are formed—this was something that he felt belonged to theoretical economics—but discusses instead the market as a form of social interaction. More precisely, a market consists according to Weber of *two* kinds of interaction: competition (among buyers on the one hand and sellers on the other) and exchange (between one particular buyer and one particular seller). By relating the market to the role played by class and status formations in modern society, Weber also succeeds in infusing quite a bit of dynamic into his analysis of the market.

The reading on the firm comes from the *General Economic History*. It is very brief, and it complements the analysis of the emergence of the shareholding corporation in chapter 1. The emphasis is primarily on the introduction of limited liability into economic life, which occurred for the first time in the Italian city-states during the Middle Ages, and which represents a very important event in the history of economic organizations. Nonetheless, in the absence of a truly modern capitalist mentality (as Weber argues in reading 2), the firm could not become the truly revolutionary organization it later was to be.

The reading that concludes Part I is a minor classic, "Class, Status, and Party." As in the reading on the market, Weber here discusses the dynamics of class versus status; the former being centered around production and "life chances," and the latter around consumption and "honor." One of the most important points that Weber makes in this text—and which leads directly to the main theme in Part II—is that the economy is not independent from the rest of society but is typically part of a political order.

Part II (Capitalism, Law, and Politics) begins with a short text devoted to a central idea in Weber's political sociology, namely that there exists some form of political domination (*Herrschaft*) in practically all societies (reading 6, "The Three Types of Legitimate Domination"). According to Weber, there exist three major forms of legitimate domination—legal domination, traditional domination, and charismatic domination—and a specific type of administration answers to each of them. Economic activities are typically played out within the broader context of political domination. There is also the fact that each type of administration has to be paid for in some manner, for example, through benefices, via taxation, or from the lord's table.

In the next two writings Weber presents material which adds to his analysis of domination and how it is related to the economy (readings 7, "The Bureaucratization of Politics and the Economy," and reading 8, "The Rational State and Its Legal System"). There is a general trend in Western society, Weber argues, toward more bureaucracy, and this goes for the modern firm as well as for state administration. But this does not mean that the bureaucrats will eventually become the new masters of society; there also exist two counterforces to the power of bureaucracy in modern society. These are the entrepreneur, in the area of the economy, and the politician, in the area of politics. Entrepreneurs and politicians have been schooled to shoulder responsibility, Weber notes, as opposed to the bureaucrats, who have been trained to follow rules.

"The Rational State and Its Legal System" comes from the *General Economic History* and is an easy-to-read introduction to the role played by law in modern capitalism. Weber was extremely interested in this topic, and a large part of *Economy and Society* is devoted to it. His basic stance was that modern rational capitalism cannot function without calculable law and sophisticated legal instruments, such as the modern contract and the notion of legal personality. In this particular reading, Weber also notes that none of the main legal institutions of capitalism comes, contrary to what is often thought, from Roman law. What Weber says on the role of law in capitalism, it should be added, is also related to his analysis of domination. This is hinted at in reading 6 on the three types of legitimate domination, but for a systematic discussion one has to go elsewhere in Weber's work (see fig. 5).

The two last readings in Part II probe deeply into the complexities of the relationship between economics and politics. Reading 9 is Weber's inaugural address as professor of economics at the University of Freiburg, which has already been discussed. Weber explains in quite some detail—and in rather strident, nationalistic tones—what he thinks the economic policy of the German state should be vis-à-vis Polish immigrant workers. But he also raises a number of interesting questions, including one on the relationship of economic theory to the rest of the social sciences. In the Germany of his day, Weber says, economics has become the ideological master science among the social sciences. Since something similar is going on today—this time under the label of "rational choice"—Weber's essay is especially interesting to read and also suitable for classroom discussion.

Reading 10, "The Social Causes of the Decay of Ancient Civilization," is one of Weber's best-written essays and pulls the reader along by means of its engaging argument. One of the issues that Weber touches on is the type of capitalism that existed in Rome, namely "political capitalism." The members of the Roman elite wanted to be rich, but since they despised industry and commerce they used the state to get what they wanted (tax farming, conquests of other countries, and so on). Weber also presents a theory of his own for the decline of the Roman Empire. One cannot say, he argues, that either economic factors or political factors constituted "the ultimate cause" for the fall of Rome; it was rather that political and economic events affected each other in a long and complicated chain of events, whose end result was the undoing of Rome. Weber's argument can be summarized as follows: the Roman Empire needed a constant supply of cheap slaves to survive, and once the wars of conquest were over, no more slaves were to be had; this in turn led to a series of economic and political events that eventually led to the erosion of the economy of the cities and also of official political power.

	LEGAL DOMINATION	CHARISMATIC DOMINATION	TRADITIONAL DOMINATION: PATRIMONIALISM	CHARISMATIC AND TRADITIONAL DOMINATION: FEUDALISM
NATURE OF LEGITIMATION	obedience is to the law and to rules, not to persons	obedience is inspired by the extraordinary character of the leader	obedience is due to the sanctity of tradition; there is a corresponding loyalty to the leader	contract of fealty between lord and vassal; a mixture of traditional and charismatic elements
TYPE OF ADMINISTRATION	bureaucracy; the official is trained, has a career and a sense of duty	followers and disciples who later become more like normal officials as a result of routinization	from household staff to more advanced officials with mostly ad hoc and stereotyped tasks	small-scale administration, similar to patrimonial staff but with a distinct status element to it; the vassal has especially military duties
LEGAL SYSTEM	law constitutes a consistent system of abstract rules that have been intentionally established	justice is made through revelation in the concrete case; there are no legal traditions or abstract legal principles	juxtaposition of legal traditionalism with arbitrary decisions by the ruler creates an unstable legal situation	the contract between lord and vassal permeates society and creates a stable legal situation
EFFECT ON THE ECONOMY, ESPECIALLY ON THE RISE OF RATIONAL CAPITALISM	indispensable to rational capitalism through its predictability; hostile to political capitalism	initially hostile to all forms of systematic economic activity; when routinized, usually a conservative force	hostile to rational capitalism because of its arbitrary element; positive to economic traditionalism and to political capitalism	the ethos of feudalism goes against all types of capitalism; deeply conservative effect on the economy

Figure 5. Major Types of Domination and Their Relation to Legal System, Type of Administration, and Form of Economy

Source: Max Weber, *Economy and Society* (1922) (Berkeley: University of California Press, 1978), pp. 212–301, 941–1211; for law, see pp. 1041, 1082, 1099, 1115.

Comment: The impact of law on the economy differs depending on what kind of domination is involved: legal, traditional, charismatic, or some mixture of these.

   Part III adds to the complexity of Weber's analysis of capitalism by looking at the impact of cultural, especially religious factors. Reading 11 ("The Evolution of the Capitalist Spirit") comes from the *General Economic History* and contains a discussion of what caused rational capitalism to emerge in the West. Weber rejects single-factor explanations, for example, that population growth or the influx of precious metals from the Americas was *the* decisive cause. Rational capitalism was rather the result of a long historical process, in which, however, two developments were particularly decisive: the emergence of certain key institutions (the firm, modern accounting, rational technology, and calculable law); and the appearance of a new way of looking at economic things (a rational mentality, rationalization of the conduct of life, and a rational economic ethos). The idea that the Jews should have been instrumental in ushering in modern capitalism is directly rejected by Weber. Judaism, however, did make a crucial contribution to the rise of rational capitalism, and that was to reject magic a few thousand years earlier—something that later would deeply influence Christianity. Weber also emphasizes how Christianity has been absolutely crucial in developing the kind of mentality that was necessary for modern capitalism to emerge. It did this by being a mass religion, and not just a religion for the few, and by later also developing the notion of work ("calling" or *Beruf*) as a way of honoring God.

   Reading 12, an excerpt from "The Protestant Sects and the Spirit of Capitalism," contains some of the most beautiful passages that Weber ever wrote and is highly recommended. Weber starts out by describing a series of observations that he made during his trip to the United States in 1904, concerning the economic role of the religious sects. Religious Americans, Weber quickly understood, were much more trusted in economic matters than those who were not members of a church. His explanation of this phenomenon was essentially that being a member of a sect constituted a form of social capital; the sects only accepted trustworthy people as members and they continuously monitored their behavior.

   Excerpts from each of Weber's three volumes for the project on *The Economic Ethics of the World Religions* have also been included. In "Kinship and Capitalism in China" (reading 13) Weber raises the question why the modern type of capitalism did not emerge spontaneously in China; and he answers it by pointing to a series of obstacles that existed in this country. One of the most important of these was the hold that the kinship group or the clan had over the individual, typically in combination with ancestor worship. While in the West, Christianity helped to shatter the power of the kinship group, in China this type of group continued to have important social, political, economic, and religious functions.

   Modern capitalism did not emerge by itself in India either, and here also there existed a number of institutional and cultural obstacles. The one that Weber singles out in reading 14 is the caste system, to which he attributes a significant role. According to Weber, it was not so much that the caste system explicitly forbade specific activities that in one way or another could have furthered the emergence of rational capitalism. Indeed, when the interests of the rich and powerful were at stake, exceptions from Hinduism were often made. It was, for example, possible for high-caste families to have low-caste servants; and members of different castes could also work together under certain circumstances. What was decisive, Weber says, was rather that the general spirit of the caste system constituted a formidable obstacle to the emergence of modern capitalism.

The last excerpt from *The Economic Ethics of the World Religions* comes from *Ancient Judaism,* which is one of Weber's most difficult books ("Charity in Ancient Palestine," reading 15). The excerpt which has been chosen here, however, is easy to read and also very modern in some respects. Weber essentially contrasts the practice of charity in ancient Palestine to that in ancient Egypt, and tries to explain why the two differed so much. He characterizes Egypt as an oppressive, patrimonial bureaucracy, whose rulers cared for their people in about the same way as cattle owners care for their animals. In Palestine, on the other hand, the people were independent peasants and there existed a unique and much more humane attitude toward poor people. What makes the charity ethics of ancient Palestine extra interesting is that also animals were included. Animals, as Weber notes, were better treated in Palestine than slaves were in Rome.

The final part of the anthology is devoted to theoretical aspects of economic sociology and how Weber viewed the science of economics, that is, social economics. The first text is an excerpt from chapter 2 of *Economy and Society,* "Sociological Categories of Economic Action," and is by far the most important reading in this part. The text is written in a very concentrated manner and is often hard to penetrate. Nonetheless, if the effort is made, the reader will be able to follow the very systematic and logical manner in which Weber tried to construct his economic sociology during his last years (1919–20). Weber begins by discussing the concept of economic action (or action directed toward utility), which represents the basic unit of analysis in theoretical economics. He then argues that in economic sociology only a special type of economic action is studied, namely economic action that is oriented to the behavior of others (*economic social action*). The idea that social action can be defined as action that is oriented to the behavior of others comes from Weber's sociology, as presented in chapter 1 of *Economy and Society* (see fig. 6).

Using economic (social) action as the basic unit in his economic sociology, Weber then proceeds to construct progressively more complex concepts, such as economic relationships and economic organizations. The former are defined as two actors directing their economic actions toward one another, and the latter as a closed economic relationship, enforced by a staff. The result is a number of interrelated concepts that are all very useful for the economic sociologist (see fig. 7).

The two last readings in this anthology are important to an understanding of Weber's general attitude to the science of economics and especially to economic theory (reading 17, "The Area of Economics, Economic Theory, and the Ideal Type," which consists of an excerpt from Weber's essay on objectivity of 1904,

A. Economic Theory
   (economic action)

B. Sociology
   (social action)

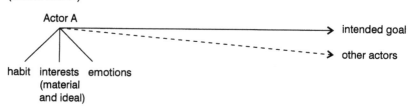

C. Economic Sociology
   (economic social action)

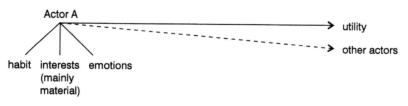

Figure 6. Economic Action, Social Action, and Economic Social Action according to Weber

Source: Max Weber, *Economy and Society* (1922) (Berkeley: University of California Press, 1978), pp. 1–24, 63–69.

Comment: Economic theory, in Weber's view, analyzes situations where the actor is driven by interests, aims at utility, but does not take the behavior of other actors into account (*economic action*). Sociology, on the other hand, looks at action driven by interests (ideal and material) but which is also oriented to the behavior of others (*social action*). Economic sociology, finally, focuses on *economic social action*, that is, action which is driven mainly by interests, which is oriented to utility, and which takes other actors into account. Emotions and habit play a role in sociology but not in economic theory.

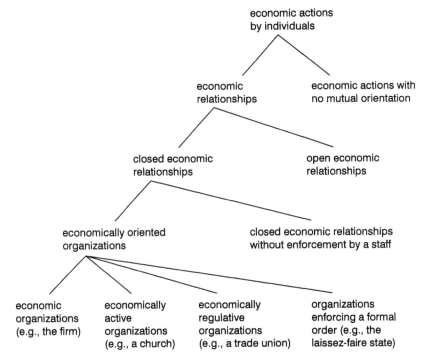

Figure 7. From Economic Actions by Individuals to Economic Organizations
Source: Max Weber, *Economy and Society* (1922) (Berkeley: University of California Press, 1978), pp. 48–50, 74–75, 341–43.
Comment: The figure shows how Weber, by using economic (social) action as his basic unit of analysis, constructs progressively more complex concepts—in this case economic relationships and economic organizations.

and reading 18, "Marginal Utility Analysis and 'The Fundamental Law of Psychophysics'"). Since both of these writings have been discussed above, I will be very brief here. Suffice it to say that the concept of the ideal type is presented in reading 17, which also contains a useful typology for how to conceptualize the area of economics; and that reading 18 contains a sharp and useful presentation of the possibilities as well as the limits of economic theory.

PART I

Modern Capitalism

Modern Capitalism: Key Characteristics and Key Institutions

THE MEANING AND PRESUPPOSITIONS OF MODERN CAPITALISM

Capitalism is present wherever the industrial provision for the needs of a human group is carried out by the method of enterprise, irrespective of what need is involved. More specifically, a rational capitalistic establishment is one with capital accounting, that is, an establishment which determines its income yielding power by calculation according to the methods of modern bookkeeping and the striking of a balance. The device of the balance was first insisted upon by the Dutch theorist Simon Stevin in the year 1698.[1]

It goes without saying that an individual economy may be conducted along capitalistic lines to the most widely varying extent; parts of the economic provision may be organized capitalistically and other parts on the handicraft or the manorial pattern. Thus at a very early time the city of Genoa had a part of its political needs, namely those for the prosecution of war, provided in capitalistic fashion, through stock companies. In the Roman empire, the supply of the population of the capital city with grain was carried out by officials, who however for this purpose, besides control over their subalterns, had the right to command the services of transport organizations; thus the leiturgical or forced contribution type of organization was combined with administration of public resources. Today, in contrast with the greater part of the past, our everyday needs are supplied capitalistically, our political needs however through compulsory contributions, that is, by the performance of political duties of citizenship such as the obligation to military service, jury duty, etc. A whole epoch can be designated as typically capitalistic only as the provision for wants is capitalistically organized to such a predominant degree that if we imagine this form of organization taken away the whole economic system must collapse.

While capitalism of various forms is met with in all periods of history, the provision of the everyday wants by capitalistic methods is characteristic of the occi-

Reprinted by permission of Transaction Publishers from Max Weber, *General Economic History* (New York: Greenberg, 1927), pp. 275–91. Translated by Frank H. Knight. The text is based on a lecture course that Weber gave in 1919–20; see *Wirtschaftsgeschichte* (1923) (Berlin: Duncker und Humblot, 1991), pp. 238–51.

[1] It is generally thought today that Simon Stevin was not the first to advocate the device of the balance in accounting, and that it had already been suggested much earlier. See Raymond de Roover, *Business, Banking, and Economic Thought* (Chicago: University of Chicago Press, 1974), p. 120 (RS).

dent alone and even here has been the inevitable method only since the middle of the 19th century. Such capitalistic beginnings as are found in earlier centuries were merely anticipatory, and even the somewhat capitalistic establishments of the 16th century may be removed in thought from the economic life of the time without introducing any overwhelming change.

The most general presupposition for the existence of this present-day capitalism is that of rational capital accounting as the norm for all large industrial undertakings which are concerned with provision for everyday wants. Such accounting involves, again, first, the appropriation of all physical means of production—land, apparatus, machinery, tools, etc. as disposable property of autonomous private industrial enterprises. This is a phenomenon known only to our time, when the army alone forms a universal exception to it. In the second place, it involves freedom of the market, that is, the absence of irrational limitations on trading in the market. Such limitations might be of a class character, if a certain mode of life were prescribed for a certain class or consumption were standardized along class lines, or if class monopoly existed, as for example if the townsman were not allowed to own an estate or the knight or peasant to carry on industry; in such cases neither a free labor market nor a commodity market exists. Third, capitalistic accounting presupposes rational technology, that is, one reduced to calculation to the largest possible degree, which implies mechanization. This applies to both production and commerce, the outlays for preparing as well as moving goods.

The fourth characteristic is that of calculable law. The capitalistic form of industrial organization, if it is to operate rationally, must be able to depend upon calculable adjudication and administration. Neither in the age of the Greek city-state (polis) nor in the patrimonial state of Asia nor in western countries down to the Stuarts was this condition fulfilled. The royal "cheap justice" with its remissions by royal grace introduced continual disturbances into the calculations of economic life. The proposition that the Bank of England was suited only to a republic, not to a monarchy, referred to above[2] was related in this way to the conditions of the time. The fifth feature is free labor. Persons must be present who are not only legally in the position, but are also economically compelled, to sell their labor on the market without restriction. It is in contradiction to the essence of capitalism, and the development of capitalism is impossible, if such a propertyless stratum is absent, a class compelled to sell its labor services to live; and it is likewise impossible if only unfree labor is at hand. Rational capitalistic calculation is possible only on the basis of free labor; only where in consequence of the existence of workers who in the formal sense voluntarily, but actually under the compulsion of the whip of hunger, offer themselves, the costs of products may be unambiguously determined by agreement in advance. The sixth and final condition is the commercialization of economic life. By this we mean the general use of commercial instruments to represent share rights in enterprise, and also in property ownership.

---

[2] See *General Economic History*, p. 265.

To sum up, it must be possible to conduct the provision for needs exclusively on the basis of market opportunities and the calculation of net income. The addition of this commercialization to the other characteristics of capitalism involves intensification of the significance of another factor not yet mentioned, namely speculation. Speculation reaches its full significance only from the moment when property takes on the form of negotiable paper.

.   .   .

THE EXTERNAL FACTS IN THE EVOLUTION OF CAPITALISM

Commercialism involves, in the first place, the appearance of paper representing shares in enterprise, and, in the second place, paper representing rights to income, especially in the form of state bonds and mortgage indebtedness. This development has taken place only in the modern western world. Forerunners are indeed found in antiquity in the share-commandite companies of the Roman *publicani,* who divided the gains with the public through such share paper. But this is an isolated phenomenon and without importance for the provision for needs in Roman life; if it had been wanting entirely, the picture presented by the economic life of Rome would not have been changed.

In modern economic life the issue of credit instruments is a means for the rational assembly of capital. Under this head belongs especially the stock company. This represents a culmination of two different lines of development. In the first place, share capital may be brought together for the purpose of anticipating revenues. The political authority wishes to secure command over a definite capital sum or to know upon what income it may reckon; hence it sells or leases its revenues to a stock company. The Bank of St. George in Genoa is the most outstanding example of such financial operations, and along the same line are the income certificates of the German cities and treasury notes (*Rentenmeisterbriefe*) especially in Flanders. The significance of this system is that in place of the original condition under which unusual state requirements were covered by compulsory law, usually without interest and frequently never repaid, loans come to be floated which appeal to the voluntary economic interests of the participants. The conduct of war by the state becomes a business operation of the possessing classes. War loans bearing a high interest rate were unknown in antiquity; if the subjects were not in a position to supply the necessary means the state must turn to a foreign financier whose advances were secured by a claim against the spoils of war. If the war terminated unfortunately his money was lost. The securing of money for state purposes, and especially for war purposes, by appeal to the universal economic interest, is a creation of the middle ages, especially of the cities.

Another and economically more important form of association is that for the purpose of financing commercial enterprise—although the evolution toward the form of association most familiar today in the industrial field, the stock company, went forward very gradually from this beginning. Two types of such organiza-

tions are to be distinguished; first, large enterprises of an inter-regional character which exceeded the resources of a single commercial house, and second,
inter-regional colonial undertakings.

For inter-regional enterprises which could not be financed by individual entrepreneurs, finance by groups was typical, especially in the operations of the
cities in the 15th and 16th centuries. In part the cities themselves carried on
inter-regional trade, but for economic history the other case is more important,
in which the city went before the public and invited share participation in the
commercial enterprise which it organized. This was done on a considerable
scale. When the city appealed to the public, compulsion was exercised on the
company thus formed to admit any citizen; hence the amount of share capital
was unlimited. Frequently the capital first collected was insufficient and an additional contribution was demanded, where today the liability of the share holder
is limited to his share. The city frequently set a maximum limit to the individual
contribution so that the entire citizenship might participate. This was often done
by arranging the citizens in groups according to the taxes paid or their wealth
and reserving a definite fraction of the capital for each class. In contrast with the
modern stock company the investment was often rescindable, while the share of
the individual was not freely transferable. Hence the whole enterprise represented a stock company only in an embryonic sense. Official supervision was exercised over the conduct of operations.

In this form the so-called "regulated" company was common, especially in the
iron trade as in Steier, and it was occasionally used in the cloth trade, as in Iglau.
A consequence of the structure of the organizations just described was the absence of fixed capital and, as in the case of the workers' association, the absence
of capital accounting in the modern sense. Share holders included not only merchants, but princes, professors, courtiers, and in general the public in the strict
sense, which participated gladly and to great profit. The distribution of the dividends was carried out in a completely irrational way, according to the gross income alone, without reserves of any kind. All that was necessary was the removal
of the official control and the modern stock company was at hand.

The great colonization companies formed another preliminary stage in the development of the modern stock company. The most significant of these were the
Dutch and English East India companies, which were not stock companies in
the modern sense. On account of the jealousy of the citizens of the provinces of
the country the Dutch East India Company raised its capital by distributing the
shares among them, not permitting all the stock to be bought up by any single
city. The government, that is the federation, participated in the administration,
especially because it reserved the right to use the ships and cannon of the company for its own needs. Modern capital accounting was absent as was free trans-
ferability of shares, although relatively extensive dealings in the latter soon took
place. It was these great successful companies which made the device of share
capital generally known and popular; from them it was taken over by all the continental states of Europe. Stock companies created by the state, and granted
privileges for the purpose, came to regulate the conditions of participation in

business enterprise in general, while the state itself in a supervisory capacity was involved in the most remote details of business activity. Not until the 18th century did the annual balance and inventory become established customs, and it required many terrible bankruptcies to force their acceptance.

Alongside the financing of state needs through stock companies stands direct financing by measures of the state itself. This begins with compulsory loans against a pledge of resources and the issue of certificates of indebtedness against anticipated revenues. The cities of the middle ages secured extraordinary income by bonds, pledging their fixed property and taxing power. These annuities may be regarded as the forerunners of the modern consols, yet only within limitations; for to a large extent the income ran for the life of the purchaser, and they were tied up with other considerations. In addition to these devices the necessity of raising money gave rise to various expedients down to the 17th century. The emperor Leopold I attempted to raise a "cavalier loan," sending mounted messengers around to the nobility to solicit subscriptions; but in general he received for answer the injunction to turn to those who had the money.

If one desires to understand the financial operations of a German city as late as the close of the middle ages, one must bear in mind that there was at that time no such thing as an orderly budget. The city, like the territorial lord, lived from week to week as is done today in a small household. Expenditures were re-adjusted momentarily as income fluctuated. The device of tax farming was of assistance in overcoming the difficulty of management without a budget. It gave the administration some security as to the sums which it might expect each year, and assisted it in planning its expenditures. Hence the tax farm operated as an outstanding instrument of financial rationalization, and was called into use by the European states occasionally at first and then permanently. It also made possible the discounting of public revenues for war purposes, and in this connection achieved especial significance. Rational administration of taxation was an accomplishment of the Italian cities in the period after the loss of their freedom. The Italian nobility is the first political power to order its finances in accordance with the principle of mercantile bookkeeping obtaining at the time, although this did not then include double entry. From the Italian cities the system spread abroad and came into German territory through Burgundy, France, and the Hapsburg states. It was especially the tax payers who clamored to have the finances put in order.

A second point of departure for rational forms of administration was the English exchequer system, of which the word "check" is a last survival and reminder. This was a sort of checker board device by means of which the payments due the state were computed, in the absence of the necessary facility in operating with figures. Regularly, however, the finances were not conducted through setting up a budget in which all receipts and disbursements were included, but a special-fund system was used. That is, certain receipts were designated and raised for the purpose of specified expenditures only. The reason for this procedure is found in the conflicts between the princely power and the citizens. The latter mistrusted the princes and thought this the only way to protect themselves against having the taxes squandered for the personal ends of the ruler.

In the 16th and 17th centuries an additional force working for the rationalization of the financial operations of rulers appeared in the monopoly policy of the princes. In part they assumed commercial monopolies themselves and in part they granted monopolistic concessions, involving of course the payment of notable sums to the political authority. An example is the exploitation of the quicksilver mines of Idria, in the Austrian province of Carniola, which were of great importance on account of the process of amalgamating silver. These mines were the subject of protracted bargaining between the two lines of the Hapsburgs and yielded notable revenues to both the German and the Spanish houses. The first example of this policy of monopoly concession was the attempt of the Emperor Frederick II to establish a grain monopoly for Sicily. The policy was most extensively employed in England and was developed in an especially systematic manner by the Stuarts, and there also it first broke down, under the protests of Parliament. Each new industry and establishment of the Stuart period was for this purpose bound up with a royal concession and granted a monopoly. The king secured important revenues from the privileges, which provided him with the resources for his struggle against Parliament. But these industrial monopolies established for fiscal purposes broke down almost without exception after the triumph of Parliament. This in itself proves how incorrect it is to regard, as some writers have done, modern western capitalism as an outgrowth of the monopolistic policies of princes.

.   .   .

THE FIRST GREAT SPECULATIVE CRISES

We have recognized as characteristics and pre-requisites of capitalistic enterprise the following: appropriation of the physical means of production by the entrepreneur, freedom of the market, rational technology, rational law, free labor, and finally the commercialization of economic life. A further motif is speculation, which becomes important from the moment when property can be represented by freely negotiable paper. Its early development is marked by the great economic crises which it called forth.

The great tulip craze of Holland in the 1630s is often numbered among the great speculative crises, but it should not be so included. Tulips had become an article of luxury among the patricians who had grown rich in colonial trade, and suddenly commanded fantastic prices. The public was misled by the wish to make easy profits until with equal suddenness the whole craze collapsed and many individuals were ruined. But all of that had no significance for the economic development of Holland; in all periods it has happened that objects connected with gaming have become subject to speculation and led to crises. It is quite otherwise with John Law and the great speculation in France and the contemporary South Sea speculation in England, in the second decade of the 18th century.

In the financial practice of the large states it had long been customary to anticipate revenues by the issue of certificates, to be redeemed later. In consequence of the War of the Spanish Succession, the financial requirements of the government rose to an extraordinary height in England as well as in France. The founding of the Bank of England supplied the financial needs of that country, but in France the state was already hopelessly in debt, and on the death of Louis XIV no one knew how the excessive debt was to be taken care of. Under the regency came forward the Scotchman, John Law, who thought he had learned something from the founding of the Bank of England, and had a theory of his own regarding financial affairs, although he had had no luck with it in England. He saw in inflation, that is the utmost possible increase in the medium of circulation, a stimulus to production.

In 1716, Law received a concession for a private bank which at first presented no exceptional character. It was merely specified that the credit obligations of the state must be received in payment for the capital, while the notes of the bank were to be accepted in the payment of taxes. In contrast with the Bank of England there was no clear plan as to the manner in which the bank was to have a regular and secure income so as to maintain the liquid character of its issues. In connection with this bank Law founded the Mississippi Company. The Louisiana territory was to be financed to the extent of a hundred million livres; the company accepted the same amount of obligations of the state as payment for stock and received in exchange the monopoly of the trade in a territory to be determined. If one examines the Louisiana plan it will be observed that a century would have been required before Louisiana would have yielded sufficient revenue to make possible the repayment of the capital. To begin with, Law intended to carry out an undertaking similar to the East India Company, entirely overlooking the fact that Louisiana was not, like India, an ancient civilized country, but a forest waste inhabited by Indians.

When, in 1718, he saw himself threatened by the competition of a stock company which wished to lease the indirect taxes, he combined the Mississippi Company with the Compagnie des Indes. The new company was to carry on the trade with India and China, but the political power was not available to secure for France the share in the Asiatic trade which England already possessed. However, the regency was induced to give to Law the right of coinage and the lease on all the taxes, involving power of life and death over the state, in exchange for a loan at 3% by means of which the gigantic floating debt was to be taken care of. At this point the public embarked on an insane course of speculation. The first year a 200% dividend was declared and the price of shares rose from 500 to 9,000. This phase of the development can be explained only by the fact that short selling was impracticable since there was as yet no systematic exchange mechanism.

In 1720 Law succeeded in getting himself appointed Comptroller General of Finances. But the whole enterprise quickly disintegrated. In vain the state decreed that only John Law notes should be legal money; in vain it sought to sustain them by drastic restriction on the trade in precious metals. Law's fall was inevitable simply because neither Louisiana nor the Chinese or East India trade had yielded sufficient profit to pay interest on even a fraction of his capital. It is true that the bank had received deposits, but it possessed no liquid external resources for repayment. The end was a complete bankruptcy and the declaration that the notes were of no value. A result was an enduring discouragement on the part of the French public, but at the same time freely transferable share certificates, made to bearer, had been popularized.

In the same years a parallel phenomena was exhibited by England, except that the course of development was not so wild as that in France. Soon after founding of the Bank of England, the idea of a competing institution became current (1696). This was the land bank project resting on the same ideas later presented in the proposals of the German agrarians, namely, of using land credit instead of bills of exchange as a cover for bank notes. But this project was not carried out because in England it was well understood that the necessary liquidity would be absent. This, however, did not prevent the occurrence that in 1711, after the fall of the Whig government, the Tories adopted a course similar to that followed a few years later by John Law.

The English nobility wished to create a centralized power in opposition to the specifically Puritan basis of the Bank of England, and at the same time the gigantic public debt was to be paid off. For this purpose was founded the South Sea Company, which made considerable advances to the state and in return received a monopoly of the South Pacific trade. The Bank of England was not shrewd enough to keep aloof from the project; it even outbid the founders and it was due only to the Tories, who on the ground of political repugnance refused it participation, that its offer was not accepted.

The course of events was similar to that of John Law's institution. Here also bankruptcy was unavoidable because the South Sea trade was not sufficient to pay interest on the sums advanced. Yet prior to this eventuality, just as in France, speculation gave rise to transferable certificates. The result was that enormous property was dissipated while many adventurers came out of it smiling, and the state—in a way none too honorable—achieved a substantial lightening of its burden of interest. The Bank of England remained standing in all its former prestige, being the only financial institution based on the rational discounting of exchange and hence possessing the requisite current liquidity. The explanation is that exchange represents nothing but goods already sold, and such a regular and sufficient turnover of goods no place in the world except London at that time could provide.

Speculative crises of a similar sort have taken place from that time forward, but never since on the same scale. The first crises in rational speculation began a full hundred years later, after the conclusion of the Wars of Liberation, and since that time they have recurred almost regularly at intervals of about 10 years—1815, 1825, 1835, 1847 etc. It was these which Karl Marx had in view when in *The Communist Manifesto* he prophesied the downfall of capitalism. The first of these crises and their periodic recurrence were based on the possibility of speculation and the resultant participation of outside interests in large business undertakings.

The collapse has resulted from the fact that in consequence of over-speculation, means of production, though not production itself, grew faster than the need for consumption of goods. In 1815 the prospect of the lifting of the continental blockade had led to a regular rage for founding factories; but the war had destroyed the buying power of the continent and it could no longer take the English products. This crisis was barely overcome, and the continent had begun to develop buying power, when in 1825 a new crisis set in because means of production, though not goods, had been speculatively produced on a scale never known before and out of correspondence with the needs.

That it was possible to create means of production to such an extent is due to the fact that with the 19th century the age of iron had begun. The discovery of the coking process, the blast furnace, and the carrying of mining operations to unprecedented depths, introduced iron as the basis of creating means of production, where the machines of the 18th century were built only of wood. Thus production was freed from the organic limitations in which nature had held it confined. At the same time, however, crises became an immanent factor of the economic order. Crises in the broader sense of chronic unemployment, destitution, glutting of the market and political disturbances which destroy all industrial life, have existed always and everywhere. But there is great difference between the fact that a Chinese or Japanese peasant is hungry and knows the while that the Deity is unfavorable to him or the spirits are disturbed and consequently nature does not give rain or sunshine at the right time, and the fact that the social order itself may be held responsible for the crisis, even to the poorest laborer. In the first case, men turn to religion; in the second, the work of men is held at fault and the laboring man draws the conclusion that it must be changed. Rational socialism would never have originated in the absence of crises.

T W O

The Spirit of Capitalism

IN THE TITLE of this study [*The Protestant Ethic and the Spirit of Capitalism*— RS] is used the somewhat pretentious phrase, the *spirit* of capitalism. What is to be understood by it? The attempt to give anything like a definition of it brings out certain difficulties which are in the very nature of this type of investigation.

If any object can be found to which this term can be applied with any understandable meaning, it can only be an historical individual, i.e. a complex of elements associated in historical reality which we unite into a conceptual whole from the standpoint of their cultural significance.

Such an historical concept, however, since it refers in its content to a phenomenon significant for its unique individuality, cannot be defined according to the formula *genus proximum, differentia specifica,* but it must be gradually put together out of the individual parts which are taken from historical reality to make it up. Thus the final and definitive concept cannot stand at the beginning of the investigation, but must come at the end. We must, in other words, work out in the course of the discussion, as its most important result, the best conceptual formulation of what we here understand by the spirit of capitalism, that is the best from the point of view which interests us here. This point of view (the one of which we shall speak later) is, further, by no means the only possible one from which the historical phenomena we are investigating can be analyzed. Other standpoints would, for this as for every historical phenomenon, yield other characteristics as the essential ones. The result is that it is by no means necessary to understand by the spirit of capitalism only what it will come to mean to *us* for the purposes of our analysis. This is a necessary result of the nature of historical concepts which attempt for their methodological purposes not to grasp historical reality in abstract general formulae, but in concrete genetic sets of relations which are inevitably of a specifically unique and individual character.[1]

Reprinted by permission of Routledge Ltd from *The Protestant Ethic and the Spirit of Capitalism* (London: Allen & Unwin, 1930), pp. 47–78; 192–204. Translated by Talcott Parsons. Originally published in 1904–5 and revised in 1920; see vol. 1 of *Gesammelte Aufsätze zur Religionssoziologie* (1920) (Tübingen: J. C. B. Mohr, 1988), pp. 30–62.

[1] These passages represent a very brief summary of some aspects of Weber's methodological views. At about the same time that he wrote this essay [i.e. *The Protestant Ethic and the Spirit of Capitalism*] he was engaged in a thorough criticism and revaluation of the methods of the social sciences, the result of which was a point of view in many ways different from the prevailing one, especially outside of Germany. In order thoroughly to understand the significance of this essay in its wider bearing on Weber's sociological work as a whole it is necessary to know what his methodological aims were. Most of his writings on this subject have been assembled since his death (in 1920) in the volume *Gesammelte Aufsätze zur Wissenschaftslehre* [part of which is translated into English as *The Methodology of the Social Sciences*]. A shorter exposition of the main position is contained in the

Thus, if we try to determine the object, the analysis and historical explanation of which we are attempting, it cannot be in the form of a conceptual definition, but at least in the beginning only a provisional description of what is here meant by the spirit of capitalism. Such a description is, however, indispensable in order clearly to understand the object of the investigation. For this purpose we turn to a document of that spirit which contains what we are looking for in almost classical purity, and at the same time has the advantage of being free from all direct relationship to religion, being thus, for our purposes, free of preconceptions.

Remember, that *time* is money. He that can earn ten shillings a day by his labour, and goes abroad, or sits idle, on half of that day, though he spends but sixpence during his diversion or idleness, ought not to reckon *that* the only expense; he has really spent, or rather thrown away, five shillings besides.

Remember, that *credit* is money. If a man lets his money lie in my hands after it is due, he gives me the interest, or so much as I can make of it during that time. This amounts to a considerable sum where a man has good and large credit, and makes good use of it.

Remember, that money is of the prolific, generating nature. Money can beget money, and its offspring can beget more, and so on. Five shillings turned is six, turned again it is seven and threepence, and so on, till it becomes a hundred pounds. The more there is of it, the more it produces every turning, so that the profits rise quicker and quicker. He that kills a breeding-sow, destroys all her offspring to the thousandth generation. He that murders a crown, destroys all that it might have produced, even scores of pounds.

Remember this saying, *The good paymaster is lord of another man's purse.* He that is known to pay punctually and exactly to the time he promises, may at any time, and on any occasion, raise all the money his friends can spare. This is sometimes of great use. After industry and frugality, nothing contributes more to the raising of a young man in the world than punctuality and justice in all his dealings; therefore never keep borrowed money an hour beyond the time you promised, lest a disappointment shut up your friend's purse for ever.

The most trifling actions that affect a man's credit are to be regarded. The sound of your hammer at five in the morning, or eight at night, heard by a creditor, makes him easy six months longer; but if he sees you at a billiard-table, or hears your voice at a tavern, when you should be at work, he sends for his money the next day; demands it, before he can receive it, in a lump.

It shows, besides, that you are mindful of what you owe; it makes you appear a careful as well as an honest man, and that still increases your credit.

Beware of thinking all your own that you possess, and of living accordingly. It is a mistake that many people who have credit fall into. To prevent this, keep an exact account for some time both of your expenses and your income. If you take the pains at first to mention particulars, it will have this good effect: you will discover how wonderfully

---

opening chapters of *Wirtschaft und Gesellschaft: Grundriss der Sozialökonomik*, III [*Economy and Society*].—Translator's note.

small, trifling expenses mount up to large sums, and will discern what might have been, and may for the future be saved, without occasioning any great inconvenience.

For six pounds a year you may have the use of one hundred pounds, provided you are a man of known prudence and honesty.

He that spends a groat a day idly, spends idly above six pounds a year, which is the price for the use of one hundred pounds.

He that wastes idly a groat's worth of his time per day, one day with another, wastes the privilege of using one hundred pounds each day.

He that idly loses five shillings' worth of time, loses five shillings, and might as prudently throw five shillings into the sea.

He that loses five shillings, not only loses that sum, but all the advantage that might be made by turning it in dealing, which by the time that a young man becomes old, will amount to a considerable sum of money.[2]

It is Benjamin Franklin [1709–90—RS] who preaches to us in these sentences, the same which Ferdinand Kürnberger satirizes in his clever and malicious *Picture of American Culture*[3] as the supposed confession of faith of the Yankee. That it is the spirit of capitalism which here speaks in characteristic fashion, no one will doubt, however little we may wish to claim that everything which could be understood as pertaining to that spirit is contained in it. Let us pause a moment to consider this passage, the philosophy of which Kürnberger sums up in the words, "They make tallow out of cattle and money out of men". The peculiarity of this philosophy of avarice appears to be the ideal of the honest man of recognized credit, and above all the idea of a duty of the individual toward the increase of his capital, which is assumed as an end in itself. Truly what is here preached is not simply a means of making one's way in the world, but a peculiar ethic. The infraction of its rules is treated not as foolishness but as forgetfulness of duty. That is the essence of the matter. It is not mere business astuteness, that sort of thing is common enough, it is an ethos. *This* is the quality which interests us.

When Jacob Fugger [1455–1525—RS], in speaking to a business associate who had retired and who wanted to persuade him to do the same, since he had made enough money and should let others have a chance, rejected that as pusillanimity and answered that "he (Fugger) thought otherwise, he wanted to make money as long as he could",[4] the spirit of his statement is evidently quite differ-

---

[2] The final passage is from *Necessary Hints to Those That Would Be Rich* (written 1736, Works, Sparks edition, II, p. 80), the rest from *Advice to a Young Tradesman* (written 1748, Sparks edition, II, pp. 87 ff.). The italics in the text are Franklin's.

[3] *Der Amerikamüde* (Frankfurt, 1855), well known to be an imaginative paraphrase of Lenau's impressions of America. As a work of art the book would to-day be somewhat difficult to enjoy, but it is incomparable as a document of the (now long since blurred-over) differences between the German and the American outlook, one may even say of the type of spiritual life which, in spite of everything, has remained common to all Germans, Catholic and Protestant alike, since the German mysticism of the Middle Ages, as against the Puritan capitalistic valuation of action.

[4] Sombart has used this quotation as a motto for his section dealing with the genesis of capitalism (*Der moderne Kapitalismus*, first edition, I, p. 193. See also p. 390).

ent from that of Franklin. What in the former case was an expression of commercial daring and a personal inclination morally neutral,[5] in the latter takes on the character of an ethically coloured maxim for the conduct of life. The concept spirit of capitalism is here used in this specific sense,[6] it is the spirit of modern capitalism. For that we are here dealing only with Western European and American capitalism is obvious from the way in which the problem was stated. Capitalism existed in China, India, Babylon, in the classic world, and in the Middle Ages. But in all these cases, as we shall see, this particular ethos was lacking.

Now, all Franklin's moral attitudes are coloured with utilitarianism. Honesty is useful, because it assures credit; so are punctuality, industry, frugality, and that is the reason they are virtues. A logical deduction from this would be that where, for instance, the appearance of honesty serves the same purpose, that would suffice, and an unnecessary surplus of this virtue would evidently appear to Franklin's eyes as unproductive waste. And as a matter of fact, the story in his autobiography of his conversion to those virtues,[7] or the discussion of the value of a strict maintenance of the appearance of modesty, the assiduous belittlement of one's own deserts in order to gain general recognition later,[8] confirms this im-

---

[5] Which, quite obviously, does not mean either that Jacob Fugger was a morally indifferent or an irreligious man, or that Benjamin Franklin's ethic is completely covered by the above quotations. It scarcely required Brentano's quotations (*Die Anfänge des modernen Kapitalismus*, pp. 150 ff.) to protect this well-known philanthropist from the misunderstanding which Brentano seems to attribute to me. The problem is just the reverse: how could such a philanthropist come to write these particular sentences (the especially characteristic form of which Brentano has neglected to reproduce) in the manner of a moralist?

[6] This is the basis of our difference from Sombart in stating the problem. Its very considerable practical significance will become clear later. In anticipation, however, let it be remarked that Sombart has by no means neglected this ethical aspect of the capitalist entrepreneur. But in his view of the problem it appears as a result of capitalism, whereas for our purposes we must assume the opposite as an hypothesis. A final position can only be taken up at the end of the investigation. For Sombart's view see *op. cit.*, pp. 357, 380, etc. His reasoning here connects with the brilliant analysis given in Simmel's *Philosophie des Geldes* (final chapter). Of the polemics which he has brought forward against me in his *Bourgeois* I shall come to speak later. At this point any thorough discussion must be postponed.

[7] "I grew convinced that truth, sincerity, and integrity in dealings between man and man were of the utmost importance to the felicity of life; and I formed written resolutions, which still remain in my journal book to practise them ever while I lived. Revelation had indeed no weight with me as such; but I entertained an opinion that, though certain actions might not be bad because they were forbidden by it, or good because it commanded them, yet probably these actions might be forbidden because they were bad for us, or commanded because they were beneficial to us in their own nature, all the circumstances of things considered." *Autobiography* (ed. F. W. Pine, Henry Holt, New York, 1916), p. 112.

[8] "I therefore put myself as much as I could out of sight and started it"—that is the project of a library which he had initiated—"as a scheme of a *number of friends*, who had requested me to go about and propose it to such as they thought lovers of reading. In this way my affair went on smoothly, and I ever after practised it on such occasions; and from my frequent successes, can heartily recommend it. The present little sacrifice of your vanity will afterwards be amply rewarded. If it remains awhile uncertain to whom the merit belongs, someone more vain than yourself will be encouraged to claim it, and then even envy will be disposed to do justice by plucking those assumed feathers and restoring them to their right owner." *Autobiography*, p. 140.

pression. According to Franklin, those virtues, like all others, are only in so far virtues as they are actually useful to the individual, and the surrogate of mere appearance is always sufficient when it accomplishes the end in view. It is a conclusion which is inevitable for strict utilitarianism. The impression of many Germans that the virtues professed by Americanism are pure hypocrisy seems to have been confirmed by this striking case. But in fact the matter is not by any means so simple. Benjamin Franklin's own character, as it appears in the really unusual candidness of his autobiography, belies that suspicion. The circumstance that he ascribes his recognition of the utility of virtue to a divine revelation which was intended to lead him in the path of righteousness, shows that something more than mere garnishing for purely egocentric motives is involved.

In fact, the *summum bonum* of this ethic, the earning of more and more money, combined with the strict avoidance of all spontaneous enjoyment of life, is above all completely devoid of any eudaemonistic, not to say hedonistic, admixture. It is thought of so purely as an end in itself, that from the point of view of the happiness of, or utility to, the single individual, it appears entirely transcendental and absolutely irrational.[9] Man is dominated by the making of money, by acquisition as the ultimate purpose of his life. Economic acquisition is no longer subordinated to man as the means for the satisfaction of his material needs. This reversal of what we should call the natural relationship, so irrational from a naïve point of view, is evidently as definitely a leading principle of capitalism as it is foreign to all peoples not under capitalistic influence. At the same time it expresses a type of feeling which is closely connected with certain religious ideas. If we thus ask, *why* should "money be made out of men", Benjamin Franklin himself, although he was a colourless deist, answers in his autobiography with a quotation from the Bible, which his strict Calvinistic father drummed into him again and again in his youth: "Seest thou a man diligent in his calling? He shall stand before kings" (Prov. xxii. 29). The earning of money within the modern economic order is, so long as it is done legally, the result and the expression of virtue and proficiency in a calling; and this virtue and proficiency are, as it is now not difficult to see, the real Alpha and Omega of Franklin's ethic, as expressed in the passages we have quoted, as well as in all his works without exception.[10]

And in truth this peculiar idea, so familiar to us to-day, but in reality so little

---

[9] Brentano (*op. cit.*, pp. 125, 127, note 1) takes this remark as an occasion to criticize the later discussion of "that rationalization and discipline" to which worldly asceticism [*innerweltliche Askese*] has subjected men. That, he says, is a rationalization toward an irrational mode of life. He is, in fact, quite correct. A thing is never irrational in itself, but only from a particular rational point of view. For the unbeliever every religious way of life is irrational, for the hedonist every ascetic standard, no matter whether, measured with respect to its particular basic values, that opposing asceticism is a rationalization. If this essay makes any contribution at all, may it be to bring out the complexity of the only superficially simple concept of the rational.

[10] In reply to Brentano's (*Die Anfänge des modernen Kapitalismus*, pp. 150 ff.) long and somewhat inaccurate apologia for Franklin, whose ethical qualities I am supposed to have misunderstood, I refer only to this statement, which should in my opinion, have been sufficient to make that apologia superfluous.

a matter of course, of one's duty in a calling, is what is most characteristic of the social ethic of capitalistic culture, and is in a sense the fundamental basis of it.[11] It is an obligation which the individual is supposed to feel and does feel towards the content of his professional[12] activity, no matter in what it consists, in particular no matter whether it appears on the surface as a utilization of his personal powers, or only of his material possessions (as capital).

Of course, this conception has not appeared only under capitalistic conditions. On the contrary, we shall later trace its origins back to a time previous to the advent of capitalism. Still less, naturally, do we maintain that a conscious acceptance of these ethical maxims on the part of the individuals, entrepreneurs or labourers, in modern capitalistic enterprises, is a condition of the further existence of present-day capitalism. The capitalistic economy of the present day is an immense cosmos into which the individual is born, and which presents itself to him, at least as an individual, as an unalterable order of things in which he must live. It forces the individual, in so far as he is involved in the system of market relationships, to conform to capitalistic rules of action. The manufacturer who in the long run acts counter to these norms, will just as inevitably be eliminated from the economic scene as the worker who cannot or will not adapt himself to them will be thrown into the streets without a job.

Thus the capitalism of to-day, which has come to dominate economic life, educates and selects the economic subjects which it needs through a process of economic survival of the fittest. But here one can easily see the limits of the concept of selection as a means of historical explanation. In order that a manner of life so well adapted to the peculiarities of capitalism could be selected at all, i.e. should come to dominate others, it had to originate somewhere, and not in isolated individuals alone, but as a way of life common to whole groups of men. This origin is what really needs explanation. Concerning the doctrine of the more naïve historical materialism, that such ideas originate as a reflection or superstructure of economic situations, we shall speak more in detail below. At this point it will suffice for our purpose to call attention to the fact that without doubt, in the country of Benjamin Franklin's birth (Massachusetts), the spirit of capitalism (in the sense we have attached to it) was present before the capitalistic order. There were complaints of a peculiarly calculating sort of profit-seeking in New England, as distinguished from other parts of America, as early as 1632. It is further undoubted that capitalism remained far less developed in some of the neighbouring colonies, the later Southern States of the United States of Amer-

[11] The concept of work as a calling (*Beruf*) is absolutely central to Weber's argument in *The Protestant Ethic*. In chapter 3 ("Luther's Conception of the Calling"), Weber explains how this term originates with Luther's translation of the Bible, and from there spread to many parts of the world. To Luther, not only work in the monastery, but *all* work, was to be seen as a task set by God (RS).

[12] The two terms "profession" and "calling" I have used in translation of the German *Beruf*, whichever seemed best to fit the particular context. "Vocation" does not carry the ethical connotation in which Weber is interested. It is especially to be remembered that "profession" in this sense is not contrasted with "business," but it refers to a particular attitude toward one's occupation, no matter what that occupation may be. This should become abundantly clear from the whole of Weber's argument.—Translator's note.

ica, in spite of the fact that these latter were founded by large capitalists for business motives, while the New England colonies were founded by preachers and seminary graduates with the help of small bourgeois, craftsmen and yeomen, for religious reasons. In this case the causal relation is certainly the reverse of that suggested by the materialistic standpoint.

But the origin and history of such ideas is much more complex than the theorists of the superstructure suppose. The spirit of capitalism, in the sense in which we are using the term, had to fight its way to supremacy against a whole world of hostile forces. A state of mind such as that expressed in the passages we have quoted from Franklin, and which called forth the applause of a whole people, would both in ancient times and in the Middle Ages[13] have been pro-

---

[13] I make use of this opportunity to insert a few anti-critical remarks in advance of the main argument. Sombart (*Bourgeois*) makes the untenable statement that this ethic of Franklin is a word-for-word repetition of some writings of that great and versatile genius of the Renaissance, Leon Battista Alberti, who besides theoretical treatises on mathematics, sculpture, painting, architecture, and love (he was personally a woman-hater), wrote a work in four books on household management (*Della Famiglia*). (Unfortunately, I have not at the time of writing been able to procure the edition of Mancini, but only the later one of Bonucci.) The passage from Franklin is printed above word for word. Where then are the corresponding passages to be found in Alberti's work, especially the maxim "time is money", which stands at the head, and the exhortations which follow it? The only passage which, so far as I know, bears the slightest resemblance to it is found towards the end of the first book of *Della Famiglia* (ed. Bonucci, II, p. 353), where Alberti speaks in very general terms of money as the *nervus rerum* of the household, which must hence be handled with special care, just as Cato spoke in *De Re Rustica*. To treat Alberti, who was very proud of his descent from one of the most distinguished cavalier families of Florence (*Nobilissimi Cavalieri, op. cit.*, pp. 213, 228, 247, etc.), as a man of mongrel blood who was filled with envy for the noble families because his illegitimate birth, which was not in the least socially disqualifying, excluded him as a bourgeois from association with the nobility, is quite incorrect. It is true that the recommendation of large enterprises as alone worthy of a *nobile è onesta famiglia* and a *libero è nobile animo*, and as costing less labor is characteristic of Alberti (p. 209; compare *Del governo della Famiglia*, IV, p. 55, as well as p. 116 in the edition for the Pandolfini). Hence the best thing is a putting-out business for wool and silk. Also an ordered and painstaking regulation of his household, i.e. the limiting of expenditure to income. This is the *santa masserizia*, which is thus primarily a principle of maintenance, a given standard of life, and not of acquisition (as no one should have understood better than Sombart). Similarly, in the discussion of the nature of money, his concern is with the management of consumption funds (money or *possessioni*), not with that of capital; all that is clear from the expression of it which is put into the mouth of Gianozzo. He recommends, as protection against the uncertainty of *fortuna*, early habituation to continuous activity, which is also (pp. 73–4) alone healthy in the long run, *in cose magnifiche è ample*, and avoidance of laziness, which always endangers the maintenance of one's position in the world. Hence a careful study of a suitable trade in case of a change of fortune, but every *opera mercenaria* is unsuitable (*op. cit.*, I, p. 209). His idea of *tranquillita dell' animo* and his strong tendency toward the Epicurean *lathe biōsas* (*vivere a sè stesso*, p. 262); especially his dislike of any office (p. 258) as a source of unrest, of making enemies, and of becoming involved in dishonourable dealings; the ideal of life in a country villa; his nourishment of vanity through the thought of his ancestors; and his treatment of the honour of the family (which on that account should keep its fortune together in the Florentine manner and not divide it up) as a decisive standard and ideal—all these things would in the eyes of every Puritan have been sinful idolatry of the flesh, and in those of Benjamin Franklin the expression of incomprehensible aristocratic nonsense. Note, further, the very high opinion of literary things (for the *industria* is applied principally to literary and scientific work), which are really most worthy of a man's efforts. And the expression of the *masserizia*, in the sense of "rational conduct of the household" as the means of living independently of others and avoiding destitution, is in general put only in the mouth of the illiterate Gianozzo as of equal value. Thus the

scribed as the lowest sort of avarice and as an attitude entirely lacking in self-respect. It is, in fact, still regularly thus looked upon by all those social groups which are least involved in or adapted to modern capitalistic conditions. This is not wholly because the instinct of acquisition was in those times unknown or undeveloped, as has often been said. Nor because the *auri sacra fames,* the greed

---

origin of this concept, which comes (see below) from monastic ethics, is traced back to an old priest (p. 249).

Now compare all this with the ethic and manner of life of Benjamin Franklin, and especially of his Puritan ancestors; the works of the Renaissance *littérateur* addressing himself to the humanistic aristocracy, with Franklin's works addressed to the masses of the lower middle class (he especially mentions clerks) and with the tracts and sermons of the Puritans, in order to comprehend the depth of the difference. The economic rationalism of Alberti, everywhere supported by references to ancient authors, is most clearly related to the treatment of economic problems in the work of Xenophon (whom he did not know), of Cato, Varro, and Columella (all of whom he quotes), except that especially in Cato and Varro, *acquisition* as such stands in the foreground in a different way from that to be found in Alberti. Furthermore, the very occasional comments of Alberti on the use of the *fattori,* their division of labour and discipline, on the unreliability of the peasants, etc., really sound as if Cato's homely wisdom were taken from the field of the ancient slave-using household and applied to that of free labour in domestic industry and the *metayer* system. When Sombart (whose reference to the Stoic ethic is quite misleading) sees economic rationalism as "developed to its farthest conclusions" as early as Cato, he is, with a correct interpretation, not entirely wrong. It is possible to unite the *diligens pater familias* of the Romans with the ideal of the *massajo* of Alberti under the same category. It is above all characteristic for Cato that a landed estate is valued and judged as an object for investment of consumption funds. The concept of *industria,* on the other hand, is differently coloured on account of Christian influence. And there is just the difference. In the conception of *industria,* which comes from monastic asceticism and which was developed by monastic writers, lies the seed of an *ethos* which was fully developed later in the Protestant worldly asceticism. Hence, as we shall often point out, the relationship of the two, which, however, is less close to the official Church doctrine of St. Thomas than to the Florentine and Siennese mendicant-moralists. In Cato and also in Alberti's own writings this *ethos* is lacking; for both it is a matter of worldly wisdom, not of ethic. In Franklin there is also a utilitarian strain. But the ethical quality of the sermon to young businessmen is impossible to mistake, and that is the characteristic thing. A lack of care in the handling of money means to him that one so to speak murder capital embryos, and hence it is an ethical defect.

An inner relationship of the two (Alberti and Franklin) exists in fact only in so far as Alberti—whom Sombart calls pious, but who actually, although he took the sacraments and held a Roman benefice, like so many humanists, did not himself (except for two quite colourless passages) in any way make use of religious motives as a justification of the manner of life he recommended—had not yet related, while Franklin on the other hand no longer related, his recommendation of economy to religious conceptions. Utilitarianism, in Alberti's preference for wool and silk manufacture, also the mercantilist social utilitarianism "that many people should be given employment" (see Alberti, *op. cit.,* p. 292), is in this field at least formally the sole justification for the one as for the other. Alberti's discussions of this subject form an excellent example of the sort of economic rationalism which really existed as a reflection of economic conditions, in the work of authors interested purely in "the thing for its own sake" everywhere and at all times; in the Chinese classicism and in Greece and Rome no less than in the Renaissance and the age of the Enlightenment. There is no doubt that just as in ancient times with Cato, Varro, and Columella, also here with Alberti and others of the same type, especially in the doctrine of *industria,* a sort of economic rationality is highly developed. But how can anyone believe that such a literary *theory* could develop into a revolutionary force at all comparable to the way in which a religious belief was able to set sanctions of salvation and damnation on the fulfillment of a particular (in this case methodically rationalized) manner of life? What, as compared with it, a really religiously oriented rationalization of conduct looks like, may be seen,

for gold, was then, or now, less powerful outside of bourgeois capitalism than within its peculiar sphere, as the illusions of modern romanticists are wont to believe. The difference between the capitalistic and pre-capitalistic spirits is not to be found at this point. The greed of the Chinese Mandarin, the old Roman aristocrat, or the modern peasant, can stand up to any comparison. And the *auri sacra fames* of a Neapolitan cab-driver or *barcaiuolo,* and certainly of Asiatic representatives of similar trades, as well as of the craftsmen of southern European or Asiatic countries, is, as anyone can find out for himself, very much more intense, and especially more unscrupulous than that of, say, an Englishman in similar circumstances.[14]

---

outside of the Puritans of all denominations, in the cases of the Jains, the Jews, certain ascetic sects of the Middle Ages, the Bohemian Brothers (an offshoot of the Hussite movement), the Skoptsi and Stundists in Russia, and numerous monastic orders, however much all these may differ from each other.

The essential point of difference is (to anticipate) that an ethic based on religion places certain psychological sanctions (not of an economic character) on the maintenance of the attitude prescribed by it, sanctions which, so long as the religious belief remains alive, are highly effective, and which mere worldly wisdom like that of Alberti does not have at its disposal. Only in so far as these sanctions work, and, above all, in the direction in which they work, which is often very different from the doctrine in the theologians, does such an ethic gain an independent influence on the conduct of life and thus on the economic order. This is, to speak frankly, the point of this whole essay, which I had not expected to find so completely overlooked.

Later on I shall come to speak of the theological moralists of the late Middle Ages, who were relatively friendly to capital (especially Anthony of Florence and Bernhard of Siena), and whom Sombart has also seriously misinterpreted. In any case Alberti did not belong to that group. Only the concept of *industria* did he take from monastic lines of thought, no matter through what intermediary links. Alberti, Pandolfini, and their kind are representative of that attitude which, in spite of all its outward obedience, was inwardly already emancipated from the tradition of the Church. With all its resemblance to the current Christian ethic, it was to a large extent of the antique pagan character, which Brentano thinks I have ignored in its significance for the development of modern economic thought (and also modern economic policy). That I do not deal with its influence here is quite true. It would be out of place in a study of the Protestant ethic and the spirit of capitalism. But, as will appear in a different connection, far from denying its significance, I have been and am for good reasons of the opinion that its sphere and direction of influence were entirely different from those of the Protestant ethic (of which the spiritual ancestry, of no small practical importance, lies in the sects and in the ethics of Wyclif and Hus). It was not the mode of life of the rising bourgeoisie which was influenced by this other attitude, but the policy of statesmen and princes; and these two partly, but by no means always, convergent lines of development should for purposes of analysis be kept perfectly distinct. So far as Franklin is concerned, his tracts of advice to business men, at present used for school reading in America, belong in fact to a category of works which have influenced practical life, far more than Alberti's large book, which hardly became known outside of learned circles. But I have expressly denoted him as a man who stood beyond the direct influence of the Puritan view of life, which had paled considerably in the meantime, just as the whole English enlightenment, the relations of which to Puritanism have often been set forth.

[14] Unfortunately Brentano (*op. cit.*) has thrown every kind of struggle for gain, whether peaceful or warlike, into one pot, and has then set up as the specific criterion of capitalistic (as contrasted, for instance, with feudal) profit-seeking, its acquisitiveness of *money* (instead of land). Any further differentiation, which alone could lead to a clear conception, he has not only refused to make, but has made against the concept of the spirit of (modern) capitalism which we have formed for our purposes, the (to me) incomprehensible objection that it already includes in its assumptions what is supposed to be proved.

The universal reign of absolute unscrupulousness in the pursuit of selfish interests by the making of money has been a specific characteristic of precisely those countries whose bourgeois-capitalistic development, measured according to Occidental standards, has remained backward. As every employer knows, the lack of *coscienziosità* of the labourers[15] of such countries, for instance Italy as compared with Germany, has been, and to a certain extent still is, one of the principal obstacles to their capitalistic development. Capitalism cannot make use of the labour of those who practise the doctrine of undisciplined *liberum arbitrium,* any more than it can make use of the business man who seems absolutely unscrupulous in his dealings with others, as we can learn from Franklin. Hence the difference does not lie in the degree of development of any impulse to make money. The *auri sacra fames* is as old as the history of man. But we shall see that those who submitted to it without reserve as an uncontrolled impulse, such as the Dutch sea-captain who "would go through hell for gain, even though he scorched his sails", were by no means the representatives of that attitude of mind from which the specifically modern capitalistic spirit as a mass phenomenon is derived, and that is what matters. At all periods of history, wherever it was possible, there has been ruthless acquisition, bound to no ethical norms whatever. Like war and piracy, trade has often been unrestrained in its relations with foreigners and those outside the group. The double ethic has permitted here what was forbidden in dealings among brothers.

Capitalistic acquisition as an adventure has been at home in all types of economic society which have known trade with the use of money and which have offered it opportunities, through *commenda,* farming of taxes, State loans, financing of wars, ducal courts and office-holders. Likewise the inner attitude of the adventurer, which laughs at all ethical limitations, has been universal. Absolute and conscious ruthlessness in acquisition has often stood in the closest connection with the strictest conformity to tradition. Moreover, with the breakdown of tradition and the more or less complete extension of free economic enterprise, even to within the social group, the new thing has not generally been ethically justified and encouraged, but only tolerated as a fact. And this fact has been treated either as ethically indifferent or as reprehensible, but unfortunately unavoidable. This has not only been the normal attitude of all ethical teachings, but, what is more important, also that expressed in the practical action of the average man of pre-capitalistic times, pre-capitalistic in the sense that the rational utilization of capital in a permanent enterprise and the rational capitalistic organization of labour had not yet become dominant forces in the determination of economic activity. Now just this attitude was one of the strongest inner ob-

[15] Compare the, in every respect, excellent observations of Sombart, *Die deutsche Volkswirtschaft im 19ten Jahrhundert,* p. 123. In general I do not need specially to point out, although the following studies go back to their most important points of view to much older work, how much they owe in their development to the mere existence of Sombart's important works, with their pointed formulations and this even, perhaps especially, where they take a different road. Even those who feel themselves continually and decisively disagreeing with Sombart's views, and who reject many of his theses, have the duty to do so only after a thorough study of his work.

stacles which the adaptation of men to the conditions of an ordered bourgeois-capitalistic economy has encountered everywhere.

The most important opponent with which the spirit of capitalism, in the sense of a definite standard of life claiming ethical sanction, has had to struggle, was that type of attitude and reaction to new situations which we may designate as traditionalism. In this case also every attempt at a final definition must be held in abeyance. On the other hand, we must try to make the provisional meaning clear by citing a few cases. We will begin from below, with the labourers.

One of the technical means which the modern employer uses in order to secure the greatest possible amount of work from his men is the device of piece-rates. In agriculture, for instance, the gathering of the harvest is a case where the greatest possible intensity of labour is called for, since, the weather being uncertain, the difference between high profit and heavy loss may depend on the speed with which the harvesting can be done. Hence a system of piece-rates is almost universal in this case. And since the interest of the employer in a speeding-up of harvesting increases with the increase of the results and the intensity of the work, the attempt has again and again been made, by increasing the piece-rates of the workmen, thereby giving them an opportunity to earn what is for them a very high wage, to interest them in increasing their own efficiency. But a peculiar difficulty has been met with surprising frequency: raising the piece-rates has often had the result that not more but less has been accomplished in the same time, because the worker reacted to the increase not by increasing but by decreasing the amount of his work. A man, for instance, who at the rate of 1 mark per acre mowed 2½ acres per day and earned 2½ marks, when the rate was raised to 1.25 marks per acre mowed, not 3 acres, as he might easily have done, thus earning 3.75 marks, but only 2 acres, so that he could still earn the 2½ marks to which he was accustomed. The opportunity of earning more was less attractive than that of working less. He did not ask: how much can I earn in a day if I do as much work as possible? but: how much must I work in order to earn the wage, 2½ marks, which I earned before and which takes care of my traditional needs? This is an example of what is here meant by traditionalism. A man does not "by nature" wish to earn more and more money, but simply to live as he is accustomed to live and to earn as much as is necessary for that purpose. Wherever modern capitalism has begun its work of increasing the productivity of human labour by increasing its intensity, it has encountered the immensely stubborn resistance of this leading trait of pre-capitalistic labour. And to-day it encounters it the more, the more backward (from a capitalistic point of view) the labouring forces are with which it has to deal.

Another obvious possibility, to return to our example, since the appeal to the acquisitive instinct through higher wage-rates failed, would have been to try the opposite policy, to force the worker by reduction of his wage-rates to work harder to earn the same amount as he did before. Low wages and high profits seem even to-day to a superficial observer to stand in correlation; everything which is paid out in wages seems to involve a corresponding reduction of profits. That road capitalism has taken again and again since its beginning. For centuries it was an article of faith, that low wages were productive, i.e. that they increased the material results of labour so that, as Pieter de la Cour, on this point, as we shall see, quite in the spirit of the old Calvinism, said long ago, the people only work because and so long as they are poor.

But the effectiveness of this apparently so efficient method has its limits.[16] Of course the presence of a surplus population which it can hire cheaply in the labour market is a necessary for the development of capitalism. But though too large a reserve army may in certain cases favour its quantitative expansion, it checks its qualitative development, especially the transition to types of enterprise which make more intensive use of labour. Low wages are by no means identical with cheap labour. From a purely quantitative point of view the efficiency of labour decreases with a wage which is physiologically insufficient, which may in the long run even mean a survival of the unfit. The present-day average Silesian mows, when he exerts himself to the full, little more than two-thirds as much land as the better paid and nourished Pomeranian or Mecklenburger, and the Pole, the further East he comes from, accomplishes progressively less than the German. Low wages fail even from a purely business point of view wherever it is a question of producing goods which require any sort of skilled labour, or the use of expensive machinery which is easily damaged, or in general wherever any great amount of sharp attention or of initiative is required. Here low wages do not pay, and their effect is the opposite of what was intended. For not only is a developed sense of responsibility absolutely indispensable, but in general also an attitude which, at least during working hours, is freed from continual calculations of how the customary wage may be earned with a maximum of comfort and a minimum of exertion. Labour must, on the contrary, be performed as if it were an absolute end in itself, a calling (*Beruf*). But such an attitude is by no means a product of nature. It cannot be evoked by low wages or high ones alone, but can only be the product of a long and arduous process of education. To-day, capitalism, once in the saddle, can recruit its labouring force in all industrial countries with comparative ease. In the past this was in every case an extremely difficult problem.[17] And even to-day it could probably not get along without the

[16] Of course we cannot here enter into the question of where these limits lie, nor can we evaluate the familiar theory of the relation between high wages and the high productivity of labour which was first suggested by Brassey, formulated and maintained theoretically by Brentano, and both historically and theoretically by Schulze-Gaevernitz. The discussion was again opened by Hasbach's penetrating studies (*Schmollers Jahrbuch*, 1903, pp. 385–91 and 417 ff.), and is not yet finally settled. For us it is here sufficient to assent to the fact which is not, and cannot be, doubted by anyone, that low wages and high profits, low wages and favourable opportunities for industrial development, are at least not simply identical, that generally speaking training for capitalistic culture, and with it the possibility of capitalism as an economic system, are not brought about simply through mechanical financial operations. All examples are purely illustrative.

[17] The establishment even of capitalistic industries has hence often not been possible without large migratory movements from areas of older culture. However correct Sombart's remarks on the difference between the personal skill and trade secrets of the handicraftsman and the scientific, objective modern technique may be, at the time of the rise of capitalism the difference hardly existed. In fact the, so to speak, ethical qualities of the capitalistic workman (and to a certain extent also of the entrepreneur) often had a higher scarcity value than the skill of the craftsman, crystallized in tra-

support of a powerful ally along the way, which, as we shall see below, was at hand at the time of its development.

What is meant can again best be explained by means of an example. The type of backward traditional form of labour is to-day very often exemplified by women workers, especially unmarried ones. An almost universal complaint of employers of girls, for instance German girls, is that they are almost entirely unable and unwilling to give up methods of work inherited or once learned in favour of more efficient ones, to adapt themselves to new methods, to learn and to concentrate their intelligence, or even to use it at all. Explanations of the possibility of making work easier, above all more profitable to themselves, generally encounter a complete lack of understanding. Increases of piece-rates are without avail against the stone wall of habit. In general it is otherwise, and that is a point of no little importance from our view-point, only with girls having a specifically religious, especially a Pietistic, background. One often hears, and statistical investigation confirms it,[18] that by far the best chances of economic education are found among this group. The ability of mental concentration, as well as the absolutely essential feeling of obligation to one's job, are here most often combined with a strict economy which calculates the possibility of high earnings, and a cool self-control and frugality which enormously increase performance. This provides the most favourable foundation for the conception of labour as an end in itself, as a calling (*Beruf*) which is necessary to capitalism: the chances of overcoming traditionalism are greatest on account of the religious upbringing. This observation of present-day capitalism[19] in itself suggests that it is worth while to ask how this connection of adaptability to capitalism with religious factors may have come about in the days of the early development of capitalism. For that they were even then present in much the same form can be inferred from numerous facts. For instance, the dislike and the persecution which Methodist workmen in the eighteenth century met at the hands of their comrades were not solely nor even principally the result of their religious eccentricities; England has seen many of those and more striking ones. It rested rather, as the destruction of their tools, repeatedly mentioned in the reports, suggests, upon their specific willingness to work as we should say to-day.

---

ditions hundreds of years old. And even present-day industry is not yet by any means entirely independent in its choice of location of such qualities of the population, acquired by long-standing tradition and education in intensive labour. It is congenial to the scientific prejudices of to-day, when such a dependent is observed to ascribe it to congenial racial qualities rather than to tradition and education, in my opinion with very doubtful validity.

[18] See my "Zur Psychophysik der gewerblichen Arbeit", *Archiv für Sozialwissenschaft und Sozialpolitik*, XXVIII.

[19] The foregoing observation might be misunderstood. The tendency of a well-known type of business man to use the belief that "religion must be maintained for the people" for his own purpose, and the earlier not uncommon willingness of large numbers, especially of the Lutheran clergy, from a general sympathy with authority, to offer themselves as black police when they wished to brand the strike as sin and trade unions as furtherers of cupidity, all these are things with which our present problem has nothing to do. The factors discussed in the text do not concern occasional but very common facts, which, as we shall see, continually recur in a typical manner.

However, let us again return to the present, and this time to the entrepreneur, in order to clarify the meaning of traditionalism in his case.

Sombart, in his discussions of the genesis of capitalism,[20] has distinguished between the satisfaction of needs and acquisition as the two great leading principles in economic history. In the former case the attainment of the goods necessary to meet personal needs, in the latter a struggle for profit free from the limits set by needs, have been the ends controlling the form and direction of economic activity. What he calls the "economy of needs" seems at first glance to be identical with what is here described as economic traditionalism. That may be the case if the concept of needs is limited to traditional needs. But if that is not done, a number of economic types which must be considered capitalistic according to the definition of capital which Sombart gives in another part of his work,[21] would be excluded from the category of acquisitive economy and put into that of needs economy. Enterprises, namely, which are carried on by private entrepreneurs by utilizing capital (money or goods with a money value) to make a profit, purchasing the means of production and selling the product, i.e. undoubted capitalistic enterprises, may at the same time have a traditionalistic character. This has, in the course even of modern economic history, not been merely an occasional case, but rather the rule, with continual interruptions from repeated and increasingly powerful conquests of the capitalistic spirit. To be sure the capitalistic form of an enterprise and the spirit in which it is run generally stand in some sort of adequate relationship to each other, but not in one of necessary interdependence. Nevertheless, we provisionally use the expression "spirit of (modern) capitalism"[22] to describe that attitude which seeks profit rationally and systematically in the manner which we have illustrated by the example of Benjamin Franklin. This, however, is justified by the historical fact that that attitude of mind has on the one hand found its most suitable expression in capitalistic enterprise, while on the other the enterprise has derived its most suitable motive force from the spirit of capitalism.

But the two may very well occur separately. Benjamin Franklin was filled with the spirit of capitalism at a time when his printing business did not differ in form from any handicraft enterprise. And we shall see that at the beginning of modern times it was by no means the capitalistic entrepreneurs of the commercial aristocracy, who were either the sole or the predominant bearers of the attitude we have here called the spirit of capitalism.[23] It was much more the rising strata

---

[20] *Der moderne Kapitalismus*, first edition, I, p. 62.

[21] *Ibid.*, p. 195.

[22] Naturally that of the modern rational enterprise peculiar to the Occident, not of the sort of capitalism spread over the world for three thousand years, from China, India, Babylon, Greece, Rome, Florence, to the present, carried on by usurers, military contractors, traders in offices, tax-farmers, large merchants, and financial magnates. See the Introduction [pp. 20–21 in *The Protestant Ethic*].

[23] The assumption is thus by no means justified a priori, that is all I wish to bring out here, that on the one hand the technique of the capitalistic enterprise, and on the other hand the spirit of professional work which gives to capitalism its expansive energy, must have had their original roots in the same social classes. Similarly with the social relationships of religious beliefs. Calvinism was his-

of the lower industrial middle classes. Even in the nineteenth century its classical representatives were not the elegant gentlemen of Liverpool and Hamburg, with their commercial fortunes handed down for generations, but the self-made parvenus of Manchester and Westphalia, who often rose from very modest circumstances. As early as the sixteenth century the situation was similar; the industries which arose at that time were mostly created by parvenus.[24]

The management, for instance, of a bank, a wholesale export business, a large retail establishment, or of a large putting-out enterprise dealing with goods produced in homes, is certainly only possible in the form of a capitalistic enterprise. Nevertheless, they may all be carried on in a traditionalistic spirit. In fact, the business of a large bank of issue cannot be carried on in any other way. The foreign trade of whole epochs has rested on the basis of monopolies and legal privileges of strictly traditional character. In retail trade—and we are not here talking of the small men without capital who are continually crying out for Government aid—the revolution which is making an end of the old traditionalism is still in full swing. It is the same development which broke up the old putting-out system, to which modern domestic labour is related only in form. How this revolution takes place and what is its significance may, in spite of the fact that these things are so familiar, be again brought out by a concrete example.

Until about the middle of the past century the life of a putter-out was, at least in many of the branches of the Continental textile industry,[25] what we should today consider very comfortable. We may imagine its routine somewhat as follows: The peasants came with their cloth, often (in the case of linen) principally or entirely made with raw material which the peasant himself had produced, to the town in which the putter-out lived, and after a careful, often official, appraisal of the quality, received the customary price for it. The putter-out's customers, for markets any appreciable distance away, were middlemen, who also came to him, generally not yet following samples, but seeking traditional qualities, and bought from his warehouse, or, long before delivery, placed orders which were probably in turn passed on to the peasants. Personal canvassing of customers took place, if at all, only at long intervals. Otherwise correspondence sufficed, though the sending of samples slowly gained ground. The number of business hours was very moderate, perhaps five to six a day, sometimes considerably less; in the rush season, where there was one, more. Earnings were moderate; enough to lead a

---

torically one of the agents of education in the spirit of capitalism. But in the Netherlands, the large moneyed interests were, for reasons which will be discussed later, not predominantly adherents of strict Calvinism, but Arminians. The rising middle and small bourgeoisie, from which entrepreneurs were principally recruited, were for the most part here and elsewhere typical representatives both of capitalistic ethics and of Calvinistic religion. But that fits in very well with our present thesis: there were at all times large bankers and merchants. But a rational capitalistic organization of industrial labour was never known until the transition from the Middle Ages to modern times took place.

[24] On this point see the good Zurich dissertation of J. Maliniak (1913).

[25] The following picture has been put together as an ideal type from conditions found in different industrial branches and at different places. For the purpose of illustration which it here serves, it is of course of no consequence that the process has not in any one of the examples we have in mind taken place in precisely the manner we have described.

respectable life and in good times to put away a little. On the whole, relations among competitors were relatively good, with a large degree of agreement on the fundamentals of business. A long daily visit to the tavern, often with plenty to drink, and a congenial circle of friends, made life comfortable and leisurely.

The form of organization was in every respect capitalistic; the entrepreneur's activity was of a purely business character; the use of capital, turned over in the business, was indispensable; and finally, the objective aspect of the economic process, the book-keeping, was rational. But it was traditionalistic business, if one considers the spirit which animated the entrepreneur: the traditional manner of life, the traditional rate of profit, the traditional amount of work, the traditional manner of regulating the relationships with labour, and the essentially traditional circle of customers and the manner of attracting new ones. All these dominated the conduct of the business, were at the basis, one may say, of the *ethos* of this group of business men.

Now at some time this leisureliness was suddenly destroyed, and often entirely without any essential change in the form of organization, such as the transition to a unified factory, to mechanical weaving, etc. What happened was, on the contrary, often no more than this: some young man from one of the putting-out families went out into the country, carefully chose weavers for his employ, greatly increased the rigour of his supervision of their work, and thus turned them from peasants into labourers. On the other hand, he would begin to change his marketing methods by so far as possible going directly to the final consumer, would take the details into his own hands, would personally solicit customers, visiting them every year, and above all would adapt the quality of the product directly to their needs and wishes. At the same time he began to introduce the principle of low prices and large turnover. There was repeated what everywhere and always is the result of such a process of rationalization: those who would not follow suit had to go out of business. The idyllic state collapsed under the pressure of a bitter competitive struggle, respectable fortunes were made, and not lent out at interest, but always reinvested in the business. The old leisurely and comfortable attitude toward life gave way to a hard frugality in which some participated and came to the top, because they did not wish to consume but to earn, while others who wished to keep on with the old ways were forced to curtail their consumption.[26]

And, what is most important in this connection, it was not generally in such cases a stream of new money invested in the industry which brought about this revolution—in several cases known to me the whole revolutionary process was set in motion with a few thousands of capital borrowed from relations—but the new spirit, the spirit of modern capitalism, had set to work. The question of the motive forces in the expansion of modern capitalism is not in the first instance a question of the origin of the capital sums which were available for capitalistic uses, but, above all, of the development of the spirit of capitalism. Where it ap-

---

[26] For this reason, among others, it is not by chance that this first period of incipient (economic) rationalism in German industry was accompanied by certain other phenomena, for instance the catastrophic degradation of taste in the style of articles of everyday use.

pears and is able to work itself out, it produces its own capital and monetary supplies as the means to its ends, but the reverse is not true.[27] Its entry on the scene was not generally peaceful. A flood of mistrust, sometimes of hatred, above all of moral indignation, regularly opposed itself to the first innovator. Often—I know of several cases of the sort—regular legends of mysterious shady spots in his previous life have been produced. It is very easy not to recognize that only an unusually strong character could save an entrepreneur of this new type from the loss of his temperate self-control and from both moral and economic shipwreck. Furthermore, along with clarity of vision and ability to act, it is only by virtue of very definite and highly developed ethical qualities that it has been possible for him to command the absolutely indispensable confidence of his customers and workmen. Nothing else could have given him the strength to overcome the innumerable obstacles, above all the infinitely more intensive work which is demanded of the modern entrepreneur. But these are ethical qualities of quite a different sort from those adapted to the traditionalism of the past.

And, as a rule, it has been neither dare-devil and unscrupulous speculators, economic adventurers such as we meet at all periods of economic history, nor simply great financiers who have carried through this change, outwardly so inconspicuous, but nevertheless so decisive for the penetration of economic life with the new spirit. On the contrary, they were men who had grown up in the hard school of life, calculating and daring at the same time, above all temperate and reliable, shrewd and completely devoted to their business, with strictly bourgeois opinions and principles.

One is tempted to think that these personal moral qualities have not the slightest relation to any ethical maxims, to say nothing of religious ideas, but that the essential relation between them is negative. The ability to free oneself from the common tradition, a sort of liberal enlightenment, seems likely to be the most suitable basis for such a business man's success. And to-day that is generally precisely the case. Any relationship between religious beliefs and conduct is generally absent, and where any exists, at least in Germany, it tends to be of the negative sort. The people filled with the spirit of capitalism to-day tend to be indifferent, if not hostile, to the Church. The thought of the pious boredom of paradise has little attraction for their active natures; religion appears to them as a means of drawing people away from labour in this world. If you ask them what is the meaning of their restless activity, why they are never satisfied with what they have, thus appearing so senseless to any purely worldly view of life, they would perhaps give the answer, if they know any at all: "to provide for my children and grandchildren". But more often and, since that motive is not peculiar to them, but was just as effective for the traditionalist, more correctly, simply: that business with its continuous work has become a necessary part of their lives. That is in fact the only possible motivation, but it at the same time expresses what is, seen from the view-point of personal happiness, so irrational about this sort of life, where a man exists for the sake of his business, instead of the reverse.

---

[27] This is not to be understood as a claim that changes in the supply of the precious metals are of no economic importance.

Of course, the desire for the power and recognition which the mere fact of wealth brings plays its part. When the imagination of a whole people has once been turned toward purely quantitative bigness, as in the United States, this romanticism of numbers exercises an irresistible appeal to the poets among business men. Otherwise it is in general not the real leaders, and especially not the permanently successful entrepreneurs, who are taken in by it. In particular, the resort to entailed estates and the nobility, with sons whose conduct at the university and in the officers' corps tries to cover up their social origin, as has been the typical history of German capitalistic parvenu families, is a product of later decadence. The ideal type[28] of the capitalistic entrepreneur, as it has been represented even in Germany by occasional outstanding examples, has no relation to such more or less refined climbers. He avoids ostentation and unnecessary expenditure, as well as conscious enjoyment of his power, and is embarrassed by the outward signs of the social recognition which he receives. His manner of life is, in other words, often, and we shall have to investigate the historical significance of just this important fact, distinguished by a certain ascetic tendency, as appears clearly enough in the sermon of Franklin which we have quoted. It is, namely, by no means exceptional, but rather the rule, for him to have a sort of modesty which is essentially more honest than the reserve which Franklin so shrewdly recommends. He gets nothing out of his wealth for himself, except the irrational sense of having done his job well.

But it is just that which seems to the pre-capitalistic man so incomprehensible and mysterious, so unworthy and contemptible. That anyone should be able to make it the sole purpose of his life-work, to sink into the grave weighed down with a great material load of money and goods, seems to him explicable only as the product of a perverse instinct, the *auri sacra fames*.

At present under our individualistic political, legal, and economic institutions, with the forms of organization and general structure which are peculiar to our economic order, this spirit of capitalism might be understandable, as has been said, purely as a result of adaptation. The capitalistic system so needs this devotion to the calling of making money, it is an attitude toward material goods which is so well suited to that system, so intimately bound up with the conditions of survival in the economic struggle for existence, that there can to-day no longer be any question of a necessary connection of that acquisitive manner of life with any single *Weltanschauung*. In fact, it no longer needs the support of any religious forces, and feels the attempts of religion to influence economic life, in so far as they can still be felt at all, to be as much an unjustified interference as its regulation by the State. In such circumstances men's commercial and social interests do tend to determine their opinions and attitudes. Whoever does not adapt his manner of life to the conditions of capitalistic success must go under, or at least cannot rise. But these are phenomena of a time in which modern capitalism has become dominant and has become emancipated from its old sup-

[28] This is only meant to refer to the type of entrepreneur (business man) whom we are making the object of our study, not any empirical average type. On the concept of the ideal type see my discussion in the *Archiv für Sozialwissenschaft und Sozialpolitik*, XIX, no 1 [reading 17 in this anthology].

ports. But as it could at one time destroy the old forms of mediaeval regulation of economic life only in alliance with the growing power of the modern State, the same, we may say provisionally, may have been the case in its relations with religious forces. Whether and in what sense that was the case, it is our task to investigate. For that the conception of money-making as an end in itself to which people were bound, as a calling, was contrary to the ethical feelings of whole epochs, it is hardly necessary to prove. The dogma *Deo placere vix potest* which was incorporated into the canon law and applied to the activities of the merchant, and which at that time (like the passage in the gospel about interest)[29]

[29] This is perhaps the most appropriate place to make a few remarks concerning the essay of F. Keller, already referred to ([*Unternehmung und Mehrwert*—RS], volume 12 of the publications of the Görres-Gesellschaft), and Sombart's observations (*Der Bourgeois*) in following it up, so far as they are relevant in the present context. That an author should criticize a study in which the canonical prohibition of interest (except in one incidental remark which has no connection with the general argument) is not even mentioned, on the assumption that this prohibition of interest, which has a parallel in almost every religious ethic in the world, is taken to be the decisive criterion of the difference between the Catholic and Protestant ethics, is almost inconceivable. One should really only criticize things which one has read, or the argument of which, if read, one has not already forgotten. The campaign against *usuraria pravitas* runs through both the Huguenots and the Dutch Church history of the sixteenth century; Lombards, i.e. bankers, were by virtue of that fact alone often excluded from communion (see Chap. I, note 17 [p. 170 in *The Protestant Ethic*]). The more liberal attitude of Calvin (which did not, however, prevent the inclusion of regulations against usury in the first plan of the ordinances) did not gain a definite victory until Salmasius. Hence the difference did not lie at this point; quite the contrary. But still worse are the author's own arguments on this point. Compared to the works of Funck and other Catholic scholars (which he has not, in my opinion, taken as fully into consideration as they deserve), and the investigations of Endemann, which, however obsolete in certain points to-day, are still fundamental, they make a painful impression of superficiality. To be sure, Keller has abstained from such excesses as the remarks of Sombart (*Der Bourgeois*, p. 321) that one noticed how the "pious gentlemen" (Bernhard of Siena and Anthony of Florence) "wished to excite the spirit of enterprise by every possible means", that is, since they, just like nearly everyone else concerned with the prohibition of interest, interpreted it in such a way as to exempt what we should call the productive investment of capital. That Sombart, on the one hand, places the Romans among the heroic peoples, and on the one other, what is for his work as a whole an impossible contradiction, considers economic rationalism to have been developed to its final consequences in Cato (p. 267), may be mentioned by the way as a symptom that this is a book with a thesis in the worst sense.

He has also completely misrepresented the significance of the prohibition of interest. This cannot be set forth here in detail. At one time it was often exaggerated, then strongly underestimated, and now, in an era which produces Catholic millionaires as well as Protestant, has been turned upside down for apologetic purposes. As is well known, it was not, in spite of Biblical authority, abolished until the last century by order of the *Congregatio S. Officii*, and then only *temporum ratione habita* and indirectly, namely, by forbidding confessors to worry their charges by questions about *usuraria pravitas*, even though no claim to obedience was given up in case it should be restored. Anyone who has made a thorough study of the extremely complicated history of the doctrine cannot claim, considering the endless controversies over, for instance, the justification of the purposes of bonds, the discounting of notes and various other contracts (and above all considering the order of the *Congregatio S. Officii*, mentioned above, concerning a municipal loan), that the prohibition of interest was only intended to apply to emergency loans, nor that it had the intention of preserving capital, or that it was even an aid to capitalist enterprise (p. 25). The truth is that the Church came to reconsider the prohibition of interest comparatively late. At the time when this happened the forms of purely business investment were not loans at fixed interests rates, but the *foenus nauticum,*

was considered genuine, as well as St. Thomas's characterization of the desire for gain as *turpitudo* (which term even included unavoidable and hence ethically justified profit-making), already contained a high degree of concession on the part of the Catholic doctrine to the financial powers with which the Church had such intimate political relations in the Italian cities,[30] as compared with the

---

commenda, societas maris, and the *dare ad proficuum de mari* (a loan in which the shares of gain and loss were adjusted according to degrees of risk), and were, considering the character of the return on loans to productive enterprise, necessarily of that sort. These were not (or only according to a few rigorous canonists) held to fall under the ban, but when investment at a definite rate of interest and discounting became possible and customary, the first sort of loans also encountered very troublesome difficulties from the prohibition, which led to various drastic measures of the merchant guilds (black lists). But the treatment of usury on the part of the canonists was generally purely legal and formal, and was certainly free from any such tendency to protect capital as Keller ascribes to it. Finally, in so far as any attitudes towards capitalism as such can be ascertained, the decisive factors were: on the one hand, a traditional, mostly inarticulate hostility towards the growing power of capital which was impersonal, and hence not readily amenable to ethical control (as is still reflected in Luther's pronouncements about the Fuggers and about the banking business); on the other hand, the necessity of accommodation to practical needs. But we cannot discuss this, for, as has been said, the prohibition of usury and its fate can have at most a symptomatic significance for us, and that only to a limited degree.

The economic ethic of the Scotists, and especially of certain mendicant theologians of the fourteenth century, above all Bernhard of Siena and Anthony of Florence, that is monks with a specifically rational type of asceticism, undoubtedly deserves a separate treatment, and cannot be disposed of incidentally in our discussion. Otherwise I should be forced here, in reply to criticism, to anticipate what I have to say in my discussion of the economic ethics of Catholicism in its positive relations to capitalism. These authors attempt, and in that anticipate some of the Jesuits, to present the profit of the merchants as a reward for his *industria,* and thus ethically to justify it. (Of course, even Keller cannot claim more.)

The concept and the approval of *industria* come, of course, in the last analysis from monastic asceticism, probably also from the idea of *masserizia,* which Alberti, as he himself says through the mouth of Gianozzo, takes over from the clerical sources. We shall later speak more fully of the sense in which the monastic ethics is a forerunner of the worldly ascetic denominations of Protestantism. In Greece, among the Cynics, as shown by late-Hellenic tombstone inscriptions, and, with an entirely different background, in Egypt, there were suggestions of similar ideas. But what is for us the most important thing is entirely lacking here and in the case of Alberti. As we shall see later, the characteristic Protestant conception of the proof of one's own salvation, the *certitudo salutis* in a calling, provided the psychological sanctions which this religious belief put behind the *industria.* But that Catholicism could not supply, because its means to salvation were different. In effect these authors are concerned with an ethical doctrine, not with motives to practical action, dependent on the desire for salvation. Furthermore, they are, as is very easy to see, concerned with concessions to practical necessity, not, as was worldly asceticism, with deductions from fundamental religious postulates. (Incidentally, Anthony and Bernhard have long ago been better dealt with than by Keller.) And even these concessions have remained an object of controversy down to the present. Nevertheless the significance of these monastic ethical conceptions as symptoms is by no means small.

But the real roots of the religious ethics which led the way to the modern conception of a calling lay in the sects and the heterodox movements, above all in Wyclif; although Brodnitz (*Englische Wirtschaftsgeschichte*), who thinks his influence was so great that Puritanism found nothing left for it to do, greatly overestimates his significance. All that cannot be gone into here. For here we can only discuss incidentally whether and to what extent the Christian ethic of the Middle Ages had in fact already prepared the way for the spirit of capitalism.

[30] The words *mēden apelpizontes* (Luke vi.35) and the translation of the Vulgate, *nihil inde sperantes,* are thought (according to A. Merx) to be a corruption of *mēdena apelpizontes* (or *neminem*

much more radically anti-chrematistic views of comparatively wide circles. But even where the doctrine was still better accommodated to the facts, as for instance with Anthony of Florence, the feeling was never quite overcome, that activity directed to acquisition for its own sake was at bottom a *pudendum* which was to be tolerated only because of the unalterable necessities of life in this world.

Some moralists of that time, especially of the nominalistic school, accepted developed capitalistic business forms as inevitable, and attempted to justify them, especially commerce, as necessary. The *industria* developed in it they were able to regard, though not without contradictions, as a legitimate source of profit, and hence ethically unobjectionable. But the dominant doctrine rejected the spirit of capitalistic acquisition as *turpitudo*, or at least could not give it a positive ethical sanction. An ethical attitude like that of Benjamin Franklin would have been simply unthinkable. This was, above all, the attitude of capitalistic circles themselves. Their life-work was, so long as they clung to the tradition of the Church, at best something morally indifferent. It was tolerated, but was still, even if only on account of the continual danger of collision with the Church's doctrine on usury, somewhat dangerous to salvation. Quite considerable sums, as the sources show, went at the death of rich people to religious institutions as conscience money, at times even back to former debtors as *usura* which had been unjustly taken from them. It was otherwise, along with heretical and other tendencies looked upon with disapproval, only in those parts of the commercial aristocracy which were already emancipated from the tradition. But even sceptics and people indifferent to the Church often reconciled themselves with it by gifts, because it was a sort of insurance against the uncertainties of what might come after death, or because (at least according to the very widely held latter view) an external obedience to the commands of the Church was sufficient to insure salvation.[31] Here the either non-moral or immoral character of their action in the opinion of the participants themselves comes clearly to light.

Now, how could activity, which was at best ethically tolerated, turn into a calling in the sense of Benjamin Franklin? The fact to be explained historically is that in the most highly capitalistic centre of that time, in Florence of the four-

---

desperantes), and thus to command the granting of loans to all brothers, including the poor, without saying anything at all about interest. The passage *Deo placere vix potest* is now thought to be of Arian origin (which, if true, makes no difference to our contentions).

[31] How a compromise with the prohibition of usury was achieved is shown, for example, in Book I, chapter 65, of the statutes of the *Arte di Calimala* (at present I have only the Italian edition in Emiliani-Guidici, *Stor. dei Com. Ital.*, III, p. 246). "Procurino i consoli con qualli frate, che parrà loro, che perdono si faccia e come fare si possa il meglio per l'amore di ciascuno, del dono, merito o guiderdono, ovvero interesse per l'anno presente e secondo che altra volta fatto fue." It is thus a way for the guild to secure exemption for its members on account of their official positions, without defiance of authority. The suggestions immediately following, as well as the immediately preceding idea to book all interest and profits as gifts, are very characteristic of the amoral attitude towards profits on capital. To the present stock exchange black list against brokers who hold back the difference between top price and actual selling price, often corresponded the outcry against those who pleaded before the ecclesiastical court with the *exceptio usurariae pravitatis*.

teenth and fifteenth centuries, the money and capital market of all the great political Powers, this attitude was considered ethically unjustifiable, or at best to be tolerated. But in the backwoods small bourgeois circumstances of Pennsylvania in the eighteenth century, where business threatened for simple lack of money to fall back into barter, where there was hardly a sign of large enterprise, where only the earliest beginnings of banking were to be found, the same thing was considered the essence of moral conduct, even commanded in the name of duty. To speak here of a reflection of material conditions in the ideal superstructure would be patent nonsense. What was the background of ideas which could account for the sort of activity apparently directed toward profit alone as a calling toward which the individual feels himself to have an ethical obligation? For it was this idea which gave the way of life of the new entrepreneur its ethical foundation and justification.

The attempt has been made, particularly by Sombart, in what are often judicious and effective observations, to depict economic rationalism as the salient feature of modern economic life as a whole. Undoubtedly with justification, if by that is meant the extension of the productivity of labour which has, through the subordination of the process of production to scientific points of view, relieved it from its dependence upon the natural organic limitations of the human individual. Now this process of rationalization in the field of technique and economic organization undoubtedly determines an important part of the ideals of life of modern bourgeois society. Labour in the service of a rational organization for the provision of humanity with material goods has without doubt always appeared to representatives of the capitalistic spirit as one of the most important purposes of their life-work. It is only necessary, for instance, to read Franklin's account of his efforts in the service of civic improvements in Philadelphia clearly to apprehend this obvious truth. And the joy and pride of having given employment to numerous people, of having had a part in the economic progress of his home town in the sense referring to figures of population and volume of trade which capitalism associated with the word, all these things obviously are part of the specific and undoubtedly idealistic satisfactions in life to modern men of business. Similarly it is one of the fundamental characteristics of an individualistic capitalistic economy that it is rationalized on the basis of rigorous calculation, directed with foresight and caution toward the economic success which is sought in sharp contrast to the hand-to-mouth existence of the peasant, and to the privileged traditionalism of the guild craftsman and of the adventurers' capitalism, oriented to the exploitation of political opportunities and irrational speculation.

It might thus seem that the development of the spirit of capitalism is best understood as part of the development of rationalism as a whole, and could be deduced from the fundamental position of rationalism on the basic problems of life. In the process Protestantism would only have to be considered in so far as it had formed a stage prior to the development of a purely rationalistic philosophy. But any serious attempt to carry this thesis through makes it evident that such a simple way of putting the question will not work, simply because of the fact that the history of rationalism shows a development which by no means follows parallel lines in the various departments of life. The rationalization of private law, for instance, if it is thought of as a logical simplification and rearrangement of the content of the law, was achieved in the highest hitherto known degree in the Roman law of late antiquity. But it remained most backward in some of the countries with the highest degree of economic rationalization, notably in England, where the Renaissance of Roman Law was overcome by the power of the great legal corporations, while it has always retained its supremacy in the Catholic countries of Southern Europe. The worldly rational philosophy of the eighteenth century did not find favour alone or even principally in the countries of highest capitalistic development. The doctrines of Voltaire are even to-day the common property of broad upper-, and what is practically more important, middle-class groups in the Romance Catholic countries. Finally, if under practical rationalism is understood the type of attitude which sees and judges the world consciously in terms of the worldly interests of the individual ego, then this view of life was and is the special peculiarity of the peoples of the *liberum arbitrium,* such as the Italians and the French are in very flesh and blood. But we have already convinced ourselves that this is by no means the soil in which that relationship of a man to his calling as a task, which is necessary to capitalism, has pre-eminently grown. In fact, one may—this simple proposition, which is often forgotten, should be placed at the beginning of every study which essays to deal with rationalism—rationalize life from fundamentally different basic points of view and in very different directions. Rationalism is an historical concept which covers a whole world of different things. It will be our task [in the rest of *The Protestant Ethic and the Spirit of Capitalism*—RS] to find out whose intellectual child the particular concrete form of rational thought was, from which the idea of a calling and the devotion to labour in the calling has grown, which is, as we have seen, so irrational from the standpoint of purely eudaemonistic self-interest, but which has been and still is one of the most characteristic elements of our capitalistic culture. We are here particularly interested in the origin of precisely the irrational element which lies in this, as in every conception of a calling (*Beruf*).

THREE

The Market

UP TO THIS POINT [in *Economy and Society*—RS] we have discussed group formations that rationalized their social action only in part, but for the rest had the most diverse structures—more amorphous or more rationally organized, more continuous or more intermittent, more open or more closed. In contrast to all of them stands, as the archetype of all rational social action (*rationales Gesellschaftshandeln*), consociation (*Vergesellschaftung*) through exchange in the *market*.

A market may be said to exist wherever there is competition, even if only unilateral, for opportunities of exchange among a plurality of potential parties. Their physical assemblage in one place, as in the local market square, the fair (the "long distance market"), or the exchange (the merchants' market), only constitutes the most consistent kind of market formation. It is, however, only this physical assemblage which allows the full emergence of the market's most distinctive feature, viz., dickering. Since the discussion of the market phenomena constitutes essentially the content of economics, it will not be presented here. From a sociological point of view, the market represents a coexistence and sequence of rational consociations, each of which is specifically ephemeral insofar as it ceases to exist with the act of exchanging the goods, unless a norm has been promulgated which imposes upon the transferors of the exchangeable goods and guaranty of their lawful acquisition as warranty of title or of quiet enjoyment. The completed barter constitutes a consociation only with the immediate partner. The preparatory dickering, however, is always a social action (*Gemeinschaftshandeln*) insofar as the potential partners are guided in their offers by the potential action of an indeterminately large group of real or imaginary competitors rather than by their own actions alone. The more this is true, the more does the market constitute social action. Furthermore, any act of exchange involving the use of money (sale) is a social action simply because the money used derives its value from its relation to the potential action of others. Its acceptability rests exclusively on the expectation that it will continue to be desirable and can be further used as a means of payment. Group formation (*Vergemeinschaftung*) through the use of money is the exact counterpart to any consociation through rationally agreed or imposed norms.

Reprinted by permission of the Regents of the University of California and the University of California Press from *Economy and Society*, where this text is published under the title "The Market: Its Impersonality and Ethic (Fragment)." See *Economy and Society: An Outline of Interpretive Sociology* (1922) (Berkeley: University of California Press, 1978), pp. 635–40. Translated by Edward Shils and Max Rheinstein. The text was originally published in 1922; see *Wirtschaft und Gesellschaft: Grundriss der verstehenden Soziologie* (Tübingen: J. C. B. Mohr, 1973), pp. 382–85.

Money creates a group by virtue of material interest relations between actual and potential participants in the market and its payments. At the fully developed stage, the so-called money economy, the resulting situation looks as if it had been created by a set of norms established for the very purpose of bringing it into being. The explanation lies in this: Within the market community every act of exchange, especially monetary exchange, is not directed, in isolation, by the action of the individual partner to the particular transaction, but the more rationally it is considered, the more it is directed by the actions of all parties potentially interested in the exchange. The market community as such is the most impersonal relationship of practical life into which humans can enter with one another. This is not due to that potentiality of struggle among the interested parties which is inherent in the market relationship. Any human relationship, even the most intimate, and even though it be marked by the most unqualified personal devotion, is in some sense relative and may involve a struggle with the partner, for instance, over the salvation of his soul. The reason for the impersonality of the market is its matter-of-factness, its orientation to the commodity and only to that. Where the market is allowed to follow its own autonomous tendencies, its participants do not look toward the persons of each other but only toward the commodity; there are no obligations of brotherliness or reverence, and none of those spontaneous human relations that are sustained by personal unions. They all would just obstruct the free development of the bare market relationship, and its specific interests serve, in their turn, to weaken the sentiments on which these obstructions rest. Market behavior is influenced by rational, purposeful pursuit of interests. The partner to a transaction is expected to behave according to rational legality and, quite particularly, to respect the formal inviolability of a promise once given. These are the qualities which form the content of market ethics. In this latter respect the market inculcates, indeed, particularly rigorous conceptions. Violations of agreements, even though they may be concluded by mere signs, entirely unrecorded, and devoid of evidence, are almost unheard of in the annals of the stock exchange. Such absolute depersonalization is contrary to all the elementary forms of human relationship. Sombart has pointed out this contrast repeatedly and brilliantly.[1]

The "free" market, that is, the market which is not bound by ethical norms, with its exploitation of constellations of interests and monopoly positions and its dickering, is an abomination to every system of fraternal ethics. In sharp contrast to all other groups which always presuppose some measure of personal fraternization or even blood kinship, the market is fundamentally alien to any type of fraternal relationship.

At first, free exchange does not occur but with the world outside of the neighborhood or the personal association. The market is a relationship which transcends the boundaries of neighborhood, kinship group, or tribe. Originally, it is indeed the only peaceful relationship of such kind. At first, fellow members did

---

[1] See, e.g., Werner Sombart, *Der moderne Kapitalismus,* vol. 3 (1927) (Berlin: Duncker und Humblot, 1969), pp. 35 ff., 657 ff. (RS).

not trade with one another with the intention of obtaining profit. There was, indeed, no need for such transactions in an age of self-sufficient agrarian units. One of the most characteristic forms of primitive trade, the "silent" trade, dramatically represents the contrast between the market community and the fraternal community. The silent trade is a form of exchange which avoids all face-to-face contact and in which the supply takes the form of a deposit of the commodity at a customary place; the counteroffer takes the same form, and dickering is effected through the increase in the number of objects being offered from both sides, until one party either withdraws dissatisfied or, satisfied, takes the goods left by the other party and departs.

It is normally assumed by both partners to an exchange that each will be interested in the future continuation of the exchange relationship, be it with this particular partner or with some other, and that he will adhere to his promises for this reason and avoid at least striking infringements of the rules of good faith and fair dealing. It is only this assumption which guarantees the law-abidingness of the exchange partners. Insofar as that interest exists, "honesty is the best policy." This proposition, however, is by no means universally applicable, and its empirical validity is irregular; naturally, it is highest in the case of rational enterprises with a stable clientele. For, on the basis of such a stable relationship, which generates the possibility of mutual personal appraisal with regard to market ethics, trading may free itself most successfully from illimited dickering and return, in the interest of the parties, to a relative limitation of fluctuation in prices and exploitation of momentary interest constellations. The consequences, though they are important for price formation, are not relevant here in detail. The fixed price, without preference for any particular buyer, and strict business honesty are highly peculiar features of the regulated local neighborhood markets of the medieval Occident, in contrast to the Near and Far East. They are, moreover, a condition as well as a product of that particular stage of capitalistic economy which is known as Early Capitalism. They are absent where this stage no longer exists. Nor are they practiced by those status and other groups which are not engaged in exchange except occasionally and passively rather than regularly and actively. The maxim of *caveat emptor* obtains, as experience shows, mostly in transactions involving feudal strata or, as every cavalry officer knows, in horse trading among comrades. The specific ethics of the market place is alien to them. Once and for all they conceive of commerce, as does any rural community of neighbors, as an activity in which the sole question is: who will cheat whom.

The freedom of the market is typically limited by sacred taboos or through monopolistic consociations of status groups which render exchange with outsiders impossible. Directed against these limitations we find the continuous onslaught of the market community, whose very existence constitutes a temptation to share in the opportunities for gain. The process of appropriation in a monopolistic group may advance to the point at which it becomes closed toward outsiders, i.e., the land, or the right to share in the commons, may have become vested definitively and hereditarily. As the money economy expands and, with it, both the growing differentiation of needs capable of being satisfied by indirect barter, and the independence from land ownership, such a situation of fixed, hereditary appropriation normally creates a steadily increasing interest of individual parties in the possibility of using their vested property rights for exchange with the highest bidder, even though he be an outsider. This development is quite analogous to that which causes the co-heirs of an industrial enterprise in the long run to establish a corporation so as to be able to sell their shares more freely. In turn, an emerging capitalistic economy, the stronger it becomes, the greater will be its efforts to obtain the means of production and labor services in the market without limitations by sacred or status bonds, and to emancipate the opportunities to sell its products from the restrictions imposed by the sales monopolies of status groups. Capitalistic interests thus favor the continuous extension of the free market, but only up to the point at which some of them succeed, through the purchase of privileges from the political authority or simply through the power of capital, in obtaining for themselves a monopoly for the sale of their products or the acquisition of their means of production, and in thus closing the market on their own part.

The breakup of the monopolies of status groups is thus the typical immediate sequence to the full appropriation of all the material means of production. It occurs where those having a stake in the capitalistic system are in a position to influence, for their own advantage, those communities by which the ownership of goods and the mode of their use are regulated; or where, within a monopolistic status group, the upper hand is gained by those who are interested in the use of their vested property interests in the market. Another consequence is that the scope of those rights which are guaranteed as acquired or acquirable by the coercive apparatus of the property-regulating community becomes limited to rights in material goods and to contractual claims, including claims to contractual labor. All other appropriations, especially those of customers or those of monopolies by status groups, are destroyed. This state of affairs, which we call free competition, lasts until it is replaced by new, this time capitalistic, monopolies which are acquired in the market through the power of property. These capitalistic monopolies differ from monopolies of status groups by their purely economic and rational character. By restricting the scope of possible sales or the permissible terms, the monopolies of status groups excluded from their field of action the mechanism of the market with its dickering and rational calculation. Those monopolies, on the other hand, which are based solely upon the power of property, rest, on the contrary, upon an entirely rationally calculated mastery of market conditions which may, however, remain formally as free as ever. The sacred, status, and merely traditional bonds, which have gradually come to be eliminated, constituted restrictions on the formation of rational market prices; the purely economically conditioned monopolies are, on the other hand, their ultimate consequence. The beneficiary of a monopoly by a status group restricts, and maintains his power against, the market, while the rational-economic monopolist rules through the market. We shall designate those interest groups which are enabled by formal market freedom to achieve power, as market–interest groups.

A particular market may be subject to a body of norms autonomously agreed upon by the participants or imposed by any one of a great variety of different groups, especially political or religious organizations. Such norms may involve limitations of market freedom, restrictions of dickering or of competition, or they may establish guaranties for the observance of market legality, especially the modes or means of payment or, in periods of interlocal insecurity, the norms may be aimed at guaranteeing the market peace. Since the market was originally a consociation of persons who are not members of the same group and who are, therefore, "enemies," the guaranty of peace, like that of restrictions of permissible modes of warfare, was ordinarily left to divine powers. Very often the peace of the market was placed under the protection of a temple; later on it tended to be made into a source of revenue for the chief or prince. However, while exchange is the specifically peaceful form of acquiring economic power, it can, obviously, be associated with the use of force. The seafarer of Antiquity and the Middle Ages was pleased to take without pay whatever he could acquire by force and had recourse to peaceful dickering only where he was confronted with a power equal to his own or where he regarded it as shrewd to do so for the sake of future exchange opportunities which might be endangered otherwise. But the intensive expansion of exchange relations has always gone together with a process of relative pacification. All of the "public peace" arrangements of the Middle Ages were meant to serve the interests of exchange. The appropriation of goods through free, purely economically rational exchange, as Oppenheimer has said time and again, is the conceptual opposite of appropriation of goods by coercion of any kind, but especially physical coercion, the regulated exercise of which is the very constitutive element of the political community.

The Beginnings of the Firm

THE FAMILY is everywhere the oldest unit supporting a continuous trading activity, in China and Babylonia, in India, and in the early middle ages. The son of a trading family was the confidential clerk and later the partner of the father. So through generations one and the same family functioned as capitalists and lenders, as did the house of Igibi in Babylonia in the 6th century B.C. It is true that in this case the transactions concerned were not extensive and complicated like those of today, but were of a simple sort. It is characteristic that we hear nothing more of bookkeeping either from Babylonia or Indian trading houses, although at least in India the position numerals were known. The reason apparently is that there, as in general in the orient and in China, the trading association remained a closed family affair and accountability was therefore unnecessary. The trading association extending beyond the members of a family first became general in the west.

The first form of group organization was occasional in character, the *commenda*, already referred to.[1] The continual participation in such ventures might gradually lead to a permanent enterprise. This evolution in fact took place, although with characteristic differences between southern and northern Europe. In the south the traveling merchant was regularly the entrepreneur, to whom the *commenda* was given, because in view of his year long absence in the orient he could not be controlled. He became the entrepreneur and received commendas from various parties, up to ten or twenty, accounting to each *commendator* separately. In the north, in contrast, the *socius* who remained at home was just as regularly the entrepreneur; he was the one who entered into relations with numerous traveling *socii* whom he provided with commendas. The traveling factor was regularly forbidden to undertake more than one commenda and this brought him into dependence upon the settled partner who thus evolved into a managerial functionary. The reason is found in the difference between the commerce of the south and the north. In the south the journeys involved notably greater risk since they led into the orient.

Reprinted by permission of Transaction Publishers from Max Weber, *General Economic History* (New York: Greenberg, Publisher, 1927), pp. 225–29. Translated by Frank H. Knight. The text is based on a lecture course Weber gave in 1919–20; see *Wirtschaftsgeschichte* (1923) (Berlin: Duncker und Humblot, 1991), pp. 200–203.

[1] See especially *General Economic History*, pp. 206–7. Weber here writes: "The commenda is found in Babylonian and Arabian as well as Italian law and in a modified form in the Hanseatic. The essence of it is that in the same [temporary] organization two types of associates are included, one of whom stays in the home while the other takes the goods overseas" (p. 206). The profit is then split according to a special scheme between the traveling entrepreneur and the partner who had advanced the capital. See also *Economy and Society*, p. 95 (RS).

With the spread of the commenda organization, developed permanent industrial enterprise. First, accountability penetrated into the family circle due to business connections with *tractators* from outside the family, since an accounting had to be made for each separate venture even when the particular commenda pertained to a member of the family. In Italy this development went forward more rapidly than in Germany, the south again taking the lead over the north. As late as the 16th century the Fuggers would indeed admit foreign capital into their affairs, but very reluctantly. (The Welsers were more broadminded in this regard.) In contrast, the association of outsiders in family business spread in Italy with increasing rapidity. Originally there was no separation between the household and the business. Such a separation gradually became established on the basis of the medieval money accounting while, as we have seen, it remained unknown in India and China. In the great Florentine commercial families such as the Medici, household expenditures and capital transactions were entered in the books indiscriminately; closing of the accounts was carried out first with reference to the outside commenda business while internally everything remained in the "family kettle" of the household community.

The prime mover in the separation of household and business accounting, and hence in the development of the early capitalistic institutions, was the need for credit. The separation remained in abeyance as long as dealings were in cash only; but as soon as transactions were suspended over a long interval, the question of guaranteeing credit intruded. To provide this guaranty, various means were used. The first was the maintenance of the wealth of the family in all its ramifications, through maintaining the house-community even to remote degrees of kinship, an objective to which for example the palaces of the great commercial families in Florence owe their origin. Associated with this was the institution of joint responsibility of those who lived together; every member of the house-community was answerable for a debt of any other member.

Apparently this joint responsibility grew out of a traditional criminal liability; in the case of high treason the house of the guilty person was razed and his family destroyed as suspect. This idea of joint responsibility no doubt passed over into the civil law. With the permeation of outside capital and outside persons into the family business for the purpose of trade, it was renewed at irregular intervals. Out of it arose the necessity for an agreed allocation of the resources at the disposal of the individual for personal use and of the power to represent the house in external matters. In the nature of the case, the house-father could everywhere bind the family, but this joint responsibility nowhere developed to such lengths as in occidental commercial law. In Italy its root was in the household community and the stages in its development are the common dwelling, the common workshop, and finally the common firm. It was otherwise in the north, where the large family community was unknown. Here the credit requirement was met by having all the participants in the trading venture sign together the document establishing the responsibility. Then each participant was responsible for the group, usually without limit, though in the reverse direction the whole was not responsible for the parts. Finally, the principle became established that each participant was responsible for every other, even if he had not signed the document. In England the same result was achieved by the common seal or the power of attorney. After the 13th century in Italy, and after the 14th in the north, joint responsibility of all the members of a company for the debts of the firm as such was fully established.

The final stage in the development established as the most effective means for securing credit standing, and the method which outlived all the rest, separation of the property of the trading company as such from the private wealth of the associates. This separation is found at the beginning of the 14th century in Florence and toward the end of the same century in the north also. The step was unavoidable since to an increasing extent persons not members of the family belonged to the trading units; in addition it could not be avoided within the family itself when the latter came repeatedly to employ outside capital. Expenses for the family on one hand and personal expenses on the other were separated from business disbursements, a specified money capital being allocated to the business. Out of the property of the firm, for which we find the designation *corpo della compagnia,* evolved the capital concept.

In detail the development took various courses. In the south the field of its development was the great family commercial houses, not only in Italy but in Germany as well, as illustrated by the Fuggers and Welsers. In the north the course of development was through small families and associations of small traders. The crucial fact was that the center of large money dealings and political money power lay in the south, as did also the bulk of the mineral trade and oriental commerce, while the north remained the abode of small capitalism. In consequence the forms of organization which developed in the two regions were quite different. The type of the southern commercial company was the *commandite,* in which one partner carried on the business and was personally responsible, the other participating through his investment and sharing in the gain. This development arose from the fact that in the south the traveling merchant holding the commenda was the typical entrepreneur, and when he took up a fixed abode he became the center of the permanent enterprise which took on the form of the commenda. In the north the relation was reversed. The sources from the Hanseatic region at first give the impression that there was no permanent enterprise but that the trade was split up into purely occasional ventures and into a number of inextricably confused individual transactions. In reality these individual ventures were permanent enterprises and are accounted for individually because the Italian (double entry) bookkeeping was not introduced until later.

The forms of organization are the *Sendeve* and the *Wedderleginge.* Under the first the traveling partner was given goods on commission, receiving a share in the gain; the latter was designed to enlist his interest in the business by ascribing to him a share in the capital of the transactions from which he was excluded.

Class, Status, and Party

ECONOMICALLY DETERMINED POWER AND THE STATUS ORDER

The structure of every legal order directly influences the distribution of power, economic or otherwise, within its respective community. This is true of all legal orders and not only that of the state. In general, we understand by "power" the chance of a man or a number of men to realize their own will in a social action even against the resistance of others who are participating in the action.

"Economically conditioned" power is not, of course, identical with "power" as such. On the contrary, the emergence of economic power may be the consequence of power existing on other grounds. Man does not strive for power only in order to enrich himself economically. Power, including economic power, may be valued for its own sake. Very frequently the striving for power is also conditioned by the social honor it entails. Not all power, however, entails social honor: The typical American Boss, as well as the typical big speculator, deliberately relinquishes social honor. Quite generally, "mere economic" power, and especially "naked" money power, is by no means a recognized basis of social honor. Nor is power the only basis of social honor. Indeed, social honor, or prestige, may even be the basis of economic power, and very frequently has been. Power, as well as honor, may be guaranteed by the legal order, but, at least normally, it is not their primary source. The legal order is rather an additional factor that enhances the chance to hold power or honor; but it can not always secure them.

The way in which social honor is distributed in a community between typical groups participating in this distribution we call the "status order." The social order and the economic order are related in a similar manner to the legal order. However, the economic order merely defines the way in which economic goods and services are distributed and used. Of course, the status order is strongly influenced by it, and in turn reacts upon it.

Now: "classes," "status groups," and "parties" are phenomena of the distribution of power within a community.

Reprinted by permission of the Regents of the University of California and the University of California Press from *Economy and Society: An Outline of Interpretive Sociology* (Berkeley: University of California Press, 1978), pp. 926–39. Translated by Hans H. Gerth. The text was originally published in 1922; see *Wirtschaft und Gesellschaft: Grundriss der verstehenden Soziologie* (Tübingen: J. C. B. Mohr, 1972), pp. 531–40.

DETERMINATION OF CLASS SITUATION BY MARKET SITUATION

In our terminology, "classes" are not communities; they merely represent possible, and frequent, bases for social action. We may speak of a "class" when (1) a
number of people have in common a specific causal component of their life
chances (*Lebenschancen*), insofar as (2) this component is represented exclusively by economic interests in the possession of goods and opportunities for income, and (3) is represented under the conditions of the commodity or labor
markets. This is "class situation."

It is the most elemental economic fact that the way in which the disposition
over material property is distributed among a plurality of people, meeting com-
petitively in the market for the purpose of exchange, in itself creates specific life
chances. The mode of distribution, in accord with the law of marginal utility, ex-
cludes the non-wealthy from competing for highly valued goods; it favors the
owners and, in fact, gives to them a monopoly to acquire such goods. Other
things being equal, the mode of distribution monopolizes the opportunities for
profitable deals for all those who, provided with goods, do not necessarily have
to exchange them. It increases, at least generally, their power in the price struggle with those who, being propertyless, have nothing to offer but their labor or
the resulting products, and who are compelled to get rid of these products in
order to subsist at all. The mode of distribution gives to the propertied a monopoly on the possibility of transferring property from the sphere of use as
"wealth"[1] to the sphere of "capital,"[2] that is, it gives them the entrepreneurial
function and all chances to share directly or indirectly in returns on capital. All
this holds true within the area in which pure market conditions prevail. "Property" and "lack of property" are, therefore, the basic categories of all class situations. It does not matter whether these two categories become effective in the
competitive struggles of the consumers or of the producers.

Within these categories, however, class situations are further differentiated:
on the one hand, according to the kind of property that is usable for returns; and,
on the other hand, according to the kind of services that can be offered in the
market. Ownership of dwellings; workshops; warehouses; stores; agriculturally
usable land in large or small holdings—a quantitative difference with possibly
qualitative consequences; ownership of mines; cattle; men (slaves); disposition
over mobile instruments of production, or capital goods of all sorts, especially
money or objects that can easily be exchanged for money; disposition over products of one's own labor or of others' labor differing according to their various distances from consumability; disposition over transferable monopolies of any
kind—all these distinctions differentiate the class situations of the propertied
just as does the "meaning" which they can give to the use of property, especially

---

[1] "Wealth" is essentially property used for consumption. See the glossary as well as sections 10–
11 of the second chapter of *Economy and Society*, reproduced in reading 16 in this anthology (RS).

[2] "Capital" is property used to acquire more property. See the glossary as well as sections 10–11
of the second chapter of *Economy and Society*, reproduced in reading 16 in this anthology (RS).

to property which has money equivalence. Accordingly, the propertied, for instance, may belong to the class of rentiers or to the class of entrepreneurs.

Those who have no property but who offer services are differentiated just as much according to their kinds of services as according to the way in which they make use of these services, in a continuous or discontinuous relation to a recipient. But always this is the generic connotation of the concept of class: that the kind of chance in the *market* is the decisive moment which presents a common condition for the individual's fate. Class situation is, in this sense, ultimately market situation. The effect of naked possession *per se,* which among cattle breeders gives the non-owning slave or serf into the power of the cattle owner, is only a fore-runner of real "class" formation. However, in the cattle loan and in the naked severity of the law of debts in such communities for the first time mere "possession" as such emerges as decisive for the fate of the individual; this is much in contrast to crop-raising communities, which are based on labor. The creditor-debtor relation becomes the basis of "class situations" first in the cities, where a "credit market," however primitive, with rates of interest increasing according to the extent of dearth and factual monopolization of lending in the hands of a plutocracy could develop. Therewith "class struggles" begin.

Those men whose fate is not determined by the chance of using goods or services for themselves on the market, e.g., slaves, are not, however, a class in the technical sense of the term. They are, rather, a status group.

SOCIAL ACTION FLOWING FROM CLASS INTEREST

According to our terminology, the factor that creates "class" is unambiguously economic interest, and indeed, only those interests involved in the existence of the market. Nevertheless, the concept of class-interest is an ambiguous one: even as an empirical concept it is ambiguous as soon as one understands by it something other than the factual direction of interests following with a certain probability from the class situation for a certain average of those people subject to the class situation. The class situation and other circumstances remaining the same, the direction in which the individual worker, for instance, is likely to pursue his interests may vary widely, according to whether he is constitutionally qualified for the task at hand to a high, to an average, or to a low degree. In the same way, the direction of interests may vary according to whether or not social action of a larger or smaller portion of those commonly affected by the class situation, or even an association among them, e.g., a trade union, has grown out of the class situation, from which the individual may expect promising results for himself. The emergence of an association or even of mere social action from a common class situation is by no means a universal phenomenon.

The class situation may be restricted in its efforts to the generation of essentially *similar* reactions, that is to say, within our terminology, of "mass behavior." However, it may not even have this result. Furthermore, often merely amorphous social action emerges. For example, the "grumbling" of workers known in ancient Oriental ethics: The moral disapproval of the work-master's conduct, which in its practical significance was probably equivalent to an increasingly typical phenomenon of precisely the latest industrial development, namely, the slowdown of laborers by virtue of tacit agreement. The degree in which "social action" and possibly associations emerge from the mass behavior of the members of a class is linked to general cultural conditions, especially to those of an intellectual sort. It is also linked to the extent of the contrasts that have already evolved, and is especially linked to the transparency of the connections between the causes and the consequences of the class situation. For however different life chances may be, this fact in itself, according to all experience, by no means gives birth to "class action" (social action by the members of a class). For that, the real conditions and the results of the class situation must be distinctly recognizable. For only then the contrast of life chances can be felt not as an absolutely given fact to be accepted, but as a resultant from either (1) the given distribution of property, or (2) the structure of the concrete economic order. It is only then that people may react against the class structure not only through acts of intermittent and irrational protest, but in the form of rational association. There have been "class situations" of the first category (1), of a specifically naked and transparent sort, in the urban centers of Antiquity and during the Middle Ages; especially then when great fortunes were accumulated by factually monopolized trading in local industrial products or in foodstuffs; furthermore, under certain conditions, in the rural economy of the most diverse periods, when agriculture was increasingly exploited in a profit-making manner. The most important historical example of the second category (2) is the class situation of the modern proletariat.

Types of Class Struggle

Thus every class may be the carrier of any one of the innumerable possible forms of class action, but this is not necessarily so. In any case, a class does not in itself constitute a group (*Gemeinschaft*). To treat "class" conceptually as being equivalent to "group" leads to distortion. That men in the same class situation regularly react in mass actions to such tangible situations as economic ones in the direction of those interests that are most adequate to their average number is an important and after all simple fact for the understanding of historical events. However, this fact must not lead to that kind of pseudo-scientific operation with the concepts of class and class interests which is so frequent these days and which has found its most classic expression in the statement of a talented author, that the individual may be in error concerning his interests but that the class is infallible about its interests.

If classes as such are not groups, nevertheless class situations emerge only on the basis of social action. However, social action that brings forth class situations is not basically action among members of the identical class; it is an action among members of different classes. Social actions that directly determine the class situation of the worker and the entrepreneur are: the labor market, the commodities market, and the capitalistic enterprise. But, in its turn, the existence of a capitalistic enterprise presupposes that a very specific kind of social action exists to protect the possession of goods *per se,* and especially the power of individuals to dispose, in principle freely, over the means of production: a certain kind of legal order. Each kind of class situation, and above all when it rests upon the power of property *per se,* will become most clearly efficacious when all other determinants of reciprocal relations are, as far as possible, eliminated in their significance. It is in this way that the use of the power of property in the market obtains its most sovereign importance.

Now status groups hinder the strict carrying through of the sheer market principle. In the present context they are of interest only from this one point of view. Before we briefly consider them, note that not much of a general nature can be said about the more specific kinds of antagonism between classes (in our meaning of the term). The great shift, which has been going on continuously in the past, and up to our times, may be summarized, although at a cost of some precision: the struggle in which class situations are effective has progressively shifted from consumption credit toward, first, competitive struggles in the commodity market and then toward wage disputes on the labor market. The class struggles of Antiquity—to the extent that they were genuine class struggles and not struggles between status groups—were initially carried on by peasants and perhaps also artisans threatened by debt bondage and struggling against urban creditors. For debt bondage is the normal result of the differentiation of wealth in commercial cities, especially in seaport cities. A similar situation has existed among cattle breeders. Debt relationships as such produced class action up to the days of Catilina. Along with this, and with an increase in provision of grain for the city by transporting it from the outside, the struggle over the means of sustenance emerged. It centered in the first place around the provision of bread and determination of the price of bread. It lasted throughout Antiquity and the entire Middle Ages. The propertyless flocked together against those who actually and supposedly were interested in the dearth of bread. This fight spread until it involved all those commodities essential to the way of life and to handicraft production. There were only incipient discussions of wage disputes in Antiquity and in the Middle Ages. But they have been slowly increasing up into modern times. In the earlier periods they were completely secondary to slave rebellions as well as to conflicts in the commodity market.

The propertyless of Antiquity and of the Middle Ages protested against monopolies, pre-emption, forestalling, and the withholding of goods from the market in order to raise prices. Today the central issue is the determination of the price of labor. The transition is represented by the fight for access to the market and for the determination of the price of products. Such fights went on between merchants and workers in the putting-out system of domestic handicraft during the transition to modern times. Since it is quite a general phenomenon we must mention here that the class antagonisms that are conditioned through the market situations are usually most bitter between those who actually and directly participate as opponents in price wars. It is not the rentier, the share-holder, and the banker who suffer the ill will of the worker, but almost exclusively the man-ufacturer and the business executives who are the direct opponents of workers in wage conflicts. This is so in spite of the fact that it is precisely the cash boxes of the rentier, the share-holder, and the banker into which the more or less un-earned gains flow, rather than into the pockets of the manufacturers or of the business executives. This simple state of affairs has very frequently been deci-sive for the role the class situation has played in the formation of political par-ties. For example, it has made possible the varieties of patriarchal socialism and the frequent attempts—formerly, at least—of threatened status groups to form alliances with the proletariat against the bourgeoisie.

STATUS HONOR

In contrast to classes, *status groups* (*Stände*) are normally groups. They are, how-ever, often of an amorphous kind. In contrast to the purely economically deter-mined "class situation," we wish to designate as *status situation* every typical component of the life of men that is determined by a specific, positive or nega-tive, social estimation of *honor.* This honor may be connected with any quality shared by a plurality, and, of course, it can be knit to a class situation: class dis-tinctions are linked in the most varied ways with status distinctions. Property as such is not always recognized as a status qualification, but in the long run it is, and with extraordinary regularity. In the subsistence economy of neighborhood associations, it is often simply the richest who is the "chieftain." However, this often is only an honorific preference. For example, in the so-called pure mod-ern democracy, that is, one devoid of any expressly ordered status privileges for individuals, it may be that only the families coming under approximately the same tax class dance with one another. This example is reported of certain smaller Swiss cities. But status honor need not necessarily be linked with a class situation. On the contrary, it normally stands in sharp opposition to the preten-sions of sheer property.

Both propertied and propertyless people can belong to the same status group, and frequently they do with very tangible consequences. This equality of social esteem may, however, in the long run become quite precarious. The equality of status among American gentlemen, for instance, is expressed by the fact that out-side the subordination determined by the different functions of business, it would be considered strictly repugnant—wherever the old tradition still pre-vails—if even the richest boss, while playing billiards or cards in his club would not treat his clerk as in every sense fully his equal in birthright, but would be-stow upon him the condescending status-conscious "benevolence" which the German boss can never dissever from his attitude. This is one of the most im-portant reasons why in America the German clubs have never been able to at-tain the attraction that the American clubs have.

In content, status honor is normally expressed by the fact that above all else a specific *style of life* is expected from all those who wish to belong to the circle. Linked with this expectation are restrictions on social intercourse (that is, intercourse which is not subservient to economic or any other purposes). These restrictions may confine normal marriages to within the status circle and may lead to complete endogamous closure. Whenever this is not a mere individual and socially irrelevant imitation of another style of life, but consensual action of this closing character, the status development is under way.

In its characteristic form, stratification by status groups on the basis of conventional styles of life evolves at the present time in the United States out of the traditional democracy. For example, only the resident of a certain street ("the Street") is considered as belonging to "society," is qualified for social intercourse, and is visited and invited. Above all, this differentiation evolves in such a way as to make for strict submission to the fashion that is dominant at a given time in society. This submission to fashion also exists among men in America to a degree unknown in Germany; it appears as an indication of the fact that a given man puts forward a *claim* to qualify as a gentleman. This submission decides, at least *prima facie,* that he will be treated as such. And this recognition becomes just as important for his employment chances in swank establishments, and above all, for social intercourse and marriage with "esteemed" families, as the qualification for dueling among Germans. As for the rest, status honor is usurped by certain families resident for a long time, and, of course, correspondingly wealthy (e.g. F.F.V., the First Families of Virginia), or by the actual or alleged descendants of the "Indian Princess" Pocahontas, of the Pilgrim fathers, or of the Knickerbockers, the members of almost inaccessible sects and all sorts of circles setting themselves apart by means of any other characteristics and badges. In this case stratification is purely conventional and rests largely on usurpation (as does almost all status honor in its beginning). But the road to legal privilege, positive or negative, is easily traveled as soon as a certain stratification of the social order has in fact been "lived in" and has achieved stability by virtue of a stable distribution of economic power.

ETHNIC SEGREGATION AND CASTE

Where the consequences have been realized to their full extent, the status group evolves into a closed caste. Status distinctions are then guaranteed not merely by conventions and laws, but also by religious sanctions. This occurs in such a way that every physical contact with a member of any caste that is considered to be lower by the members of a higher caste is considered as making for a ritualistic impurity and a stigma which must be expiated by a religious act. In addition, individual castes develop quite distinct cults and gods.

In general, however, the status structure reaches such extreme consequences only where there are underlying differences which are held to be "ethnic." The caste is, indeed, the normal form in which ethnic communities that believe in blood relationship and exclude exogamous marriage and social intercourse usually associate with one another. As mentioned before[3], such a caste situation is part of the phenomenon of pariah peoples and is found all over the world. These people form communities, acquire specific occupational traditions of handi-crafts or of other arts, and cultivate a belief in their ethnic community. They live in a diaspora strictly segregated from all personal intercourse, except that of an unavoidable sort, and their situation is legally precarious. Yet, by virtue of their economic indispensability, they are tolerated, indeed frequently privileged, and they live interspersed in the political communities. The Jews are the most im-pressive historical example.

A status segregation grown into a caste differs in its structure from a mere eth-nic segregation: the caste structure transforms the horizontal and unconnected coexistences of ethnically segregated groups into a vertical social system of super- and subordination. Correctly formulated: a comprehensive association in-tegrates the ethnically divided communities into one political unit. They differ precisely in this way: ethnic coexistence, based on mutual repulsion and disdain, allows each ethnic community to consider its own honor as the highest one; the caste structure brings about a social subordination and an acknowledgement of "more honor" in favor of the privileged caste and status groups. This is due to the fact that in the caste structure ethnic distinctions as such have become "func-tional" distinctions within the political association (warriors, priests, artisans that are politically important for war and for building, and so on). But even pariah peoples who are most despised (for example, the Jews) are usually apt to con-tinue cultivating the belief in their own specific "honor," a belief that is equally peculiar to ethnic and to status groups.

However, with the negatively privileged status groups the sense of dignity takes a specific deviation. A sense of dignity is the precipitation in individuals of social honor and of conventional demands which a positively privileged status group raises for the deportment of its members. The sense of dignity that char-acterizes positively privileged status groups is naturally related to their "being" which does not transcend itself, that is, it is related to their "beauty and excel-lence" (*kalokagathia*). Their kingdom is "of this world." They live for the present and by exploiting their great past. The sense of dignity of the negatively privi-leged strata naturally refers to a future lying beyond the present, whether it is of this life or of another. In other words, it must be nurtured by the belief in a prov-idential mission and by a belief in a specific honor before God. The chosen peo-ple's dignity is nurtured by a belief either that in the beyond "the last will be the first," or that in this life a Messiah will appear to bring forth into the light of the world which has cast them out the hidden honor of the pariah people. This sim-ple state of affairs, and not the resentment which is so strongly emphasized in Nietzsche's much-admired construction in the *Genealogy of Morals*, is the

---

[3] See *Economy and Society*, pp. 492 ff. Weber defines "pariah people"—a controversial term—as follows: "In our usage, 'pariah people' denotes a distinct hereditary social group lacking au-tonomous political organization and characterized by internal prohibitions against commensality and intermarriage originally founded upon magical tabooistic and ritual injunctions. Two additional traits of a pariah people are political and social disprivilege, and a far-reaching distinctiveness in economic functioning" (p. 493) (RS).

source of the religiosity cultivated by pariah status groups; moreover, resentment applies only to a limited extent; for one of Nietzsche's main examples, Buddhism, it is not at all applicable.

For the rest, the development of status groups from ethnic segregations is by no means the normal phenomenon. On the contrary. Since objective "racial differences" are by no means behind every subjective sentiment of an ethnic community, the question of an ultimately racial foundation of status structure is rightly a question of the concrete individual case. Very frequently a status group is instrumental in the production of a thoroughbred anthropological type. Certainly status groups are to a high degree effective in producing extreme types, for they select personally qualified individuals (e.g. the knighthood selects those who are fit for warfare, physically and psychically). But individual selection is far from being the only, or the predominant, way in which status groups are formed: political membership or class situation has at all times been at least as frequently decisive. And today the class situation is by far the predominant factor. After all, the possibility of a style of life expected for members of a status group is usually conditioned economically.

STATUS PRIVILEGES

For all practical purposes, stratification by status goes hand in hand with a monopolization of ideal and material goods or opportunities, in a manner we have come to know as typical. Besides the specific status honor, which always rests upon distance and exclusiveness, honorific preferences may consist of the privilege of wearing special costumes, of eating special dishes taboo to others, of carrying arms—which is most obvious in its consequences—the right to be a dilettante, for example, to play certain musical instruments. However, material monopolies provide the most effective motives for the exclusiveness of a status group; although, in themselves, they are rarely sufficient, almost always they come into play to some extent. Within a status circle there is the question of intermarriage: the interest of the families in the monopolization of potential bridegrooms is at least of equal importance and is parallel to the interest in the monopolization of daughters. The daughters of the members must be provided for. With an increased closure of the status group, the conventional preferential opportunities for special employment grow into a legal monopoly of special offices for the members. Certain goods become objects for monopolization by status groups, typically, entailed estates, and frequently also the possession of serfs or bondsmen and, finally, special trades. This monopolization occurs positively when the status group is exclusively entitled to own and to manage them; and negatively when, in order to maintain its specific way of life, the status group must *not* own and manage them. For the decisive role of a style of life in status honor means that status groups are the specific bearers of all conventions. In whatever way it may be manifest, all stylization of life either originates in status groups or is at least conserved by them. Even if the principles of status conventions differ greatly, they reveal certain typical traits, especially among the most privileged strata. Quite generally, among privileged status groups there is a status disqualification that operates against the performance of common physical labor. This disqualification is now "setting in" in America against the old tradition of esteem for labor. Very frequently every rational economic pursuit, and especially entrepreneurial activity, is looked upon as a disqualification of status. Artistic and literary activity is also considered degrading work as soon as it is exploited for income, or at least when it is connected with hard physical exertion. An example is the sculptor working like a mason in his dusty smock as against the painter in his salon-like studio and those forms of musical practice that are acceptable to the status group.

Economic Conditions and Effects of Status Stratification

The frequent disqualification of the gainfully employed as such is a direct result of the principle of status stratification, and of course, of this principle's opposition to a distribution of power which is regulated exclusively through the market. These two factors operate along with various individual ones, which will be touched upon below.

We have seen above [in reading 3—RS] that the market and its processes know no personal distinctions: "functional" interests dominate it. It knows nothing of honor. The status order means precisely the reverse: stratification in terms of honor and styles of life peculiar to status groups as such. The status order would be threatened at its very root if mere economic acquisition and naked economic power still bearing the stigma of its extra-status origin could bestow upon anyone who has won them the same or even greater honor as the vested interests claim for themselves. After all, given equality of status honor, property *per se* represents an addition even if it is not overtly acknowledged to be such. Therefore all groups having interest in the status order react with special sharpness precisely against the pretensions of purely economic acquisition. In most cases they react the more vigorously the more they feel themselves threatened. Calderon's respectful treatment of the peasant, for instance, as opposed to Shakespeare's simultaneous ostensible disdain of the *canaille* illustrates the different way in which a firmly structured status order reacts as compared with a status order that has become economically precarious. This is an example of a state of affairs that recurs everywhere. Precisely because of the rigorous reactions against the claims of property *per se*, the "parvenu" is never accepted, personally and without reservation, by the privileged status groups, no matter how completely his style of life has been adjusted to theirs. They will only accept his descendants who have been educated in the conventions of their status group and who have never besmirched its honor by their own economic labor.

As to the general *effect* of the status order, only one consequence can be stated, but it is a very important one: the hindrance of the free development of the market. This occurs first for those goods that status groups directly withhold from free exchange by monopolization, which may be effected either legally or conventionally. For example, in many Hellenic cities during the "status era" and also originally in Rome, the inherited estate (as shown by the old formula for placing spendthrifts under a guardian) was monopolized, as were the estates of knights, peasants, priests, and especially the clientele of the craft and merchant guilds. The market is restricted, and the power of naked property *per se,* which gives its stamp to class formation, is pushed into the background. The results of this process can be most varied. Of course, they do not necessarily weaken the contrasts in the economic situation. Frequently they strengthen these contrasts, and in any case, where stratification by status permeates a community as strongly as was the case in all political communities of Antiquity and of the Middle Ages, one can never speak of a genuinely free market competition as we understand it today. There are wider effects than this direct exclusion of special goods from the market. From the conflict between the status order and the purely economic order mentioned above, it follows that in most instances the notion of honor peculiar to status absolutely abhors that which is essential to the market: hard bargaining. Honor abhors hard bargaining among peers and occasionally it taboos it for the members of a status group in general. Therefore, everywhere some status groups, and usually the most influential, consider almost any kind of overt participation in economic acquisition as absolutely stigmatizing.

With some over-simplification, one might thus say that classes are stratified according to their relations to the production and acquisition of goods; whereas status groups are stratified according to the principles of their *consumption* of goods as represented by special styles of life.

An "occupational status group," too, is a status group proper. For normally, it successfully claims social honor only by virtue of the special style of life which may be determined by it. The differences between classes and status groups frequently overlap. It is precisely those status communities most strictly segregated in terms of honor (viz. the Indian castes) who today show, although within very rigid limits, a relatively high degree of indifference to pecuniary income. However, the Brahmins seek such income in many different ways.

As to the general economic conditions making for the predominance of stratification by status, only the following can be said. When the bases of the acquisition and distribution of goods are relatively stable, stratification by status is favored. Every technological repercussion and economic transformation threatens stratification by status and pushes the class situation into the foreground. Epochs and countries in which the naked class situation is of predominant significance are regularly the periods of technical and economic transformations. And every slowing down of the change in economic stratification leads, in due course, to the growth of status structures and makes for a resuscitation of the important role of social honor.

PARTIES

Whereas the genuine place of classes is within the economic order, the place of status groups is within the social order, that is, within the sphere of the distribution of honor. From within these spheres, classes and status groups influence one another and the legal order and are in turn influenced by it. *"Parties"* reside in the sphere of power. Their action is oriented toward the acquisition of social power, that is to say, toward influencing social action no matter what its content may be. In principle, parties may exist in a social club as well as in a state. As against the actions of classes and status groups, for which this is not necessarily the case, party-oriented social action always involves association. For it is always directed toward a goal which is striven for in a planned manner. This goal may be a cause (the party may aim at realizing a program for ideal or material purposes), or the goal may be personal (sinecures, power, and from these, honor for the leader and the followers of the party). Usually the party aims at all these simultaneously. Parties are, therefore, only possible within groups that have an associational character, that is, some rational order and a staff of persons available who are ready to enforce it. For parties aim precisely at influencing this staff, and if possible, to recruit from it party members.

In any individual case, parties may represent interests determined through class situation or status situation, and they may recruit their following respectively from one or the other. But they need be neither purely class nor purely status parties; in fact, they are more likely to be mixed types, and sometimes they are neither. They may represent ephemeral or enduring structures. Their means of attaining power may be quite varied, ranging from naked violence of any sort to canvassing for votes with coarse or subtle means: money, social influence, the force of speech, suggestion, clumsy hoax, and so on to the rougher or more artful tactics of obstruction in parliamentary bodies.

The sociological structure of parties differs in a basic way according to the kind of social action which they struggle to influence; that means, they differ according to whether or not the community is stratified by status or by classes. Above all else, they vary according to the structure of domination. For their leaders normally deal with its conquest. In our general terminology, parties are not only products of modern forms of domination. We shall also designate as parties the ancient and medieval ones, despite the fact that they differ basically from modern parties. Since a party always struggles for political control (*Herrschaft*), its organization too is frequently strict and "authoritarian." Because of these variations between the forms of domination, it is impossible to say anything about the structure of parties without discussing them first. Therefore, we shall now turn to this central phenomenon of all social organization.

Before we do this,[4] we should add one more general observation about classes, status groups and parties: The fact that they presuppose a larger association, especially the framework of a polity, does not mean that they are confined to it. On the contrary, at all times it has been the order of the day that such association (even when it aims at the use of military force in common) reaches beyond the state boundaries. This can be seen in the [interlocal] solidarity of interests of oligarchs and democrats in Hellas, of Guelphs and Ghibellines in the Middle Ages,

---

[4] See the discussion of the different types of domination in *Economy and Society*, pp. 941–1372 (RS).

and within the Calvinist party during the age of religious struggles; and all the way up to the solidarity of landlords (International Congresses of Agriculture), princes (Holy Alliance, Karlsbad Decrees [of 1819]), socialist workers, conservatives (the longing of Prussian conservatives for Russian intervention in 1850). But their aim is not necessarily the establishment of a new territorial dominion. In the main they aim to influence the existing polity.

PART II

Capitalism, Law, and Politics

The Three Types of Legitimate Domination

DOMINATION (*Herrschaft*)[1] means the probability that a specific command will be obeyed. Such obedience may feed on diverse motives. It may be determined by sheer interest situation, hence by the compliant actor's calculation of expediency; by mere custom, that is, the actor's inarticulate habituation to routine behavior; or by mere affect, that is, purely personal devotion of the governed. A structure of power, however, if it were to rest on such foundations alone, would be relatively unstable. As a rule both rulers and ruled uphold the internalized power structure as "legitimate" by right, and usually the shattering of this belief in legitimacy has far-reaching ramifications.

There are but three clear-cut grounds on which to base the belief in legitimate domination. Given pure types each is connected with a fundamentally different sociological structure of executive staff and means of administration.

I

Legal domination rests on enactment; its pure type is best represented by bureaucracy. The basic idea is that laws can be enacted and changed at pleasure by formally correct procedure. The governing body is either elected or appointed and constitutes as a whole and in all its sections rational organizations. A heteronomous[2] and heterocephalous[3] sub-unit we shall call "public authorities" (*Behörde*). The administrative staff consists of officials appointed by the ruler; the law-abiding people are members of the body politic ("fellow citizens").

Obedience is not owed to anybody personally but to enacted rules and regulations which specify to whom and to what rule people owe obedience. The person in authority, too, obeys a rule when giving an order, namely, "the law," or "rules and regulations" which represent abstract norms. The person in command typically is the "superior" within a functionally defined "competency" or "juris-

Reprinted by permission from the *Berkeley Journal of Sociology* 4 (1958): 1–10. Translated by Hans H. Gerth. The text was originally published in 1922; see *Gesammelte Aufsätze zur Wissenschaftslehre* (Tübingen: J. C. B. Mohr, 1988), pp. 475–88.

[1] The German term *Herrschaft* has been translated into English in a variety of ways, including "authority," "rule" and "domination." The last of these—*domination*—has been used here. For the close connection between the structure of domination and the structure of the economy, see, e.g., fig. 5, p. 35 in the introduction (RS).

[2] "Heteronomous" means that the order governing an organization has been imposed by an outside agency. Weber, *Economy and Society*, pp. 49–50 (RS).

[3] "Heterocephalous" means that the chief and the staff of an organization are appointed by outsiders. Weber, *Economy and Society*, p. 50 (RS).

diction," and his right to govern is legitimized by enactment. Specialization sets limits with regard to functional purpose and required skill of the office incumbent.

The typical official is a trained specialist whose terms of employment are contractual and provide a fixed salary scaled by rank of office, not by amount of work, and the right to a pension according to fixed rules of advancement. His administration represents vocational work by virtue of impersonal duties of office; ideally the administrator proceeds *sine ira et studio,* not allowing personal motive or temper to influence conduct, free of arbitrariness and unpredictability; especially he proceeds "without regard to person," following rational rules with strict formality. And where rules fail he adheres to "functional" considerations of expediency. Dutiful obedience is channeled through a hierarchy of offices which subordinates lower to higher offices and provides a regular procedure for lodging complaints. Technically, operation rests on organizational discipline.

1. Naturally this type of "legal" domination comprises not only the modern structure of state and city government but likewise the power relations in private capitalist enterprises, in public corporations and voluntary associations of all sorts, provided that an extensive and hierarchically organized staff of functionaries exists. Modern political bodies merely represent the type preeminently. Domination in a private capitalist organization is partially heteronomous, its order is partly prescribed by the state, and it is completely heterocephalous as regards the machinery of coercion. Normally the courts and police take care of these functions. Private enterprise, however, is autonomous in its increasingly bureaucratic organization of management. The fact that, formally speaking, people enter into the power relationship (*Herrschaftsverband*) voluntarily and are likewise "free" to give notice does not affect the nature of private enterprise as a power structure since conditions of the labor market normally subject the employees to the code of the organization. Its sociological affinity to modern state domination will be clarified further in the discussion of the economic bases of power and authority. The "contract" as constitutive for the relations of authority in capitalist enterprise makes this a pre-eminent type of "legal domination."

2. Technically, bureaucracy represents the purest type of legal domination. No structure of domination, however, is exclusively bureaucratic, to wit, is managed by contractually hired and appointed officials alone. That is quite impossible. The top positions of the body politic may be held by "monarchs" (hereditary charismatic rulers), or by popularly elected "presidents" (hence plebiscitarian charismatic rulers), or by parliamentary elected presidents. In the latter case the actual rulers are members of parliament or rather the leaders of the prevailing parliamentary parties. These leaders in turn may stand close to the type of charismatic leadership or to that of notabilities. More of this below.

Likewise the administrative staff is almost never exclusively bureaucratic but usually notables and agents of interest groups participate in administration in manifold ways. This holds most of all for the so-called self-government. It is decisive that regular administrative work is predominantly and increasingly performed by bureaucratic forces. The historical development of the modern state is identical indeed with that of modern officialdom and bureaucratic organization (cf. below), just as the development of modern capitalism is identical with the increasing bureaucratization of economic enterprise. The part played by bureaucracy becomes bigger in all structures of power.

3. Bureaucracy does not represent the only type of legal domination. Other types comprise rotating office holders or office holders chosen by lot or popularly elected officers. Parliamentary and committee administration and all sorts of collegiate and administrative bodies are included under the type if and when their competency rests on enacted rules and if the use they make of their prerogative follows the type of legal administration. During the rise of the modern state collegiate bodies have made essential contributions to the development of legal authority, especially the concept of "public authorities" originated with them. On the other hand, elected officialdom has played an important role in the pre-history of the modern civil service and still does so today in the democracies.

II

Traditional domination rests on the belief in the sacredness of the social order and its prerogatives as existing of yore. Patriarchal domination represents its pure type. The body politic is based on communal relationships, the man in command is the "lord" ruling over obedient "subjects." People obey the lord personally since his dignity is hallowed by tradition; obedience rests on piety. Commands are substantively bound by tradition, and the lord's inconsiderate violation of tradition would endanger the legitimacy of his personal rule, which rests merely upon the sacredness of tradition. The creation of new law opposite traditional norms is deemed impossible in principle. Actually this is done by way of "recognizing" a sentence as "valid of yore" (the *Weistum* of ancient Germanic law). Outside the norms of tradition, however, the lord's sway in a given case is restricted only by sentiments of equity, hence by quite elastic bonds. Consequently the rule of the lord divides into a strictly tradition-bound sphere and one of free favor and arbitrariness where he rules at pleasure as sympathy or antipathy moves him, following purely personal considerations subject especially to the influence of "good turns."

So far as principles are followed in administration and settlement of disputes, they rest on substantive considerations of ethical equity, justice, or utilitarian expediency, not on formal considerations characteristic of the rule of law. The lord's administrative staff proceeds in the same way. It consists of personally dependent men (members of the household or domestic officials), of relatives, of personal friends (favorites), or associates bound by personal allegiance (vassals, tributary princes). The bureaucratic concept of "competency" as a functionally delimited jurisdictional sphere is absent. The scope of the "legitimate" prerogatives of the individual servant is defined from case to case at the pleasure of the lord on whom the individual servant is completely dependent as regards his employment in more important or high ranking roles. Actually this depends largely on what the servant may dare do opposite the more or less docile subjects. Personal loyalty of the faithful servant, not functional duty of office and office discipline, control the interrelationship of the administrative staff.

One may, however, observe two characteristically different forms of positional relationships, the patriarchal structure and that of estates.

1. In the purely patriarchal structure of administration the servants are completely and personally dependent on the lord; they are either purely patrimonially recruited as slaves, bondsmen-serfs, eunuchs, or extra patrimonially as favorites and plebeians from among strata lacking all rights. Their administration is entirely heteronomous and heterocephalous, the administrators have no personal right to their office, there is neither merit selection nor status honor; the material means of administration are managed under, and on account of, the lord. Given the complete dependency of the administrative staff on the lord, there is no guarantee against the lord's arbitrariness, which in this set-up can therefore have its greatest possible sway. Sultanistic domination represents the pure type. All genuine "despotism" was of this nature. Prerogatives are considered as ordinary property rights of the lord.

2. In the estate system the servants are not personal servants of the lord but independent men whose social position makes them presumably socially prominent. The lord, actually or according to the legitimacy fiction, bestows office on them by privilege or concession; or they have contractually, by purchase, tenancy or lease, acquired a title to their office which cannot be arbitrarily taken away from them; hence within limits, their administration is autocephalous and autonomous. Not the lord but they dispose over the material means of administration. This represents estate rule.

The competition of the officeholders for larger bailiwicks (and income) then determines the mutual delimitation of their actual bailiwicks and takes the place of "competency." Privilege often breaks through the hierarchic structure (*de non evocando, non apellando*). The category of "discipline" is absent. Tradition, privilege, feudal or patrimonial bonds of allegiance, status honor and "good will" regulate the web of inter-relations. The power prerogatives of the lord hence are divided between the lord and the privileged administrative staff, and this division of powers among the estates to a great extent locks the administration into one and the same pattern.

Patriarchal domination (of the family father, sib chief, father of the people) represents but the purest type of traditional domination. Any "authorities" who claim legitimacy successfully by virtue of mere habituation represent the most typical contrast, on the one hand, to the position of a contractually employed worker in business enterprise; on the other, to the way a faithful member of a religious community emotionally relates to a prophet. Actually the domestic group (*Hausverband*) is the nucleus of traditionalist power structures. The typical "officials" of the patrimonial and feudal state are domestic officers with originally purely domestic tasks (dapifer, chamberlain, marshall, cupbearer, seneschal, major domo).

The co-existence of the strictly tradition-bound and the free sphere of conduct is a common feature of all traditionalistic forms of domination. Within the free sphere, action of the lord or of his administrative staff must be bought or earned by personal relations. (This is one of the origins of the institution of fees.) It is decisive that formal law is absent and that substantive principles of administration and arbitration take its place. This likewise is a common feature of all traditionalist power structures and has far-reaching ramifications, especially for economic life.

The patriarch, like the patrimonial ruler, governs and decides according to the principles of "*kadi* justice": on the one hand, decisions are strictly bound by tradition; however, where these fetters give leeway, decisions follow juristically informal and irrational considerations of equity and justice from case to case, also taking individual differences into account. All codifications and laws of patrimonial rulers embody the spirit of the so-called "welfare state." A combination of social ethical with social utilitarian principles prevails, breaking through all rigor of formal law.

The sociological distinction between the patriarchal power structure and that of the estates in traditional domination is fundamental for all states of the pre-bureaucratic epoch. (The contrast will become fully clear only in connection with its economic aspect, that is, with the separation of the administrative staff from the material means of administration or with their appropriation by the staff.) This has been historically decisive for the question whether and what status groups existed as champions of ideas and culture values.

Patrimonial dependents (slaves, bondsmen) as administrators are to be found throughout the Mideastern orient and in Egypt down to the time of the Mamelukes; they represent the most extreme and what would seem to be the most consistent type of the purely patriarchal rule devoid of estates. Plebeian freedom as administrators stand relatively close to rational officialdom. The administration by literati can vary greatly in accordance with their nature: typical is the contrast between Brahmins and Mandarins, and both in turn stand opposite Buddhist and Christian clerics—yet their administration always approximates the estate type of power structure.

The rule of estates is most clearly represented by aristocracy, in purest form by feudalism, which puts in the place of the functional and rational duty of office the personal allegiance and the appeal to status honor of the enfeoffed.

In comparison to patriarchalism, all estate rule, based upon more or less stable appropriation of administrative power, stands closer to legal domination as the guarantees surrounding the prerogatives of the privileged assume the form of special "rights" (a result of the "division of power" among the estates). This rationale is absent in patriarchal structures, with their administration completely dependent on the lord's arbitrary sway. On the other hand, the strict discipline and the lack of rights of the administrative staff within patriarchalism is more closely related to the discipline of legal authority than is the administration of estates, which is fragmented and stereotyped through the appropriation of the means of administration by the staff. Plebeians (used as jurists) in Europe's princely service have been pacemarkers of the modern state.

III

Charismatic domination rests on the affectual and personal devotion of the follower to the lord and his gifts of grace (charisma). They comprise especially magical abilities, revelations of heroism, power of the mind and of speech. The eternally new, the non-routine, the unheard of and the emotional rapture from it are sources of personal devotion. The purest types are the rule of the prophet, the warrior hero, the great demagogue. The body politic consists in the communal relationship of a religious group or following. The person in command is typically the "leader"; he is obeyed by the "disciple." Obedience is given exclusively to the leader as a person, for the sake of his nonroutine qualities, not because of enacted position or traditional dignity. Therefore obedience is forthcoming only so long as people ascribe these qualities to him, that is, so long as his charisma is proven by evidence. His rule falls if he is "forsaken" by his god or deprived of his heroic strength, or if the masses lose faith in his leadership capacity. The administrative staff is selected according to charisma and personal devotion, hence selection does not consider special qualification (as in the case of the civil servant) nor rank and station (as in the case of administration by estates) nor domestic or other forms of personal dependency (as, in contrast to the above, holds for the patriarchal administrative staff). The rational concept of "competency" is lacking as is the status idea of "privilege." Decisive for the legitimation of the commissioned follower or disciple is alone the mission of the lord and his followers' personal charismatic qualification. The administration—so far as this word is adequate—lacks all orientation to rules and regulations whether enacted or traditional. Spontaneous revelation or creation, deed and example, decision from case to case, that is—at least measured against enacted orders—irrational decisions are characteristic of charismatic domination. It is not bound to tradition: "It is written but I say unto you" holds for the prophet. For the warrior hero the legitimate orders vanish opposite new creations by power of the sword, for the demagogue by virtue of his annunciation or suggestion of revolutionary "natural law." In the genuine form of charismatic justice and arbitration the lord or "sage" speaks the law and the (military or religious) following gives it recognition, which is obligatory, unless somebody raises a counter claim to charismatic validity. This case presents a struggle of leaders which in the last analysis can solely be decided by the confidence of the community; only one side can be right; the other side must be wrong and be obliged to make amends.

A. The type of charismatic domination has first been developed brilliantly by R. Sohm in his *Kirchenrecht* for the early Christian community without his recognizing that it represents a type of authority. The term has since been used repeatedly without recognition of its bearing.

Early history shows alongside a few beginnings of "enacted" domination, which are by no means entirely absent, the division of all power relationships under tradition and charisma. Besides the "economic chief" (sachem) of the Indians, an essentially traditional figure, stands the charismatic warrior prince (corresponding to the Germanic "duke") with his following. Hunting and war campaigns, both demanding a leader of extraordinary personal endowments, are the secular; magic is the "sacred" place of charismatic leadership. Throughout the ages charismatic authority exercised by prophets and warrior princes has held sway over men. The charismatic politician—the "demagogue"—is the product of the occidental city state. In the city state of Jerusalem he emerged only in religious costume as a prophet. The constitution of Athens, however, was completely cut out for his existence after the innovations of Pericles and Ephialtes, since without the demagogue the state machine would not function at all.

B. Charismatic authority rests on the "faith" in the prophet, on the "recognition" which the charismatic warrior hero, the hero of the street or the demagogue, finds personally, and this authority falls with him. Yet, charismatic authority does not derive from this recognition by the subjects. Rather the reverse obtains: the charismatically legitimized leader considers faith in the acknowledgement of his charisma obligatory and punishes its violation. Charismatic authority is even one of the great revolutionary forces in history, but in pure form it is thoroughly authoritarian and lordly in nature.

C. It should be understood that the term "charisma" is used here in a completely value-neutral sense. For the sociologist the manic seizure and rage of the Nordic berserk, the miracles and revelations of any pettifogging prophecy, the demagogic talents of Cleon are just as much "charisma" as the qualities of a Napoleon, Jesus, Pericles. Decisive for us is only whether they were considered charismatics and whether they were effective, that is, gained recognition. Here, "proof" is the basic prerequisite. The charismatic lord has to prove his being sent "by the grace of god" by performing miracles and being successful in securing the good life for his following or subjects. Only as long as he can do so will he be recognized. If success fails him, his authority falters. Wherever this charismatic concept of rule by the grace of god has existed, it has had decisive ramifications. The Chinese monarch's position was threatened as soon as drought, floods, military failure or other misfortune made it appear questionable whether he stood in the grace of Heaven. Public self-impeachment and penance, in cases of stubborn misfortune, removal and possible sacrifice threatened him. Certification by miracles was demanded of every prophet (the Zwickau people demanded it still from Luther).

So far as the belief in legitimacy matters for the stability of basically legal structures of domination, this stability rests mostly on mixed foundations. Traditional habituation of "prestige" (charisma) fuses with the belief in formal legality which in the last analysis is also a matter of habit. The belief in the legitimacy of domination is shattered alike through extraordinary misfortunes whether this exacts unusual demands from the subjects in the light of tradition, or destroys the prestige or violates the usual formal legal correctness. But with all structures of domination the obedience of the governed as a stable condition depends above all on the availability of an administrative staff and especially its continuous operation to maintain order and (directly or indirectly) enforce submission to the rule. The term "organization" means to guarantee the pattern of conduct which realizes the structure of domination. The solidarity of its (ideal and material) interests with those of the lord is decisive for the all important loyalty of the staff to the lord. For the relation of the lord to the executive staff it generally holds that the lord is the stronger opposite the resisting individual because of the isolation of the individual staff member and his solidarity with the lord. The lord is weak opposite the staff members as a whole when they band themselves together, as has happened occasionally in the past and present. Deliberate agreement of the staff is requisite in order to frustrate the lord's action and rule through obstruction or deliberate counter action. Likewise the opposition requires an administrative staff of its own.

D. Charismatic domination represents a specifically extraordinary and purely personal relationship. In the case of continued existence, however, at least when the personal representative of charisma is eliminated, the structure of domination has the tendency to routinize. This is the case when the charisma is not extinguished at once but continues to exist in some form and the authority of the lord, hence, is transferred to successors. This routinization of charisma proceeds through

1. Traditionalization of the orders. The authority of precedents takes the place of the charismatic leader's or his staff's charismatic creativity in law and administration. These precedents either protect the successors or are attributed to them.
2. The charismatic staff of disciples or followers changes into a legal or estate-like staff by taking over internal prerogatives or those appropriated by privilege (fiefs, prebends).
3. The meaning of charisma itself may undergo a change. Decisive in this is the way in which the problem of successorship is solved, which is a burning question for ideological and indeed often material reasons. This question can be solved in various ways: the merely passive tarrying for a new charismatically certified or qualified master usually gives way to an active search for a successor, especially if none readily appears and if any strong interests are vested in the continuity of the structure of domination.

   a) In this endeavor people may search for characteristic traits of the charismatic qualification. A rather pure type is represented by the search for a new Dalai Lama. The strictly personal, extraordinary character of the charisma thus is transformed into a regularly determinable quality.

   b) People may use the lot, oracles, or other indicative techniques. Thus, the belief in the qualified charismatic shifts to a belief in the respective techniques.

   c) People may designate the qualified charismatic leader:

(ca) The charismatic leader himself may do so. In this case we have successorship by designation, which occurs frequently among prophets and warlords. Therewith the belief in the personal legitimacy of charisma changes into the belief in the legitimate acquisition of power prerogatives by lawful and divine designation.

(cb) The charismatically qualified disciples or following may designate the successor and have the religious or military community accede to it by granting recognition. The conception of this procedure as a right to "elect" or "nominate" the successor is secondary. The modern concepts of election and nomination must be kept out of this. The original idea was not that of "voting" for an electoral candidate of one's choice but to determine and recognize the "right one," that is the charismatically qualified master who has a call to successorship. A "wrong" election, hence, was an atonable wrong. The basic postulate was that unanimity must be attainable, lack of unanimity was error and weakness.

In any case belief then no longer was belief in the person *per se* but in the person of the master as "correctly" and "validly designated" (possibly enthroned) or otherwise inaugurated into power like into possession of a property object.

(cc) People may believe in "hereditary charisma" and think that the charismatic qualification is in the blood. This suggestive idea represents, first, the notion of a "hereditary right" in prerogatives. The idea has become dominant in the occident only during the middle ages. Frequently charisma attaches only to the sib and its new depository must first be determined according to one of the aforementioned rules and methods (ca, cb, or cc). Where fixed rules exist with regard to the person they are not homogeneous. Only in the medieval occident and in Japan the right to inherit the crown by primogeniture has clearly won out and has greatly contributed to the stability of supreme authority, as all other forms give rise to internal conflicts.

The belief then is no longer belief in the person *per se* but in the "legitimate" heir of the dynasty: the timely and extraordinary nature of charisma is strongly transformed in a traditionalist direction; the idea of the divine right of kings ruling by the grace of God has also changed its meaning completely: now the lord reigns in his own right, not by virtue of "personal" charisma acknowledged by the subjects. The right to rule then is completely independent of personal qualities.

(cd) Charisma may be depersonalized as objectified into ritual. Then people believe that charisma is a magical quality which can be transferred or produced by a special kind of hierurgy, anointment, laying on of hands or other sacramental acts.

Then people no longer believe in the charismatic person but in the efficacy of the respective sacramental act. The claim to authority is completely independent of the charismatic's personal qualities, as is especially obvious in the Catholic principle of the *character indelebilis* of the priest.

(ce) The charismatic principle of legitimation, which is primarily authoritarian in meaning, may be re-interpreted in an anti-authoritarian direction. The empirical validity of charismatic rule rests on whether or not the person of the charismatic is recognized as qualified by the governed and has proven his charisma. According to the genuine conception of charisma people owe this recognition to the legitimate pretender because of his quality. This relationship can, however, easily be reversed to mean that the free recognition of the part of the governed be the presupposition of legitimacy and its basis (democratic legitimacy). Then recognition becomes an "election" and the lord, legitimate by virtue of his own charisma, becomes the ruler by grace of the ruled and the mandate. Designation by the following, acclamation by the (military or religious) community, and the plebiscite have historically often assumed the nature of an election by vote. Thus they have made the chosen lord or charismatic claimant into an official of the governed whom they elect at their pleasure.

A comparable development can be observed in the transformation of the principle of charismatic law. Originally the military or religious community had to recognize the pronounced law. Thus the competition of possible diverse and contradictory laws might be decided by charismatic means, as a last resort by commitment of the community to the "right" law. This charismatic principle could easily change to the—legal—idea that the governed should freely determine the law to be enforced by freely expressing their will and intention, and that vote counting, hence, majority decision, be the legitimate means for so doing.

The difference between a chosen *leader* and an elected official then consists only in the meaning which the person elected, given his personal qualities, can and does attach to his behavior opposite the staff and the governed. The official will wholly behave as the mandatary of his master—here the voters. The leader will behave as solely responsible to himself. Hence as long as the leader can successfully claim their confidence, he will act as he sees fit (leader-democracy) and not as the official, who follows the expressed or presumed will of the voters as an imperative mandate.

The Bureaucratization of Politics and the Economy

BUREAUCRACY AND POLITICS

In a modern state the actual ruler is necessarily and unavoidably the bureaucracy, since power is exercised neither through parliamentary speeches nor monarchical enunciations but through the routines of administration. This is true of both the military and civilian officialdom. Even the modern higher-ranking officer fights battles from the "office." Just as the so-called progress toward capitalism has been the unequivocal criterion for the modernization of the economy since medieval times, so the progress toward bureaucratic official-dom—characterized by formal employment, salary, pension, promotion, specialized training and functional division of labor, well-defined areas of jurisdiction, documentary procedures, hierarchical sub- and super-ordination—has been the equally unambiguous yardstick for the modernization of the state, whether monarchic or democratic; at least if the state is not a small canton with rotating administration, but comprises masses of people. The democratic state no less than the absolute state eliminates administration by feudal, patrimonial, patrician or other notables holding office in honorary or hereditary fashion, in favor of employed civil servants. It is they who decide on all our everyday needs and problems. In this regard the military power-holder, the officer, does not differ from the civilian official. The modern mass army, too, is a bureaucratic army, and the officer is a special type of official, distinct from the knight, the *condottiere*, the chieftain, or the Homeric hero. Military effectiveness rests on bureaucratic discipline. The advance of bureaucratism in municipal administration differs little from the general development; it is the more rapid, the larger the community is, or the more it loses local autonomy to technical and economic associations. In the Church the most important outcome [of the Vatican Council] of 1870 was not the much-discussed dogma of infallibility, but the universal episcopate [of the pope] which created the ecclesiastic bureaucracy and turned the bishop and the parish priest, in contrast to the Middle Ages, into mere officials of the central power, the Roman *Curia*. The same bureaucratic trend prevails in

Reprinted by permission of the Regents of the University of California and the University of California Press from "Parliament and Government in a Reconstructed Germany," pp. 1393–95, 1400–1404 in *Economy and Society: An Outline of Interpretive Sociology* (1922) (Berkeley: University of California Press, 1978). Translated by Guenther Roth and Claus Wittich. The text was originally published in 1917–18; see *Gesammelte Politische Schriften* (1921) (Tübingen: J. C. B. Mohr, 1988), pp. 320–23, 328–33.

the big private enterprises of our time, the more so, the larger they are. Private salaried employees grow statistically faster than the workers.

It is simply ridiculous if our literati believe that non-manual work in the private office is in the least different from that in a government office. Both are basically identical. Sociologically speaking, the modern state is an "enterprise" (*Betrieb*) just like a factory: This exactly is its historical peculiarity. Here as there the authority relations have the same roots. The relative independence of the artisan, the producer under the putting-out system, the free seigneurial peasant, the travelling associate in a *commenda* relationship, the knight and vassal rested on their ownership of the tools, supplies, finances and weapons with which they fulfilled their economic, political and military functions and maintained themselves. In contrast, the hierarchical dependence of the wage worker, the administrative and technical employee, the assistant in the academic institute *as well as* that of the civil servant and the soldier is due to the fact that in their case the means indispensable for the enterprise and for making a living are in the hands of the entrepreneur or the political ruler. The majority of the Russian soldiers, for example, did not want to continue the war [in 1917]. But they had no choice, for both the means of destruction and of maintenance were controlled by persons who used them to force the soldiers into the trenches, just as the capitalist owner of the means of production forces the workers into the factories and the mines. This all-important economic fact: the "separation" of the worker from the material means of production, destruction, administration, academic research, and finance in general is the common basis of the modern state, in its political, cultural and military sphere, and of the private capitalist economy. In both cases the disposition over these means is in the hands of that power whom the *bureaucratic apparatus* (of judges, officials, officers, supervisors, clerks and non-commissioned officers) directly obeys or to whom it is available in case of need. This apparatus is nowadays equally typical of all those organizations; its existence and function are inseparably cause and effect of this concentration of the means of operation—in fact, the apparatus is its very form. Increasing public ownership in the economic sphere today unavoidably means increasing bureaucratization.

The "progress" toward the bureaucratic state, adjudicating and administering according to rationally established law and regulation, is nowadays very closely related to the modern capitalist development. The modern capitalist enterprise rests primarily on *calculation* and presupposes a legal and administrative system, whose functioning can be rationally predicted, at least in principle, by virtue of its fixed general norms, just like the expected performance of a machine. The modern capitalist enterprise cannot accept what is popularly called "*kadi*-justice": adjudication according to the judge's sense of equity in a given case or according to the other irrational means of law-finding that existed everywhere in the past and still exist in the Orient.[1] The modern enterprise also finds incompatible the theocratic or patrimonial governments of Asia and of our own past, whose administrations operated in a patriarchal manner according to their

---

[1] See also reading 6, "The Three Types of Legitimate Domination," pp. 104–5 (RS).

own discretion and, for the rest, according to inviolably sacred but irrational tradition. The fact that *kadi*-justice and the corresponding administration are so often venal, precisely because of their irrational character, permitted the development, and often the exuberant prosperity, of the capitalism of traders and government purveyors and of all the pre-rational types known for four thousand years, especially the capitalism of the adventurer and booty-seeker, who lived from politics, war and administration. However, the specific features of modern capitalism, in contrast to these ancient forms of capitalist acquisition, the strictly rational organization of work embedded in rational technology, nowhere developed in such irrationally constructed states, and could never have arisen within them because these modern organizations, with their fixed capital and precise calculations, are much too vulnerable to irrationalities of law and administration. They could arise only in such circumstances as: 1) In England, where the development of the law was practically in the hands of the lawyers who, in the service of their capitalist clients, invented suitable forms for the transaction of business, and from whose midst the judges were recruited who were strictly bound to precedent, that means, to calculable schemas; or 2) where the judge, as in the bureaucratic state with its rational laws, is more or less an automaton of paragraphs: the legal documents, together with the costs and fees, are dropped in at the top with the expectation that the judgment will emerge at the bottom together with more or less sound arguments—an apparatus, that is, whose functioning is by and large *calculable* or predictable. . . .[2]

.　.　.

BUREAUCRATIZATION AND THE NAIVETÉ OF THE LITERATI

Just as the Italians and after them the English masterly developed the modern capitalist forms of economic organization, so the Byzantines, later the Italians, then the territorial states of the absolutist age, the French revolutionary centralization and finally, surpassing all of them, the Germans perfected the rational, functional and specialized bureaucratic organization of all forms of domination from factory to army and public administration. For the time being the Germans have been outdone only in the techniques of party organization, espe-

---

[2] The idea that Roman law promoted capitalism is part of the nursery school lore of the amateurish literati: Every student must know that all characteristic legal institutions of modern capitalism (from the share, the bond, the modern mortgage, the bill of exchange and all kinds of transaction forms to the capitalist forms of association in industry, mining and commerce) were completely unknown to Roman law and are of medieval, in part of Germanic origin. Moreover Roman law never got a foothold in England, where modern capitalism originated. The reception of Roman law became possible in Germany because of the absence of the great national guilds of lawyers, which in England resisted this development, and because of the bureaucratization of law and administration. Early modern capitalism did not *originate* in the bureaucratic model states where bureaucracy was a product of the state's rationalism. Advanced capitalism, too, was at first not limited to these countries, in fact, not even primarily located in them; it arose where the judges were recruited from the ranks of the lawyers. Today, however, capitalism and bureaucracy have found one another and belong intimately together.

cially by the Americans. The present world war means the world-wide triumph of this form of life, which was advancing at any rate. Already before the war, the universities, polytechnical and business colleges, trade schools, military academies and specialized schools of all conceivable kinds (even for journalism) reverberated with urgent demands propelled by the schools' recruitment interests and the graduates' mania for benefices: The professional examination was to be the precondition for all well-paying and, above all, secure positions in public and private bureaucracies; the diploma was to be the basis of all claims for social prestige (of *connubium* and social *commercium* with the circles that consider themselves "society"); the socially proper, guaranteed "salary" [rather than the "wage"], followed by a pension, was to be the form of compensation; finally, salary increases and promotion were to be dependent on seniority. The effects can be seen inside and outside of governmental institutions, but we are here only interested in the consequences for political life. It is this sober fact of universal bureaucratization that is behind the so-called "German ideas of 1914," behind what the literati euphemistically call the "socialism of the future," behind the slogans of "organized society," "cooperative economy," and all similar contemporary phrases. Even if they aim at the opposite, they always promote the rise of bureaucracy. It is true that bureaucracy is by far not the only modern form of organization, just as the factory is by far not the only type of commercial enterprise, but both determine the character of the present age and of the foreseeable future. The future belongs to bureaucratization, and it is evident that in this regard the literati pursue their calling—to provide a salvo of applause to the up-and-coming powers—just as they did in the age of laissez-faire, both times with the same naiveté.

Bureaucracy is distinguished from other historical agencies of the modern rational order of life in that it is far more persistent and "escape-proof." History shows that wherever bureaucracy gained the upper hand, as in China, Egypt and, to a lesser extent, in the later Roman empire and Byzantium, it did not disappear again unless in the course of the total collapse of the supporting culture. Yet these were still, relatively speaking, highly irrational forms of bureaucracy: "Patrimonial bureaucracies." In contrast to these older forms, modern bureaucracy has one characteristic which makes its "escape-proof" nature much more definite: rational specialization and training. The Chinese mandarin was not a specialist but a "gentleman" with a literary and humanistic education. The Egyptian, Late-Roman or Byzantine official was much more of a bureaucrat in our sense of the word. But compared to the modern tasks, his were infinitely simple and limited; his attitude was in part tradition-bound, in part patriarchally, that means, irrationally oriented. Like the businessman of the past, he was a pure empiricist. The modern official receives a professional training which unavoidably increases in correspondence with the rational technology of modern life. All bureaucracies in the world proceed on this path. Our superiority on this score was due to the fact that before the war other bureaucracies had not gone as far. The old American patronage official, for example, was a campaign "expert" with the pertinent "know-how," but he was by no means an expertly trained official.

Not democracy as such, as our literati allege, but lack of professional training was the source of corruption, which is as alien to the university-trained civil service now emerging as it is to the modern English bureaucracy, which increasingly replaces self-government through notables ("gentlemen"). Wherever the modern specialized official comes to predominate, his power proves practically indestructible since the whole organization of even the most elementary want satisfaction has been tailored to his mode of operation. A progressive elimination of private capitalism is theoretically conceivable, although it is surely not so easy as imagined in the dreams of some literati who do not know what it is all about; its elimination will certainly not be a consequence of this war. But let us assume that some time in the future it will be done away with. What would be the practical result? The destruction of the steel frame of modern industrial work? No! The abolition of private capitalism would simply mean that also the *top management* of the nationalized or socialized enterprises would become bureaucratic. Are the daily working conditions of the salaried employees and the workers in the state-owned Prussian mines and railroads really perceptibly different from those in big business enterprises? It is true that there is even less freedom, since every power struggle with a state bureaucracy is hopeless and since there is no appeal to an agency which as a matter of principle would be interested in limiting the employer's power, such as there is in the case of a private enterprise. *That* would be the whole difference.

State bureaucracy would rule *alone* if private capitalism were eliminated. The private and public bureaucracies, which now work next to, and potentially against, each other and hence check one another to a degree, would be merged into a single hierarchy. This would be similar to the situation in ancient Egypt, but it would occur in a much more rational—and hence unbreakable—form.

An inanimate machine is mind objectified. Only this provides it with the power to force men into its service and to dominate their everyday working life as completely as is actually the case in the factory. Objectified intelligence is also that animated machine, the bureaucratic organization, with its specialization of trained skills, its division of jurisdiction, its rules and hierarchical relations of authority. Together with the inanimate machine it is busy fabricating the shell of bondage which men will perhaps be forced to inhabit some day, as powerless as the fellahs of ancient Egypt. This might happen *if* a technically superior administration *were to be the ultimate and sole value* in the ordering of their affairs, and that means: a rational bureaucratic administration with the corresponding welfare benefits, for this bureaucracy can accomplish much better than any other structure of domination. This shell of bondage, which our unsuspecting literati praise so much, might perhaps be reinforced by fettering every individual to his job (notice the beginnings in the system of fringe benefits), to his class (through the increasing rigidity of the property distribution), and maybe to his occupation (through liturgic methods of satisfying state requirements, and that means: through burdening occupational associations with state functions). It would be made all the more indestructible if in the social sphere a status order were then to be imposed upon the ruled, linked to the bureaucracy and in truth subordinate to it, as in the forced-labor states of the past. An "organic" social stratification, similar to the Oriental-Egyptian type, would then arise, but in contrast to the latter it would be as austerely rational as a machine. Who would want to deny that such a potentiality lies in the womb of the future? In fact, this has often been said before, and the very muddled anticipation of it also throws its shadow upon the productions of our literati. Let us assume for the moment that this possibility were our "inescapable" fate: Who would then not smile about the fear of our literati that the political and social development might bring us *too much* "individualism" or "democracy" or other such-like things, and about their anticipation that "true freedom" will light up only when the present "anarchy" of economic production and the "party machinations" of our parliaments will be abolished in favor of social "order" and "organic stratification"—that means, in favor of the pacifism of social impotence under the tutelage of the only really inescapable power: the bureaucracy in state and economy.

The Political Limitations of Bureaucracy

Given the basic fact of the irresistible advance of bureaucratization, the question about the future forms of political organization can only be asked in the following way:

1. How can one possibly save *any remnants* of "individualist" freedom in any sense? After all, it is a gross self-deception to believe that without the achievements of the age of the Rights of Man any one of us, including the most conservative, can go on living his life. But this question shall not concern us here, for there is another one:

2. In view of the growing indispensability of the state bureaucracy and its corresponding increase in power, how can there be any guarantee that any powers will remain which can check and effectively control the tremendous influence of this stratum? How will democracy even in this limited sense be *at all possible?* However, this too is not the only question with which we are concerned here.

3. A third question, and the most important of all, is raised by a consideration of the inherent limitations of bureaucracy proper. It can easily be seen that its effectiveness has definite limitations in the public and governmental realm as well as in the private economy. The "directing mind," the "moving spirit"—that of the entrepreneur here and of the politician there—differs in substance from the civil-service mentality of the official. It is true that the entrepreneur, too, works in an office, just like the army leader, who is formally not different from other officers. If the president of a large enterprise is a salaried employee of a joint stock corporation, then he is *legally* an official like many others. In political life the same is true of the head of a political agency. The governing minister is *formally* a salaried official with pension rights. The fact that according to all constitutions he can be dismissed or resign at any time differentiates his position from that of most, but not all other officials. Far more striking is the fact that he, and he alone, does not need to prove formal specialized training. This

indicates that the meaning of his position distinguishes him, after all, from other officials, as it does the entrepreneur and the corporation president in the private economy. Actually, it is more accurate to say that he is *supposed* to be something different. And so it is indeed. If a man in a leading position is an "official" in the spirit of his performance, no matter how qualified—a man, that is, who works dutifully and honorably according to rules and instruction—then he is as useless at the helm of a private enterprise as of a government. Unfortunately, our own government [in Germany during World War I—RS] has proven this point.

The difference is rooted only in part in the kind of performance expected. Independent decision-making and imaginative organizational capabilities in matters of detail are usually also demanded of the bureaucrat, and very often expected even in larger matters. The idea that the bureaucrat is absorbed in subaltern routine and that only the "director" performs the interesting, intellectually demanding tasks is a preconceived notion of the literati and only possible in a country that has no insight into the manner in which its affairs and the work of its officialdom are conducted. The difference lies, rather, in the kind of *responsibility,* and this does indeed determine the different demands addressed to both kinds of positions. An official who receives a directive which he considers wrong can and is supposed to object to it. If his superior insists on its execution, it is his duty and even his honor to carry it out as if it corresponded to his innermost conviction, and to demonstrate in this fashion that his sense of duty stands above his personal preference. It does not matter whether the imperative mandate originates from an "agency," a "corporate body" or an "assembly." This is the ethos of *office.* A political leader acting in this way would deserve contempt. He will often be compelled to make compromises, that means, to sacrifice the less important to the more important. If he does not succeed in demanding of his master, be he a monarch or the people: "You either give me now the authorization I want from you, or I will resign," he is a miserable *Kleber* [one who sticks to his post]—as Bismarck called this type—and not a leader. "To be above parties"—in truth, to remain outside the realm of the struggle for power—is the official's role, while this struggle for personal power, and the resulting personal responsibility, is the lifeblood of the politician as well as of the entrepreneur.

The Rational State and Its Legal System

THE STATE in the sense of the rational state has existed only in the western world. Under the old regime in China a thin stratum of so-called officials, the mandarins, existed above the unbroken power of the clans and commercial and industrial guilds. The mandarin is primarily a humanistically educated literatus in the possession of a benefice[1] but not in the least degree trained for administration; he knows no jurisprudence but is a fine writer, can make verses, knows the age-old literature of the Chinese and can interpret it. In the way of political service no importance is attached to him. Such an official performs no administrative work himself; administration lies rather in the hands of the chancery officials. The mandarin is continually transferred from one place to another to prevent his obtaining a foothold in his administrative district, and he could never be assigned to his home province. As he does not understand the dialect of his province he cannot communicate with the public. A state with such officials is something different from the occidental state.

In reality everything is based on the magical theory that the virtue of the emperor and the merits of the officials, meaning their perfection in literary culture, keep things in order in normal times. If a drought sets in or any untoward event takes place an edict is promulgated intensifying the examinations of verse-making, or speeding up legal trials in order to quiet the spirits. The empire is an agrarian state; hence the power of the peasant clans who represent nine-tenths of the economic life—the other one-tenth belonging to commercial and trading guild organizations—is entirely unbroken. In essence things are left to take care of themselves. The officials do not rule but only interfere in the event of disturbances or untoward happenings.

Very different is the rational state in which alone modern capitalism can flourish. Its basis is an expert officialdom and rational law. The Chinese state changed over to administration through trained officials in the place of humanistically cultured persons as early as the 7th and 11th centuries but the change could be only temporarily maintained; then the usual eclipse of the moon arrived and arrangements were transformed in reverse order. It cannot be seriously asserted, however, that the spirit of the Chinese people could not tolerate an administration

Reprinted by permission of Transaction Publishers from Max Weber, *General Economic History* (New York: Greenberg, Publisher, 1927), pp. 338–43. Translated by Frank H. Knight. The text is based on a lecture course Weber gave in 1919–20; see *Wirtschaftsgeschichte* (1923) (Berlin: Duncker und Humblot, 1991), pp. 289–93.

[1] "The benefice is a life-long, not a hereditary, remuneration for its holder in exchange for his real or presumed services; the remuneration is an attribute of the office, not the incumbent." *Economy and Society*, p. 1073 (RS).

of specialists. Its development, and that of the rational state, was rather prevented by the persistence of reliance upon magic. In consequence of this fact the power of the clans could not be broken, as happened in the occident through the development of the cities and of Christianity.

The rational law of the modern occidental state, on the basis of which the trained official renders his decisions, arose on its formal side, though not as to its content, out of Roman law. The latter was to begin with a product of the Roman city state, which never witnessed the dominion of democracy and its justice in the same form as the Greek city. A Greek heliast court administered a petty justice; the contestants worked upon the judges through pathos, tears, and abusing their opponents. This procedure was also known in Rome in political trials, as the orations of Cicero show, but not in civil trials where the praetor appointed an *iudex* to whom he gave strict instructions as to the conditions requiring a judgment against the accused or the throwing out of the case. Under Justinian the Byzantine bureaucracy brought order and system into this rational law, in consequence of the natural interest of the official in a law which would be systematic and fixed and hence easier to learn.

With the fall of the Roman empire in the west, law came into the hands of the Italian notaries. These, and secondarily the universities, have on their conscience the revival of Roman law. The notaries adhered to the old contractual forms of the Roman empire and re-interpreted them according to the needs of the time. At the same time a systematic legal doctrine was developed in the universities. The essential feature in the development, however, was the rationalization of procedure. As among all primitive peoples the ancient German legal trial was a rigidly formal affair. The party which pronounced wrongly a single word in the formula lost the case, because the formula possessed magical significance and supernatural evils were feared. This magical formalism of the German trial fitted in with the formalism of Roman law. At the same time the French kingdom played a part through the creation of the institution of the representative or advocate whose task it was especially to pronounce the legal formulas correctly, particularly in connection with the canon law. The magnificent administrative organization of the church required fixed forms for its disciplinary ends in relation to the laity and for its own internal discipline. No more than the bourgeoisie could it take up with the Germanic ordeal or judgment of God. The business man could not permit commercial claims to be decided by a competition in reciting formulas, and everywhere secured exemptions from this legalistic contest and from the ordeal. The church also, after hesitating at first, ended by adopting the view that such procedure was heathenish and not to be tolerated, and established the canonical procedure on lines as rational as possible. This two-fold rationalization of procedure from the profane and spiritual sides spread over the western world.

In the revival of the Roman law has been seen the basis for the downfall of the peasant class, as well as for the development of capitalism. It is true that there were cases in which the application of Roman law principles was disadvantageous to the peasant. An example is the transformation of the old mark community rights into feudal obligations, the individual who stood at the head of the mark community (*Obermärker*) being recognized as a proprietor in the Roman sense and the holdings of the associates burdened with feudal dues. On the other hand, however, it was especially through the jurists trained in the Roman law that in France the monarchy was able to obstruct the eviction of peasants by the lords.

As little is the Roman law the basis without qualification for the development of capitalism. England, the home of capitalism, never accepted the Roman law, for the reason that in connection with the royal courts existed a class of advocates who guarded the national legal institutions against corruption. This class controlled the development of legal doctrine, for from its ranks were chosen, as they still are, the judges. It prevented Roman law from being taught in English universities, in order that persons from outside the class might not reach the judicial bench.

In fact all the characteristic institutions of modern capitalism have other origins than Roman law. The annuity bond, whether arising out of a personal debt or a war loan, came from medieval law, in which Germanic legal ideas played their part. Similarly the stock certificate arose out of medieval and modern law and was unknown to the law of antiquity. Likewise the bill of exchange, to the development of which Arabic, Italian, German, and English law contributed. The commercial company is also a medieval product; only the commenda enterprise was current in antiquity. So also the mortgage, with the security of registration, and the deed of trust, as well as the power of attorney, are medieval in origin and do not go back to antiquity.

The reception of the Roman law was crucial only in the sense that it created formal juristic thinking. In its structure every legal system is based either on formal-legalistic or on material principles. By material principles are to be understood utilitarian and economic considerations, such for example as those according to which the Islamic *kadi* conducts his administration. In every theocracy and every absolutism justice is materially directed as by contrast in every bureaucracy it is formal-legalistic. Frederick the Great hated the jurists because they constantly applied in a formalistic sense his decrees which were based on material principles, and so turned them to ends with which he would have nothing to do. In this connection, as in general, the Roman law was the means of crushing the material legal system in favor of the formal.

This formalistic law, is however, calculable. In China it may happen that a man who has sold a house to another may later come to him and ask to be taken in because in the meantime he has been impoverished. If the purchaser refuses to heed the ancient Chinese command to help a brother, the spirits will be disturbed; hence the impoverished seller comes into the house as a renter who pays no rent. Capitalism cannot operate on the basis of a law so constituted. What it requires is law which can be counted upon, like a machine; ritualistic-religious and magical considerations must be excluded.

The creation of such a body of law was achieved through the alliance between the modern state and the jurists for the purpose of making good its claims to power. For a time in the 16th century it attempted to work with the humanists, and the first Greek gymnasia were established with the idea that men educated in them would be suitable for state officials; for political contests were carried out to a large extent through the exchange of state papers and only one schooled in Latin and Greek had the necessary equipment. This illusion was shortlived. It was soon found that the products of the gymnasia were not on that account alone equipped for political life, and the jurists were the final resort. In China, where the humanistically cultured mandarin ruled the field, the monarch had no jurists at his disposal, and the struggle among the different philosophical schools as to which of them formed the best statesmen waged to and fro until finally orthodox Confucianism was victorious. India also had writers but no trained jurists. In contrast the western world had at its disposal a formally organized legal system, the product of the Roman genius, and officials trained in this law were superior to all others as technical administrators. From the standpoint of economic history this fact is significant in that the alliance between the state and formal jurisprudence was indirectly favorable to capitalism.

NINE

The National State and Economic Policy
(Freiburg Address)

THE TITLE I have chosen promises much more than I can achieve today, or wish to achieve. What I intend is first of all this: to use a *single example* to make clear the role played by racial differences of a physical and psychological nature, as between nationalities, in the economic struggle for existence. I should then like to add some reflections on the situation of a state which rests on a national basis—such as our own—within the framework of a consideration of economic policy. I am choosing for my example a set of events which although they are occurring a long way from us have repeatedly come to the notice of the public in the last ten years. Allow me, then, to conduct you to the eastern marches of the *Reich*, to the open country of the Prussian province of *West Prussia*. This setting combines the character of a national borderland with some unusually sharp variations in the conditions of economic and social existence, and this recommends it for our purpose. Unfortunately I cannot avoid calling on your forbearance initially while I recite a series of dry data.

The rural areas of the province of West Prussia contain three different types of contrast, as follows: First, extraordinary variations in the *quality of agricultural land.* From the sugar-beet country of the Vistula plain to the sandy uplands of Cassubia the estimates of the gross tax yield vary in a ratio of 10 or 20 to 1. Even the average values at district level fluctuate between 4¾ and 33⅔ marks per hectare.

Then there are contrasts in the *social stratification* of the population which cultivates this land. As in general in the East, the official statistics refer alongside the 'rural parish' (*Landgemeinde*) to a second form of communal unit, unknown to the South: the 'estate district' (*Gutsbezirk*). And, correspondingly, the estates of the nobility stand out in bold relief in the landscape between the villages of the peasants. These are the places of residence of the class which gives the East its social imprint—the Junkers. Everywhere there are manor-houses, surrounded by the single-storey cottages the lord of the manor (*Gutsherr*) has allotted to the day-labourers, plus a few strips of arable land and pasture: these people are obliged to work on the manor the whole year round. The area of the province of West Prussia is divided between these two categories in roughly equal proportions. But in particular districts the share of the manorial estates can vary from a few per cent to two thirds of the whole area.

Reprinted by permission from *Economy and Society* 9(1980): 428–49. Translated by Ben Fowkes. This lecture was originally published in 1895; see *Gesammelte Politische Schriften* (1921) (Tübingen: J. C. B. Mohr, 1988), pp. 1–25.

Finally, within this population which is subject to a twofold social stratification, there exists a third contrast; it is between the *nationalities*. And the national composition of the population of the individual communities also varies from region to region. It is *this kind of variation* which is of interest to us today. In the first place, the proportion of Poles is naturally greater as you approach the boundary of the *Reich*. But this proportion of Poles also *increases* as the quality of the soil *deteriorates*. Any language-map will show that. One will at first wish to explain this historically from the form taken by the German occupation of these lands, which initially spread over the fertile plain of the Vistula. And this would not be entirely incorrect. But let us now ask the further question: what *social strata* are the repositories of Germanism (*Deutschtum*) and Polonism (*Polentum*) in the country districts? In answer to this question, the figures of the most recently published population census (that of 1885)[1] present us with a curious picture. Admittedly we cannot directly extract the national composition of each parish from these figures, but we can do this indirectly, provided we are content to achieve only approximate accuracy. The intermediate step is the figure for religious affiliation, which, for the nationally mixed district we are concerned with, coincides to within a few per cent with nationality. If we separate the economic categories of the peasant village and the manorial estate in each district, by identifying them with the corresponding administrative units of the rural parish and the estate district,[2] we find that their national composition is related *inversely* to the quality of the soil; in the fertile districts the Catholics, i.e. the Poles, are relatively most numerous on the *estates,* and the Protestants, i.e. the *Germans,* are to be found in greater proportions in the *villages*. In districts where the soil is inferior the situation is precisely the opposite of this. For example, if we take the districts with an average net tax yield of under 5 marks per hectare, we find only 35.5 per cent Protestants in the villages and 50.2 per cent Protestants on the estates; if on the other hand we take the group of districts which provide an average of 10 to 15 marks per hectare, we find the proportion of Protestants rising to 60.7 per cent in the villages and falling to 42.1 per cent on the estates. Why is this? Why are the estates the reservoirs of Polonism on the plain, and the villages the reservoirs of Polonism in the hills? One thing is immediately evident: *the Poles have a tendency to collect together in that stratum of the population which stands lowest both economically and socially.* On the good soil, like that of the Vistula plain, the peasant's standard of living has always been higher than that of the day-labourer on an estate; on the bad soil, which could only be rationally exploited on a large scale, the manorial estate (*Rittergut*) was the repository of civilization and hence of Germanism; there the miserable small peasants still live *below* the level of the day-labourers on the estates. If we did not know that anyway, the age-structure of the population would lead

[1] *Gemeindelexikon,* Berlin, 1887.

[2] This administrative subdivision is more characteristic evidence of social stratification than a division on the basis of the size of the enterprise. In the plains manorial enterprises of less than 100 hectares are not uncommon, nor, conversely, are peasant enterprises of more than 200 hectares in the hills.

us to that presumption. If we look at the *villages* we find that as one rises from the plain to the hilltops, and as the quality of the soil deteriorates the proportion of children under 14 years old rises from 35–36 per cent to 40–41 per cent. If we compare the *estates,* we find that the proportion of children is higher on the plain than in the villages, that it increases as the height above sea-level increases, though more slowly than this happens in the villages, and finally that *on* the hilltops the proportion is lower than the proportion in the hilltop villages. As usual, a large number of children follows hard on the heels of a low standard of living, since this tends to obliterate any calculations of future welfare. Economic advance (*wirtschaftliche Kultur*), a relatively high standard of living and *Germanism* are in West Prussia identical.

And yet the two nationalities have competed for centuries on the same soil, and with essentially the same opportunities. What then is the basis of the distinction? One is immediately tempted to believe that the two nationalities differ in their *ability to adapt* to different economic and social conditions of existence. And this is in fact so—as is proved by the tendency of development revealed by shifts in the population and changes in its national composition. This also allows us to perceive how fateful that difference in the ability to adapt is for the Germanism of the East.

It is true that we only have at our disposal the figures of 1871 and 1885 for a comparative examination of the displacements which have occurred in the individual parishes, and these figures allow us to perceive only the indistinct beginnings of a development which has since then, according to all indications, been extraordinarily reinforced. Apart from this, the clarity of the numerical picture naturally suffers under the enforced but not entirely correct assumption of an identity between religious affiliation and nationality on one side, and administrative subdivisions and social structure on the other. Despite all of this, we can still gain a clear enough view of the relevant changes. The rural population of West Prussia, like that of large parts of the whole of eastern Germany, showed a tendency to *fall* during the period between 1880 and 1885; this fall amounted to 12,700 people, i.e. there was a decline of 1¼ per cent, while the overall population of the German *Reich* was increasing by about 3½ per cent. This phenomenon, like the phenomena we have already discussed, also occurred unevenly: in some districts there was actually an increase in the rural population. And indeed the *manner in which* these phenomena were distributed is highly characteristic. If we take first the different soil qualities, one would normally assume that the decline hit the *worst* land hardest, for there the pressure of falling prices would be first to render the margin of subsistence too narrow. If one looks at the figures, however, one sees that the *reverse* is the case: precisely the most well-favoured districts, such as Stuhm and Marienwerder, with an average net yield of around 15–17 marks, experienced the greatest *population loss*, a loss of 7–8 per cent, whereas in the hilly country the district of Konitz and Tuchel, with a net yield of 5–6 marks, experienced the biggest *increase*, an increase which had been going on since 1871. One looks for an explanation, and one asks first: from which social strata did the population loss originate, and which social strata gained from the increase? Let us look at the districts where the figures demonstrate a great reduction in population: Stuhm, Marienwerder, Rosenberg. These are without exception districts where *large-scale landowner-ship* predominates particularly strongly, and if we take the *estate districts* of the whole province together, we find that although in 1880 they exhibited a total population two thirds smaller than the villages (on the same area of land) their share in the fall of the rural population between 1880 and 1885 comes to over 9,000 people, which is almost three quarters of the total reduction over the whole province: the population of the estate districts has fallen by about 3¾ per cent. But this fall in population is also distributed unevenly *within* the category referred to: in some places the population actually increased, and when one isolates the areas where the population was sharply reduced, one finds that it was precisely the estates on *good* soil which experienced a particularly severe loss of population.

In contrast to this, the *increase* of population which took place on the bad soils of the uplands worked chiefly in favour of the *villages,* and indeed this was most pronounced in the villages on *bad* soils, as opposed to the villages of the plain. The tendency which emerges from these figures is therefore towards a *decrease in the numbers of day-labourers* on the estates situated on the *best* land, and an *increase in the numbers of peasants* on land *of inferior quality.* What is at stake here, and how the phenomenon is to be explained, becomes clear when one finally asks how the *nationalities* are affected by these shifts in population.

In the first half of the century the Polish element appeared to be in retreat, slowly but continuously. However, since the 1860s, as is well known, it has just as continuously, and just as slowly, been advancing. Despite their inadequate basis, the language data for West Prussia make the latter point extremely plain. Now a shift in the boundary between two nationalities can occur in two ways, which are fundamentally distinct. It may on the one hand happen that the language and customs of the majority gradually impose themselves on national minorities in a nationally mixed region, that these minorities get 'soaked up'. This phenomenon can be found as well in eastern Germany: the process is statistically demonstrable in the case of Germans of the Catholic confession. Here the ecclesiastical bond is stronger than the national one, memories of the *Kulturkampf* also play their part, and the lack of a German-educated clergy means that the German Catholics are lost to the cultural community of the nation. But the second form of nationality-displacement is more important, and more relevant for us: *economic extrusion.* And this is how it is in the present case. If one examines the changes in the proportion of adherents of the two faiths in the rural parish units between 1871 and 1885, one sees this: the migration of day-labourers away from the estates is in the lowlands regularly associated with a relative decline of Protestantism, while in the hills the increase of the village population is associated with a relative increase of Catholicism.[3] *It is chiefly German day-labourers who move out of the districts of progressive cultivation;*

---

[3] For example the manorial estates of the district of Stuhm experienced a decline in population of 6.7 per cent between 1871 and 1885, and the proportion of Protestants in the Christian population fell from 33.4 per cent to 31.3 per cent. The villages of the district of Konitz and Tuchel increased in population by 8 per cent and the proportion of Catholics rose from 84.7 per cent to 86.0 per cent.

it is chiefly Polish peasants who multiply in the districts where cultivation is on a low level.

But both processes—here emigration, there increase in numbers,—lead back ultimately to one and the same reason: *a lower expectation of living standards,* in part physical, in part mental, which the Slav race either possesses as a gift from nature or has acquired through breeding in the course of its past history. This is what has helped it to victory.

Why do the German day-labourers move out? Not for material reasons: the movement of emigration does not draw its recruits from districts with low levels of pay or from categories of worker who are badly paid. Materially there is hardly a more secure situation than that of agricultural labourer on the East German estates. Nor is it the much-bruited longing for the diversions of the big city. This is a reason for the planless wandering off of the younger generation, but not for the emigration of long-serving families of day-labourers. Moreover, why would such a longing arise precisely among the people on the big estates? Why is it that the emigration of the day-labourers demonstrably falls off in proportion as the *peasant village* comes to dominate the physiognomy of the landscape? The reason is as follows: there are only masters and servants, and nothing else, on the estates of his homeland for the day-labourer, and the prospect for his family, down to the most distant of his progeny, is to slave away on someone else's land from one chime of the estate-bell to the next. In this deep, half-conscious impulse towards the distant horizon there lies hidden an element of primitive idealism. He who cannot decipher this does not know the magic of *freedom.* Indeed, the spirit of freedom seldom touches us today in the stillness of the study. The naive youthful ideals of freedom are faded, and some of us have grown prematurely old and all too wise, and believe that one of the most elemental impulses of the human breast has been borne to its grave along with the slogans of a dying conception of politics and economic policy.

We have here an occurrence of a mass-psychological character: the German agricultural labourers can no longer adjust themselves to the *social* conditions of life in their homeland. We have reports of West Prussian landowners complaining about their labourers' 'self-assertiveness'. The old patriarchal relationship between lord and vassal is disappearing. But this is what attached the day-labourer directly to the interests of the agricultural producers as a small cultivator with a right to a share in the produce. Seasonal labour in the beet-growing districts requires seasonal workers and payment in money. They are faced with a purely proletarian existence, but without the possibility of that energetic advance to economic independence which gives added self-confidence to the industrial proletarians who live cheek by jowl in the cities of the West. Those who replace the Germans on the estates of the East are better able to submit to these conditions of existence: I mean the itinerant Polish workers, troops of nomads recruited by agents in Russia, who cross the frontier in tens of thousands in spring, and leave again in autumn. They first emerge in attendance upon the sugar-beet, a crop which turns agriculture into a seasonal trade, then they are everywhere, because one can save on workers' dwellings, on poor rates, on social obligations by using them, and further because they are in a precarious position as foreigners and therefore in the hands of the landowners. These are accompanying circumstances of the economic death-struggle of Old Prussian Junkerdom. On the sugar-beet estates a stratum of industrial businessmen steps into the shoes of the patriarchally ruling lord of the manor, while in the uplands the lands of the manorial estates crumble away under the pressure of the crisis in the agrarian economy. Tenants of small parcels and colonies of small peasants arise on their outfields. The economic foundations of the power of the old landed nobility vanish, and the nobility itself becomes something other than what it was.

And why is it the *Polish* peasants who are gaining the land? Is it their superior economic intelligence, or their greater supply of capital? It is rather the opposite of both these factors. Under a climate, and on a soil, which favour the growing of cereals and potatoes above all, alongside extensive cattle-raising, the person who is least threatened by an unfavourable market is the one who brings his products to the place where they are least devalued by a collapse in prices: his own stomach. This is the person who produces *for his own requirements.* And once again, the person who can set his own requirements *at the lowest level,* the person who makes the smallest physical and mental demands for the maintenance of his life, is the one with the advantage. The small Polish peasant in East Germany is a type far removed from the bustling peasant owner of a dwarf property, whom one may see here in the well-favoured valley of the Rhine as he forges links with the towns via greenhouse cultivation and market-gardening. The small Polish peasant gains more land, because he as it were eats the very grass from off of it, he gains not *despite* but *on account of* the low level of his physical and intellectual habits of life.

We therefore seem to see a *process of selection* unfolding. Both nationalities have for a long time been embedded in the same conditions of existence. The consequence of this has *not* been what vulgar materialists might have imagined, that they took on the same physical and psychological qualities, but rather that one yielded the ground to the other, that victory went to the nationality which possessed the greater ability to adapt itself to the given economic and social conditions of existence.

This difference in the ability to adapt seems to be present ready-made, as a fixed magnitude. The nations' respective abilities to adapt might perhaps undergo further shifts in the course of many generations, through the millennial process of breeding which no doubt originally produced the difference, but for any reflections on the present situation it is a factor with which we have to reckon, as given.[4]

---

[4] I need hardly point out the irrelevance for the above comments of the disputes in natural science over the significance of the principles of selection, or over the general application *in natural science* of the concept of 'breeding', and all the discussions which have taken this as their starting-point. This is in any case not my field. However, the *concept* of 'selection' is today common ground, just as much as is, e.g., the heliocentric hypothesis, and the idea of 'breeding' human beings is as old as the Platonic state. Both these concepts are employed e.g. by F. A. Lange in his *Arbeiterfrage* [*Die Arbeiterfrage in ihrer Bedeutung für Gegenwart und Zukunft,* (Duisburg, 1865)] and they have long

The free play of the forces of selection does not always work out, as the optimists among us think, in favour of the nationality which is more highly developed or more gifted economically. We have just seen this. Human history does not lack examples of the victory of less developed types of humanity and the extinction of fine flowers of intellectual and emotional life, when the human community which was their repository lost its ability to adapt to the conditions of existence, either by reason of its social organization or its racial characteristics. In our case it is the transformation of the forms of agricultural enterprise and the tremendous crisis in agriculture which is bringing to victory the less economically developed nationality. The rise of sugar-beet cultivation and the unprofitability of cereal production for the market are developments running parallel and in the same direction: the first breeds the Polish seasonal worker, the second the small Polish peasant.

On looking back at the facts presented here, I am in no position, as I shall willingly concede, to develop theoretically the significance of the various general points which may be derived from them. The immensely difficult question, certainly insoluble at present, of *where to place the limit* of the variability of physical and psychological qualities in a population under the influence of its given conditions of existence is something I shall not even venture to touch on.

Instead of this, everyone will automatically want to ask, above all else: what can and should be done in this situation?

You will however permit me to abstain from an exhaustive discussion of this on the present occasion, and to content myself with briefly indicating the two demands which in my view should be posed from the standpoint of Germanism, and are in fact being posed with growing unanimity. The first is the demand for the closing of the Eastern frontier. This was accomplished under Prince Bismarck, and then reversed after his resignation in 1890: permanent settlement remained forbidden to the aliens, but they were permitted entry as migratory workers. A 'class-conscious' landowner at the head of the Prussian government excluded them in the interests of the maintenance of our nationality, and the hated opponent of the Agrarians [Caprivi] let them in, in the interests of the big landowners, who are the *only people* to gain from this influx. This demonstrates that the 'economic class-standpoint' is not always decisive in matters of economic

---

been so familiar to us that a misunderstanding of their meaning is impossible for anyone who knows our literature. More difficult to answer is the question of how much lasting value should be attached to the latest attempts by anthropologists to extend Darwin's and Weissman's selection concept to the field of economic investigation. They are ingenious, but arouse considerable reservations as to method and factual results, and are no doubt mistaken in a number of exaggerated versions. Nevertheless the writings of e.g. Otto Ammon ('Natural selection in man', 'The social order and its natural basis') deserve more attention than they have been given, irrespective of all the reservations that have to be made. One weakness of most of the contributions made from natural-scientific quarters to the illumination of the problems of our science consists in their mistaken ambition to provide above all a 'refutation' of socialism. Their eagerness to attain this goal leads to the involuntary conversion of what was intended to be a 'natural-scientific theory' of the social order into an apology for it.

policy—*here* it was the circumstance that the helm of the ship of state fell from a strong hand into a weaker one. The other demand is for a policy of systematic land purchase on the part of the state, i.e. the extension of crown lands on the one hand, and systematic colonization by German peasants on suitable land, particularly on suitable crown land, on the other hand. Large-scale enterprises which can only be preserved at the expense of Germanism deserve from the point of view of the nation to go down to destruction. To leave them as they are without assistance means to allow unviable Slav hunger colonies to arise by way of gradual fragmentation of the estates into small parcels. And it is not only our interest in stemming the Slav flood which requires the transfer of considerable parts of the land of eastern Germany into the hands of the state, but also the annihilating criticism the big landowners themselves have made of the continued existence of their private property by demanding the removal of the risk they run, their personal responsibility for their own property, which is its sole justification. I refer to the proposal for the introduction of a corn monopoly [the Kanitz proposal of 1894 for a state monopoly on the import of corn into Germany] and the granting of a state contribution of half a billion marks a year.[5]

But, as I said earlier, I would prefer not to discuss this practical question of Prussian agrarian policy today. I would rather start from the fact that such a question arises at all, the fact that we all consider the German character of the East to be something that *should* be protected, and that the economic policy of the state *should* also enter into the lists in its defence. Our state is a *national*

---

[5] The same train of thought as mine led Professor Schmoller too to pose the demand for state purchase of land in his journal (*Schmollers Jahrbuch*, 19, 1895, pp. 625 ff.). In fact that part of the stratum of big landowners whose retention as agricultural managers is desirable from the state's point of view cannot in most cases be allowed to keep their land in full ownership but only as tenants of the crown demesne. I am certainly of the opinion that the purchase of land only has long-term validity if organically combined with the colonization of suitable crown lands, with the result that a part of the land in the East passes through the hands of the state and while it is in this position undergoes an energetic course of improvement with the assistance of state credits. The Settlement Commission [set up in 1886 to buy Polish estates and settle German farmers on them] has to contend with two difficulties in this connection. One is that it is burdened with the 'after-effects of the cure', in the shape of the colonists who have been planted and who ought preferably to be handed over after a while, along with their requests to postpone repayment to the ordinary state treasury, which is somewhat more hardhearted than the Commission. The other difficulty derives from the fact that the estates which have been purchased have been for the most part in the hands of crown tenants for over a decade. Now the improvement must be carried out at breakneck speed and with great losses of the administration itself, although certainly a large number of crown lands would be suitable for immediate colonization. The consequent dilatoriness of the procedure does not by any means justify the judgment of Hans Delbrück on the national-political impact, delivered in his many well-known articles in the *Preussische Jahrbücher.* A merely mechanical calculation, comparing the number of peasant farms founded with the number of Poles, is not conclusive proof for anyone who has observed the civilising effect of colonization on the spot: a few villages with a dozen German farms each will eventually *Germanise* many square miles, naturally with the pre-condition that the flood of proletarian reinforcements from the East is dammed up, and that we do not cut the ground from under the feet of those who are bringing progress, by leaving the big estates to the free play of the forces which are leading to their fragmentation and ruin, and are acting with even less restraint now thanks to the laws on renting land in perpetuity.

state, and it is this circumstance which makes us feel we have a right to make this demand.

However, how does the attitude assumed by economics relate to this? Does it treat such nationalist value-judgments as prejudices, of which it must carefully rid itself in order to be able to apply its own specific standard of value to the economic facts, without being influenced by emotional reflexes? And *what is* this standard of value peculiar to economic policy (*Volkswirtschaftspolitik*)? I should like to try to get closer to this question by making one or two further observations.

As we have seen, the economic struggle between the nationalities follows its course even under the semblance of 'peace'. The German peasants and day-labourers of the East are not being pushed off the land in an open conflict by politically superior opponents. Instead they are getting the worst of it in the silent and dreary struggle of everyday economic existence, they are abandoning their homeland to a race which stands on a lower level, and moving towards a dark future in which they will sink without trace. There can be no truce even in the *economic* struggle for existence; only if one takes the semblance of peace for its reality can one believe that peace and prosperity will emerge for our successors at some time in the distant future. Certainly, the vulgar conception of political economy is that it consists in working out recipes for making the world happy; the improvement of the 'balance of pleasure' in human existence is the sole purpose of our work that the vulgar conception can comprehend. However the deadly seriousness of the population problem prohibits eudaemonism; it prevents us from imagining that peace and happiness lie hidden in the lap of the future, it prevents us from believing that elbow-room in this earthly existence can be won in any other way than through the hard struggle of human beings with each other.

It is certain that there can be no work in political economy on any other than an altruistic basis. The overwhelming majority of the fruits of the economic, social and political endeavours of the present are garnered not by the generation now alive but by the generations of the future. If our work is to retain any meaning it can only be informed by this: concern for the *future,* for *those who will come after us.* But there can also be no real work in political economy on the basis of optimistic dreams of happiness. Abandon hope all ye who enter here: these words are inscribed above the portals of the unknown future history of mankind. So much for the dream of peace and happiness.

The question which leads us beyond the grave of our own generation is not 'how will human beings *feel* in the future' but 'how will they *be*'. In fact this question underlies all work in political economy. We do not want to train up feelings of well-being in people, but rather those characteristics we think constitute the greatness and nobility of our human nature.

The doctrines of political economy have alternately placed in the forefront or naively identified as standards of value either the technical economic problem of the production of commodities or the problem of their distribution, in other words 'social justice'. Yet again and again a different perception, in part unconscious, but nevertheless all-dominating, has raised itself above both these standards of value: the perception that a *human* science, and that is what political economy is, investigates above all else the *quality of the human beings* who are brought up in those economic and social conditions of existence. And here we must be on our guard against a certain illusion.

As a science of explanation and analysis political economy is *international*, but as soon as it makes *value judgments* it is bound up with the distinct imprint of humanity we find in our own nature. We are often most bound to our own nature on precisely those occasions when we think we have escaped our fleshly limitations. And if—to use a somewhat fanciful image—we could arise from the grave thousands of years hence, we would seek the distant traces of our own nature in the physiognomy of the race of the future. Even our highest, our ultimate, terrestrial ideals are mutable and transitory. We cannot presume to impose them on the future. But we can hope that the future recognises in our nature the nature of *its own ancestors*. We wish to make ourselves the forefathers of the race of the future with our labour and our mode of existence.

The economic policy of a German state, and the standard of value adopted by a German economic theorist, can therefore be nothing other than a German policy and a German standard.

Has this situation perhaps changed since economic development began to create an all-embracing economic community of nations, going beyond national boundaries? Is the 'nationalistic' standard of evaluation to be thrown on the scrapheap along with 'national egoism' in economic policy? Has the struggle for economic survival, for the maintenance of one's wife and children, been surmounted now that the family has been divested of its original function as an association for production, and meshed into the network of the national economic community? We know that this is *not* the case: the struggle has taken on *other forms*, forms about which one may well raise the question of whether they should be viewed as a mitigation or indeed rather an intensification and a sharpening of the struggle. In the same way, the world-wide economic community is only another form of the struggle of the nations with each other, and it *aggravates* rather than mitigates the struggle for the maintenance of one's own culture, because it calls forth in the very bosom of the nation material interests *opposed* to the nation's future, and throws them into the ring in alliance with the nation's enemies.

We do not have peace and human happiness to bequeath to our posterity, but rather the *eternal struggle* for the maintenance and improvement by careful cultivation of our national character. And we should not abandon ourselves to the optimistic expectation that we have done what is necessary once we have developed economic progress to the highest possible level, and that the process of selection in the freely conducted and 'peaceful' economic struggle will thereupon automatically bring the victory to the more highly developed human type.

Our successors will not hold us responsible before history for the kind of economic organization we hand over to them, but rather for the amount of elbow-room we conquer for them in the world and leave behind us. Processes of economic development are in the final analysis also *power struggles*, and the ultimate and decisive interests at whose service economic policy must place it-self are the interests of national *power*, where these interests are in question. The science of political economy is a *political* science. It is a servant of politics, not the day-to-day politics of the individuals and classes who happen to be rul-ing at a particular time, but the lasting power-political interests of the nation. And for us the *national state* is not, as some people believe, an indeterminate entity raised higher and higher into the clouds in proportion as one clothes its nature in mystical darkness, but the temporal power-organization of the nation, and in this national state the ultimate standard of value for economic policy is 'reason of state'. There is a strange misinterpretation of this view current to the effect that we advocate 'state assistance' instead of 'self-help', state regulation of economic life instead of the free play of economic forces. We do not. Rather we wish under this slogan of 'reason of state' to raise the demand that for questions of German economic policy—including the question of whether, and how far, the state should intervene in economic life, and when it should rather untie the economic forces of the nation and tear down the barriers in the way of their free development—the ultimate and decisive voice should be that of the economic and political interests of our nation's power, and the vehicle of that power, the German national state.

Has it been superfluous to recall things that appear to go without saying? Or was it unnecessary for precisely a younger representative of economic science to recall these matters? I do not think so, for it appears that our generation is li-able very easily to lose sight of these simple bases for judgment. We have wit-nessed a hitherto unimaginable growth in the present generation's interest in the burning issues of our field of science. Everywhere we find an advance in the pop-ularity of the economic method of approach. Social policy has become the cen-tral pre-occupation instead of politics, economic relations of power instead of legal relations, cultural and economic history instead of political history. In the outstanding works of our historical colleagues we find that today instead of telling us about the warlike deeds of our ancestors they dilate at length about 'mother-right', that monstrous notion, and force into a subordinate clause the victory of the Huns on the Catalaunian Plain. One of our most ingenious theo-rists was self-confident enough to believe he could characterize jurisprudence as 'the handmaiden of political economy'. And one thing is certainly true: the economic form of analysis has penetrated into jurisprudence itself. Even its most intimate regions, the treatises on the Pandects, are beginning to be quietly haunted by economic ideas. And in the verdicts of the courts of law it is not rare to find so-called 'economic grounds' put in where legal concepts are unable to fill the bill. In short, to use the half-reproachful phrase of a legal colleague: we have 'come into fashion'. A method of analysis which is so confidently forging ahead is in danger of falling into certain illusions and exaggerating the signifi-cance of its own point of view. This exaggeration occurs in a quite specific di-rection. Just as the extension of the material of *philosophical* reflection—already made apparent externally through the fact that nowadays we frequently find e.g. prominent physiologists occupying the old Chairs of Philosophy—has led laymen to the opinion that the old questions of the nature of human knowledge are no longer the ultimate and central questions of philosophy, so in the field of political economy the notion has grown in the minds of the coming generation that the work of economic science has not only immensely extended our *knowledge* of the nature of human communities, but also provided a completely new *standard* by which these phenomena can ultimately be *evaluated,* that political economy is in a position to extract from its material its own specific ideals. The notion that there exist independent economic or 'socio-political' ideals is revealed as an optical illusion as soon as one seeks to establish these 'peculiar' canons of evaluation by using the literature produced by our science. We are confronted instead with a *chaotic mass* of standards of value, partly eudaemonistic, partly ethical, and often both present together in an ambiguous identification. Value judgments are made everywhere in a nonchalant and spontaneous manner, and if we abandon the evaluation of economic phenomena we in fact abandon the very accomplishment which is being demanded of us. But it is not the general rule, in fact it is well-nigh exceptional, for the maker of a judgment to clarify for others and *for himself* the nature of the ultimate subjective core of his judgments, to make clear the *ideals* on the basis of which he proceeds to judge the events he is observing; there is a lack of conscious self-inspection, the internal contradictions of his judgment do not come to the writer's notice, and where he seeks to give a general formulation of his specifically 'economic' principle of judgment he falls into vagueness and indeterminacy. In truth, the ideals we introduce into the substance of our science are not peculiar to it, nor have we worked them out independently: they are *old-established human ideals of a general type.* Only he who proceeds exclusively from the pure Platonic interest of the technologist, or, inversely, the actual interests of a particular class, whether a ruling or a subject class, can expect to derive his own standard of judgment from the material itself.

And is it so unnecessary for us, the younger representatives of the German historical school, to keep in sight these extremely simple truths? By no means, for we in particular are liable to fall victim to a special kind of illusion: the illusion that we can *entirely do without* conscious value judgments of our own. The result is of course, and the evidence is quite convincing on this point, that we do not remain true to this intention but rather fall prey to uncontrolled instincts, sympathies, and antipathies. And it is still more likely to happen that the point of departure we adopt in analysing and *explaining* economic events unconsciously becomes determinant in our *judgment* of the events. We shall perhaps have to be on our guard lest the very qualities of the dead and living masters of our school to which they and their science owed its success turn in our case into weaknesses. In practice we have essentially to consider the following two different points of departure in economic analysis.

Either we look at economic development mainly from above: we proceed from the heights of the administrative history of the larger German states, pursuing to its origins the way they have administered economic and social affairs and their attitude to these matters. In that case we involuntarily become their apologists. If—let us keep to our original example—the administration decides to close the Eastern border, we are ready and inclined to view the decision as the conclusion of a historical development, which as a result of the gigantic reverberations of the past has posed great tasks the present-day state must fulfil in the interest of the maintenance of our national culture. If on the other hand that decision is not taken it is very easy for us to believe that radical interventions of that kind are in part unnecessary and in part do not correspond any longer to present-day views.

Or, and this is the other starting-point, we may view economic development more from below, we may look at the great spectacle of the emancipatory struggles of rising classes emerging from the chaos of conflicts of economic interest, we may observe the way in which the balance of economic power shifts in their favour. Then we unconsciously take sides with the rising classes, because they are the stronger, or are beginning to be so. They seem to prove, precisely because they are victorious, that they represent a type of humanity that stands on a higher level 'economically': it is all too easy for the historian to succumb to the idea that the victory of the *more highly developed* element in the struggle is a matter of course, and that defeat in the struggle for existence is a symptom of 'backwardness'. And every new sign of the shift of power gives satisfaction to the historian, not only because it confirms his observations, but because, half unconsciously, he senses it as a personal triumph: history is honouring the bills he has drawn on it. Without being aware of it, he observes the resistance that development finds in its path with a certain animosity; it seems to him to be not simply the natural result of the interplay of various inevitably divergent interests, but to some extent a rebellion against the 'judgment of history' as formulated by the historian. But criticism must also be made of processes which appear to us to be the unreflected result of tendencies of historical development; and precisely here, where there is most need of it, the critical spirit deserts us. In any case, there is a very obvious temptation on the historian to become a part of the camp-following of the victor in the economic struggle for power, and to *forget that economic power and the vocation for political leadership of the nation do not always coincide.*

With this we now arrive at a final series of reflections belonging more to the realm of practical politics. There is only one *political standard of value* which is supreme for us economic nationalists, and it is by this standard that we also measure the classes which either have the leadership of the nation in their hands or are striving for it. What we are concerned with is their *political maturity*, i.e. their understanding of the lasting economic and political interests of the nation's *power* and their ability to place these interests above all other considerations if the occasion demands. A nation is favoured by destiny if the naive identification of the interests of one's own class with the general interest also corresponds to the interests of national power. And it is one of the delusions which arise from the modern over-estimation of the 'economic' in the usual sense of the word when people assert that feelings of political community cannot maintain themselves in face of the full weight of divergent economic interests, indeed that very possibly these feelings are *merely* the reflection of the economic basis underlying those changing interests. This is approximately accurate only in times of fundamental social transformation. One thing can certainly be said: among nations like the English, who are not confronted daily with the dependence of their economic prosperity on their situation of political power, the instinct for these specifically political interests does *not*, at least not as a rule, dwell in the broad *masses* of the people, for they are occupied in the fight to secure their daily needs. It would be unfair to expect them to possess this understanding. But in great moments, in the case of war, their souls too become conscious of the significance of national power. Then it emerges that the national state rests on deep and elemental psychological foundations within the broad economically subordinate strata of the nation as well, that it is by no means a mere 'superstructure', the organisation of the economically dominant classes. It is just that in normal times this political instinct sinks below the level of consciousness for the masses. In that case the specific function of the economically and politically leading strata is to be the repositories of political understanding. This is in fact the *sole* political justification for their existence.

At all times it has been the *attainment of economic power* which has led to the emergence within a given class of the notion that it has a *claim to political leadership*. It is dangerous, and in the long term incompatible with the interests of the nation when an economically declining class is politically dominant. But it is still more dangerous when classes which are beginning to achieve economic power and thereby the expectation of political domination are not yet politically mature enough to assume the direction of the state. Germany is at present under threat from both these directions, and this is in truth the key to understanding the present dangers of our situation. The changes in the social structure of eastern Germany, with which the phenomena discussed at the outset are linked, also belong within this larger context.

Right up to the present time in Prussia the dynasty has been politically based on the social stratum of the Prussian *Junkers*. The dynasty created the Prussian state against them, but only with their assistance was it possible. I know full well that the word 'Junker' resonates harshly in South German ears. It will perhaps be thought that if I now say a word in their favour, I shall be speaking a 'Prussian' language. I cannot be sure. Even today in Prussia the Junkers have open to them many paths to influence and power, many ways to the ear of the monarch, which are not available to every citizen; they have not always used this power in accordance with their responsibility before history, and there is no reason for a bourgeois scholar like myself to love them. But despite all this the strength of their political instincts is one of the most tremendous resources which could have been applied to the service of the state's power-interests. They have done their work now, and today are in the throes of an economic death-struggle, and no kind of economic policy on the part of the state could bring back their old social character. Moreover the tasks of the present are quite different from those they might be able to solve. The last and greatest of the Junkers stood at the head of Germany for a quarter of a century, and the future will very likely find the tragic element in his career as a statesman, alongside his incomparable greatness, in something which even today is hidden from view for many people: in the fact that the work of his hands, the nation to which he gave unity, gradually and irresistibly altered its economic structure even while he was in office, and became something different, a people compelled to demand other institutions than those he could grant to them, or those his autocratic nature could adapt itself to. In the final analysis it is this fate which brought about the partial failure of his life's work. For this was intended to lead not just to the external but to the inner unification of the nation, and, as every one of us knows, that has not been achieved. With his means he could not achieve it. And when, last winter, ensnared by the graciousness of his monarch, he made his way into the splendidly decorated capital of the *Reich,* there were many people who felt—I can vouch for this—as if the Kyffhäuser legend was about to come true, felt that the Sachsenwald had opened up and the long-lost hero was emerging from its depths.[6] But this feeling was not shared by everyone. For it seemed as if the cold breath of historical impermanence could be sensed in the January air. A strangely oppressive feeling overcame us, as if a ghost had stepped down from a great past epoch and were going about among a new generation, and through a world become alien to it.

The manors of the East were the points of support for the ruling class of Prussia, which was scattered over the countryside, they were the social point of contact for the bureaucracy. But with their decline, with the disappearance of the social character of the old landed nobility, the centre of gravity of the political intelligentsia is shifting irresistibly towards the towns. This displacement is the decisive *political* aspect of the agrarian development of the East.

But whose are the hands into which the political function of the Junkers is passing, and what kind of political vocation do they have?

I am a member of the bourgeois classes. I feel myself to be a bourgeois, and I have been brought up to share their views and ideals. But it is the task of precisely our science to say what people do not like to hear—to those above us, to those below us, and also to our own class—and when I ask myself whether the German bourgeoisie is at present ripe to be the leading political class of the nation, I cannot answer this question in the affirmative *today*. The German state was not created by the bourgeoisie with its own strength, and when it had been created, there stood at the head of the nation that Caesar-like figure hewn out of quite other than bourgeois timber. Great power-political tasks were not set a second time for the nation to accomplish: only much later on, timidly, and half unwillingly, did an overseas 'power policy' begin, a policy which does not deserve the name.

And after the nation's unity had thus been achieved, and its political 'satiation' was an established fact, a peculiarly 'unhistorical' and unpolitical mood came over the growing race of German bourgeois, drunk as it was with success and thirsty for peace. German history appeared to have come to an end. The present

---

[6] This is a reference by Weber to the old German legend that the Emperor Frederick Barbarossa was not dead but waiting in the heart of the Kyffhäuser mountains in Thuringia to come forth and lead the German people against their enemies. Bismarck's own estate was located in the Sachsenwald [Trans.].

was the complete fulfilment of past millennia. Who was inclined to question whether the future might judge otherwise? Indeed it seemed as if modesty forbade world history from going over to the order of the day, from resuming its day-to-day course after these successes of the German nation. Today we are more sober, and it is seemly to make the attempt to lift the veil of illusions which has hidden the position of our generation in the historical development of the fatherland. And it seems to me that if we do this we shall judge differently. Over our cradle stood the most frightful curse history has ever handed to any race as a birthday-gift: the hard destiny of the political *epigone*.

Do we not see his miserable countenance wherever we look in the fatherland? Those of us who have retained the capacity to hate pettiness have recognised, with passionate and furious sorrow, the petty manoeuvring of political epigones in the events of the last few months, for which bourgeois politicians are responsible first and foremost, in far too much of what has been said recently *in* the German parliament, and in a certain amount of what has been said *to* it. The gigantic sun which stood at its zenith in Germany and caused the German name to shine forth in the furthest corners of the earth was too strong for us, it might almost seem, and burnt out the bourgeoisie's slowly developing sense of political judgment. For where is this to be seen at the present moment?

One section of the haute bourgeoisie longs all too shamelessly for the coming of a new Caesar, who will protect them in two directions: from beneath against the rising masses of the people, from above against the socio-political impulses they suspect the German dynasties of harbouring.

And another section has long been sunk in that political Philistinism from which broad strata of the lower middle classes have never awakened. Already when the first positive political task began to come on the nation's horizon, after the wars of unification—I mean the idea of overseas expansion—this section of the bourgeoisie lacked the simplest *economic* understanding of what it means for Germany's trade in far-off oceans when the German flag waves on the surrounding coasts.

The political immaturity of broad strata of the German bourgeoisie is not due to economic causes, nor is it due to the much-bruited 'interest politics', which is present in no less a degree in other nations than the German. The explanation lies in its unpolitical past, in the fact that one cannot make up in a decade for a missing century of political education, and that the domination of a great man is not always an appropriate instrument for such a process. And this is now the vital question for the political future of the German bourgeoisie: is it *too late* for it to catch up on its political education? No *economic* factor can make up for this loss.

Will other classes become the repositories of a politically greater future? The modern proletariat is self-confidently announcing itself as the heir of the ideals of the middle classes. What then of its claim to inherit the political leadership of the nation?

If anyone were to say of the German working class at present that it was politically mature, or on the road to political maturity, he would be a flatterer, a seeker after the dubious accolade of popularity.

The highest strata of the German working class are far more mature *economically* than the possessing classes in their egoism would like to admit, and it is with justification that the working class demands the freedom to put forward its interests in the form of the openly organised struggle for economic power. *Politically* the German working class is infinitely less mature than a clique of journalists, who would like to monopolise its leading positions, are trying to make the working class itself believe. In the circles of these *déclassé* bourgeois they like to amuse themselves with reminiscences of an epoch now one hundred years in the past. In some cases they have even succeeded in convincing other people: here and there anxious souls see in them the spiritual successors of the men of the Convention. But they are infinitely more harmless than they appear to themselves, for there lives in them not one glimmer of that Catiline energy *of the deed* which agitated the halls of the Convention. By the same token however they possess no trace of the Convention's tremendous *national* passion. Wretched political manipulators—that is what they are. They lack the grand *power* instincts of a class destined for political leadership. The workers are led to believe that only the upholders of capital's interests are at present politically opposed to giving them a share in state power. It is not so. They would find very few traces of a community of interest with capital if they investigated the study-rooms of Germany's scholars and intellectuals.

However the *workers too* must be asked about their *political maturity*. There is nothing more destructive for a great nation than to be led by politically uneducated philistines, and the German proletariat has not yet lost this character of philistinism; that is why we are politically opposed to the proletariat. Why is the proletariat of England and France constituted differently, in part? The reason is not only the longer period of *economic* education accomplished by the English workers' organised fight for their interests; we have once again what is above all a *political* element to bear in mind: *the resonance of a position of world power.* This constantly poses for the state great power-political tasks and gives the individual a political training which we might call 'chronic', whereas with us the training is only received when our borders are threatened, i.e. in 'acute' cases. The question of whether a policy on the grand scale can again place before us the significance of the great political issues of power is also decisive for *our* development. We must understand that the unification of Germany was a youthful prank committed by the nation at an advanced age, and should rather have been avoided on grounds of excessive cost if it was to form the conclusion instead of the point of departure for a policy of German world power.

The *threatening danger* in our situation is this: the bourgeois classes, as repositories of the *power*-interests of the nation, seem to be withering, and there is still no sign that the workers have begun to mature so that they can take their place.

The danger does *not* lie with the masses, as is believed by people who stare as if hypnotised at the depths of society. The final content of the *socio*-political problem is not the question of the *economic* situation of the *ruled* but of the *political* qualifications of the *ruling and rising* classes. The aim of our socio-political activity is not world happiness but the *social unification* of the nation, which has been split apart by modern economic development, for the severe struggles of the future. At present the bourgeoisie is carrying the burden of these struggles, but it is becoming too heavy. Only if we were in fact to succeed in creating a 'labour aristocracy', of the kind we now miss in the workers' movement, which would be the repository of its political sense, only then could the burden be transferred to the broader shoulders of the workers. But that moment still seems a long way away.

For the present, however, one thing is clear: there is an immense labour of *political* education to be performed, and no more serious duty exists for us than that of fulfilling *this* task, each of us in his narrow circle of activity. The ultimate goal of our science must remain that of cooperating in the *political* education of our nation. The economic development of periods of transition threatens the natural political instincts with decomposition; it would be a misfortune if economic science also moved towards the same objective, by breeding a weak eudaemonism, in however intellectualised a form, behind the illusion of independent 'socio-political' ideals.

Of course we do have to remember, and for that very reason, that it is the opposite of political education when one seeks to formulate a vote of no confidence, paragraph by paragraph, against the nation's future social peace, or when the secular arm reaches for the hand of the church to give support to the temporal authorities. But the opposite of political education is also proclaimed by the stereotyped yelping of the ever growing chorus of the social politicians of the woods and fields—if I may be forgiven the expression. And the same may be said of that softening of attitude which is human, amiable, and worthy of respect, but at the same time unspeakably narrowing in its effects, and leads people to think they can replace political with 'ethical' ideals, and to identify these in turn harmlessly with optimistic expectations of felicity.

In spite of the great misery of the masses, which burdens the sharpened social conscience of the new generation, we have to confess openly that one thing weighs on us even more heavily today: the sense of our responsibility *before history*. Our generation is not destined to see whether the struggle we are engaged in will bear fruit, whether posterity will recognise us as *its forerunners*. We shall not succeed in exorcising the curse that hangs over us: the curse of being posthumous to a great political epoch. Instead we shall have to learn how to be something different: the precursors of an even greater epoch. Will that be our place in history? I do not know, and all I will say is this: youth has the right to stand up for itself and for its ideals. And it is not years which make a man old. He is young as long as he is able to remain sensitive to the grand passions nature has placed within us. And so—you will allow me to conclude with this—a great nation does not age beneath the burden of a thousand years of glorious history. It remains young if it has the capacity and the courage to keep faith with itself and with the grand instincts it has been given, and when its leading strata are able to raise themselves into the hard and clear atmosphere in which the sober activity of German politics flourishes, an atmosphere which is also pervaded by the solemn splendour of national sentiment.

The Social Causes of the Decay
of Ancient Civilization

THE ROMAN EMPIRE was not destroyed from without; its destruction was not caused by the numerical superiority of its opponents nor by the inadequacy of its political leaders. In the last century of its existence Rome had her iron chancellors: heroic figures, like Stilicho, men who combined Teutonic boldness with the art of cunning diplomacy, were at the head of the state. Why could they not accomplish what the illiterate princes of the Merovingian, Carolingian, and Saxon houses were able to achieve and to defend against Saracens and Huns? The Empire had, long before, undergone a change in its very essence; when it disintegrated, it did not suddenly collapse under one powerful blow. The Teutonic invaders brought to its logical climax a development that had been long in the making.

But most important: the decay of ancient *civilization* was not caused by the destruction of the Roman *Empire*. The Empire as a political structure survived by centuries the acme of Roman culture. This culture had vanished much earlier. As early as the beginning of the third century Roman literature had come to an end. The art of the jurists decayed together with their schools. Greek and Roman poetry were dead. Historiography languished and almost disappeared. The Latin language was soon in a state of full degeneration. When, one and a half centuries later, with the extinction of the office of the emperor in the West, the books are closed, it becomes obvious that barbarism, long ago, has conquered the Empire from within. The barbarian invaders, moreover, are far from establishing completely new conditions on the soil of the demolished Empire; the Merovingian kingdom, in Gaul at least, continues for some time the pattern of the Roman province. The problem, therefore, arises for us: What has caused the decline of ancient civilization?

Quite a few different explanations have been offered by different scholars, some missing the point completely, others getting off to a good start, but making a wrong use of correct premises.

Some authors maintain that despotism necessarily strangled the soul of the ancient Romans and so destroyed their state and their civilization. But the despotism of Frederick the Great was, on the contrary, a powerful force of growth.

Reprinted by permission of The Pennsylvania State University Press from *Journal of General Education* 5 (1949–51): 75–88. Translated by Christian Mackauer. Copyright 1949 by The Pennsylvania State University. Originally published in 1896; see *Gesammelte Aufsätze zur Sozial- und Wirtschaftsgeschichte* (1924) (Tübingen: J. C. B. Mohr, 1988), pp. 289–311.

Others assert that the alleged luxury and the undeniable decline of morality in the highest social ranks called forth the revenge of History. But both phenomena are symptoms themselves. We shall see that much more powerful factors than the guilt of individuals destroyed ancient civilization.

Still others believe that the foundations of society were dissolved by the emancipation of the Roman woman and the loosening of the ties of marriage in the ruling classes. The fables told by a biased reactionary like Tacitus about the Germanic woman, that miserable slave of a peasant-warrior, are repeated by modern reactionaries. In fact, the ubiquitous "German woman" decided the victory of the Germanic invaders as little as the ubiquitous "Prussian schoolmaster" decided the battle of Königgrätz. On the contrary, we shall see that the *reestablishment* of the family among the *lower* classes of society was connected with the decay of ancient civilization.

Pliny, an eye-witness, assures us: *Latifundia perdidere Italiam* ["the large estates have ruined Italy"]: "Here you see it," one school among the moderns says, "it was the Junkers who ruined Rome." "Yes," their opponents reply, "but only because they were ruined themselves by grain imports from foreign countries." If the Romans had protected their agriculture with high tariff walls, the Caesars, apparently, would still be on their throne today. But we shall see that the destruction of ancient civilization was a first step on the way towards the *reestablishment* of a *peasant* class.

There is even what people call a "Darwinistic" hypothesis: a quite recent author contends that the process of selection by which the strongest men were drafted into the army and so condemned to celibacy led to the degeneration of the Roman race. We shall rather see that increasing recruiting of the army from its own ranks was a symptom of the decay of the Roman Empire.

But enough of these examples. Only one more remark before we take up our proper subject:

The interest in a story is always keener when the audience has the feeling: *de te narratur fabula*, and when the story-teller can conclude his yarn with a *discite moniti!* Unfortunately, the discussion which follows does not fall into this enviable category. We can learn little or nothing for our contemporary social problems from ancient history. A modern proletarian and a Roman slave would be as unable to understand one another as a European and a Chinese. Our problems are of a completely different character. The drama we are going to study has only an *historical* interest; but it presents one of the most singular historical phenomena, indeed, the internal dissolution of an old civilization.

Our first task will be to understand those peculiarities of the social structure of ancient society that we have just mentioned. We shall see how they determined the cycle of ancient civilization.

The civilization of classical antiquity is, in its essence, first of all an urban civilization. The city is the foundation of political life as well as of art and literature. With regard to its economic system, also, the ancient world, at least during its earlier period, represents what we call today a "city economy." The ancient city during the Greek period, is not essentially different from the medieval city. As far as differences exist, they can be explained by the differences between the climate and race of the Mediterranean, on the one hand, and those of Central Europe, on the other, just as even today English workers are different from Italian workers and German craftsmen from Italian ones. Originally, the economic basis of the ancient, just as of the medieval city, is the exchange in the urban market of the products of urban craftsmanship for those of its immediate rural neighborhood. Almost the whole demand is satisfied by this direct exchange between producer and consumer, without any importation from outside. Aristotle's ideal of urban autarchy had been realized in the majority of Greek cities.

To be sure, since very ancient times, an international trade has been built on these local foundations; it comprises a vast area and numerous objects. Our historical reports are almost exclusively concerned with those cities whose ships are engaged in this trade; but because we hear just about them, we are prone to forget how insignificant, quantatively, this trade was. In the first place, the civilization of European antiquity is a *coastal* civilization, just as European ancient history remains for a long time the history of coastal towns. Side by side with the technically highly developed urban exchange economy, and in sharp contrast to it, there presents itself the "natural economy" of the barbaric peasants of the inland regions, entrammeled in tribal communities or bent under the rule of feudal patriarchs. A steady and regular international traffic is carried on only by sea or on large rivers. No inland traffic comparable to that even of the Middle Ages existed in ancient Europe. The glorified Roman highways never carried a traffic even remotely reminiscent of modern conditions; the same applies to the Roman postal service. There is an immense difference in revenue between estates lying inland and those located on rivers or on the sea shore. To be close to a highway was generally considered not an advantage in Roman times but rather a nuisance because of billeting and of—vermin: Roman highways are military not commercial roads.

On the ground of such a still intact "natural economy" international exchange is unable to strike deep roots. Only a small number of high-priced articles such as precious metals, amber, valuable textiles, some iron ware and pottery, are objects of regular trade. Such a trade just cannot be compared to modern commerce. It would be the same as if today nothing but champagne and silk were exchanged, while all trade statistics show that *mass* demand alone accounts for the big figures in the balance of international trade. At some time or other, to be sure, cities like Athens and Rome become dependent on imports for their grain supply. But such conditions are highly abnormal; and in all these cases the *community* takes over the responsibility of supplying these goods. The citizens are not inclined to leave this task to uncontrolled private trade nor can they afford to do so.

Not the masses with their day-by-day needs, but a small group of well-to-do people are interested in international commerce. This has one implication: increasing differentiation of wealth is a prerequisite of the development of commerce in the ancient world. This differentiation—and here we reach a third, decisive point—takes a quite definite form and direction: ancient civilization is a *slave* civilization. From the very beginning, unfree labor in the countryside exists side by side with free labor in the city; unfree division of labor on the rural estate, producing for the master's own use, side by side with the free division of labor regulated by the conditions of exchange in the urban market, just as in the Middle Ages. And in the ancient world, as in the Middle Ages, these two forms of productive co-operation were naturally antagonistic. Progress is based on progressing division of labor. Under conditions of free labor, this progress is, in its beginnings, identical with a progressive growth of the market, extensively through geographical, intensively through personal extension of the area of exchange; the citizens of the towns, therefore, try to destroy the manorial estates and to include the serfs in the process of free exchange. Where unfree labor prevails, however, economic progress takes place through the progressive accumulation of human beings; the more slaves or serfs are combined on one estate, the higher the degree of specialization which can be attained with unfree workers. But while during the Middle Ages the development leads more and more to the victory of free labor and of free exchange, the outcome in the ancient world is exactly the opposite. What is the reason for this difference? It is the same reason which determines the limits of technological progress in antiquity: the "cheapness" of human beings resulting from the character of the uninterrupted warfare in the ancient world. Wars in ancient times are always slave raids; they continuously throw new supplies upon the slave market and so favor unfree labor and the accumulation of human beings as in no other period of history. The development of free handicraft, therefore, was arrested at the level of non-capitalistic wage-work for a narrowly defined local clientele. No competition arose between (capitalistic) free enterprisers and free (non-capitalistic) wage-work for supplying the market, and so the economic premium on labor-saving inventions was absent which has called forth such inventions in our modern epoch. In the ancient world, on the contrary, the economic importance of unfree labor in the *oikos* (the autarchic estate) is all the time on the increase. Only slave-owners are able to satisfy their economic needs by division of labor, through slave labor, and so to raise their standard of living. Only they can—in addition to satisfying their own needs—more and more produce for the market.

This determines the peculiar economic development of the ancient world and its difference from that of the Middle Ages. In medieval Europe, free division of labor first expands *intensively* within the economic area of the city, in the form of production for a clientele and for the local market. Later, increasing external trade on the basis of a geographical division of labor creates new forms of production for foreign markets; making use of free labor, it takes the form first of the putting-out system, then of manufacture. And the development of a *modern* system of economy is accompanied by the phenomenon that the masses increasingly satisfy their demand through interlocal and finally international exchange of goods. In the ancient world, as we see, development of international commerce is accompanied, on the contrary, by the conglomeration of unfree labor on the big slave-estates. So, under the superstructure of the exchange economy one finds a ceaselessly expanding substructure of an economy without exchange (a "natural economy"): the slave-combines, constantly absorbing human beings and satisfying their demand essentially not in the market but by their own production. The higher the standard of living of the slave-owning top-stratum of society rises and the more, therefore, the *extensive* development of commerce increases, the more this commerce loses in *intensity;* it is transformed into a thin net spread out over a substructure of a "natural economy," a net whose meshes become finer while its thread becomes thinner and thinner all the time. During the Middle Ages, the transition from production for a local clientele to production for an interlocal market is prepared by the slow infiltration of (capitalistic) enterprise and the principle of competition from the circumference towards the center of the local economic community; during the ancient period, however, international commerce leads to the growth of the *oikoi* which stifle the *local* exchange economy

This development has reached its most gigantic dimension in the Roman Empire. Rome is first—after the victory of the *plebs*—a conquering state of peasants or better: of townsmen cultivating their own land. Every war ends with the annexation of more land for colonization. The younger sons of land-owning citizens, who cannot expect to inherit their father's estate, fight in the army for an estate of their own and so, at the same time, for full citizenship. This is the secret of Rome's expansive strength. This development comes to an end with the extension of Roman conquests to territories overseas. Now, the peasants' interest in acquiring new land for settlement is no longer decisive, but rather the interest of the aristocracy in exploiting the newly conquered province. The purpose of these wars consists in slave raids and in the confiscation of land to be exploited by the farmer of state land or the tax-farmer. In addition, the Second Punic War decimated the peasantry in the homeland—the consequences of its decline are partly a belated triumph of Hannibal. The reaction following the Gracchan movement finally decides the victory of slave-labor in agriculture. From this time on, the slave-owners alone are the representatives of a rising standard of living, of an increase in buying-power, of the development of production for the market. This does not mean that free labor completely disappears; but the slave-using enterprises alone represent the *progressive* element. The Roman agricultural writers presuppose slave-labor as the natural basis of the labor system.

The cultural importance of unfree labor was finally decisively re-enforced through the inclusion of large inland areas—like Spain, Gaul, Illyria, the Danubian countries—into the Roman world. The center of gravity of the Roman Empire shifted into the inland regions. This means that ancient civilization made an attempt to change its scene of action, to turn from a coastal into an inland civilization. It expanded over an immense economic area which even in the course of centuries could not have been converted into an exchange and market economy similar to that existing along the coasts of the Mediterranean. Even in these coastal areas, as we have pointed out, interlocal exchange of commodities was only a superficial net, getting thinner all the time; in the inland regions, the meshes of the net of exchange were, of necessity, much looser still. In these inland regions, progress of civilization in the way of a free division of labor through the development of an *intensive* exchange of commodities was virtually *impossible*. Only through the rise of a landed aristocracy, based on slave-ownership and unfree division of labor (the *oikos*), could these regions gradually be drawn into the orbit of Mediterranean civilization. In the inland regions, to a higher degree still than along the coasts, the immensely more expensive commerce could serve only the luxury needs of the uppermost social stratum, the slave-owners; and, at the same time, the possibility of producing for the market was restricted to a small number of large slave-owning enterprises.

Thus the slave-owner became the economic representative of ancient civilization; the organization of slave-labor forms the indispensable basis of Roman society. We have to study, therefore, somewhat more closely its specific social character.

Our sources are mostly concerned with the *agricultural* enterprises of the late republican and early imperial periods. Large land-ownership constitutes, anyway, the main form of wealth; even wealth that is speculatively used rests on this basis: the large-scale Roman speculator is, as a rule, also a great landowner; if for no other reason, than because security in the form of landed property was legally required for the most lucrative kinds of speculation, tax-farming and contracting.

The typical large Roman land-owner is not a gentleman-farmer, supervising his own estate, but a man who lives in town, devotes his time to political activity, and is interested above all in receiving a money rent. The supervision of his estate is entrusted to unfree bailiffs (*villici*). The methods of cultivation are influenced mainly by the following circumstances.

Production of grain for the market is, in most cases, not profitable. The market of the city of Rome, e.g., is closed to private producers because of public grain distributions; transportation of grain from inland estates to distant markets is impossible anyway because the price cannot support the costs. In addition, slave-labor is not suited to grain production, especially since the Roman agricultural technique requires scrupulous and intensive work and therefore presupposes a personal interest on the worker's part. For this reason, land for grain production is mostly, at least in part, leased to *coloni*, small tenants, the descendants of the free peasantry who are deprived of their former property. But such a *colonus* is, even in earlier times, not an independent tenant and self-responsible farmer. The owner provides the inventory, the *villicus* controls the cultivation. From the very beginning, apparently, it was a frequent practice that the tenant had to do a certain amount of work on the owner's estate, especially during harvest time. Leasing of land to *coloni* is considered a form of cultivation of the land by the *owner* "by means of" the tenants (*per colonos*).

The part of the estate under direct management by the owner produces for the market primarily high-priced products like olive-oil and wine, and secondarily garden vegetables, cattle-raising, poultry, and luxuries for the table of the highest stratum of Roman society, for the people who alone have the money to purchase them. By these products grain is pushed back to the less fertile land which is in the hands of the *coloni*. The master's own estate resembles a plantation, and the workers on it are slaves. *Coloni* and a herd of slaves (the *familia*), side by side, represent, under the Empire as well as during the late Republic, the normal population of a large estate.

We first turn to the slaves. What is their condition?

Let us look at the ideal pattern which the agricultural writers describe. The lodging of the "talking inventory" (*instrumentum vocale*), i.e., the slave stable, is found close to that of the cattle (*instrumentum semi-vocale*). It contains the dormitories, in addition a hospital (*valetudinarium*), a lockup (*carcer*), a workshop for the craftsmen (*ergastulum*). Whoever has worn the king's colors will be reminded by this picture of a familiar experience: the barracks. And indeed, the life of a slave normally is a barracks life. The slaves sleep and eat together, under supervision of the *villicus;* their better piece of clothing is left at the store-room with the bailiff's wife (*villica*) who takes the place of the store-room sergeant; every month the clothing is inspected at a roll-call. The work is disciplined in a strictly military manner: squads (*decuriae*) are formed every morning; they march to work under supervision of the "drivers" (*monitores*). This was absolutely necessary. It never has been possible to use unfree labor for market production on a permanent basis without resorting to the lash. For us one implication of this form of life is of special importance: the slave in his barracks is not only without property but without family as well. Only the *villicus* lives permanently together with his wife in his special cell in some form of slave-marriage (*contubernium*), comparable to the married sergeant or staff-sergeant in modern barracks; according to the agricultural writers, this is even a "standing regulation" for the *villicus*, in the interest of the master. And as the institutions of private property and private family always go hand in hand, so it is here: the slave who owns property owns a family as well. The *villicus*—and only the *villicus*, as the agricultural writers seem to indicate—has a *peculium*, originally, as the name tells, his own cattle which he grazes on the master's pasture, just as the agricultural laborer does today on the large estates of eastern Germany. As the masses of the slaves have no *peculium*, they also do not live in monogamous sexual relations. Sexual intercourse for them is a kind of controlled prostitution with bounties awarded to female slaves for the raising of children—some masters granted them liberty when they had raised three children. This last practice already indicates what the consequences of the absence of monogamous marriage were. Human beings thrive only in the circle of the family. The slave barracks were unable to reproduce themselves, they depended for their recruitment on the continuous purchase of slaves, and the agricultural writers assume, indeed, that new slaves are bought regularly. The ancient slave estate devours human beings as the modern blast-furnace devours coal. A slave market and its regular and ample supply with human material is the indispensable presupposition of slave barracks producing for the market. The buyer looked for cheap ware: Varro recommends that one should choose criminals and similar cheap material; the reason he gives is characteristic: such rabble, he maintains, is mostly "sharper" (*velocior est animus hominum improborum*). So this form of enterprise depends on the regular supply of the slave market with human cattle. What would happen if this supply should collapse? The effect on the slave barracks must be the same as that of an exhaustion of the coal deposits on the blast-furnaces. And the time came when it happened. Here we have reached the turning-point in the development of ancient civilization.

When we are being asked from which event we should date the—first latent, soon manifest—decline of Roman power and civilization, it is difficult, at least for a German, not to think of the battle in the Forest of Teutoburg. There is, indeed, a kernel of truth in this popular conception, although it seems to be contradicted by the obvious facts which show the Roman Empire at the zenith of its power at the time of Trajan. To be sure, the battle itself was not decisive—a reverse like this occurs in every war of expansion waged against barbarians; decisive was the aftermath: the suspension of offensive warfare on the Rhine by Tiberius. This brought to an end the expansive tendencies of the Roman Empire. With the internal and in the main also external pacification of the area of ancient civilization, the regular supply of the slave-markets with human cattle begins to shrink. As a result of this, an immense *acute* scarcity of labor seems to have developed already at the time of Tiberius. We are told that under his regime it was necessary to inspect the *ergastula* of the large estates because the large land-owners resorted to kidnapping; like the robber-barons of later times, it seems, they were lying in ambush along the highways, on the look-out, not for merchants' goods, but for hands to work on their deserted land. More important was the slow but steadily spreading *long-run* result: it became impossible to continue production on the basis of slave barracks. They presupposed a continuous supply of new slaves; they could not provide for their own needs. They were liable to break down when this supply came to a permanent stand-still. From later agricultural writers we get the impression that the decline in the "cheapness" of human cattle first led to an improvement in agricultural technique: one tried to raise the performance of the workers by careful training. But when the last offensive wars of the second century were over (they had already acquired the character of slave-raids), the large plantations with their celibate and property-less slaves were bound to dwindle away.

That this really happened and how it happened we learn from a comparison of the conditions of the slaves on large estates as described by the Roman writers with the conditions prevailing on the estates of the Carolingian epoch about which we known from Charlemagne's regulations for the royal demesnes (*capitulare de villis imperialibus*) and from the surveys of monasteries of this time. In either epoch we find the slaves as agricultural laborers; in either case they are equally without rights, especially equally subject to the unlimited exploitation of their labor-power by their master. No change has occurred in this regard. In addition, numerous individual traits have been taken over from the Roman estate; even in the terminology used we rediscover, e.g., the women's house (*gy-*

naikeion) of the Romans under the name of *genitium*. But one thing has changed fundamentally: the Roman slaves live in "communistic" slave barracks, the *servus* of the Carolingian epoch has his own cottage (*mansus servilis*) on the land which he holds from his master; he is a small tenant, subject to service on the lord's demesne. He has a family, and with the family individual property has returned. This separation of the slave from the *oikos* occurred in late-Roman times; and it was bound to occur, indeed, as the result of the lacking self-recruitment of the slave barracks. By restoring the individual family and by making the slave his hereditary serf, the lord secured for himself the offspring and so a permanent labor supply which could not be provided any more through purchases in the shrinking slave market whose last remnants disappeared during the Carolingian epoch. The risk of the maintenance of the slave (which on the plantations the master had to carry) was now shifted to the slave himself. The impact of this slow but irreversible development was deep. We are faced here with a gigantic process of change in the lower strata of society: family and individual property were given back to them. I can only indicate with one word here how this development runs parallel to the victory of Christianity: in the slave barracks Christian religion could hardly have taken roots, but the unfree African peasants of the time of St. Augustine already were supporters of a sectarian movement.

While in this way the slave advanced in his social status and became a serf, the *colonus*, at the same time, slides down into serfdom. The reason for this change in his social position was that his relation to the land-owner more and more took on the character of a *labor* relation. *Originally*, the lord is mainly interested in the *rent* which the tenant pays, although, as we have pointed out, there probably were some cases from the very beginning where he had to work on the lord's own land, in addition. But already early in the Empire the agricultural writers put the main emphasis on the *labor* of the *colonus*, and this interest was bound to increase as slave labor became scarcer. African inscriptions of the time of Commodus show that there the *colonus* already had become a kind of serf who, in return for the use of the land he held, was forced to render certain services. This *economic* change in the position of the *colonus* was followed soon by a *legal* change which expressed in legal terms his treatment as part of the *labor* force of the estate: he was tied to the soil. In order to understand how this happened we have to discuss in a few words some concepts of Roman public administration.

The basis of Roman public administration, at the end of the Republic and the beginning of the Empire, was the *city*, the *municipium*, just as the city was the *economic* basis of ancient civilization. The Romans had all the areas which they incorporated into their empire consistently organized in the form of urban communities (in various gradations of political dependence) and so had expanded the administrative form of the *municipium* over the whole empire. The city regularly was the lowest administrative unit. The city magistrates were responsible to the State for taxes and military recruitment. In the course of the imperial epoch, however, the development takes a new turn. The great estates successfully attempt to escape incorporation into the urban communities. The more the center of gravity of the empire moves inland (with the increase of population in the inland regions), the more the rural inland population supplies the recruits for the army. But these same circumstances more and more make the interests of the "agrarians" of Antiquity, of the great land-owners, the controlling factor in State politics. Whereas today we meet with strong resistance in our attempt to integrate the large estates of Eastern Germany in the rural communities, the government of the Roman Empire hardly resisted the tendency of the large estates to withdraw from the urban communities of which they formed a part. In great numbers the *saltus* and *territoria* appear side by side with the cities, administrative districts in which the landowner is the local government, just like the squire of Eastern Germany in the so-called "manorial districts." The landowner, in those districts, was responsible to the State for the taxes of the *territorium*—in some cases he advanced them for his "vassals" and then collected from them—and he supplied the contingent of recruits imposed upon his estate. Supplying recruits, therefore, was soon considered, like any other assessment, as an impost on the estate whose labor force—the *coloni*—was decimated by it.

Those developments paved the road for the legal fettering of the *colonus* to the estate.

The right of free movement never was legally guaranteed to all inhabitants of the Roman Empire. We all remember how familiar an idea it is to the author of the Gospel of Luke that, for the purpose of taxation, everybody can be ordered to return to his home community (*origo*)—to his "place of settlement," as we would say—as Christ's parents returned to Bethlehem. The *origo* of the *colonus*, however, is the estate of his lord.

Quite early we see it happen that a man is forced to return to his community for the performance of public duties. The senator, to be sure, who played truant all year long, was just fined. But the councilor of a provincial town, the *decurio*, who shirked his duties, did not escape so lightly; he was brought back if his community required it. Such a request was often enough necessary, for the position of the councilor—who was accountable for the tax arrears of his community—was not an enviable one. Later when, with the decay and mixture of all legal forms, these claims for return were resolved into the one concept of the claim for restitution (the old "real action": *vindicatio*), the communities chased their run-away councilors just like a run-away parish bull.

What was good for the *decurio* was good for the *colonus*. No distinction was made between his public obligations and the statute-labor he owed to his lord because lord and magistrate were the same person, and he was forced to return to his duties when he tried to escape. So, in the way of administrative practice, he became a real serf, permanently tied to the estate and therefore subject to the manorial rule of the landowner. In his relation to the State he was, so to speak, "mediatized." And above the ranks of these new serfs there arose the group of independent seigneurs (the *possessores*) which we meet, as a well established social type, in the later Roman Empire as well as in the Ostrogothian and Merovingian kingdoms. A *caste order* had taken the place of the old simple distinction of free and unfree. This was the result of an almost imperceptible development which was forced upon society by the change in economic conditions. The signs of *feudal society* were already apparent in the later Roman Empire.

So, on the late-imperial estate, two categories of tenants existed side by side: those who were unfree (*servi*) with "indefinite" service obligations, and those who were personally free (*cloni, tributarii*) with strictly defined money payments, payments in kind, later on more and more frequently payments in form of a fixed share of the produce, and, in addition—not always, but as a rule—regular labor duties. It is apparent that such an estate already represents the type of the medieval manor.

Under the economic conditions of the ancient world, production *for the market* could not be based on statute-labor of free or unfree tenants. Well-disciplined slave barracks were the precondition of any market production. Especially in the inland regions, market production disappeared as soon as the peasants' cottages took the place of the barracks; the thin threads of commerce which were spun over the substratum of a "natural economy" were bound to become looser still and finally to break. This is quite evident already in an argument of the last important agricultural writer, Palladius, who advises the owner to see to it that as far as possible the estate provides through its own labor for all its needs in order that any buying be made superfluous. Spinning and weaving as well as the grinding and baking of the grain has always been done by the women of the estate under the estate's own management; but now, smiths, joiners, stone masons, carpenters, and other unfree craftsmen were added, and they finally produced the total supply on the estate itself. By this development, the small group of urban craftsmen who mostly worked for wages plus board, lost still further in relative importance; the economically prominent households of the great landowners provided for their needs without any resort to exchange.

Supplying the landowner's own needs, on the basis of an internal division of labor, necessarily became the proper economic purpose of the *oikos*. The large estates dissociate themselves from the urban market. The majority of the medium-sized and small towns thereby more and more lose their economic basis, the exchange of services and commodities with the surrounding countryside, this very essence of the city economy. The resulting decay of the cities remains visible to us even through the dim and broken glass of late Roman legal sources. Again and again the emperors inveigh against the flight from the city, they especially take the *possessores* to task for giving up and tearing down their town residences and conveying wainscotting and furniture to their country seats.

This collapse of the cities is re-enforced by the financial policy of the government. As its financial needs increase, the state increasingly adopts the pattern of a "natural economy"; the exchequer becomes an *oikos*, it purchases as little as possible in the market and covers its needs as far as possible through its own production. This prevents the accumulation of private fortunes in money form. For the subjects it was a boon that one of the main forms of speculative enterprise, tax-farming, was abolished and tax collection by State officials took its place.

Transporting the public grain supply on ships whose owners were rewarded by land grants was perhaps more efficient than leaving it to private enterprise. The increasing monopolization of numerous lucrative trades and management of the mines by the government brought certain financial advantages with it. But all these measures naturally hindered the accumulation of private capital and nipped in the bud the development of a social class comparable to our modern bourgeoisie. And such a financial system on a "natural economy" basis was increasingly emerging the more the Empire developed from a conglomeration of cities exploiting the countryside and having its economic point of gravity on the coast and in coastal traffic into a political system that tried to incorporate and to organize large inland regions which had not advanced beyond the stage of a "natural economy." This expansion led to an enormous increase in public expenses, and the shell of exchange was much too thin to make possible the satisfaction of the growing public needs by means of a money economy. Hence, the scope of "natural economy" within public finance was bound to expand.

The provinces always had paid their taxes largely in kind, especially in grain, which was stored in the public warehouses. During the Empire, even the manufactured products needed by the government were less and less frequently bought in the market or procured by contracts, but their supply was assured by forcing urban craftsmen to deliver them *in natura;* they were often forced, for this purpose, to form compulsory guilds. This development made of the wretched free craftsman actually a hereditary serf of his guild. This income in kind was used up by the exchequer through corresponding expenses in kind. In this way, especially the two main expense items in the budget were taken care of without resort to money payments: the bureaucracy and the army. But here the "natural economy" reached its limit.

A large inland state can be ruled permanently only by means of a salaried bureaucracy, an institution unknown to the ancient city states. Since Diocletian's time salaries of state officials are very largely paid in kind; they are somewhat similar—only on a much larger scale—to the emoluments of an agricultural laborer on a contemporary Mecklenburgian estate: a few thousand bushels of grain, so and so many heads of cattle, corresponding quantities of salt, olive oil, etc.; in short, whatever the official needs for his food, clothing, and other sustenance, he draws from the imperial warehouses, in addition to relatively modest pocket money in cash. But in spite of this unmistakable preference for direct satisfaction of material needs, the maintenance of a numerous bureaucracy made considerable money expenses unavoidable. This was true, to a still higher degree, of the military requirements of the Empire.

A continental state with neighbours threatening its frontiers cannot be without a standing army. Already at the end of the Republic, the old citizen militia, based on conscription and self-equipment of all landowners, had been replaced by an army recruited from the ranks of the proletariat and equipped by the state—the main pillar of the power of the Caesars. The emperors created what was, not only in fact but legally, a standing *professional* army. To maintain such an army two things are needed: recruits and money. The need for recruits was the reason why the mercantilist rulers during the epoch of "enlightened despotism" curbed big enterprise in agriculture and prevented enclosures. This was not done for humanitarian reasons and not out of sympathy with the peasants. Not the individual peasant was protected—the squire could drive him out without any scruples by putting another peasant in his place. But if, in the words of Frederick William I, "a surplus of peasant lads" was to be the source of soldiers, such a surplus had to *exist*. Therefore, any reduction in the number of peasants through enclosures was prevented because it would endanger the recruitment of soldiers and depopulate the countryside. For quite similar reasons, the Roman emperors regulated the status of the *coloni* and prohibited, e.g., an increase in the duties imposed on them. There is one difference, however. The mercantilist rulers of the 18th century strongly fostered the big manufacturers because they increased the population and, secondly, brought money into the country. Frederick the Great chased with warrants not only his deserting soldiers, but also his deserting workers and—manufacturers. This part of mercantilist policy the Caesars could not adopt since large industries using free labor and producing for the market did not exist and could not develop in the Roman Empire. On the contrary, with the decay of cities and commerce and with the relapse into a "natural economy," the country became more and more unable to pay the ever increasing taxes in cash. And under the prevailing scarcity of labor, which resulted from the drying up of the slave market, recruitment of the *coloni* for the army threatened the large estates with ruin, a menace from which they tried to escape by all possible means. The draftee flees from the decaying city to the countryside into the safety of serfdom, because the *possessor*—under the pressure of the existing scarcity of labor—is interested in hiding him from the draft. The later Caesars fight against the flight of townsmen to the countryside exactly as the later Hohenstaufen fight against the flight of the serfs into the cities.

The repercussions of this scarcity of recruits are distinctly reflected in the army of the imperial epoch. Since Vespasian, Italy is no longer subject to the draft; since Hadrian, the units of the army are no longer composed of contingents from different local districts; in order to save money, one tries to recruit each army, as far as possible, from the district in which it is stationed—the first symptom of the decomposition of the Empire. But the process goes far beyond this: when we study the places of birth of the soldiers as given in their discharge documents through the centuries, we discover that the number of those characterized as "natives of the camp" (*castrenses*) rises during the imperial epoch from a few per cent of the total to almost one half—in other words, the Roman army increasingly reproduces itself. Just as the peasant with his individual family takes the place of the celibate barracks slave, so—partly at least—the professional and actually hereditary mercenary soldier, who enjoys a kind of substitute marriage, replaces the celibate barracks soldier, or rather, camp soldier, of the earlier period. The increasing recruitment of the army from the ranks of barbarians was dictated by the same principal purpose: by the desire to preserve the labor force of the country, especially of the large estates. Finally, for the defense of the frontiers, the Romans completely turn away from the principles of money economy: land-grants are made to barbarians, carrying with them the obligation of military service, and this device, the remote forerunner of the fief, is used with increasing frequency. In this way the army, which controls the Empire, is changed into a horde of barbarians, maintaining weaker and weaker ties with the native population. The victorious invasions by the barbarians *from without,* therefore, meant for the inhabitants of the provinces, at first, nothing but a change in the force billeted on them: even the Roman pattern of billeting was preserved. In some parts of Gaul, the barbarians, far from being feared as conquerors, apparently were welcomed as liberators from the pressure of the Roman administration. And this we can well understand.

For not only was it difficult for the aging Empire to recruit soldiers from the ranks of its own population, but the provinces, relapsing as they were into a "natural economy," virtually collapsed under the pressure of the money taxes without which a mercenary army cannot possibly be maintained. Raising of money increasingly becomes the sole aim of political administration; and it becomes more and more apparent that the *possessores,* now producing almost exclusively for their own needs, are economically unable to pay *money* taxes. It would have been a different story if the emperor had told them: "Well, gentlemen, make your *coloni* forge arms for yourselves, mount your horses, and protect with me the soil on which you live!" To *this* task they would have been economically equal. But this would have meant the beginning of the Middle Ages and the feudal army. The feudal organization of the army was, indeed, like the feudal structure of society, the end towards which the late-Roman development was tending and which—after the short and only local reverse in favor of colonizing peasant armies during the Age of Migrations—was already attained, on the whole, in the Carolingian epoch. But although with feudal armies of knights one can conquer foreign crowns and defend a restricted territory, one cannot preserve with them the unity of a world empire nor hold hundreds of miles of frontiers against the attacks of land-hungry invaders. A transition, therefore, to that army pattern which would have conformed to the "natural economy" basis of society was impossible during the late-Roman epoch. This was the reason why Diocletian had to attempt the reorganization of public finances on the basis of uniform *money* taxes, and why, to the very end, the *city* officially remained the lowest cell of the State organism. But the *economic* basis of the great majority of Roman cities was withering away: in the interest of a money-hungry state administration they were sitting, like cupping-glasses, on a soil covered with a net of seigneuries. The fall of the Empire was the necessary political result of the gradual disappearance of commerce and the spread of a "natural economy." This fall essentially meant the abolition of that state administration and, hence, of the political superstructure with its money economy character which was no longer adapted to its changed economic basis.

When, after half a millennium, the belated executor of Diocletian's will, Charlemagne, revived the political unity of the Occident, this development took place on the basis of a strictly "natural" economy. Whoever studies the instructions he gave to the administrators of his domains (the *villici*)—the famous *ca-*

pitulare de villis, in its practical sense and the tartness of its language reminiscent of the ukases of Frederick William I of Prussia—will find this fact most impressively illustrated. At the side of the king, the queen appears in a dominant position: the king's wife is his minister of finance. And justly so; "administration of finance" here principally is concerned with the needs of the royal table and household which is identical with the "state household." We read there what the bailiffs have to provide for the king's court: grain, meat, textiles, surprisingly large quantities of soap, etc.; in short whatever the king needs for his own use, for that of his companions, and for political functions, like horses and vehicles for warfare. The standing army has disappeared; so has the salaried bureaucracy and, with it, the very concept of taxation. The king feeds his officials on his own table or he endows them with land. The self-equipped army is about to become, for good, an army on horseback and so a military caste of landowning knights. Interlocal exchange of commodities has disappeared as well; the threads of commerce connecting the self-sufficient cells of economic life are broken, trade is reduced to peddling, carried on by foreigners, Greeks and Jews.

Above all, the *city* has disappeared; the Carolingian epoch does not know this term as a specific concept of administrative law. The seigneuries are the vehicles of civilization; they also form the basis of the monasteries. The seigneurs are the political officials; the king himself is a seigneur, the biggest of all—rural and illiterate. His castles are situated in the countryside; therefore he has no fixed residence: for the sake of his livelihood he travels even more than some modern monarchs do; for he continuously moves from castle to castle and eats up what has been stored for him. Civilization has become rural, indeed.

The cycle of the economic development of antiquity is now completed. The intellectual achievements of the ancients seem to be totally lost. Gone with commercial traffic is the marble splendor of the ancient cities and, with them, all the intellectual values based on them: art and literature, science and the elaborate forms of ancient commercial law. And on the estates of the *possessores* and seigneurs the songs of the troubadours are not yet heard. We hardly can suppress a feeling of sadness when we witness a culture that seems to aim at perfection lose its material foundation and collapse. But what is it actually that we are witnessing in this gigantic process? In the depth of society organic structural changes occur (and had to occur) which, if we look at them as a whole, must be interpreted as an immense process of recovery. Individual family life and private property were restored to the masses of unfree people; they themselves were raised again, from the position of "speaking inventory" up into the circle of human beings. The rise of Christianity surrounded their family life with firm moral guarantees: already late-Roman laws for the protection of the peasants recognize the unity of the unfree family to a degree not known before. To be sure, at the same time one sector of the free population was sinking down into actual serfdom, and the highly cultivated aristocracy of the ancient world declined into barbarism. As we have seen: the spread of unfree labor and the increasing differentiation of wealth based on slave-ownership had formed the foundation for the evolution of ancient civilization. But later, when the center of political gravity had shifted from the coast to the inland regions and when the supply of human cattle had dwindled away, this new system of "natural economy" as it had become established on the big estates had forced its own semi-feudal structure upon the exchange economy originally developed in the coastal cities. So, the threadbare wrap of ancient civilization disappeared, and the intellectual life of western man sank into a long night. But that fall reminds us of that giant in Greek mythology who gained new strength whenever he rested on the bosom of mother earth. If one of the old classical authors had arisen from his manuscript in Carolingian times and had examined the world through the window of the monk's cell in which he found himself, his surroundings would have looked strange to him, indeed: the dung-heap odor of the manor-yard would have hit his nostrils. But those classics were deep asleep now, as was all civilization, hidden away under the cover of an economic life which had returned to rural forms. Neither the songs nor the tournaments of feudal society roused it out of this sleep. Only when, on the basis of free division of labor and of commercial exchange the *city* had arisen again in the Middle Ages, when, later still, the transition to a national economy prepared the ground for civil liberty and broke the fetters imposed by the external and internal authorities of the feudal age, only then the old giant arose and carried with him the intellectual inheritance of antiquity up to the new light of our modern middle-class civilization.

PART III

Capitalism, Culture, and Religion

The Evolution of the Capitalist Spirit

IT IS A widespread error that the increase of population is to be included as a really crucial agent in the evolution of western capitalism. In opposition to this view, Karl Marx made the assertion that every economic epoch has its own law of population, and although this proposition is untenable in so general a form, it is justified in the present case. The growth of population in the west made most rapid progress from the beginning of the 18th century to the end of the 19th. In the same period China experienced a population growth of at least equal extent—from 60 or 70 to 400 millions, allowing for the inevitable exaggerations; this corresponds approximately with the increase in the west. In spite of this fact, capitalism went backward in China and not forward. The increase in the population took place there in different strata than with us. It made China the seat of a swarming mass of small peasants; the increase of a class corresponding to our proletariat was involved only to the extent that a foreign market made possible the employment of coolies ("coolie" is originally an Indian expression, and signifies neighbor or fellow member of a clan). The growth of population in Europe did indeed favor the development of capitalism, to the extent that in a small population the system would have been unable to secure the necessary labor force, but in itself it never called forth that development.

Nor can the inflow of precious metals be regarded, as Sombart suggests, as the primary cause of the appearance of capitalism. It is certainly true that in a given situation an increase in the supply of precious metals may give rise to price revolutions, such as that which took place after 1530 in Europe, and when other favorable conditions are present, as when a certain form of labor organization is in process of development, the progress may be stimulated by the fact that large stocks of cash come into the hands of certain groups. But the case of India proves that such an importation of precious metal will not alone bring about capitalism. In India in the period of the Roman power, an enormous mass of precious metal—some twenty-five million *sestertii* annually—came in in exchange for domestic goods, but this inflow gave rise to commercial capitalism to only a slight extent. The greater part of the precious metal disappeared in the hoards of the rajahs instead of being converted into cash and applied in the establishment of enterprises of a rational capitalistic character. This fact proves that it depends entirely upon the nature of the labor system what tendency will result from an inflow of precious metal. The gold and silver from America, after the discovery,

Reprinted by permission of Transaction Publishers from Max Weber, *General Economic History* (New York: Greenberg, 1927), pp. 352–69, 381. Translated by Frank H. Knight. The text is based on a lecture course Weber gave in 1919–20; see *Wirtschaftsgeschichte* (1923) (Berlin: Duncker und Humblot, 1991), pp. 300–315.

flowed in the first place to Spain; but in that country a recession of capitalistic development took place parallel with the importation. There followed, on the one hand, the suppression of the *communeros* and the destruction of the commercial interests of the Spanish grandees, and, on the other hand, the employment of the money for military ends. Consequently, the stream of precious metal flowed through Spain, scarcely touching it, and fertilized other countries, which in the 15th century were already undergoing a process of transformation in labor relations which was favorable to capitalism.

Hence neither the growth of population nor the importation of precious metal called forth western capitalism. The external conditions for the development of capitalism are rather, first, geographical in character. In China and India the enormous costs of transportation, connected with the decisively inland commerce of the regions, necessarily formed serious obstructions for the classes who were in a position to make profits through trade and to use trading capital in the construction of a capitalistic system, while in the west the position of the Mediterranean as an inland sea, and the abundant interconnections through the rivers, favored the opposite development of international commerce. But this factor in its turn must not be over-estimated. The civilization of antiquity was distinctively coastal. Here the opportunities for commerce were very favorable, (thanks to the character of the Mediterranean Sea), in contrast with the Chinese waters with their typhoons, and yet no [rational—RS] capitalism arose in antiquity. Even in the modern period the capitalistic development was much more intense in Florence than in Genoa or in Venice. Capitalism in the west was born in the industrial cities of the interior, not in the cities which were centers of sea trade.

Military requirements were also favorable, though not as such but because of the special nature of the particular needs of the western armies. Favorable also was the luxury demand, though again not in itself. In many cases rather it led to the development of irrational forms, such as small work shops in France and compulsory settlements of workers in connection with the courts of many German princes. In the last resort the factor which produced [modern—RS] capitalism is the rational permanent enterprise, rational accounting, rational technology and rational law, but again not these alone. Necessary complementary factors were *a rational mentality, the rationalization of the conduct of life in general,* and *a rational economic ethos.*[1]

At the beginning of all ethics and the economic relations which result, is traditionalism, the sanctity of tradition, the exclusive reliance upon such trade and industry as have come down from the fathers. This traditionalism survives far down into the present; only a human lifetime in the past it was futile to double the wages of an agricultural laborer in Silesia who mowed a certain tract of land on a contract, in the hope of inducing him to increase his exertions. He would simply have reduced by half the work expended because with this half he would

---

[1] See Max Weber, *Gesammelte Aufsätze zur Religionssoziologie*, I, pp. 30 ff. [reproduced in this anthology as reading 2—RS].

have been able to earn just as much as before (*sic*). This general incapacity and indisposition to depart from the beaten paths is the motive for the maintenance of tradition.

Primitive traditionalism may, however, undergo essential intensification through two circumstances. In the first place, material interests may be tied up with the maintenance of the tradition. When for example in China, the attempt was made to change certain roads or to introduce more rational means or routes of transportation, the perquisites of certain officials were threatened; and the same was the case in the middle ages in the west, and in modern times when railroads were introduced. Such special interests of officials, landholders and merchants assisted decisively in restricting a tendency toward rationalization. Stronger still is the effect of the stereotyping of trade on magical grounds, the deep repugnance to undertaking any change in the established conduct of life because supernatural evils are feared. Generally some injury to economic privilege is concealed in this opposition, but its effectiveness depends on a general belief in the potency of the magical processes which are feared.

Traditional obstructions are not overcome by the economic impulse alone. The notion that our rationalistic and capitalistic age is characterized by a stronger economic interest than other periods is childish; the moving spirits of modern capitalism are not possessed of a stronger economic impulse than, for example, an oriental trader. The unchaining of the economic interest merely as such has produced only irrational results; such men as Cortez and Pizarro, who were perhaps its strongest embodiment, were far from having an idea of a rationalistic economic life. If the economic impulse in itself is universal, it is an interesting question as to the relations under which it becomes rationalized and rationally tempered in such fashion as to produce rational institutions of the character of capitalistic enterprise.

Originally, two opposite attitudes toward the pursuit of gain exist in combination. Internally, there is attachment to tradition and to the pietistic relations of fellow members of tribe, clan, and house-community, with the exclusion of the unrestricted quest of gain within the circle of those bound together by religious ties; externally, there is absolutely unrestricted play of the gain spirit in economic relations, every foreigner being originally an enemy in relation to whom no ethical restrictions apply; that is, the ethics of internal and external relations are categorically distinct. The course of development involves on the one hand the bringing in of calculation into the traditional brotherhood, displacing the old religious relationship. As soon as accountability is established within the family community, and economic relations are no longer strictly communistic, there is an end of the naive piety and its repression of the economic impulse. This side of the development is especially characteristic in the west. At the same time there is a tempering of the unrestricted quest of gain with the adoption of the economic principle into the internal economy. The result is a regulated economic life with the economic impulse functioning within bounds.

In detail, the course of development has been varied. In India, the restrictions upon gain-seeking apply only to the two uppermost strata, the Brahmins and the

Rajputs. A member of these castes is forbidden to practice certain callings. A Brahmin may conduct an eating house, as he alone has clean hands; but he, like the Rajput, would be unclassed if he were to lend money for interest. The latter, however, is permitted to the mercantile castes, and within it we find a degree of unscrupulousness in trade which is unmatched anywhere in the world. Finally, antiquity had only legal limitations on interest, and the proposition *caveat emptor* characterizes Roman economic ethics. Nevertheless no modern capitalism developed there.

The final result is the peculiar fact that the germs of modern capitalism must be sought in a region where officially a theory was dominant which was distinct from that of the east and of classical antiquity and in principle strongly hostile to capitalism. The *ethos* of the classical economic morality is summed up in the old judgment passed on the merchant, which was probably taken from primitive Arianism: *homo mercator vix aut numquam potest Deo placere;* he may conduct himself without sin but cannot be pleasing to God. This proposition was valid down to the 15th century, and the first attempt to modify it slowly matured in Florence under pressure of the shift in economic relations.

The typical antipathy of Catholic ethics, and following that the Lutheran, to every capitalistic tendency, rests essentially on the repugnance of the impersonality of relations within a capitalist economy. It is this fact of impersonal relations which places certain human affairs outside the church and its influence, and prevents the latter from penetrating them and transforming them along ethical lines. The relations between master and slave could be subjected to immediate ethical regulation; but the relations between the mortgage creditor and the property which was pledged for the debt, or between an endorser and the bill of exchange, would at least be exceedingly difficult if not impossible to moralize.[2] The final consequence of the resulting position assumed by the church was that medieval economic ethics excluded higgling, overpricing and free competition, and were based on the principle of just price and the assurance to everyone of a chance to live.

For the breaking up of this circle of ideas the Jews cannot be made responsible as Sombart does.[3] The position of the Jews during the middle ages may be compared sociologically with that of an Indian caste in a world otherwise free from castes; they were an outcast people. However, there is the distinction that according to the promise of the Indian religion the caste system is valid for eternity. The individual may in the course of time reach heaven through a course of reincarnations, the time depending upon his deserts; but this is possible only within the caste system. The caste organization is eternal, and one who attempted to leave it would be accursed and condemned to pass in hell into the bowels of a dog. The Jewish promise, on the contrary, points toward a reversal of caste relations in the future world as compared with this. In the present world the Jews are stamped as an outcast people, either as punishment for the sins of

[2] Ibid., I, p. 544.

[3] Werner Sombart, *The Jews and Modern Capitalism* (trans. by M. Epstein) London, 1913.

their fathers, as Deutero-Isaiah holds, or for the salvation of the world, which is the presupposition of the mission of Jesus of Nazareth; from this position they are to be released by a social revolution. In the middle ages the Jews were a guest-people standing outside of political society; they could not be received into any town citizenship group because they could not participate in the communion of the Lord's Supper, and hence could not belong to the *coniuratio.*

The Jews were not the only guest-people[4]; besides them the Caursines, for example, occupied a similar position. These were Christian merchants who dealt in money and in consequence were, like the Jews, under the protection of the princes and on consideration of a payment enjoyed the privilege of carrying on monetary dealings. What distinguished the Jews in a striking way from the Christian guest-peoples was the impossibility in their case of entering into *commercium* and *conubium* with the Christians. Originally the Christians did not hesitate to accept Jewish hospitality, in contrast with the Jews themselves who feared that the ritualistic prescriptions as to food would not be observed by their hosts. On the occasion of the first outbreak of medieval anti-semitism the faithful were warned by the synods not to conduct themselves unworthily and hence not to accept entertainment from the Jews who on their side despised the hospitality of the Christians. Marriage with Christians was strictly impossible, going back to Ezra and Nehemiah.[5]

A further ground for the outcast position of the Jews arose from the fact that Jewish craftsmen existed; in Syria there had even been a Jewish knightly class, though only exceptionally Jewish peasants, for the conduct of agriculture was not to be reconciled with the requirements of the ritual. Ritualistic considerations were responsible for the concentration of Jewish economic life in monetary dealings.[6] Jewish piety set a premium on the knowledge of the law and continuous study was very much easier to combine with exchange dealings than with other occupations. In addition, the prohibition against usury on the part of the church condemned exchange dealings, yet the trade was indispensable and the Jews were not subject to the ecclesiastical law.

Finally, Judaism had maintained the originally universal dualism of internal and external moral attitudes, under which it was permissible to accept interest from foreigners who did not belong to the brotherhood or established association. Out of this dualism followed the sanctioning of other irrational economic

---

[4] See Max Weber, *General Economic History,* pp. 196, 217.

[5] Living as they did sometime between the mid-fifth and early fourth centuries B.C., Ezra and Nehemiah naturally never issued prohibitions against the marriage of Jews with Christians. Rather, what they prohibited was marriages of Jews with members of contemporary non-Jewish peoples of the Middle East (Ezra 9:1–2; Neh. 13:23–31). Most likely, Weber said that the later prohibition against marriage with Christians continued the tradition of the earlier decrees of Ezra and Nehemiah, but he was misunderstood by the students on whose lecture notes the text of the *General Economic History* is based (see above, p. 27) (RS).

[6] Earlier in *General Economic History,* Weber writes: "A strict adherent of Jewish ritual could not become an agriculturalist. . . . In this turning to trade, dealing with money was preferred because it alone permitted complete devotion to the study of the Law" (p. 196; see also p. 217) (RS).

affairs, especially tax farming and political financing of all sorts. In the course of the centuries the Jews acquired a special skill in matters which made them useful and in demand. But all this was pariah capitalism, not rational capitalism such as originated in the west. In consequence, hardly a Jew is found among the creators of the modern economic situation, the large entrepreneurs; this type was Christian and only conceivable in the field of Christianity. The Jewish manufacturer, on the contrary, is a modern phenomenon. If for no other reason, it was impossible for the Jews to have a part in the establishment of rational capitalism because they were outside the craft organizations. But even alongside the guilds they could hardly maintain themselves, even where, as in Poland, they had command over a numerous proletariat which they might have organized in the capacity of entrepreneurs in domestic industry or as manufacturers. After all, the genuine Jewish ethic is specifically traditionalism, as the Talmud shows. The horror of the pious Jew in the face of any innovation is quite as great as that of an individual among any primitive people with institutions fixed by the belief in magic.

However, Judaism was none the less of notable significance for modern rational capitalism, insofar as it transmitted to Christianity the latter's hostility to magic. Apart from Judaism and Christianity, and two or three oriental sects (one of which is in Japan), there is no religion with the character of outspoken hostility to magic. Probably this hostility arose through the circumstance that what the Israelites found in Canaan was the magic of the agricultural god Baal, while Jahweh was a god of volcanoes, earthquakes, and pestilences. The hostility between the two priesthoods and the victory of the priests of Jahweh discredited the fertility magic of the priests of Baal and stigmatized it with a character of decadence and godlessness. Since Judaism made Christianity possible and gave it the character of a religion essentially free from magic, it rendered an important service from the point of view of economic history. For the dominance of magic outside the sphere in which Christianity has prevailed is one of the most serious obstructions to the rationalization of economic life. Magic involves a stereotyping of technology and economic relations. When attempts were made in China to inaugurate the building of railroads and factories a conflict with geomancy ensued. The latter demanded that in the location of structures on certain mountains, forests, rivers, and cemetery hills, care should be taken in order not to disturb the rest of the spirits.[7]

Similar is the relation to capitalism of the castes in India. Every new technical process which an Indian employs signifies for him first of all that he leaves his caste and falls into another, necessarily lower. Since he believes in the transmigration of souls, the immediate significance of this is that his chance of pu-

---

[7] As soon as the mandarins realized the chances for gain open to them, these difficulties suddenly ceased to be insuperable; today they are the leading stockholders in the railways. In the long run, no religious-ethical conviction is able of barring the way to the entry of capitalism, when it stands in full armor before the gate; but the fact that it is able to leap over magical barriers does not prove that genuine capitalism could have originated in circumstances where magic played such a role.

rification is put off until another re-birth. He will hardly consent to such a change. An additional fact is that every caste makes every other impure. In consequence, workmen who dare not accept a vessel filled with water from each other's hands, cannot be employed together in the same factory room. Not until the present time, after the possession of the country by the English for almost a century, could this obstacle be overcome. Obviously, capitalism could not develop in an economic group thus bound hand and foot by magical beliefs.

In all times there has been but one means of breaking down the power of magic and establishing a rational conduct of life; this means is great rational prophecy. Not every prophecy by any means destroys the power of magic; but it is possible for a prophet who furnishes credentials in the shape of miracles and otherwise, to break down the traditional sacred rules. Prophecies have released the world from magic and in doing so have created the basis for our modern science and technology, and for [rational—RS] capitalism. In China such prophecy has been wanting. What prophecy there was has come from the outside as in the case of Lao-Tse and Taoism. India, however, produced a religion of salvation; in contrast with China it has known great prophetic missions. But they were prophecies by example; that is, the typical Hindu prophet, such as Buddha, lives before the world the life which leads to salvation, but does not regard himself as one sent from God to insist upon the obligation to lead it; he takes the position that whoever wishes salvation, as an end freely chosen, should lead the life. However, one may reject salvation, as it is not the destiny of everyone to enter at death into Nirvana, and only philosophers in the strictest sense are prepared by hatred of this world to adopt the stoical resolution and withdraw from life.

The result was that Hindu prophecy was of immediate significance for the intellectual classes. These became forest dwellers and poor monks. For the masses, however, the significance of the founding of a Buddhistic sect was quite different, namely the opportunity of praying to the saints. There came to be holy men who were believed to work miracles, who must be well fed so that they would repay this good deed by guaranteeing a better reincarnation or through granting wealth, long life, and the like, that is, this world's goods. Hence Buddhism in its pure form was restricted to a thin stratum of monks. The laity found no ethical precepts according to which life should be molded; Buddhism indeed had its decalogue, but in distinction from that of the Jews it gave no binding commands but only recommendations. The most important act of service was and remained the physical maintenance of the monks. Such a religious spirit could never be in a position to displace magic but at best could only put another magic in its place.

In contrast with the ascetic religion of salvation of India and its defective action upon the masses, are Judaism and Christianity, which from the beginning have been plebeian religions and have deliberately remained such. The struggle of the ancient church against the Gnostics was nothing else than a struggle against the aristocracy of the intellectuals, such as is common to ascetic religions, with the object of preventing their seizing the leadership in the church. This struggle was crucial for the success of Christianity among the masses, and hence for the fact that magic was suppressed among the general population to the greatest possible extent. True, it has not been possible even down to today to overcome it entirely, but it was reduced to the character of something unholy, something diabolic.

The germ of this development as regards magic is found far back in ancient Jewish ethics, which is much concerned with views such as we also meet with in the proverbs and the so-called prophetic texts of the Egyptians. But the most important prescriptions of Egyptian ethics were futile when by laying a scarab on the region of the heart one could prepare the dead man to successfully conceal the sins committed, deceive the judge of the dead, and thus get into paradise. The Jewish ethics knows no such sophisticated subterfuges and as little does Christianity. In the Eucharist the latter has indeed sublimated magic into the form of a sacrament, but it gave its adherents no such means for evading the final judgment as were contained in Egyptian religion. If one wishes to study at all the influence of a religion on life one must distinguish between its official teachings and this sort of actual procedure upon which in reality, perhaps against its own will, it places a premium, in this world or the next.

It is also necessary to distinguish between the virtuoso religion of adepts and the religion of the masses. Virtuoso religion is significant for everyday life only as a pattern; its claims are of the highest, but they fail to determine everyday ethics. The relation between the two is different in different religions. In Catholicism, they are brought into harmonious union insofar as the claims of the religious virtuoso are held up alongside the duties of the laymen as *consilia evangelica*. The really complete Christian is the monk; but his mode of life is not required of everyone, although some of his virtues in a qualified form are held up as ideals. The advantage of this combination was that ethics was not split asunder as in Buddhism. After all the distinction between monk ethics and mass ethics meant that the most worthy individuals in the religious sense withdrew from the world and established a separate community.

Christianity was not alone in this phenomenon, which rather recurs frequently in the history of religions, as is shown by the powerful influence of asceticism, which signifies the carrying out of a definite, methodical conduct of life. Asceticism has always worked in this sense. The enormous achievements possible to such an ascetically determined methodical conduct of life are demonstrated by the example of Tibet. The country seems condemned by nature to be an eternal desert; but a community of celibate ascetics has carried out colossal construction works in Lhasa and saturated the country with the religious doctrines of Buddhism. An analogous phenomenon is present in the middle ages in the west. In that epoch the monk is the first human being who lives rationally, who works methodically and by rational means toward a goal, namely the future life. Only for him did the clock strike, only for him were the hours of the day divided—for prayer. The economic life of the monastic communities was also rational. The monks in part furnished the officialdom for the early middle ages; the power of the doges of Venice collapsed when the investiture struggle deprived them of the possibility of employing churchmen for oversea enterprises.

But the rational mode of life remained restricted to the monastic circles. The Franciscan movement indeed attempted through the institution of the tertiaries to extend it to the laity, but the institution of the confessional was a barrier to such an extension. The church domesticated medieval Europe by means of its system of confession and penance, but for the men of the middle ages the possibility of unburdening themselves through the channel of the confessional, when they had rendered themselves liable to punishment, meant a release from the consciousness of sin which the teachings of the church had called into being. The unity and strength of the methodical conduct of life were thus in fact broken up. In its knowledge of human nature the church did not reckon with the fact that the individual is a closed unitary ethical personality, but steadfastly held to the view that in spite of the warnings of the confessional and of penances, however strong, he would again fall away morally; that is, it shed its grace on the just and the unjust.

The Reformation made a decisive break with this system. The dropping of the *consilia evangelica* by the Lutheran Reformation meant the disappearance of the dualistic ethics, of the distinction between a universally binding morality and a specifically advantageous code for virtuosi. The other-worldly asceticism came to an end. The stern religious characters who had previously gone into monasteries had now to practice their religion in the life of the world. For such an asceticism within the world the ascetic dogmas of protestantism created an adequate ethics. Celibacy was not required, marriage being viewed simply as an institution for the rational bringing up of children. Poverty was not required, but the pursuit of riches must not lead one astray into reckless enjoyment. Thus Sebastian Franck was correct in summing up the spirit of the Reformation in the words, "you think you have escaped from the monastery, but everyone must now be a monk throughout his life."

The wide significance of this transformation of the ascetic ideal can be followed down to the present in the classical lands of protestant ascetic religiosity. It is especially discernible in the importance of the religious denominations in America. Although state and church are separated, still, as late as fifteen or twenty years ago [that is, 1900–1905] no banker or physician took up a residence or established connections without being asked to what religious community he belonged, and his prospects were good or bad according to the character of his answer. Acceptance into a sect was conditioned upon a strict inquiry into one's ethical conduct. Membership in a sect which did not recognize the Jewish distinction between internal and external moral codes guaranteed one's business honor and reliability and this in turn guaranteed success. Hence the principle "honesty is the best policy" and hence among Quakers, Baptists, and Methodists the ceaseless repetition of the proposition based on experience that God would take care of his own. "The Godless cannot trust each other across the road; they turn to us when they want to do business; piety is the surest road to wealth." This is by no means "cant," but a combination of religiosity with consequences which were originally unknown to it and which were never intended.

It is true that the acquisition of wealth, attributed to piety, led to a dilemma, in all respects similar to that into which the medieval monasteries constantly fell; the religious guild led to wealth, wealth to fall from grace, and this again to the necessity of re-constitution. Calvinism sought to avoid this difficulty through the idea that man was only an administrator of what God had given him; it condemned enjoyment, yet permitted no flight from the world but rather regarded working together, with its rational discipline, as the religious task of the individual. Out of this system of thought came our word "calling" (*Beruf*), which is known only to the languages influenced by the protestant translation of the Bible.[8] It expresses the value placed upon rational activity carried on according to the rational capitalistic principle, as the fulfillment of a God-given task. Here lay also in the last analysis the basis of the contrast between the Puritans and the Jews. The ideas of both were capitalistically directed; but in a characteristic way the Jew was for the Puritan the embodiment of everything repugnant because he devoted himself to irrational and illegal occupations such as war loans, tax farming, and leasing of offices, in the fashion of the court favorite.[9]

This development of the concept of the calling quickly gave to the modern entrepreneur a fabulously clear conscience—and also industrious workers; he gave to his employees as the wages of their ascetic devotion to the calling and of cooperation in his ruthless exploitation of them through capitalism the prospect of eternal salvation, which in an age when ecclesiastical discipline took control of the whole of life to an extent inconceivable to us now, represented a reality quite different from any it has today. The Catholic and Lutheran churches also recognized and practiced ecclesiastical discipline. But in the protestant ascetic communities admission to the Lord's Supper was conditioned on ethical fitness, which again was identified with business honor, while into the content of one's faith no one inquired. Such a powerful, unconsciously refined organization for the production of capitalistic individuals has never existed in any other church or religion, and in comparison with it what the Renaissance did for capitalism shrinks into insignificance. Its practitioners occupied themselves with technical problems and were experimenters of the first rank. From art and mining experimentation was taken over into science.

The world-view of the Renaissance, however, determined the policy of rulers in a large measure, though it did not transform the soul of man as did the innovations of the Reformation. Almost all the great scientific discoveries of the 16th and even the beginning of the 17th century were made against the background of Catholicism. Copernicus was a Catholic, while Luther and Melanchthon repudiated his discoveries. Scientific progress and protestantism must not

[8] Max Weber, *Gesammelte Aufsätze zur Religionssoziologie,* I, p. 63 ff., 163 ff., 207 ff.

[9] In a general way, though with necessary reservations, the contrast may be formulated by saying that Jewish capitalism was speculative pariah-capitalism, while Puritan capitalism consisted in the organization of citizen labor. See Max Weber, *Gesammelte Aufsätze zur Religionssoziologie,* I, pp. 181 ff., note 2.

at all be unquestioningly identified. The Catholic church has indeed occasionally obstructed scientific progress; but the ascetic sects of protestantism have also been disposed to have nothing to do with science, except in a situation where material requirements of everyday life were involved. On the other hand it is its specific contribution to have placed science in the service of technology and economics.[10]

The religious root of modern economic humanity is dead; today the concept of the calling is a *caput mortuum* in the world. Ascetic religiosity has been displaced by a pessimistic though by no means ascetic view of the world, such as that portrayed in Mandeville's *Fable of the Bees,* which teaches that private vices may under certain conditions be for the good of the public. With the complete disappearance of all the remains of the original enormous religious pathos of the sects, the optimism of the Enlightenment which believed in the harmony of interests, appeared as the heir of Protestant asceticism in the field of economic ideas; it guided the hands of the princes, statesmen, and writers of the later 18th and early 19th century. Economic ethics arose against the background of the ascetic ideal; now it has been stripped of its religious import. It was possible for the working class to accept its lot as long as the promise of eternal happiness could be held out to it. When this consolation fell away it was inevitable that those strains and stresses should appear in economic society which since then have grown so rapidly. This point had been reached at the end of the early period of capitalism, at the beginning of the age of iron, in the 19th century.

[10] See also Ernst Troeltsch, *The Social Teachings of the Christian Churches,* 2 vols., Tübingen 1912 (reprinted 1919; trans. 1931). Among the opponents of the above conceptions of Max Weber regarding the significance of Calvinism should be mentioned Lujo Brentano (*Die Anfänge des modernen Kapitalismus,* Munich, 1916, pp. 117 ff.) and Georg Brodnitz (*Englische Wirtschaftsgeschichte,* I, pp. 282 ff.).

TWELVE

The Protestant Sects and the Spirit of Capitalism

FOR SOME TIME in the United States a principled 'separation of state and church' has existed.[1] This separation is carried through so strictly that there is not even an official census of denominations, for it would be considered against the law for the state even to ask the citizen for his denomination. We shall not here discuss the practical importance of this principle of the relation between religious organizations and the state.[2] We are interested, rather, in the fact that scarcely two and a half decades ago the number of 'persons without church affiliation' in the U.S.A. was estimated to be only about 6 per cent;[3] and this despite the absence of all those highly effective premiums which most of the European states then placed upon affiliation with certain privileged churches and despite the immense immigration to the U.S.A.

It should be realized, in addition, that church affiliation in the U.S.A. brings with it incomparably higher financial burdens, especially for the poor, than anywhere in Germany. Published family budgets prove this, and I have personally known of many burdened cases in a congregation in a city on Lake Erie, which was almost entirely composed of German immigrant lumberjacks. Their regular contributions for religious purposes amounted to almost $80 annually, being paid out of an average annual income of about $1,000. Everyone knows that even a small fraction of this financial burden in Germany would lead to a mass exo-

Reprinted by permission of Oxford University Press, Inc. from *From Max Weber: Essays in Sociology* by Max Weber. Edited and translated by H. H. Gerth and C. Wright Mills. Translation copyright © 1946, 1958 by H. H. Gerth and C. Wright Mills. This excerpt is taken from pp. 302–13 and 450–51. Originally published in 1920; see *Gesammelte Aufsätze zur Religionssoziologie*, vol. 1 (Tübingen: J. C. B. Mohr, 1988), pp. 207–20.

[1] This is a new and greatly enlarged draft of an article published in *Frankfurter Zeitung*, Easter 1906, then somewhat enlarged in the *Christliche Welt*, 1906, pp. 558 ff., 577 ff., under the title, 'Churches and Sects' [for a translation, see *Sociological Theory* 3(1958): 7–13—RS]. I have repeatedly referred to this article as supplementing *The Protestant Ethic and the Spirit of Capitalism*. The present rewriting is motivated by the fact that the concept of sect as worked out by myself (as a contrasting conception to 'church') has, in the meanwhile and to my joy, been taken over and treated thoroughly by Troeltsch in his *Soziallehren der christlichen Kirchen* [*The Social Teachings of the Christian Churches*, trans. by O. Wyon, 2 vols., London, 1931]. Hence, conceptual discussions can more easily be omitted as what is necessary has been said already in *The Protestant Ethic and the Spirit of Capitalism*, pp. 254 ff., note 173. This essay contains only the barest data supplementing that essay.

[2] The principle is often only theoretical; note the importance of the Catholic vote, as well as subsidies to confessional schools.

[3] Details are of no interest here. Reference should be made to the respective volumes of the 'American Church History Series', which is, to be sure, of very uneven value.

dus from the church. But quite apart from that, nobody who visited the United States fifteen or twenty years ago, that is, before the recent Europeanization of the country began, could overlook the very intense church-mindedness which then prevailed in all regions not yet flooded by European immigrants.[4] Every old travel book reveals that formerly church-mindedness in America went unquestioned, as compared with recent decades, and was even far stronger. Here we are especially interested in one aspect of this situation.

Hardly a generation ago when businessmen were establishing themselves and making new social contacts, they encountered the question: 'To what church do you belong?' This was asked unobtrusively and in a manner that seemed to be apropos, but evidently it was never asked accidentally. Even in Brooklyn, New York's twin city, this older tradition was retained to a strong degree, and the more so in communities less exposed to the influence of immigration. This question reminds one of the typical Scotch *table d'hôte*, where a quarter of a century ago the continental European on Sundays almost always had to face the situation of a lady's asking, 'What service did you attend today?' Or, if the Continental, as the oldest guest, should happen to be seated at the head of the table, the waiter when serving the soup would ask him: 'Sir, the prayer, please." In Portree (Skye) on one beautiful Sunday I faced this typical question and did not know any better way out than to remark: 'I am a member of the *Badische Landeskirche* and could not find a chapel of my church in Portree.' The ladies were pleased and satisfied with the answer. 'Oh, he doesn't attend any service except that of his own denomination!'

If one looked more closely at the matter in the United States, one could easily see that the question of religious affiliation was almost always posed in social life and in business life which depended on permanent and credit relations. However, as mentioned above, the American authorities never posed the question. Why?

First, a few personal observations [from 1904] may serve as illustrations. On a long railroad journey through what was then Indian territory, the author, sitting next to a traveling salesman of 'undertaker's hardware' (iron letters for tombstones), casually mentioned the still impressively strong church-mindedness. Thereupon the salesman remarked, 'Sir, for my part everybody may believe or not believe as he pleases; but if I saw a farmer or a businessman not belonging to any church at all, I wouldn't trust him with fifty cents. Why pay me, if he doesn't believe in anything?' Now that was a somewhat vague motivation.

The matter became somewhat clearer from the story of a German-born nose-and-throat specialist, who had established himself in a large city on the Ohio River and who told me of the visit of his first patient. Upon the doctor's request, he lay down upon the couch to be examined with the [aid of a] nose reflector. The patient sat up once and remarked with dignity and emphasis, 'Sir, I am a member of the ——— Baptist Church in ——— Street.' Puzzled about what

---

[4] The opening by prayer of not only every session of the U.S. Supreme Court but also of every Party Convention has been annoying ceremonial for quite some time.

meaning this circumstance might have for the disease of the nose and its treatment, the doctor discreetly inquired about the matter from an American colleague. The colleague smilingly informed him that the patient's statement of his church membership was merely to say: 'Don't worry about the fees.' But *why* should it mean precisely that? Perhaps this will become still clearer from a third happening.

On a beautiful clear Sunday afternoon early in October I attended a baptism ceremony of a Baptist congregation. I was in the company of some relatives who were farmers in the backwoods some miles out of M. [a county seat] in North Carolina. The baptism was to take place in a pool fed by a brook which descended from the Blue Ridge Mountains, visible in the distance. It was cold and it had been freezing during the night. Masses of farmers' families were standing all around the slopes of the hills; they had come, some from great distances, some from the neighborhood, in their light two-wheeled buggies.

The preacher in a black suit stood waist deep in the pond. After preparations of various sorts, about ten persons of both sexes in their Sunday-best stepped into the pond, one after another. They avowed their faith and then were immersed completely—the women in the preacher's arms. They came up, shaking and shivering in their wet clothes, stepped out of the pond, and everybody 'congratulated' them. They were quickly wrapped in thick blankets and then they drove home. One of my relatives commented that 'faith' provides unfailing protection against sneezes. Another relative stood beside me and, being unchurchly in accordance with German traditions, he looked on, spitting disdainfully over his shoulder. He spoke to one of those baptised, 'Hello, Bill, wasn't the water pretty cool?' and received the very earnest reply, 'Jeff, I thought of some pretty hot place (Hell!), and so I didn't mind the cool water.' During the immersion of one of the young men, my relative was startled.

'Look at him,' he said. 'I told you so!'

When I asked him after the ceremony, 'Why did you anticipate the baptism of that man?' he answered, 'Because he wants to open a bank in M.'

'Are there so many Baptists around that he can make a living?'

'Not at all, but once being baptised he will get the patronage of the whole region and he will outcompete everybody.'

Further questions of 'why' and 'by what means' led to the following conclusion: Admission to the local Baptist congregation follows only upon the most careful 'probation' and after closest inquiries into conduct going back to early childhood (Disorderly conduct? Frequenting taverns? Dance? Theatre? Card playing? Unpunctual meeting of liability? Other frivolities?) The congregation still adhered strictly to the religious tradition.

Admission to the congregation is recognized as an absolute guarantee of the moral qualities of a gentleman, especially of those qualities required in business matters. Baptism secures to the individual the deposits of the whole region and unlimited credit without any competition. He is a 'made man.' Further observation confirmed that these, or at least very similar phenomena, recur in the most varied regions. In general, *only* those men had success in business who belonged to Methodist or Baptist or other *sects* or sectlike conventicles. When a sect member moved to a different place, or if he was a traveling salesman, he carried the certificate of his congregation with him; and thereby he found not only easy contact with sect members but, above all, he found credit everywhere. If he got into economic straits through no fault of his own, the sect arranged his affairs, gave guarantees to the creditors, and helped him in every way, often according to the Biblical principle, *mutuum date nihil inde sperantes.* (Luke VI:35)

The expectation of the creditors that his sect, for the sake of their prestige, would not allow creditors to suffer losses on behalf of a sect member was not, however, decisive for his opportunities. What was decisive was the fact that a fairly reputable sect would only accept for membership one whose 'conduct' made him appear to be morally *qualified* beyond doubt.

It is crucial that sect membership meant a certificate of moral qualification and especially of business morals for the individual. This stands in contrast to membership in a 'church' into which one is 'born' and which lets grace shine over the righteous and the unrighteous alike. Indeed, a church is a corporation which organizes grace and administers religious gifts of grace, like an endowed foundation. Affiliation with the church is, in principle, obligatory and hence proves nothing with regard to the member's qualities. A sect, however, is a voluntary association of only those who, according to the principle, are religiously and morally qualified. If one finds voluntary reception of his membership, by virtue of religious *probation,* he joins the sect voluntarily.

It is, of course, an established fact that this selection has often been very strongly counteracted, precisely in America, through the proselyting of souls by competing sects, which, in part, was strongly determined by the material interests of the preachers. Hence, cartels for the restriction of proselyting have frequently existed among the competing denominations. Such cartels were formed, for instance, in order to exclude the easy wedding of a person who had been divorced for reasons which, from a religious point of view, were considered insufficient. Religious organizations that facilitated remarriage had great attraction. Some Baptist communities are said at times to have been lax in this respect, whereas the Catholic as well as the Lutheran (Missouri) churches were praised for their strict correctness. This correctness, however, allegedly reduced the membership of both churches.

Expulsion from one's sect for moral offenses has meant, economically, loss of credit and, socially, being declassed.

Numerous observations during the following months confirmed not only that church-mindedness *per se,* although still (1904) rather important, was rapidly dying out; but the particularly important trait, mentioned above, was definitely confirmed. In metropolitan areas I was spontaneously told, in several cases, that a speculator in undeveloped real estate would regularly erect a church building, often an extremely modest one; then he would hire a candidate from one of the various theological seminaries, pay him $500 to $600, and hold out to him a splendid position as a preacher for life if he would gather a congregation and thus preach the building terrain 'full.' Deteriorated churchlike structures which marked failures were shown to me. For the most part, however, the preachers were said to be successful. Neighborly contact, Sunday School, and so on, were said to be indispensable to the newcomer, but above all association with 'morally' reliable neighbors.

Competition among sects is strong, among other things, through the kind of material and spiritual offerings at evening teas of the congregations. Among genteel churches also, musical presentations contribute to this competition. (A tenor in Trinity Church, Boston, who allegedly had to sing on Sundays *only*, at that time received $8,000.) Despite this sharp competition, the sects often maintained fairly good mutual relations. For instance, in the service of the Methodist church which I attended, the Baptist ceremony of the baptism, which I mentioned above, was recommended as a spectacle to edify everybody. In the main, the congregations refused entirely to listen to the preaching of 'dogma' and to confessional distinctions. 'Ethics' alone could be offered. In those instances where I listened to sermons for the middle classes, the typical bourgeois morality, respectable and solid, to be sure, and of the most homely and sober kind, was preached. But the sermons were delivered with obvious inner conviction; the preacher was often moved.

Today the kind of denomination [to which one belongs] is rather irrelevant. It does not matter whether one be Freemason,[5] Christian Scientist, Adventist, Quaker, or what not. What is decisive is that one be admitted to membership by 'ballot,' after an *examination* and an ethical *probation* in the sense of the virtues which are at a premium for the inner-worldly asceticism of protestantism and hence, for the ancient puritan tradition. Then, the same effect could be observed.

Closer scrutiny revealed the steady progress of the characteristic process of 'secularization,' to which in modern times all phenomena that originated in religious conceptions succumb. Not only religious associations, hence sects, had this effect on American life. Sects exercised this influence, rather, in a steadily decreasing proportion. If one paid some attention it was striking to observe (even fifteen years ago) that surprisingly many men among the American middle classes (always outside of the quite modern metropolitan areas and the immigration centers) were wearing a little badge (of varying color) in the buttonhole, which reminded one very closely of the rosette of the French Legion of Honor.

When asked what it meant, people regularly mentioned an association with a sometimes adventurous and fantastic name. And it became obvious that its significance and purpose consisted in the following: Almost always the association functioned as a burial insurance, besides offering greatly varied services. But often, and especially in those areas least touched by modern disintegration, the association offered the member the (ethical) claim for brotherly help on the part

---

[5] An assistant in Semitic languages at an eastern university told me that he regretted not having become 'master of the chair,' for then he would go back into business. When asked what good that would do the answer was: As a traveling salesman or seller he could present himself in a role famous for respectability. He could beat any competition and would be worth his weight in gold.

of every brother who had the means. If he faced an economic emergency for which he himself was not to be blamed, he could make this claim. And in several instances that came to my notice at the time, this claim again followed the very principle, *mutuum date nihil inde sperantes,* or at least a very low rate of interest prevailed. Apparently, such claims were willingly recognized by the members of the brotherhood. Furthermore—and this is the main point in this instance—membership was again acquired through balloting after investigation and a determination of moral worth. And hence the badge in the buttonhole meant, 'I am a gentleman patented after investigation and probation and guaranteed by my membership.' Again, this meant, in business life above all, tested *credit worthiness.* One could observe that business opportunities were often decisively influenced by such legitimation.

All these phenomena, which seemed to be rather rapidly disintegrating—at least the religious organizations—were essentially confined to the middle classes. Some cultured Americans often dismissed these facts briefly and with a certain angry disdain as 'humbug' or backwardness, or they even denied them; many of them actually did not know anything about them, as was affirmed to me by William James. Yet these survivals were still alive in many different fields, and sometimes in forms which appeared to be grotesque.

These associations were especially the typical vehicles of social ascent into the circle of the entrepreneurial middle class. They served to diffuse and to maintain the bourgeois capitalist business ethos among the broad strata of the middle classes (the farmers included).

As is well known, not a few (one may well say the majority of the older generation) of the American 'promoters,' 'captains of industry,' of the multimillionaires and trust magnates belonged formally to sects, especially to the Baptists. However, in the nature of the case, these persons were often affiliated for merely conventional reasons, as in Germany, and only in order to legitimate themselves in personal and social life—not in order to legitimate themselves as businessmen; during the age of the Puritans, such 'economic supermen' did not require such a crutch, and *their* 'religiosity' was, of course, often of a more than dubious sincerity. The middle classes, above all the strata ascending with and out of the middle classes, were the bearers of that specific religious orientation which one must, indeed, beware viewing among them as only opportunistically determined.[6] Yet one must never overlook that without the universal diffusion of these qualities and principles of a methodical way of life, qualities which were maintained through these religious communities, capitalism today, even in America, would not be what it is. In the history of any economic area on earth there is no epoch, [except] those quite rigid in feudalism or patrimonialism, in

---

[6] 'Hypocrisy' and conventional opportunism in these matters were hardly stronger developed in America than in Germany where, after all, an officer or civil servant 'without religious affiliation or preference' was also an impossibility. And a Berlin ('Aryan!') Lord Mayor was not confirmed officially because he failed to have one of his children baptised. Only the direction in which conventional 'hypocrisy' moved differed: official careers in Germany, business opportunities in the United States.

which capitalist figures of the kind of Pierpont Morgan, Rockefeller, Jay Gould, *et al.* were absent. Only the technical *means* which they used for the acquisition of wealth have changed (of course!). *They* stood and they stand 'beyond good and evil.' But, however high one may otherwise evaluate their importance for economic transformation, they have never been decisive in determining what economic mentality was to dominate a given epoch and a given area. Above all, they were not the creators and they were not to become the bearers of the specifically Occidental bourgeois mentality.

This is not the place to discuss in detail the political and social importance of the religious sects and the numerous similarly exclusive associations and clubs in America which are based upon recruitment by ballot. The entire life of a typical Yankee of the last generation led through a series of such exclusive associations, beginning with the Boys' Club in school, proceeding to the Athletic Club or the Greek Letter Society or to another student club of some nature, then onward to one of the numerous notable clubs of businessmen and the bourgeoisie, or finally to the clubs of the metropolitan plutocracy. To gain admission was identical to a ticket of ascent, especially with a certificate before the forum of one's self-feeling; to gain admission meant to have 'proved' oneself. A student in college who was not admitted to *any* club (or quasi-society) whatsoever was usually a sort of pariah. (Suicides because of failure to be admitted have come to my notice.) A businessman, clerk, technician, or doctor who had the same fate usually was of questionable ability to serve. Today, numerous clubs of this sort are bearers of those tendencies leading toward aristocratic status groups which characterize contemporary American development. These status groups develop alongside of and, what has to be well noted, partly in contrast to the naked plutocracy.

In America mere 'money' in itself also purchases power, but not social honor. Of course, it is a means of acquiring social prestige. It is the same in Germany and everywhere else; except in Germany the appropriate avenue to social honor led from the purchase of a feudal estate to the foundation of an entailed estate, and acquisition of titular nobility, which in turn facilitated the reception of the *grandchildren* in aristocratic 'society.' In America, the old tradition respected the self-made man more than the heir, and the avenue to social honor consisted in affiliation with a genteel fraternity in a distinguished college, formerly with a distinguished sect (for instance, Presbyterian, in whose churches in New York one could find soft cushions and fans in the pews). At the present time, affiliation with a distinguished club is essential above all else. In addition, the kind of home is important (in 'the street' which in middle-sized cities is almost never lacking) and the kind of dress and sport. Only recently descent from the Pilgrim fathers, from Pocahontas and other Indian ladies, et cetera has become important. This is not the place for a more detailed treatment. There are masses of translating bureaus and agencies of all sorts concerned with reconstructing the pedigrees of the plutocracy. All these phenomena, often highly grotesque, belong in the broad field of the Europeanization of American 'society.'

In the past and up to the very present, it has been a characteristic precisely of the specifically American democracy that it did *not* constitute a formless sand heap of individuals, but rather a buzzing complex of strictly exclusive, yet voluntary associations. Not so long ago these associations still did not recognize the prestige of birth and *inherited* wealth, of the office and educational diploma; at least they recognized these things to such a low degree as has only very rarely been the case in the rest of the world. Yet, even so, these associations were far from accepting anybody with open arms as an equal. To be sure, fifteen years ago an American farmer would not have led his guest past a plowing farmhand (American born!) in the field without making his guest 'shake hands' with the worker after formally introducing them.

Formerly, in a typical American club nobody would remember that the two members, for instance, who play billiards once stood in the relation of boss and clerk. Here equality of gentlemen prevailed absolutely.[7] To be sure, the American worker's wife accompanying the trade unionist to lunch had completely accommodated herself in dress and behavior, in a somewhat plainer and more awkward fashion, to the bourgeois lady's model.

He who wished to be fully recognized in this democracy, in whatever position, had not only to conform to the conventions of bourgeois society, the very strict men's fashions included, but as a rule he had to be able to show that he had succeeded in gaining admission by ballot to one of the sects, clubs, or fraternal societies, no matter *what* kind, were it only recognized as sufficiently legitimate. And he had to maintain himself in the society by proving himself to be a gentleman. The parallel in Germany consists in the importance of the *Couleur*[8] and the commission of an officer of the reserve for *commercium* and *connubium,* and the great status significance of qualifying to give satisfaction by duel. The thing is the same, but the direction and material consequence characteristically differ.

He who did not succeed in joining was no gentleman; he who despised doing so, as was usual among Germans,[9] had to take the hard road, and especially so in business life.

However, as mentioned above, we shall not here analyze the social significance of these conditions, which are undergoing a profound transformation. First, we are interested in the fact that the modern position of the secular clubs and societies with recruitment by ballot is largely the product of a process of *secularization.* Their position is derived from the far more exclusive importance of the prototype of these voluntary associations, to wit, the sects. They stem, indeed, from the sects in the homeland of genuine Yankeedom, the North Atlantic states. Let us recall, first, that the universal and equal franchise within Ameri-

---

[7] This was not always the case in the German-American clubs. When asking young German merchants in New York (with the best Hanseatic names) why they all strove to be admitted to an American club instead of the very nicely furnished German one, they answered that their (German-American) bosses would play billiards with them occasionally, however not without making them realize that they (the bosses) thought themselves to be 'very nice' in doing so.

[8] Student fraternity, comparable to a 'Greek letter society' (Translator's Note).

[9] But note above. Entry into an American club (in school or later) is always the decisive moment for the loss of German nationality.

can democracy (of the Whites! for Negroes and all mixtures have, even today, no *de facto* franchise) and likewise the 'separation of state and church' are only achievements of the recent past, beginning essentially with the nineteenth century. Let us remember that during the colonial period in the central areas of New England, especially in Massachusetts, full citizenship status in the church congregation was the precondition for full citizenship in the state (besides some other prerequisites). The religious congregation indeed determined admission or non-admission to political citizenship status.[10]

The decision was made according to whether or not the person had *proved* his religious qualification through conduct, in the broadest meaning of the word, as was the case among all Puritan sects. The Quakers in Pennsylvania were not in any lesser way masters of that state until some time before the War of Independence. This was actually the case, though *formally* they were not the only full political citizens. They were political masters only by virtue of extensive gerrymandering.

The tremendous social significance of admission to full enjoyment of the rights of the sectarian congregation, especially the privilege of being admitted to the *Lord's Supper,* worked among the sects in the direction of breeding that ascetist professional ethic which was adequate to modern capitalism during the period of its origin. It can be demonstrated that everywhere, including Europe, the religiosity of the ascetic sects has for several centuries worked in the same way as has been illustrated by the personal experiences mentioned above for [the case of] America.

When focusing on the religious background[11] of these Protestant sects, we

---

[10] The organization of the religious congregation during the immigration to New England often preceded the creation of a political association (in the fashion of the well-known pact of the Pilgrim Fathers). Thus, the Dorchester Immigrants of 1619 first bound themselves together by organizing a church congregation *before* emigrating, and they elected a parson and a teacher. In the colony of Massachusetts, the church was formally a completely autonomous corporation, which admitted, however, only citizens for membership, and affiliation with which, on the other hand, was a prerequisite of citizenship. Likewise, at first, church membership and good conduct (meaning admission to the Lord's Supper) were prerequisites of citizenship in New Haven (before it was incorporated in Connecticut despite resistance against incorporation). In Connecticut, however (in 1650), the township was obliged to maintain the church (a defection from the strict principles of Independentism to Presbyterianism).

This at once meant a somewhat laxer practice, for after the incorporation of New Haven the church there was restricted to giving out certificates stating that the respective person was religiously inoffensive and of sufficient means. Even during the seventeenth century, on the occasion of the incorporation of Maine and New Hampshire, Massachusetts had to depart from the full strictness of the religious qualification of political rights. On the question of church membership compromises also had to be made, the most famous of which is the Half-way Covenant of 1657. In addition, those who could not prove themselves to be regenerate were nevertheless admitted to membership. But, until the beginning of the eighteenth century, they were not admitted to communion.

[11] Some references from the older literature which is not very well known in Germany may be listed. A sketch of Baptist history is present in: Vedder, *A Short History of the Baptists* (Second ed. London, 1897). Concerning Hanserd Knollys: Culross, *Hanserd Knollys,* vol. II of the Baptist Manuals edited by P. Gould (London, 1891).

For the history of Anabaptism: E. B. Bax, *Rise and Fall of the Anabaptists* (New York, 1902). Confind in their literary documents, especially among those of the Quakers and Baptists up to and throughout the seventeenth century, again and again jubilation over the fact that the sinful 'children of the world' distrust one another in business but that they have confidence in the religiously determined righteousness of the pious.[12]

Hence, they give credit and deposit their money only with the pious, and they make purchases in their stores because there, and there alone, they are given honest and *fixed prices*. As is known, the Baptists have always claimed to have first raised this price policy to a principle. In addition to the Baptists, the Quakers raise the claim, as the following quotation shows, to which Mr. Eduard Bernstein drew my attention at the time:

> But it was not only in matters which related to the law of the land where the primitive members held their words and engagements sacred. This trait was remarked to be true of them in their concerns of trade. On their first appearance as a society, they suffered as tradesmen because others, displeased with the peculiarity of their manners, withdrew their custom from their shops. But in a little time the great outcry against them was that they got the trade of the country into their hands. This outcry arose in part from a strict exemption of all commercial agreements between them and others and *because they never asked two prices for the commodities they sold.*[13]

The view that the gods bless with riches the man who pleases them, through sacrifice or through his kind of conduct, was indeed diffused all over the world. However, the Protestant sects consciously brought this idea into connection with this *kind* of religious conduct, according to the principle of early capitalism:

---

cerning Smyth: Henry M. Dexter, *The True Story of John Smyth, the Se-Baptist, as Told by Himself and His Contemporaries* (Boston, 1881). The important publications of the Hanserd Knollys Society (printed for the Society by J. Hadden, Castle Street, Finsbury, 1846–54) have been cited already. Further official documents in *The Baptist Church Manual* by J. Newton Brown, D.D. (Philadelphia, American Baptist Publishing Society, 30 S. Arch Street). Concerning the Quakers, besides the cited work of Sharpless: A. C. Applegarth, *The Quakers in Pennsylvania*, ser. x, vol. VIII, IX of the Johns Hopkins University Studies in History and Political Science. G. Lorimer, *Baptists in History* (New York, 1902), J. A. Seiss, Baptist System Examined (Lutheran Publication Society, 1902).

Concerning New England (besides Doyle): The Massachusetts Historical Collections; furthermore, Weeden, *Economic and Social History of New England, 1620–1789*, 2 vols. Daniel W. Howe, *The Puritan Republic* (Indianapolis, Bobbs-Merrill Co.).

Concerning the development of the 'Covenant' idea in older Presbyterianism, its church discipline, and its relation to the official church, on the one hand, and to Congregationalists and sectarians on the other hand, see: Burrage, *The Church Covenant Idea* (1904), and *The Early English Dissenters* (1912). Furthermore, W. M. Macphail, *The Presbyterian Church* (1918), J. Brown, *The English Puritans* (1910). Important documents in Usher, *The Presbyterian Movement, 1584–89* (Com. Soc., 1905). We give here only an extremely provisional list of what is relevant for us.

[12] During the seventeenth century this was so much taken for granted that Bunyan, as mentioned previously, makes 'Mr. Money-Love' argue that one may even become pious *in order to* get rich, especially in order to add to one's patronage; for it should be irrelevant for what reason one had become pious (*Pilgrim's Progress*, Tauchnitz ed., p. 114).

[13] Thomas Clarkson, *Portraiture of the Christian Profession and Practice of the Society of Friends.* Third edition (London, 1867), p. 276. (The first edition appeared around 1830.)

'Honesty is the best policy.' This connection is found, although not quite exclusively, among these Protestant sects, but with characteristic continuity and consistency it is found *only* among them.

The whole typically bourgeois ethic was from the beginning common to all ascetic sects and conventicles and it is identical with the ethic practiced by the sects in America up to the very present. The Methodists, for example, held to be forbidden:

1. to make words when buying and selling ('haggling')
2. to trade with commodities before the custom tariff has been paid·on them
3. to charge rates of interest higher than the law of the country permits
4. 'to gather treasures on earth' (meaning the transformation of investment capital into 'funded wealth'
5. to borrow without being sure of one's ability to pay back the debt
6. luxuries of all sorts

But it is not only this ethic, already discussed in detail,[14] which goes back to the early beginnings of ascetic sects. Above all, the social premiums, the means of discipline, and, in general, the whole organizational basis of Protestant sectarianism with all its ramifications reach back to those beginnings. The survivals in contemporary America are the derivatives of a religious regulation of life which once worked with penetrating efficiency.[15]

[14] In *The Protestant Ethic and the Spirit of Capitalism.*

[15] In the second half of this article Weber surveys the nature of the ascetic sects and how they operated; see Gerth and Mills, *From Max Weber,* pp. 313–22 (RS).

Kinship and Capitalism in China

IN THE PERIOD of the Warring States, the politically determined capitalism which is common in patrimonial states, based on money-lending and contracting for the princes, seems to have been of considerable significance and to have functioned at high rates of profit, as always under such conditions. Mines and trade are also cited as sources of capital accumulation. Under the Han dynasty, there are reputed to have been multi-millionaires, reckoned in terms of copper. But China's political unification into a world-empire, like the unification of the known world by Imperial Rome, had the obvious consequence that this form of capitalism, which was essentially rooted in the state and its competition with other states, went into decline. The development of a purely market capitalism, directed towards free exchange, on the other hand, remained at an embryonic stage. In all sections of industry, of course, even in the cooperative undertakings to be discussed presently, the merchant, here as elsewhere, was conspicuously superior to the technician. This clearly showed itself even in the usual proportions in which profits were distributed within associations. The interlocal industries also, it is plain, often brought in considerable speculative profits. The ancient classical disposition to set a high value on agriculture, as the truly hallowed calling, hence did not prevent a higher valuation being placed, even as early as the first century B.C., on the opportunities for profit from industry than on those from agriculture (just as in the Talmud), nor did it prevent the highest valuation of all being placed on those from trade.

But that did not mean that there were any beginnings of development towards a modern capitalism. Precisely those characteristic institutions which were developed by the bourgeoisie which flourished in the medieval cities of the West have, right up to the present day, either been entirely absent or taken characteristically different forms. There did not exist in China the legal forms, or the sociological basis, of the permanent capitalist enterprise, with its rational depersonalisation of the economy, such as existed already, in its first unmistakable beginnings, in the commercial law of the Italian city-states. The liability of members of a kinship group for their fellow members, which had existed in China in the more distant past and had represented a first step towards the development of personal credit, was preserved only in fiscal and political criminal law. Development proceeded no further. To be sure, the association of heirs in a business

Reprinted by permission of Cambridge University Press from W. G. Runciman, ed., *Max Weber: Selections in Translation* (Cambridge: Cambridge University Press, 1978), pp. 315–20. The text was originally published in 1915 and revised in 1920; see *Gesammelte Aufsätze zur Religionssoziologie*, vol. 1 (Tübingen: J. C. B. Mohr, 1988), pp. 373–79.

partnership, based on the household communities, played a similar role, precisely among the propertied classes, to that played by the Western household associations, from which later (at least in Italy) our 'public trading company' emerged. But its economic meaning was characteristically different. As always in a patrimonial state, it was the official, both in that capacity and as tax-farmer (as officials actually were), who had the best opportunities for accumulating wealth.[1] Discharged officials invested their more or less legally acquired wealth in the purchase of land. Their sons, in order to maintain the power derived from their wealth, remained in partnership as joint heirs and raised the means to enable some members of the family again to study, so as to make it possible for them to obtain lucrative posts and so once again enrich the members of the hereditary partnership and create posts for their kinsmen (for the greatest possible number, it goes without saying). Thus, on the basis of political accumulation of wealth, there developed a patriciate, however unstable, and a class of great landowners leasing out plots of land, which was neither feudal nor bourgeois in type but speculated in opportunities for purely political exploitation of office. As is typical in patrimonial states, therefore, the accumulation of wealth, especially of land, was dominated, not primarily by rational economic acquisition, but by trade—which again led to the investment of the money acquired in land—and above all by a form of capitalism based on the exploitation of internal political opportunities. For the officials acquired their wealth, as we have seen, by, among other things, speculation in taxes—that is, by arbitrarily fixing the exchange rate at which the due payments were to be converted at current prices. Examinations also gave the right to expect to be fed at this trough. As a result, they were constantly being freshly shared out among the provinces, although only exceptionally was there a fixed quota. Suspension of examinations in a particular province was an extremely effective, because economically painful, punishment for the families of notables who were involved. It is plain that this kind of familial business partnership tended to develop in a diametrically opposite direction to that of the rational economic enterprise. Above all, however, it was also very closely bound up with the kinship group. At this point we must attempt a connected discussion of the significance of the kinship associations, which has already been touched on a number of times.

Kinship, which in Western medieval society had virtually lost all significance, remained important in China both for the local administration of the smallest units and for the character of economic association; it had indeed developed to an extent unknown elsewhere, even in India. The patrimonial government from above clashed with the kinship organisations from below, which were firmly structured as a counterweight to it. A very significant fraction of all politically dangerous 'secret societies' has, even up to the present day, consisted of kins-

---

[1] The 'hoppo' (inspector and farmer of customs) in Canton was famous for his tremendous opportunities for accumulation: the income of his first year (200,000 *taels*) went to pay for the purchase of his office, that of the second year was spent on 'gifts', that of his third and last year he kept for himself (calculations from the 'North China Herald').

men.[2] The villages were often called after the name of a kinship group[3] which was either exclusively or predominantly represented in them. Or else they were actual confederations of kinship groups. The old boundary stones show that the land was not allotted to individuals, but to kinship groups, and the sense of community in the kinship groups preserved this state of affairs to a considerable extent. From the numerically most powerful kinship group was chosen the—often salaried—village headman. 'Elders' of the kinship groups stood at his side and claimed the right of dismissal. The individual kinship group, however, of which we must first speak now, claimed, as such and independently, the power to punish its members and exercised this power, however little the modern state authorities may have officially recognised it.[4]

The cohesiveness of the kinship group and its continued existence, despite the relentless encroachments of the patrimonial administration, with its mechanically constructed liability associations, its resettlements, redistributions of land and groupings of the population according to *ting* (individuals capable of work) was without doubt entirely dependent on the significance of the ancestor-cult, as the only undoubtedly classical and ancient 'folk-cult', performed, not by the Caesaro-papist government and its officials, but by the head of the household, in his capacity as house priest, assisted by the family. Already in the 'men's house' of the early militarist period the spirits of the ancestors seem to have played a role. It may be remarked in passing that this seems hardly compatible with true totemism, and perhaps points to the following, and the hereditary charisma of the prince and his retinue developed from that following, under the form of the men's house as the oldest form of organisation which we can infer with any degree of probability.[5] However that may be, in the historical period the absolutely fundamental belief of the Chinese people has always been the belief in the spirits of one's ancestors (not only, but principally, one's own[6]), in their role, as at-

---

[2] This was the core of the Taiping 'rebels' of 1858–64. Even as late as 1895, the Hung Yi Tang, the kinship group of the founder of the Taiping religion, was persecuted as a secret society (source: 'Peking Gazette').

[3] E.g. (Conrady in Pflugk-Harkkung, ed., *Weltgeschichte*, III), *Chang chia tsung* was the village of the family Chang.

[4] Official recognition was given only to the jurisdiction of the Imperial kinship group over its members and to domestic authority.

[5] Perhaps both types of men's house, the 'comradely' and the 'seigneurial', existed regionally side by side, though it is right to say, on the other hand, that the notes collected by von Quistorp (*Mitteilungen des Seminars für Orientalische Sprachen*, XVIII [1915]) *on the whole* tend rather to suggest the former. Nevertheless, the legendary Emperor Yao handed over his authority to his successor Shun in the temple of his ancestors. An Emperor threatens his vassals with the wrath of the spirits of their ancestors. Such examples, collected by Hirth in his *Ancient History of China*, support the latter hypothesis, as does the fact that the spirit of one of the Emperor's ancestors appears when he is guilty of misgovernment and demands an account; so also does the speech of Emperor P'an Keng in *Shu Ching* (Legge, *Prolegomena*, p. 238). Survivals of totemism are collected in Conrady, *Weltgeschichte*, III: they are not really convincing, though they are impressive.

[6] The protection given, as already mentioned, to the last descendant of an overthrown dynasty results from the concern to avoid annoying the spirits of his ancestors, who would after all be powerful, as former Emperors. (Cf. even the 'Peking Gazette' of 13 April and 31 July 1883: the com-

tested in ritual and literature, as intermediaries for the wishes of their descendants with the spirit of Heaven (or God),[7] and in the absolute necessity of appeasing them and gaining their favour by means of sacrifices. The ancestral spirits of the Emperors were the following, almost equal in rank, of the spirit of Heaven.[8] A Chinese who had no male descendants must necessarily have recourse to adoption, and if he neglected to do so, then his family would undertake a posthumous fictitious adoption on his behalf[9]—less in his interest than in their own, so as to be at peace with his spirit. The social effect of these all-pervasive ideas is clearly evident. First, there was the enormous strengthening of patriarchal power.[10] Then there was the cohesiveness of the kinship group as such. In Egypt, where the cult of the dead, but not that of the ancestors, dominated everything, the cohesiveness of the kinship group broke down (as in Mesopotamia, but considerably earlier) under the pressure of bureaucratisation and fiscalism. In China, it survived and grew stronger until it became a force equal to the political power.

In principle, every kinship group had (and still has up to the present) the hall of its ancestors[11] in the village. Apart from the ritual objects of the cult, it often contained a table of the 'moral rules' recognised by the kinship group. For the right to lay down its own statutes was never in fact questioned for the kinship group, and it was exercised not only independently of the law, but also in certain circumstances, even in regard to ritual questions, contrary to the law.[12] The kin-

---

plaint of the Chang Tuan, the representative of the Ming dynasty, about building on the Ming ancestral land). Similarly with the official state sacrifices, mentioned above, for the spirits of those who have died without issue and (also discussed above) the adoptions.

[7] See the speech of the Prince of Chou in the *Shu Ching* (Legge, *Prolegomena*, p. 175) and the prayer offered for the sick Emperor—to his ancestors, not to Heaven (*ibid.*, p. 391 ff.).

[8] That the spirit of Heaven was treated merely as 'first among equals' seems very clearly to follow from the evidence cited by de Groot in his *Universalismus*. It was the 'spirits of the ancestors', according to the report published in the 'Peking Gazette' of 29 September 1898, who condemned the attempts at reform made by the Emperor and K'ang Yu-Wei, which had at that time come to grief. Heaven is concerned, not only with what is due to itself, but also with what is due to one's ancestors (de Groot, *The Religion of the Chinese*, New York, 1910, pp. 27, 28). Hence also the Confucian doctrine that Heaven regards impassively the sins of a dynasty for a little while and only intervenes when total degeneration has set in. This was of course a rather convenient 'theodicy'.

[9] There are cases in which an adoption has been annulled, because the death sacrifices of the natural father have been endangered ('Peking Gazette', 26 April 1878).

[10] 'Patricide' was considered such a dreadful act (to be punished by a 'lingering death') that the Governor of the affected province was deposed in the same way as after natural catastrophes ('Peking Gazette', 7 August 1894). According to the 'Peking Gazette' of 12 July, 1895, a drunkard's murder of his grandfather in that year led to the punishment also of the murderer's father, for not bringing up his son in such a way that 'he could tolerate the most severe punishment from an elder'.

[11] In some cases, subdivisions of the kinship group had their own subordinate hall of ancestors.

[12] According to classical ritual, adoption might take place only within the kinship group. But the family statutes made a variety of arrangements for this, even within the same village. Several modifications of the old ritual had come almost universally into vogue. For instance, the daughter-in-law no longer mourned only, as officially prescribed, for her parents-in-law, but also for her own parents. Or again, 'deep' mourning was now the custom, not only for the father, as officially prescribed, but also for the mother.

ship group maintained its solidarity in relation to the outside world. Although, as previously explained, joint liability did not exist outside the criminal law, it was usual for the group, whenever possible, to settle the debts of a member. Under the chairmanship of the elder, it pronounced sentences, not only of flogging and excommunication (which meant civil death), but also, like the Russian commune, of exile. The often pronounced need for consumer loans was likewise met essentially within the kinship group, where it was considered a moral duty for the members with means to help in times of distress. Admittedly, a non-member was also supposed to be granted a loan if he made sufficiently many kow-tows, for it was impossible to take the risk of calling down the vengeance of the man's spirit if, in his desperation, he committed suicide,[13] and no one seems readily to have paid back a loan of his own free will, at least if he knew he had a strong kinship group behind him. Nevertheless, a clearly regulated obligation to help the needy and system of assistance with credit existed primarily only within the kinship group. When necessary, the kinship group conducted feuds with outsiders.[14] The reckless bravery shown here, where it was a matter of personal interests and personal ties, contrasted in the most glaring way with the frequently mentioned 'cowardice' of the government armies, manned as they were by conscripts or mercenaries. Wherever necessary, the kinship group provided for medicines, doctors and the burial of the dead; it looked after the old and the widows, and above all it provided the schools. The kinship group owned property, especially landed property (*shih t'ien* or 'ancestral land'[15]), and often, if it was particularly well-to-do, extensive endowed lands. It utilised this by leasing it (usually by auction for three years), but alienation of such land was only permitted with the consent of a three-quarters majority. The revenue was assigned to the heads of households. The typical method was to grant every man and every widow one unit each, those from the age of fifty-nine upward, two units, and from the age of sixty-nine upward, three units. Within the kinship group the principle of hereditary charisma was combined with that of democracy. All married men had equal voting rights; unmarried men could speak in discussion, but had no right to vote; women were excluded both from inheritance (they had only a right to claim a dowry) and from taking part in the deliberations of the group. The elders, chosen annually according to families but by an electorate consist-

---

[13] Hence A. Merx's reading, *mēdena apelpizontes* in place of *mēden apelpizontes* is very plausible: in this case too there is anxiety about 'crying' to God and, in the case of suicide, about the 'spirit' of the desperate man.

[14] Occasions for such feuds were offered by re-allocations of taxes, vendettas and especially by conflicts provoked by the *fêng shui*, or 'geomancers', among neighbours. It will be explained later that every building and, above all, every new grave could injure the spirits of the ancestors already buried in existing graves or agitate the spirits of the rocks, streams, hills and so on. In such cases, it was often almost impossible to settle such feuds because of the geomantic interests involved on both sides.

[15] In the 'Peking Gazette' there is a case, for instance, of the purchase of 2,000 *mou* for 17,000 *taels* (1 *mou* = 5.62 ares). Express mention is made in this case, not only of sacrifices, but also of the relief of widows and orphans and the maintenance of the children's school out of rents (14 December 1883).

ing of all members of the kinship group, functioned as an executive committee which had to collect revenues, utilise property and distribute the income, and most important of all, take care of the sacrifices to the ancestors and the maintenance in proper order of ancestral halls and schools. The outgoing elders proposed the motion of election, according to seniority; in case of refusal, the next in order of seniority was offered the post.

The Caste System in India

WE ARE NOW in a position to enquire into the effects of the caste system on the economy. These effects were essentially negative and must rather be inferred than inductively assessed. Hence we can but phrase a few generalizations. Our sole point is that this order by its nature is completely traditionalistic and anti-rational in its effects. The basis for this, however, must not be sought in the wrong place.

Karl Marx has characterized the peculiar position of the artisan in the Indian village—his dependence upon fixed payment in kind instead of upon production for the market—as the reason for the specific "stability" of the Asiatic peoples. In this, Marx was correct.

In addition to the ancient village artisan, however, there was the merchant and also the urban artisan; and the latter either worked for the market or was economically dependent upon merchant guilds, as in the Occident. India has always been predominantly a country of villages. Yet the beginnings of cities were also modest in the Occident, especially inland, and the position of the urban market in India was regulated by the princes in many ways "mercantilistically"—in a sense similar to the territorial states at the beginnings of modern times. In any case, insofar as social stratification is concerned, not only the position of the village artisan but also the caste order as a whole must be viewed as the bearer of stability. One must not think of this effect too directly. One might believe, for instance, that the ritual caste antagonisms had made impossible the development of "large-scale enterprises" with a division of labor in the same workshop, and might consider this to be decisive. But such is not the case.

The law of caste has proved just as elastic in the face of the necessities of the concentration of labor in workshops as it did in the face of a need for concentration of labor and service in the noble household. All domestic servants required by the upper castes were ritually clean, as we have seen. The principle, "the artisan's hand is always clean in his occupation,"[1] is a similar concession to the necessity of being allowed to have fixtures made or repair work done, personal services, or other work accomplished by wage workers or by itinerants not belonging to the household. Likewise, the workshop[2] (*ergasterion*) was recog-

Reprinted with the permission of The Free Press, a Division of Simon & Schuster, from *The Religion of India* by Max Weber. Translated by Hans H. Gerth and Don Martindale. Copyright © 1950, 1958 by The Free Press; copyright renewed 1980 by The Free Press. This excerpt is taken from pp. 111–14 and 350–51. The text was originally published in 1916–17; see *Gesammelte Aufsätze zur Religionssoziologie*, vol. 2 (1921) (Tübingen: J. C. B. Mohr, 1988), pp. 109–13.

[1] Budhayana's *Sacred Books of the East*, I, 5, 9, i.

[2] Budhayana, I, 5, 9, 3. Mines and workshops except distilleries of alcohol are ritually clean.

nized as "clean." Hence no ritual factor would have stood in the way of jointly using different castes in the same large workroom, just as the ban upon interest during the Middle Ages, as such, hindered little the development of industrial capital, which did not even emerge in the form of investment for fixed interest. The core of the obstacle did not lie in such particular difficulties, which every one of the great religious systems has placed, or has seemed to place, in the way of the modern economy. The core of the obstruction was rather imbedded in the "spirit" of the whole system. In modern times it had not always been easy, but eventually it has been possible to employ Indian caste labor in modern factories. And even earlier it was possible to exploit the labor of Indian artisans capitalistically in the forms usual elsewhere in colonial areas, after the finished mechanism of modern capitalism once could be imported from Europe. Even if all this has come about, it must still be considered extremely unlikely that the modern organization of industrial capitalism would ever have *originated* on the basis of the caste system. A ritual law in which every change of occupation, every change in work technique, may result in ritual degradation is certainly not capable of giving birth to economic and technical revolutions from within itself, or even of facilitating the first germination of capitalism in its midst.

The artisan's traditionalism, great in itself, was necessarily heightened to the extreme by the caste order. Commercial capital, in its attempts to organize industrial labor on the basis of the putting-out system, had to face an essentially stronger resistance in India than in the Occident. The traders themselves in their ritual seclusion remained in the shackles of the typical oriental merchant class, which by itself has never created a modern capitalist organization of labor. This situation is as if none but different guest peoples, like the Jews, ritually exclusive toward one another and toward third parties, were to follow their trades in one economic area. Some of the great Hindu merchant castes, particularly, for instance, the Vania, have been called the "Jews of India," and, in this negative sense, rightly so. They were, in part, virtuosi in unscrupulous profiteering.

Nowadays a considerable tempo in the accumulation of wealth is singularly evident among castes which were formerly considered socially degraded or unclean and which therefore were especially little burdened with (in our sense) "ethical" expectations addressed to themselves. In the accumulation of wealth, such castes compete with others which formerly monopolized the positions of scribes, officials, or collectors of farmed-out taxes, as well as similar opportunities for politically determined earnings typical of patrimonial states. Some of the capitalist entrepreneurs also derive from the merchant castes. But in capitalist enterprise they could keep up with the castes of literati only to the extent to which they acquired the "education" nowadays necessary—as has been occasionally noticed above.[3] The training for trade is among them in part so intense—as far as the reports allow for insight—that their specific "gift" for trad-

---

[3] The relations of the Indian sects and salvation religions to the banking and commercial circles of India are discussed later [in *The Religion of India*, e.g. pp. 193 ff. (RS)].

ing must by no means rest upon any "natural disposition."[4] That ancient castes with strong occupational mobility often drift into occupations whose demands on "natural disposition" form the greatest psychological contrast imaginable to the previous mode of activity, but which stand close to one another through the common usefulness of certain forms of knowledge and aptitudes acquired through training, speaks against imputations of "natural disposition." Thus, the frequent shift, mentioned above, from the ancient caste of surveyors—whose members naturally know the roads particularly well—to the occupation of chauffeur may be referred to among many similar examples. However, in spite of the adaptability of some of the castes we have no indication that by themselves they could have created the rational enterprise of modern capitalism.

Finally, modern capitalism undoubtedly would never have originated from the circles of the completely traditionalist Indian trades. The Hindu artisan, is nevertheless, famous for his extreme industry; he is considered to be essentially more industrious than the Indian artisan of Islamic faith. And, on the whole, the Hindu caste organization has often developed a very great intensity of work and of property accumulation within the ancient occupational castes. The intensity of work holds more for handicraft and for individual ancient agricultural castes. By the way, the Kunbis (for instance, those in South India) achieve a considerable accumulation of wealth, and nowadays, as a matter of fact, it takes modern forms.

Modern industrial capitalism, in particular the factory, made its entry into India under the British administration and with direct and strong incentives. But, comparatively speaking, how small is the scale and how great the difficulties. After several hundred years of English domination there are today only about 980,000 factory workers, that is, about one-third of 1 per cent of the population.[5] In addition, the recruitment of labor is difficult, even in those manufacturing industries with the highest wages. (In Calcutta, labor often has to be recruited from the outside. In one near-by village, hardly one-ninth of the people speak the native language of Bengal.) Only the most recent acts for the protection of labor have made factory work somewhat more popular. Female labor is found only here and there, and then it is recruited from among the most despised castes, although there are textile industries where women can accomplish twice as much as men.

Indian factory labor shows exactly those traditionalist traits which also characterized labor in Europe during the early period of capitalism. The workers want to earn some money quickly in order to establish themselves independently. An increase in wage rate does not mean for them an incentive for more work or for a higher standard of living, but the reverse. They then take longer holidays because they can afford to do so, or their wives decorate themselves with ornaments. To stay away from work as one pleases is recognized as a mat-

---

[4] Cf. Census report for Bengal (1911) concerning the training for commerce among the Baniyas.
[5] These figures are from the 1911 Census.

ter of course, and the worker retires with his meagre savings to his home town as soon as possible.[6] He is simply a mere casual laborer. "Discipline" in the European sense is an unknown idea to him. Hence, despite a fourfold cheaper wage, competition with Europe is maintained easily only in the textile industry, as two-and-a-half times as many workers and far more supervision are required. One advantage for the entrepreneurs is that the caste division of the workers has so far made any trade union organization and any real "strike" impossible. As we have noticed, the work in the workshop is "clean" and is performed jointly. Only separate drinking cups at the well are necessary, at least one for the Hindus and one for the Islamites, and in sleeping quarters only men of the same caste sleep together. A fraternization of labor, however, has (so far) been as little possible as a *conjuratio* (sworn confederation) of the citizens.[7]

[6] V. Delden, *Die Indische Jute-Industrie* (1915), p. 96.
[7] V. Delden, *ibid.*, pp. 114–25.

Charity in Ancient Palestine

ONE CHARACTERISTIC element of the old Israelite ethic, shared with others, requires somewhat closer attention. The ethical prescriptions thus far discussed
[in *Ancient Judaism*—RS] show, in part, striking features of the charity generally characteristic of the present revision of the Torah. Particularly noteworthy
are numerous stipulations for the benefit of the poor, the *metics*, widows and
waifs which are already present in the older collections, but particularly
Deuteronomy. Its god is an incorruptible judge "which regardeth not persons"
and "doth execute the judgment" of the prescriptions mentioned above (Deut.
10:17f.). The formal law of debt bondage was, as noted, supplemented in the
moral exhortation by far-reaching stipulations concerning payment of wages,
debt remission, limitation on pledges, and general charity. The most general formulations of these duties may well be the following: "Thou shalt open thine hand
wide" (Deut. 15:11), and extend aid to the needy, the poor, the robbed (Jer.
22:16), and the oppressed (Is. 1:17). The stipulations, discussed previously, re-
specting gleaning and a fallow year appear to be integrated into this orbit. The
sources allow us to discern the steadily increasing importance of these elements
of moral exhortation parallel with increasing hierocratic influence on the Israelite ethic which was originally by no means sentimental. Whence did this
characteristic originate?

India and Egypt were the two areas where classically charity developed. In
India, Jainism and Buddhism were its preeminent exponents. In general, Indian
charity rested on the conception of all life as a unity. This was reinforced by the
belief in *Samsara*. Indian charity, as expressed also in the Decalogues of the Bud-
dhists, soon adopted a formal and almost purely ritualistic character.

In Egypt charity was strongly influenced by the bureaucratic structure of the
state and the economy. The kings of the "Old" and the "New" Kingdoms, and
the feudal princes of the "Middle" Kingdom employed forced labor and had an
interest in the preservation of the labor power of man and beast. They sought to
protect them against the inconsiderate brutality of the officials and taskmasters.
The Egyptian sources show clearly how strongly this contributed to the development of poor laws.[1] The officials, who were responsible to the king for the

---

Reprinted with the permission of The Free Press, a Division of Simon & Schuster, from *Ancient Judaism* by Max Weber. Translated by Hans H. Gerth and Don Martindale. Copyright © 1952 by The
Free Press; copyright renewed 1980 by The Free Press. This excerpt is taken from pp. 255–63 and
454–55. The text was originally published in 1917–20; see *Gesammelte Aufsätze zur Religionssoziologie*, vol. 3 (1921) (Tübingen: J. C. B. Mohr, 1988), pp. 271–80.

[1] See, for instance, the prohibition against depriving a poor man of his position during his corvée
service for the king (nineteenth Dynasty). Breastead, *Records*, vol. III, p. 51.

economic and demographic condition of the country, were exposed to complaints of the subjects who apparently could address complaints directly to the king. In the inscriptions the officials, even of the Old Kingdom, boast that they gave aid during famine, took no land away from anyone, did not abuse the subordinates of other officials, never settled a dispute dishonestly, neither took away nor raped anybody's daughter, violated no property, did not oppress the widows; or that they fed the hungry, clothed the naked, shipped people who had no boat across the river, filled the stables of their subordinates with cattle.[2] This always refers to the population belonging to the bailiwick entrusted by the Pharaoh to the official.

Generally the officials also express themselves as follows: they "never did evil to anybody," but rather did "what was pleasing to all." Suspicion against and tabooing of gifts for judges is almost as common with the Egyptian religious poets and moralists as with the Israelite prophets. The fear of the king, who, after all, like the Czar in Russia, was far away, was supplemented by the fear of complaints to higher authorities, that is, the gods. A monarch of the fifth dynasty said that he had not harmed anybody so that he "had complained to the god of the city." The curse of the poor was feared, directly because of the possible intervention of the god, indirectly because of the danger to one's good name in posterity, which was quite important to the Egyptian mind. The belief in the magical efficacy of a curse based on an actual wrong was obviously common in the Middle East: hence, also, the last and the poorest could avail himself of this "weapon of democracy."

The Egyptian official, therefore, did not fail to emphasize that the people "loved" him, because he did what pleased them. Any responsibility of the great to the people was possibly still more remote to the Egyptian mind than to the Israelite. Yet an official will be "like god" if his workers trust him, if he treats them "like a crocodile" he will be cursed. Hence, Ptah-hetep's ethic of the genteel scribe emphasizes that the practice of charity will be payed for by the permanence of one's position, originally probably that of the Pharaoh, then that of god. The memorial stones of little men (artisans) of the thirteenth and twelfth centuries find comfort in the hope that Amon usually listens to the voice of the poor in his grief (in contrast to the "impertinent" great man, warrior, official). For God guides and protects all his creatures including fish and birds.[3]

In the earliest inscriptions, the kings behaved exactly like the officials, not only the Egyptian but all Mid-Eastern kings. Besides all sorts of offenses against divine property and the state, according to Urukagina, the harsh oppression of the economically weak has brought God's wrath upon his predecessors and legit-

---

[2] Breastead, *Records*, vol. I, pp. 239, 240, 281, 328 ff., 459, 523. All these inscriptions stem from the time of the Old Kingdom and begin with the first Dynasty.

[3] For documents of Egyptian popular piety of the time of the Rameses, see Erman, *Sitzungs-Berichte der Berliner Akademie der Wissenschaflen*, philosophisch-historische Klasse, vol. II, p. 1086ff. For the growing belief in compensation in the New Kingdom, see Poertner, "Die ägyptischen Totenstelen als Zeugen des sozialen und religiösen Lebens ihrer Zeit", in *Studien zur Geschichte und Kritik des Altertums*, vol. 4, no. 3 (Paderborn, 1911).

imizes his own usurpation. In this case, the reference is to the hardships of the transition to a money economy in the city kingship: to indebtedness and enslavement as in Israel. The usurpers, as noted with Abimelech, always rule with the demos [people—RS] against the great sibs. In Egypt and the later Mesopotamian great kingdoms the usual patrimonial-bureaucratic legend of the welfare state gives its stamp to the meanwhile formalist royal charity. Rameses IV boasts of having harmed no waif and no poor man and of not having taken anybody's hereditary land. Nebuchadnezzar expresses himself similarly. Cyrus presumes that the inordinate taxation of the Babylonian people of Nabunadin caused god's wrath to come upon his king and Darius, in the Behistun inscription, takes his stand likewise on the ground of welfare policy and protectionism for the poor. These policies hence were common to all patrimonial states of the Orient and to the majority of such monarchies. In the direct neighborhood of Israel and here, probably, under Egyptian influence a Phoenician royal inscription (the oldest thus far existing) shows the very same features.[4] These ultimately formalistically rigidified, but therefore not necessarily ineffectual maxims will have probably reached from here the scribes of the kings of Israel.

This charity ethic grew out of the patrimonial welfare policy and its projection into the heavenly rule of the world. In Egypt this ethic appears to have been developed first quite consciously by the petty patrimonial princes and feudal lords of the Middle Kingdom from ever present beginnings. Later it was systematized by the scribes, priests, and priestly influenced moralists in correspondence with the general type of hierocratic welfare policy. The declaration to have coerced no one to work beyond his fixed measure (E. 5) stands at the head of all the detailed assurances which the dead in the 125th chapter of the Book of the Dead has to give in the "hall of truth." The derivation from the corvée administration is obvious. Then follow the assurances to have brought to no one fear, poverty, suffering, misfortune, hunger, mourning, not to have caused a master to abuse his slave (E. 6), not to have withheld milk from the suckling babe, not to have maltreated cattle (E. 9), and not to have harmed the sick (B. 26). At the end of the entire confession (B. 38) stands the assurance of having obliged god by one's "charity" (*mer*), "to having given bread to the hungry, water to the thirsty, clothes to the naked, and a boat to him in want of it." To this must be added the previously mentioned ethical prohibition of inflicting pain upon another or of frightening him, of doing evil to one's neighbor and the prescription of doing good also to one's enemy. The appearance of this prescription in Egyptian ethics seems, however, controversial. In substance these commandments anticipate largely the charity of the Gospels.

Presumably the development of old Israelite charity was influenced by Egypt directly or by way of Phoenicia. This influence was strongest in Deuteronomic times. Even in pre-Deuteronomic times the conviction prevailed that Yahwe protected the weak *per se*, woman against man, the concubine against the wife, the outcast son against the father (Gen. 16:5, 7; 21:14; I. Sam. 24:13). It is to be

---

[4] On Kalumus' inscription, see Littmann, *SBAW*, November 16, 1911, p. 973 ff.

found with the Yahwist as well as the Elohist and had the same religious foundation as the Egyptian conception. The poor and oppressed "cries of Yahwe" (Deut. 24:15) who as heavenly king may take revenge on the oppressor. In Exile the conception came to prevail in Israelite ethic that it was best to suffer oppression because such behavior would insure the revenge of God. At the time it was due to the social impotence of the oppressed classes, but it probably goes back to the significance of one's name which was to become a blessing for the descendants. For the efficacy of the curse negatively corresponds to the blessing of the poor, when treated according to the charity commandments; and it "shall be righteousness unto thee before Yahwe" (Deut. 24:13). Charity was continuously developed in increasingly systematic fashion through the moral exhortation of the Levites; the Shechemite cursing formula, influenced by them; the *debarim,* joined to the Book of the Covenant; and then Deuteronomy and the priestly law.

Despite many striking and hardly accidental similarities, the substantive demands of Israelite charity differed in tenor from Egyptian charity demands. It rested on a priestly influenced community of free peasant and herdsmen sibs, not on a priestly influenced patrimonial bureaucracy, although devout kings, following foreign example in their ethic of the welfare state, were perhaps the first to express these demands. Naturally, in Israel, too, oppressions by royal officials occurred in Egyptian fashion. Even the king might commit acts of oppression which in Egypt was officially impossible. The paradigm of the priestly revision has Yahwe react against this through prophetic pronouncements of doom. The primary evil to be fought was not oppression by a bureaucracy but by an urban patriciate, and conditions were far simpler than in Egypt. The sublimation of charity into ethical absolutism, hence, does not extend as far as in Egypt. Individual prescriptions were more in agreement with the patriarchal nature of the household and neighborhood relations than was the case with the abstractions of Egyptian scribes. Only the pacifistic, urban epoch of the Torah directly prior to and during the Exile produced the abstractions of the Holiness Code. We note the injunction of replacing candid discussion by hatred and vindictiveness against one's "neighbor," that is (Lev. 19:18) against the children of one's people and, according to 19:34, against the *ger.* This is related to the principle: "thou shalt love thy neighbor as thyself" (Lev. 19:18).

This tabooing of vindictiveness might appear to be a reaction to the Levitical exhortation against the promises of some prophets strongly encouraging (political) vindictiveness. The prescription of neighborly love for one's compatriots shows however by the reenforcing addition: "I am the Lord" that this was identical with the frequently repeated prescription to leave vengeance to God (Deut. 32:35). The hope was that God would consummate it the more thoroughly. The leaving of revenge to God has no genuine ethical significance. The prescription originated in the feeling of plebeian and, at that, politically impotent strata. Obviously, the study of David and Nabal (I. Sam. 25:24, 33) was composed as a paradigm for this even more satisfying revenge. The reservation of vengeance for God was for the Torah teachers the natural ethical parallel to abolishing blood revenge in law. The positive command to "love" one's neighbor was for them a transfer of the principles of ancient sib brotherliness to the fellow believer. Only the rabbinical interpretation made of it the positive prescription that one must not even covertly hate and pursue the neighbor with thoughts of revenge. In practice though, even in their own feeling, this proved none too successful.[5]

In Israel, as occasionally in Egyptian charity, protection of those afflicted with disease and infirmities stood alongside the protection of the poor. One shall not curse them "nor put a stumbling block before the blind" or lead them astray (Lev. 19:14). Egyptian charity, too, prescribed aid to those who had gone astray and prohibited harm to the diseased; it did not deal in detail with those afflicted with infirmities. The prophets of hope of the "great kings" usually ascribed to their ruling monarchy the defense against afflictions, disease, and similar misery. In this he proved his charisma. The peculiar saying for David (II. Sam. 5:6, 8) at the conquest of Jerusalem is probably related to the same idea of the miraculous power of a charismatic ruler. In the Levitical Torah, however, one has to locate the reason for the protection of the infirm in the fact that quite a few of them were numbered among the confessants of the Levites and their devoutness was too often experienced to permit unconditional retention of the ancient magical notion that the afflicted were personally hateful to God because of an offense. One could think of him as suffering for the sins of his forebears and with the deaf and the blind the assumption that they were subject to a mysterious divine verdict, could readily lead to the conception that they might also command forces which others lacked, as indicated by the widespread esteem for the blind. To hurt them seemed in any case apt to provoke the wrath of God.

Finally, there are a number of stipulations for the protection of animals to be found in Deuteronomy like the one protecting the mother bird (22:6, 7) and the famous prohibition (25:4) not to "muzzle the ox when he treadeth out the corn," whereas on Roman plantations the slaves at the millstone wore muzzles. To this must be added the evaluation of the Sabbath as a day of rest also for cattle and of the Sabbath year as giving animals the opportunity to feed freely. The Israelite sources do not permit discernment of the extent to which these theological constructions hang together with the ubiquitous Mid-Eastern belief in an original and hoped-for paradisiacal state of peace between man and beast or whether they are related to some sort of ancient ritualistic vegetarianism which perhaps sprang from local agricultural cults, or whether they simply resulted from the commandment of love. Balaam's talking ass was simply an animal of popular fable to be found elsewhere like the prophetic lamb under Bocchoris in Egypt. In Egypt the prohibition against the ill-treatment of cattle probably originally goes back to the interest of the king in its labor power. With Rameses II we find the characteristic promise to the horses having saved him from the battle of Kadesh that they shall be fed, henceforth, in his presence in the palace just as

---

[5] In his polemic against Protestant scholars Büchler presents R. Chanina as a model of Jewish morality. Chanina died wrapped in a Torah scroll, because he believed that way to be better assured of God's vengeance on his tormentors.

he promised his workers correct payment of their wages. This resulted from the typical relation of the rider or stable master to his animals. The priestly systematized, popular animal worship and the ability of the souls of the dead to assume animal forms was hardly the source of this friendly attitude toward animals. But these conceptions naturally promoted charity toward animals.

As its absence in the legend (II. Ki. 4:23) indicates, in Israel the Sabbath rest for cattle, as for slaves, was only a product of late kingly, presumably Deuteronomic times. Possibly the kindness toward animals, at least its general direction, was due to Egyptian influence. All in all it is quite probable that Israelite ethics and charity in late pre-exilic times have been influenced in many details by the example of the great culture areas, especially by Egypt, directly or by way of Phoenicia. The decisive features of this sort of charity have also developed without borrowing wherever priestly interest in physically afflicted or unfortunate patrons was strong enough to promote a rationalization of welfare work for the weak. The Israelite Torah has independently refashioned the commandments even where the assumption of external influence suggests itself.

More important than all individual differences is the previously emphasized fact that magic formed no substitute for fulfillment of the commandments. Egyptian priestly teaching, for instance, might raise ethical or charity commandments of whatever content. What reenforcement could it provide, if simple magical means were at hand allowing the dead to hide his sins in the decisive moment before the judge of the dead? This, indeed, was the case. The plea to one's own heart in the Book of the Dead (ch. 30, L. 1) not to testify against the dead was later reenforced by providing the dead with a consecrated scarabaeus, which enabled the heart to resist the magical power of the judges of the dead and to conceal sins. Hence, one outwitted the gods. Things were not as crass in Babylon. But in neo-Babylonian times, magic of all sorts was the specific, popular means of influencing the invisible powers. With increasing rationalization of the culture feelings of sinfulness became also more intensive in Mesopotamia particularly among the pacifistic bourgeois population. Later, however, the expressive Sumerian and old Babylonian penitential psalms were used purely as magical formulae and often without regard to their meaning. This happened after the evil spirits as cause of all evil in popular belief had taken the place of the great deities. In ancient Yahwism this kind of magic was absent and therefore the once-accepted ethical commandments necessarily had greater practical importance. This was due to the different turn given to the problem of theodicy and to the frequently adduced circumstance that each and every individual in Israel had to fear the vengeance of god if violation of his commandments were tolerated in their very midst. For Israel was an association of free compatriots who, by virtue of *berith*, were jointly responsible for keeping the commandments of the god of the covenant. Hence, in Israel people reacted against sin by means of casting out the unreconciled sinner, by banning and by stoning him.

Capital punishment without mercy was obligatory for certain serious offenders, because it was the one and only means of expurgating the community. This motive was indeed absent in bureaucratic monarchies and especially where professional magicians were present. It is analogous to the responsibility of the early Christian and puritan communion of the Lord's Supper for removing the obvious reprobate from the table of the Lord in contrast to Catholicism, Anglicanism, and Lutheranism. The specific ethical turn of the Levitical Torah was necessarily greatly reenforced by the steady pressure of this interest. The attitude of the Levites, however, originated in relation to their private clientele. Moses' establishment of the ancient *berith* and the assumption of the oracular functions gave the first impetus to all this. Hence to this extent Moses is rightly considered the founder of this important ethical development.

PART IV

Theoretical Aspects of Economic Sociology

Sociological Categories of Economic Action

PREFATORY NOTE

What follows is not intended in any sense to be "economic theory." Rather, it consists only in an attempt to define certain concepts which are frequently used and to analyze certain of the simplest sociological relationships in the economic sphere. As in the first chapter [of *Economy and Society*—RS], the procedure here has been determined entirely by considerations of convenience. It has proved possible entirely to avoid the controversial concept of "value." The usage here, in the relevant sections on the division of labor [see sections 15–21, not reproduced here; *Economy and Society*, pp. 114–37—RS], has deviated from the terminology of Karl Bücher[1] only so far as seemed necessary for the purposes of the present undertaking. For the present all questions of dynamic process will be left out of account.

1. THE CONCEPT OF ECONOMIC ACTION

Action will be said to be "economically oriented" so far as, according to its subjective meaning, it is concerned with the satisfaction of a desire for "utilities" (*Nutzleistungen*). "Economic action" (*Wirtschaften*) is any peaceful exercise of an actor's control over resources which is in its main impulse oriented towards economic ends. "Rational economic action" requires instrumental rationality in this orientation, that is, deliberate planning. We will call autocephalous[2] economic action an "economy" (*Wirtschaft*), and an organized system of continuous economic action an "economic establishment" (*Wirtschaftsbetrieb*).

Reprinted by permission of the Regents of the University of California and the University of California Press from chapter 2 of *Economy and Society* ("Sociological Categories of Economic Action"). See *Economy and Society: An Outline of Interpretive Sociology* (1922) (Berkeley: University of California Press, 1978), pp. 63–75, 82–100, 107–13, 161–66, 202–6. Translated by A. M. Henderson and Talcott Parsons. The text was originally published in 1921; see *Wirtschaft und Gesellschaft: Grundriss der verstehenden Soziologie* (1921) (Tübingen: J. C. B. Mohr, 1972), pp. 31–37, 43–53, 58–62, 94–97, 119–21.

[1] Karl Bücher (1847–1930), a well-known German economic historian, was the author of the popular *Industrial Evolution* (1893; translated into English 1901). Bücher contributed to Weber's handbook of economics, *Grundriss der Sozialökonomik* (RS).

[2] "Autocephalous means that the chief and his staff are selected according to the autonomous order of the organization itself." Weber, *Economy and Society*, p. 50 (RS).

1. It was pointed out above that economic action as such need not be social action.[3]

2. The definition of economic action must be as general as possible and must bring out the fact that all "economic" processes and objects are characterized as such entirely by the *meaning* they have for human action in such roles as ends, means, obstacles, and by-products. It is not, however, permissible to express this by saying, as is sometimes done, that economic action is a "psychic" phenomenon. The production of goods, prices, or even the "subjective valuation" of goods, if they are empirical processes, are far from being merely psychic phenomena.[4] But underlying this misleading phrase is a correct insight. It is a fact that these phenomena have a peculiar type of subjective *meaning*. This alone defines the unity of the corresponding processes, and this alone makes them accessible to subjective interpretation.

The definition of "economic action" must, furthermore, be formulated in such a way as to include the operation of a modern business enterprise run for profit. Hence the definition cannot be based directly on "consumption needs" and the "satisfaction" of these needs, but must rather, start out on the one hand from the fact that there is a *desire* (demand) for utilities (which is true even in the case of orientation to purely monetary gains), and on the other hand from the fact that *provision* is being made to furnish the supplies to meet this demand (which is true even in the most primitive economy merely "satisfying needs," and regardless of how primitive and frozen in tradition the methods of this provision are).

3. As distinguished from "economic action" as such, the term "economically oriented action" will be applied to two types: (a) every action which, though primarily oriented to other ends, takes account, in the pursuit of them, of economic considerations; that is, of the consciously recognized necessity for economic prudence. Or (b) that which, though primarily oriented to economic ends, makes use of physical force as a means. It thus includes all primarily non-economic action and all non-peaceful action which is influenced by economic considerations. "Economic action" thus is a *conscious, primary* orientation to economic considerations. It must be conscious, for what matters is not the objective necessity of making economic provision, but the belief that is is necessary. Robert Liefmann[5] has rightly laid emphasis on the subjective understandable orientation of action which makes it economic action. He is not, however, correct in attributing the contrary view to all other authors.[6]

4. Every type of action, including the use of violence, may be economically

---

[3] The reference is to chapter 1, section 1:B of *Economy and Society*, where Weber defines social action as action that is oriented to the behavior of others. Weber also points out that all economic actions are not social: "the economic activity of an individual is social only if it takes account of the behavior of someone else" (p. 22) (RS).

[4] For an elaboration of this point, see "Marginal Utility Analysis and 'The Fundamental Law of Psychophysics'" (reading 18 in this anthology) (RS).

[5] Robert Liefmann (1874–1941), German economist (RS).

[6] Robert Liefmann, *Grundsätze der Volkswirtschaftslehre* (Stuttgart 1917), Vol. 1, pp. 24 ff., 109 ff., 118 ff., 287 ff., 299 ff.

oriented. This is true, for instance, of war-like action, such as marauding expeditions and trade wars. Franz Oppenheimer,[7] in particular, has rightly distinguished "economic" means from "political" means.[8] It is essential to distinguish the latter from economic action. The use of force is unquestionably very strongly opposed to the spirit of economic acquisition in the usual sense. Hence the term "economic action" will not be applied to the direct appropriation of goods by force and the direct coercion of the other party by threats of force. It goes without saying, at the same time, that exchange is not the *only* economic means, though it is one of the most important. Furthermore, the formally peaceful provision for the means and the success of a projected exercise of force, as in the case of armament production and economic organization for war, is just as much economic action as any other.

Every rational course of political action is economically oriented with respect to provision for the necessary means, and it is always possible for political action to serve the interest of economic ends. Similarly, though it is not necessarily true of every economy, certainly the modern economic order under modern conditions could not continue if its control of resources were not upheld by the legal compulsion of the state; that is, if its formally "legal" rights were not upheld by the threat of force. But the fact that an economy thus dependent on protection by force, does not mean that it is itself an example of the use of force.

How entirely untenable it is to maintain that the economy, however defined, is only a *means,* by contrast, for instance, with the state, becomes evident from the fact that it is possible to define the state itself only in terms of the means which it today monopolizes, namely, the use of force. If anything, the most essential aspect of economic action for practical purposes is the prudent choice *between ends.* This choice is, however, oriented to the scarcity of the means which are available or could be procured for these various ends.

5. Not every type of action which is rational in its choice of means will be called "rational economic action," or even "economic action" in any sense; in particular, the term "economy" will be distinguished from that of "technology."[9] The "technique" of an action refers to the means employed as opposed to the meaning or end to which the action is, in the last analysis, oriented. "Rational" technique is a choice of means which is consciously and systematically oriented to the experience and reflection of the actor, which consists, at the highest level of rationality, in scientific knowledge. What is concretely to be treated as a "technique" is thus variable. The ultimate meaning of a concrete act may, seen in the total context of action, be of a "technical" order, that is, it may be significant only as a means in this broader context. Then the "meaning" of the concrete act (viewed from the larger context) lies in its technical function; and, conversely, the means which are applied in order to accomplish this are its "techniques." In

---

[7] Franz Oppenheimer (1864–1953), German economist and sociologist (RS).

[8] See, e.g., Franz Oppenheimer, *The State* (Indianapolis: Bobbs-Merrill, 1914), pp. 24–27 (RS).

[9] The German word *Technik* which Weber uses here covers both the meanings of the English word "technique" and of "technology". Since the distinction is not explicitly made in Weber's terminology, it will have to be introduced according to the context in the translation. (Note by Parsons.)

this sense there are techniques of every conceivable type of action, techniques of prayer, of asceticism, of thought and research, of memorizing, of education, or exercising political or hierocratic domination, of administration, of making love, of making war, of musical performances, of sculpture and painting, of arriving at legal decisions. All these are capable of the widest variation in degree of rationality. The presence of a "technical question" always means that there is some doubt over the choice of the most rational *means* to an end. Among others, the standard of rationality for a technique may be the famous principle of "least effort," the achievement of an optimum *in the relation* between the result and the means to be expended on it (and not the attainment of a result with the *absolute* minimum of means). Seemingly the same principle, of course, applies to economic action—or to any type of rational action. But there it has a different *meaning*. As long as the action is purely "technical" in the present sense, it is oriented only to the selection of the means which, with equal quality, certainty, and permanence of the result, are comparatively most "economical" of effort in the attainment of a *given* end; comparatively, that is, insofar as there are at all directly comparable expenditures of means in different methods of achieving the end. The end itself is accepted as beyond question, and a purely technical consideration ignores other wants. Thus, in a question of whether to make a technically necessary part of a machine out of iron or platinum, a decision on technical grounds alone would, so long as the requisite quantities of both metals for their particular purpose were available, consider only which of the two would in this case best bring about the given result and would at the same time minimize the other comparable expenditure of resources, such as labor. But once consideration is extended to take account of the relative scarcity of iron and platinum in relation to their potential uses, as today every technician is accustomed to do even in the chemical laboratory, the action is no longer in the present sense purely technical, but *also* economic. From the economic point of view, "technical" questions always involve the consideration of "costs." This is a question of crucial importance for economic purposes and in this context always takes the form of asking what would be the effect on the satisfaction of other wants if this particular means were not used for satisfaction of one given want. The "other wants" may be qualitatively different present wants or qualitatively identical future wants. (A similar position is taken by Friedrich von Gottl-Ottlilienfeld[10] in [Book I, Part I of—RS] *Grundriss der Sozialökonomik* [Tübingen 1914]; an extensive and very good discussion of this issue in R. Liefmann, *Grundsätze der Volkswirtschaftslehre*, vol. I [1917], p. 334 ff. Any attempt to reduce all means to "ultimate expenditures of labor" is erroneous.)

For the answer to the question, what is, in comparative terms, the "cost" of using various means for a given technical end, depends in the last analysis on their potential usefulness as means to other ends. This is particularly true of labor. A *technical* problem in the present sense is, for instance, that of what equipment is necessary in order to move loads of a particular kind or in order to

---

[10] Friedrich von Gottl-Ottlilienfeld (1868–1958), German economist. Gottl contributed to Weber's handbook of economics, *Grundriss der Sozialökonomik* (RS).

raise mineral products from a given depth in a mine, and which of the alternatives is the most "suited," that is, among other things, which achieves a given degree of success with the least expenditure of effort. It is, on the other hand, an
economic problem whether, on the assumption of a market economy, these expenditures will pay off in terms of money obtained through the sale of the goods;
or, on the assumption of a planned economy, whether the necessary labor and
other means of production can be provided without damage to the satisfaction
of other wants held to be more urgent. In both cases, it is a problem of the comparison of *ends*. Economic action is primarily oriented to the problem of choosing the *end* to which a thing shall be applied; technology, to the problem, given
the end, of choosing the appropriate *means*. For purposes of the theoretical (not,
of course, the practical) definition of technical rationality it is wholly indifferent
whether the product of a technical process is in any sense useful. In the present
terminology we can conceive of a rational technique for achieving ends which
no one desires. It would, for instance, be possible, as a kind of technical amuse-
ment, to apply all the most modern methods to the production of atmospheric
air. And no one could take the slightest exception to the purely technical rationality of the action. Economically, on the other hand, the procedure would under
normal circumstances be clearly irrational because there would be no demand
for the product. (On all this, compare v. Gottl-Ottlilienfeld, *op. cit.*)

The fact that what is called the technological development of modern times
has been so largely oriented economically to profit-making is one of the fundamental facts of the history of technology. But however fundamental it has been,
this economic orientation has by no means stood alone in shaping the development of technology. In addition, a part has been played by the games and cogi-
tations of impractical ideologists, a part by other-worldly interests and all sorts
of fantasies, a part by preoccupation with artistic problems, and by various other
non-economic motives. None the less, the main emphasis at all times, and especially the present, has lain in the economic determination of technological development. Had not rational calculation formed the basis of economic activity,
had there not been certain very particular conditions in its economic background, rational technology could never have come into existence.

The fact that the aspects of economic orientation which distinguish it from
technology were not explicitly brought into the initial definition, is a consequence of the sociological starting point. From a sociological point of view, the
weighing of alternative ends in relation to each other and to costs is a consequence of "continuity." This is true at least so far as costs mean something other
than altogether giving up one end in favor of more urgent ones. An economic
theory, on the other hand, would do well to emphasize this criterion from the
start.

6. It is essential to include the criterion of power of control and disposal (*Verfügungsgewalt*)[11] in the sociological concept of economic action, if for no other
reason than that at least a modern market economy (*Erwerbswirtschaft*) essen-

---

[11] Power of control and disposal exists in the market, according to Weber, while there is domination (*Herrschaft*) inside most economic organizations (RS).

tially consists in a complete network of exchange contracts, that is, in deliberate planned acquisitions of powers of control and disposal. This, in such an economy, is the principal source of the relation of economic action to the law. But any other type of organization of economic activities would involve some kind of *de facto* distribution of powers of control and disposal, however different its underlying principles might be from those of the modern private enterprise economy with its legal protection of such powers held by autonomous and autocephalous economic units. Either the central authority, as in the case of socialism, or the subsidiary parts, as in anarchism, must be able to count on having some kind of control over the necessary services of labor and of the means of production. It is possible to obscure this fact by verbal devices, but it cannot be interpreted out of existence. For purposes of definition it is a matter of indifference in what way this control is guaranteed; whether by convention or by law, or whether it does not even enjoy the protection of any external sanctions at all, but its security rests only on actual expectations in terms of custom or self-interest. These possibilities must be taken into account, however essential legal compulsion may be for the modern economic order. The indispensability of powers of control for the concept of social action in its economic aspects thus does not imply that *legal* order is part of that concept by definition, however important it may be held to be on empirical grounds.

7. The concept of powers of control and disposal will here be taken to include the possibility of control over the actor's own labor power, whether this is in some way enforced or merely exists in fact. That this is not to be taken for granted is shown by its absence in the case of slaves.

8. It is necessary for the purposes of a sociological theory of the economy to introduce the concept of "goods" at an early stage, as is done in section 2. For this theory is concerned with a type of action which is given its specific *meaning* by the *results* of the actors' deliberations, which themselves can be isolated only in theory. Economic theory, the theoretical insights of which provide the basis for economic sociology (*Wirtschaftssoziologie*), might (perhaps) be able to proceed differently; the latter may find it necessary to create its own theoretical constructs.

2. The Concept of Utility

By "utilities" (*Nutzleistungen*) will always be meant the specific and concrete, real or imagined, opportunities (*Chancen*) for present or future use as they are estimated and made an object of specific provision by one or more economically acting individuals. The action of these individuals is oriented to the estimated importance of such utilities as means for the ends of their economic action.

Utilities may be the services of non-human or inanimate objects or of human beings. Non-human objects which are the sources of potential utilities of whatever sort will be called "goods." Utilities derived from a human source, so far as this source consists in active conduct, will be called "services" (*Leistungen*). Social relationships which are valued as a potential source of present or future disposal over utilities are, however, also objects of economic provision. The opportunities in this respect, which are made available by custom, by the constellation of interest, or by a conventional or legal order for the purposes of an economic unit, will be called "economic opportunities."

On the following comments, compare E. von Böhm-Bawerk, *Rechte und Verhältnisse vom Standpunkt der volkswirtschaftlichen Güterlehre* (Innsbruck 1881).[12]

1. The categories of goods and services do not exhaust those aspects of the environment which may be important to an individual for economic purposes and which may hence be an object of economic concern. Such things as "good will," or the tolerance of economic measures on the part of individuals in a position to interfere with them, and numerous other forms of behavior, may have the same kind of economic importance and may be the object of economic provision and, for instance, of contracts. It would, however, result in a confusion of concepts to try to bring such things under either of these two categories. This choice of concepts is thus entirely determined by consideration of convenience.

2. As Böhm-Bawerk has correctly pointed out, it would be equally imprecise if all *concrete* objects of life and of everyday speech were without distinction designated as "goods," and the concept of a good were then equated to that of a material utility. In the strict sense of utility, it is not a "horse" or a "bar of iron" which is an economic "good," but the specific ways in which they can be put to desirable and practical uses, for instance the power to haul loads or to carry weights, or something of the sort. Nor can we, in the present terminology, call *goods* such potential future opportunities (*Chancen*) which appear as objects of exchange in economic transactions, as "good will," "mortgage," "property." Instead, for simplicity's sake, we shall call the services of such potential powers of control and disposal over the utilities of goods and services, promised or guaranteed by the traditional or legal order, "economic opportunities" (*Chancen*) or simply "advantages" wherever this is not likely to be misunderstood.

3. The fact that only active conduct, and not mere acquiescence, permission, or omission, are treated as "services" is a matter of convenience. But it must be remembered that it follows from this that goods and services do not constitute an exhaustive classification of all economically significant utilities.

On the concept of "labor," see below, section 15 [not reproduced here; see *Economy and Society*, pp. 114–18—RS].

3. MODES OF THE ECONOMIC ORIENTATION OF ACTION

Economic orientation may be a matter of tradition or of goal-oriented rationality. Even in cases where there is a high degree of rationalization of action, the

---

[12] Eugen von Böhm-Bawerk (1851–1914), famous member of the founding generation of the Austrian school of economics. The work Weber refers to has been translated as "Whether Legal Rights and Relationships are Economic Goods", pp. 25–138 in *Shorter Classics of Eugen von Böhm-Bawerk* (South Holland, Ill.: Libertarian Press, 1962) (RS).

element of traditional orientation remains considerable. For the most part, rational orientation is primarily significant for "managerial" action, no matter under what form of organization. (See below, section 15 [not reproduced here; see *Economy and Society*, pp. 114–18—RS].) The development of rational economic action from the instinctively reactive search for food or traditional acceptance of inherited techniques and customary social relationships has been to a large extent determined by non-economic events and actions, including those outside everyday routine, and also by the pressure of necessity in cases of increasing absolute or relative limitations on subsistence.

1. Naturally there cannot in principle be any scientific standard for any such concept as that of an "original economic state." It would be possible to agree arbitrarily to take the economic state on a given technological level, as, for instance, that characterized by the lowest development of tools and equipment known to us, and to treat it and analyze it as the most primitive. But there is no scientific justification for concluding from observations of living primitive peoples on a low technological level that the economic organization of all peoples of the past with similar technological standing has been the same as, for instance, that of the Vedda or of certain tribes of the Amazon region. For, from a purely economic point of view, this level of technology has been just as compatible with large-scale organization of labor as with extreme dispersal in small groups (see section 16 [not reproduced here; see *Economy and Society*, pp. 118–20—RS]). It is impossible to infer from the economic aspects of the natural environment alone, which of these would be more nearly approached. Various non-economic factors, for instance, military, could make a substantial difference.

2. War and migration are not in themselves economic processes, though particularly in early times they have been largely oriented to economic considerations. At all times, however, indeed up to the present, they have often been responsible for radical changes in the economic system. In cases where, through such factors as climatic changes, inroads of sand, or deforestation, there has been an absolute decrease in the means of subsistence, human groups have adapted themselves in widely differing ways, depending on the structure of interests and on the manner in which non-economic factors have played a role. The typical reactions, however, have been a fall in the standard of living and an absolute decrease in population. Similarly, in cases of relative impoverishment in means of subsistence, as determined by a given standard of living and of the distribution of opportunities for acquisition, there have also been wide variations [see below, section 11—RS]. But on the whole, this type of situation has, more frequently than the other, been met by the increasing rationalization of economic activities. Even in this case, however, it is not possible to make general statements. So far as the "statistical" information can be relied upon, there was a tremendous increase of population in China after the beginning of the eighteenth century, but it had exactly the opposite effect from the similar phenomenon of about the same time in Europe. It is, however, possible to say at least something about the reasons for this. The chronic scarcity of the means of subsistence in the Arabian

desert has only at certain times resulted in a change in the economic and political structure, and these changes have been most prominent when non-
economic (religious) developments have played a part.

3. A high degree of traditionalism in habits of life, such as characterized the
laboring classes in early modern times, has not prevented a great increase in the
rationalization of economic enterprise under capitalistic direction. But it was
also compatible with, for instance, the rationalization of public finances in Egypt
on a state-socialistic model. Nevertheless, this traditionalist attitude had to be at
least partly overcome in the Western World before the further development to
the specifically modern type of rational capitalistic economy could take place.

4. TYPICAL MEASURES OF RATIONAL ECONOMIC ACTION

The following are typical measures of rational economic action:

(1) The systematic allocation between present and future utilities, on the control of which the actor for whatever reason feels able to count. (These are the
essential features of saving.)

(2) The systematic allocation of available utilities to various potential uses in
the order of their estimated relative urgency, ranked according to the principle
of marginal utility.

These two cases, the most definitely "static," have been most highly developed
in times of peace. Today, for the most part, they take the form of the allocation
of money incomes.

(3) The systematic procurement through production or transportation of
such utilities for which all the necessary means of production are controlled by
the actor himself. Where action is rational, this type of action will take place so
far as, according to the actor's estimate, the urgency of his demand for the expected result of the action exceeds the necessary expenditure, which may consist in (a) the irksomeness of the requisite labor services, and (b) the other potential uses to which the requisite goods could be put; including, that is, the
utility of the potential alternative products and their uses. This is "production"
in the broader sense, which includes transportation.

(4) The systematic acquisition, by agreement (*Vergesellschaftung*) with the
present possessors or with competing bidders, of assured powers of control and
disposal over utilities. The powers of control may or may not be shared with others. The occasion may lie in the fact that utilities themselves are in the control
of others, that their means of procurement are in such control, or that third persons desire to acquire them in such a way as to endanger the actor's own supply.

The relevant rational association with the present possessor of a power of control or disposal may consist in (a) the establishment of an organization with an
order to which the procurement and use of utilities is to be oriented, or (b) in
exchange. In the first case the purpose of the organization may be to ration the
procurement, use, or consumption, in order to limit competition of procuring
actors. Then it is a "regulative organization." Or, secondly, its purpose may be to

set up a unified authority for the systematic administration of the utilities which had hitherto been subject to a dispersed control. In this case there is an "administrative organization."

"Exchange" is a compromise of interests on the part of the parties in the course of which goods or other advantages are passed as reciprocal compensation. The exchange may be traditional or conventional, and hence, especially in the latter case, not economically rational. Or, secondly, it may be economically rational both in intention and in result. Every case of a rationally oriented exchange is the resolution of a previously open or latent conflict of interests by means of a compromise. The opposition of interests which is resolved in the compromise involves the actor potentially in two different conflicts. On the one hand, there is the conflict over the price to be agreed upon with the partner in exchange; the typical method is bargaining. On the other hand, there may also be competition with actual or potential rivals, either in the present or in the future, who are competitors in the same market. Here, the typical method is competitive bidding and offering.

1. Utilities, and the goods or labor which are their sources, are under the control of an economically acting individual (*Eigenverfügung*) if he is in a position to be able in fact to make use of them at his convenience (at least, up to a point) without interference from other persons, regardless of whether this ability rests on the legal order, on convention, on custom or on a complex of interests. It is by no means true that only the legal assurance of powers of disposal is decisive, either for the concept or in fact. It is, however, today empirically an indispensable basis for economic activity with the *material* means of production.

2. The fact that goods are not as yet consumable may be a result of the fact that while they are, as such, finished, they are not yet in a suitable place for consumption; hence the transportation of goods, which is naturally to be distinguished from trade, a change in the control over the goods, may here be treated as part of the process of production.

3. When there is a lack of control over desired utilities, it is in principle indifferent whether the individual is typically prevented from forcibly interfering with the control of others by a legal order, convention, custom, his own self-interest, or his consciously-held moral standards.

4. Competition in procurement may exist under the most various conditions. It is particularly important when supplies are obtained by seizure, as in hunting, fishing, lumbering, pasturage, and clearing new land. It may also, and most frequently does, exist within an organization which is closed to outsiders. An order which seeks to restrain such competition then always consists in the rationing of supplies, usually combined with the appropriation of the procurement possibilities thus guaranteed for the benefit of a limited number of individuals or, more often, households. All medieval *Mark* and fishing associations, the regulation of forest clearing, pasturage and wood gathering rights in the common fields and wastes, the grazing rights on Alpine meadows, and so on, have this character.

Various types of hereditary property-rights in land owe their development to this type of regulation.

5. Anything which may in any way be transferred from the control of one person to that of another and for which another is willing to give compensation, may be an object of exchange. It is not restricted to goods and services, but includes all kinds of potential economic opportunities; for instance, "good will," which exists only by custom or self-interest and cannot be enforced; in particular, however, it includes all manner of opportunities, claims to which are enforceable under some kind of order. Thus objects of exchange are not necessarily presently existing utilities.

For present purposes, by "exchange" in the broadest sense will be meant every case of a formally voluntary agreement involving the offer of any sort of present, continuing, or future utility in exchange for utilities of any sort offered in return. Thus it includes the turning over of the utility of goods or money in exchange for the future return of the same kind of goods. It also includes any sort of permission for, or tolerance of, the use of an object in return for "rent" or "hire," or the hiring of any kind of services for wages or salary. The fact that the last example today involves, from a sociological point of view, the subjection of the "worker," as defined in section 15 below [not reproduced here; see *Economy and Society*, pp. 114–18—RS], under a form of domination will, for preliminary purposes, be neglected, as will the distinction between loan and purchase.

6. The conditions of exchange may be traditional, partly traditional though enforced by convention, or rational. Examples of conventional exchanges are exchanges of gifts between friends, heroes, chiefs, princes; as, for instance, the exchange of armor between Diomedes and Glaucus.[13] It is not uncommon for these to be rationally oriented and controlled to a high degree, as can be seen in the Tell el-Amarna documents.[14] Rational exchange is only possible when both parties expect to profit from it, or when one is under compulsion because of his own need or the other's economic power. Exchange may serve either purposes of consumption or of acquisition (see below, section 11). It may thus be oriented to provision for the personal use of the actor or to opportunities for profit. In the first case, its conditions are to a large extent differentiated from case to case, and it is in *this* sense irrational. Thus, for instance, household surpluses will be valued according to the individual marginal utilities of the particular household economy and may on occasion be sold very cheaply, and the fortuitous desires of the moment may establish the marginal utility of goods which are sought in exchange at a very high level. Thus the exchange ratios, as determined by marginal utility, will fluctuate widely. Rational competition develops only in the case of "marketable goods" (see section 8) and, to the highest degree, when goods are used and sold in a profit system (see section 11).

---

[13] According to Greek legend, Glaucus took part in the Trojan War and when he found himself opposed in combat to his friend Diomedes, they stopped fighting and exchanged armor (RS).

[14] The reference is to the famous cuneiform tablets discovered in 1887 at Tell el-Amarna in Egypt (RS).

7. The modes of intervention of a regulatory system mentioned above under point (4) are not the only possible ones, but merely those which are relevant here because they are the most immediate consequences of a tightening of the supply basis. The regulation of marketing processes will be discussed below.

5. TYPES OF ECONOMIC ORGANIZATIONS

According to its relation to the economy, an economically oriented organization may be: (a) an "economically active organization" (*wirtschaftender Verband*) if the primarily non-economic organized action oriented to its order includes economic action; (b) an "economic organization" (*Wirtschaftsverband*) if its organized action, as governed by the order, is *primarily* autocephalous[15] economic action of a given kind; (c) an "economically regulative organization" (*wirtschafts-regulierender Verband*) if the autocephalous economic activity of the members is directly oriented to the order governing the group; that is, if economic action is heteronomous in that respect; (d) an "organization enforcing a formal order" (*Ordnungsverband*) if its order merely guarantees, by means of formal rules, the autocephalous and autonomous economic activities of its members and the corresponding economic advantages thus acquired.[16]

1. The state, except for the socialistic or communist type, and all other organizations like churches and voluntary associations are economically active groups if they manage their own financial affairs. This is also true of educational institutions and all other organizations which are not primarily economic.

2. In the category of "economic organizations" in the present sense are included not only business corporations, co-operative associations, cartels, partnerships, and so on, but all permanent economic establishments (*Betriebe*) which involve the activities of a plurality of persons, all the way from a workshop run by two artisans to a conceivable communistic organization of the whole world.

3. "Economically regulative organizations" are the following: medieval village associations, guilds, trade unions, employers' associations, cartels, and all other groups, the directing authorities of which carry on an "economic policy" which seeks to regulate both the ends and the procedures of economic activity. It thus includes the villages and towns of the Middle Ages, just as much as a modern state which follows such a policy.

4. An example of a group confined to the "enforcement of a formal order" is the pure laissez-faire state, which would leave the economic activity of individ-

---

[15] "Autocephalous means that the chief and his staff are selected according to the autonomous order of the organization itself, not, as in the case of heterocephaly, that they are appointed by outsiders." Weber, *Economy and Society,* p. 50 (RS).

[16] An organization in general (*Verband*) is defined in chapter 1 of *Economy and Society* as follows: "A social relationship which is either closed or limits the admission of outsiders will be called an organization (*Verband*) when its regulations are enforced by specific individuals: a chief and, possibly, an administrative staff, which normally also has representative powers" (p. 48).

ual households and enterprises entirely free and confine its regulation to the formal function of settling disputes connected with the fulfillment of free contractual obligations.

5. The existence of organizations "regulating economic activity" or merely "enforcing a formal order" presupposes in principle a certain amount of autonomy in the field of economic activity. Thus there is in principle a domain of free disposal over economic resources, though it may be limited in varying degrees by means of rules to which the actors are oriented. This implies, further, the (at least relative) appropriation of economic opportunities, over which the actors then have autonomous control. The purest type of a group "enforcing a formal order" is thus present when all *human* action is autonomous with respect to content, and oriented to regulation only with respect to form, and when all *non-human* sources of utility are completely appropriated so that individuals can have free disposal of them, in particular by exchange, as is the case in a modern property system. Any other kind of limitation on appropriation and autonomy implies "regulation of economic activity," because it restricts the orientation of human activities.

6. The dividing line between "regulation of economic activity" and mere "enforcement of a formal order" is vague. For, naturally, the type of "formal" order not only may, but must, in some way also exert a material influence on action; in some cases, a fundamental influence. Numerous modern legal ordinances, which claim to do no more than set up formal rules, are so drawn up that they actually exert a material influence (see the section on the sociology of law[17]). Indeed, a really strict limitation to purely formal rules is possible only in theory. Many of the recognized "overriding" principles of law, of a kind which cannot be dispensed with, imply to an appreciable degree important limitations on the content of economic activity. Especially "enabling provisions" can under certain circumstances, as in corporate law, involve quite appreciable limitations on economic autonomy.

7. The limits of the material regulation of economic activity may be reached when it results in (a) the abandonment of certain kinds of economic activity, as when a tax on turnover leads to the cultivation of land only for consumption; or (b) in evasion, in such cases as smuggling, bootlegging, etc. . . .

. . .

8. THE MARKET

By the "market situation" (*Marktlage*) for any object of exchange is meant all the opportunities of exchanging it for money which are known to the participants in exchange relationships and aid their orientation in the competitive price struggle.

[17] A final version of Weber's planned section on the sociology of law for *Economy and Society* was never produced. For an early version that was found among his papers, however, see *Economy and Society*, pp. 641–900 (RS).

"Marketability" (*Marktgängigkeit*) is the degree of regularity with which an object tends to be an object of exchange on the market.

"Market freedom" is the degree of autonomy enjoyed by the parties to market relationships in the price struggle and in competition.

"Regulation of the market," on the contrary, is the state of affairs where there is a substantive restriction, effectively enforced by the provisions of an order, on the marketability of certain potential objects of exchange or on the market freedom of certain participants. Regulation of the market may be determined (1) traditionally, by the actors' becoming accustomed to traditionally accepted limitations on exchange or to traditional conditions; (2) by convention, through social disapproval of treating certain utilities as marketable or of subjecting certain objects of exchange to free competition and free price determination, in general or when undertaken by certain groups of persons; (3) by law, through legal restrictions on exchange or on the freedom of competition, in general or for particular groups of persons or for particular objects of exchange. Legal regulations may take the form of influencing the market situation of objects of exchange by price regulation, or of limiting the possession, acquisition, or exchange of rights of control and disposal over certain goods to certain specific groups of persons, as in the case of legally guaranteed monopolies or of legal limitations on economic action. (4) By voluntary action arising from the structure of interests. In this case there is substantive regulation of the market, though the market remains formally free. This type of regulation tends to develop when certain participants in the market are, by virtue of the totally or approximately exclusive control of the possession of or opportunities to acquire certain utilities—that is, of their monopolistic powers—in a position to influence the market situation in such a way as actually to abolish the market freedom of others. In particular, they may make agreements with each other and with typical exchange partners for regulating market conditions. Typical examples are market quota agreements and price cartels.

1. It is convenient, though not necessary, to confine the term "market situation" to cases of exchange for money, because it is only then that uniform numerical statements of relationships become possible. Opportunities for exchange *in kind* are best described simply as "exchange opportunities." Different kinds of goods are and have been marketable in widely different and variable degrees, even where a money economy was well developed. The details cannot be gone into here. In general, articles produced in standardized form in large quantities and widely consumed have been the most marketable; unusual goods, only occasionally in demand, the least. Durable consumption goods which can be used up over long periods and means of production with a long or indefinite life, above all, agricultural and forest land, have been marketable to a much less degree than finished goods of everyday use or means of production which are quickly used up, which can be used only once, or which give quick returns.

2. Rationality of the regulation of markets has been historically associated with the growth of formal market freedom and the extension of marketability of goods. The original modes of market regulation have been various, partly tradi-

tional and magical, partly dictated by kinship relations, by status privileges, by military needs, by welfare policies, and not least by the interests and requirements of the governing authorities of organizations. But in each of these cases the dominant interests have not been primarily concerned with maximizing the opportunities of acquisition and economic provision of the participants in the market themselves; have, indeed, often been in conflict with them. (1) Sometimes the effect has been to exclude certain objects from market dealings, either permanently or for a time. This has happened in the magical case, by taboo; in that of kinship, by the entailing of landed property; on the basis of social status, as with knightly fiefs. In times of famine the sale of grain has been temporarily prohibited. In other cases permission to sell has been made conditional on a prior offer of the good to certain persons, such as kinsmen, co-members of the status group, of the guild, or of the town association; or the sale has been limited by maximum prices, as is common in war time, or by minimum prices. Thus, in the interests of their status dignity magicians, lawyers, or physicians may not be allowed to accept fees below a certain minimum. (2) Sometimes certain categories of persons, such as members of the nobility, peasants, or sometimes even artisans, have been excluded from market trade in general or with respect to certain commodities. (3) Sometimes the market freedom of consumers has been restricted by regulations, as by the sumptuary laws regulating the consumption of different status groups, or by rationing in case of war or famine. (4) Another type is the restriction of the market freedom of potential competitors in the interest of the market position of certain groups, such as the professions or the guilds. Finally, (5) certain economic opportunities have been reserved to the political authorities (royal monopolies) or to those holding a charter from such authorities. This was typical for the early capitalistic monopolies.

Of all these, the fifth type of market regulation had the highest "market-rationality," and the first the lowest. By "rationality" we here mean a force which promotes the orientation of the economic activity of strata interested in purchase and sale of goods on the market to the market situations. The other types of regulation fit in between these two with respect to their rationality-impeding effect. The groups which, relative to these forms of regulation, have been most interested in the freedom of the market, have been those whose interest lay in the greatest possible extension of the marketability of goods, whether from the point of view of availability for consumption, or of ready opportunities for sale. Voluntary market regulation first appeared extensively and permanently only on behalf of highly developed profit-making interests. With a view to the securing of monopolistic interests, this could take several forms: (1) the pure regulation of opportunities for purchase and sale, which is typical of the widespread phenomena of trading monopolies; (2) the regulation of transportation facilities, as in shipping and railway monopolies; (3) the monopolization of the production of certain goods; and (4) that of the extension of credit and of financing. The last two types generally are accompanied by an increase in the regulation of economic activity by organizations. But unlike the primitive, irrational forms of regulation, this is apt to be oriented in a methodical manner to the market situation. The starting point of voluntary market regulation has in general been the

fact that certain groups with a far-reaching degree of actual control over economic resources have been in a position to take advantage of the formal freedom of the market to establish monopolies. Voluntary associations of consumers,
such as consumers' co-operatives, have, on the other hand, tended to originate
among those who were in an economically weak position. They have hence often
been able to accomplish savings for their members, but only occasionally and
limited to particular localities have they been able to establish an effective system of market regulation.

9. Formal and Substantive Rationality of Economic Action

The term "formal rationality of economic action" will be used to designate the
extent of quantitative calculation or accounting which is technically possible and
which is actually applied. The "substantive rationality," on the other hand, is the
degree to which the provisioning of given groups of persons (no matter how delimited) with goods is shaped by economically oriented social action under some
criterion (past, present, or potential) of ultimate values, regardless of the nature
of these ends. These may be of a great variety.

1. The terminology suggested above is thought of merely as a means of securing greater consistency in the use of the word "rational" in this field. It is actually only a more precise form of the meanings which are continually recurring
in the discussion of "nationalization" and of the economic calculus in money and
in kind.[18]

2. A system of economic activity will be called "formally" rational according
to the degree in which the provision for needs, which is essential to every rational economy, is capable of being expressed in numerical, calculable terms, and
is so expressed. In the first instance, it is quite independent of the technical form
these calculations take, particularly whether estimates are expressed in money
or in kind. The concept is thus unambiguous, at least in the sense that expression in money terms yields the highest degree of formal calculability. Naturally,
even this is true only relatively, so long as other things are equal.

3. The concept of "substantive rationality," on the other hand, is full of am-
biguities. It conveys only one element common to all "substantive" analyses:
namely, that they do not restrict themselves to note the purely formal and (relatively) unambiguous fact that action is based on "goal-oriented" rational calculation with the technically most adequate available methods, but apply certain
criteria of ultimate ends, whether they be ethical, political, utilitarian, hedonistic, feudal, egalitarian, or whatever, and measure the results of the economic action, however formally "rational" in the sense of correct calculation they may be,
against these scales of "value rationality" or "*substantive* goal rationality." There
is an infinite number of possible value scales for this type of rationality, of which

---

[18] Weber is here referring to a political discussion in Germany just after World War I (RS).

the socialist and communist standards constitute only one group. The latter, although by no means unambiguous in themselves, always involve elements of social justice and equality. Others are criteria of status distinction, or of the capacity for power, especially of the war capacity, of a political unit; all these and many others are of potential "substantive" significance. These points of view are, however, significant only as bases from which to judge the *outcome* of economic action. In addition and quite independently, it is possible to judge from an ethical, ascetic, or esthetic point of view the *mentality* of economic activity as well as the *instruments* of economic activity. All of these approaches may consider the "purely formal" rationality of calculation in monetary terms as of quite secondary importance or even as fundamentally inimical to their respective ultimate ends, even before anything has been said about the consequences of the specifically modern calculating attitude. There is no question in this discussion of attempting value judgments in this field, but only of determining and delimiting what is to be called "formal." In this context the concept "substantive" is itself in a certain sense "formal"; that is, it is an abstract, generic concept.

10. THE RATIONALITY OF MONETARY ACCOUNTING. MANAGEMENT AND BUDGETING

From a purely technical point of view, money is the most "perfect" means of economic calculation. That is, it is formally the most rational means of orienting economic activity. Calculation in terms of money, and not its actual use, is thus the specific means of rational, economic provision. So far as it is completely rational, money accounting has the following primary consequences:

(1) The valuation of all the means of achieving a productive purpose in terms of the present or expected market situation. This includes everything which is needed at present or is expected to be needed in the future; everything actually in the actor's control, which he may come to control or may acquire by exchange from the control of others; everything lost, or in danger of damage or destruction; all types of utilities, of means of production, or any other sort of economic opportunity.

(2) The quantitative statement of (a) the expected advantages of every projected course of economic action and (b) the actual results of every completed action, in the form of an account comparing money costs and money returns and the estimated net profit to be gained from alternatives of action.

(3) A periodical comparison of all the goods and other assets controlled by an economic unit at a given time with those controlled at the beginning of a period, both in terms of money.

(4) An *ex-ante* estimate and an *ex-post* verification of receipts and expenditures, either those in money itself, or those which can be valued in money, which the economic unit is likely to have available for its use during a period if it maintains the money value of the means at its disposal intact.

(5) The orientation of consumption to these data by the utilization of the

money available (on the basis of point 4) during the accounting period for the acquisition of the requisite utilities in accordance with the principle of marginal utility.

The continual utilization and procurement of goods, whether through production or exchange, by an economic unit for purposes of its own *consumption* or to procure other goods for *consumption* will be called "budgetary management" (*Haushalt*).[19] Where rationality exists, its basis for an individual or for a group economically oriented in this way is the "budget" (*Haushaltsplan*), which states systematically in what way the needs expected for an accounting period— needs for utilities or for means of procurement to obtain them—can be covered by the anticipated income.

The "income" (*Einkommen*) of a "budgetary unit" is the total of goods valued in money, which, as estimated according to the principle stated above in point (4), has been available during a previous period or on the availability of which the unit is likely to be able to count on the basis of a rational estimate for the present or for a future period. The total estimated value of the goods at the disposal of a budgetary unit which are normally utilized over a longer period, either directly or as a source of income, will be called its "wealth" (*Vermögen*).[20] The possibility of complete monetary budgeting for the budgetary unit is dependent on the possibility that its income and wealth consist either in money or in goods which are at any time subject to exchange for money; that is, which are in the highest degree marketable.

A rational type of management and budgeting of a budgetary unit is possible also where calculation is carried out in terms of physical units, as will be further discussed below. It is true that in that case there is no such thing as "wealth" capable of being expressed in a single sum of money, nor is there a single "income" in the same sense. Calculation is in terms of "holdings" of concrete goods and, where acquisition is limited to peaceful means, of concrete "receipts" from the expenditure of available real goods and services, which will be administered with a view to attaining the optimum provision for the satisfaction of wants. If the wants are strictly given, this involves a comparatively simple problem from the technical point of view so long as the situation does not require a very precise estimate of the comparative utility to be gained from the allocation of the available resources to each of a large number of very heterogeneous modes of use. If the situation is markedly different, even the simple self-sufficient household is faced with problems which are only to a very limited degree subject to a formally exact solution by calculation. The actual solution is usually found partly by the application of purely traditional standards, partly by making very rough estimates, which, however, may be quite adequate where both the wants concerned and the conditions of provision for them are well known and readily comparable. When the "holdings" consist in heterogeneous goods, as must be the

---

[19] An alternative translation would be "householding." The opposite of *Haushalt* is profit-making (*Erwerben*), which will be discussed in the next section (RS).

[20] The opposite of wealth is capital (*Kapital*), just as the opposite of budgetary management is profit-making (RS).

case in the absence of exchange, a formally exact calculable comparison of the state of holdings at the beginning and the end of a period, or of the comparison of different possible ways of securing receipts, is possible only for categories of goods which are qualitatively identical. The typical result is that all available goods are treated as forming a totality of physical holdings, and certain quantities of goods are treated as available for consumption, so long as it appears that this will not in the long run diminish the available resources. But every change in the conditions of production—as, for instance, through a bad harvest—or any change in wants necessitates a new allocation, since it alters the scale of relative marginal utilities. Under conditions which are simple and adequately understood, this adaptation may be carried out without much difficulty. Otherwise, it is technically more difficult than if money terms could be used, in which case any change in the price situation in principle influences the satisfaction only of the wants which are marginal on the scale of relative urgency and are met with the last increments of money income.

As calculation in kind becomes completely rational and is emancipated from tradition, the estimation of marginal utilities in terms of the relative urgency of wants encounters grave complications; whereas, if it were carried out in terms of monetary wealth and income, it would be relatively simple. In the latter case the question is merely a "marginal" one, namely whether to apply *more* labor or whether to satisfy or sacrifice, as the case may be, one or more wants, rather than others. For when the problems of budgetary management are expressed in money terms, this is the form the "costs" take. But if calculations are in physical terms, it becomes necessary to take into account, besides the scale of urgency of the wants, also (1) the alternative modes of utilization of *all* means of production, including the *entire* amount of labor hitherto expended, which means different (according to the mode of utilization) and variable ratios between want satisfaction and the expenditure of resources, and therefore, (2), requires a consideration of the volume and type of *additional* labor which the householder would have to expend to secure additional receipts and, (3), of the mode of utilization of the material expenditures if the goods to be procured can be of various types. It is one of the most important tasks of economic theory to analyse the various possible ways in which these evaluations can be rationally carried out. It is, on the other hand, a task for economic history to pursue the ways in which the budgetary management in physical terms has been actually worked out in the course of various historical epochs. In general, the following may be said: (1) that the degree of formal rationality has, generally speaking, fallen short of the level which was even empirically possible, to say nothing of the theoretical maximum. As a matter of necessity, the calculations of money-less budgetary management have in the great majority of cases remained strongly bound to tradition. (2) In the later units of this type, precisely because an expansion and refinement of everyday wants has not taken place, there has been a tendency to employ surpluses for uses of a non-routine nature—above all, for artistic purposes. This is an important basis for the artistic, strongly stylized cultures of epochs with a "natural economy."

1. The category of "wealth" includes more than physical goods. Rather, it covers *all* economic opportunities over which the budgetary unit has an assured control, whether that control is due to custom, to the play of interests, to convention, or to law. The "good will" of a profit-making organization, whether it be a medical or legal practice, or a retail shop, belongs to the "wealth" of the owner if it is, for whatever reason, relatively stable since, if it is legally appropriated, it can constitute "property" in the terms of the definition in chapter 1, section 10.[21]

2. Monetary calculation can exist without the actual use of money or with its use limited to the settlement of balances which cannot be paid in kind in the goods being exchanged on both sides. Evidence of this is common in the Egyptian and Babylonian records. The use of money accounting as a measure for payments in kind is found in Hammurabi's Code and in provincial Roman and early Medieval law in the permission that a debtor may pay an amount due expressed in money "in whatever form he will be able" (*in quo potuerit*). The establishment of equivalents must in such cases have been carried out on the basis of traditional prices or of prices laid down by decree.

3. Apart from this, the above discussion contains only commonplaces, which are introduced to facilitate the formation of a precise concept of the rational budgetary unit as distinguished from that of a rational profit-making enterprise—the latter will be discussed presently. It is important to state explicitly that both can take rational forms. The satisfaction of needs is not something more "primitive" than profit-seeking, "wealth" is not necessarily a more primitive category than capital; "income," than profit. It is, however, true that historically the budgetary unit has been prior and has been the dominant form in most periods of the past.

4. It is indifferent what unit is the bearer of a budgetary management economy. Both the budget of a state and the family budget of a worker fall under the same category.

5. Empirically the administration of budgetary units and profit-making are not mutually exclusive alternatives. The business of a consumers' cooperative, for instance, is normally oriented to the economical provision for wants; but in the form of its activity, it is a "profit-making organization" without being oriented to profit as a substantive end. In the action of an individual, the two elements may be so intimately intertwined, and in the past have typically been so, that only the concluding act—namely, the sale or the consumption of the product—can serve as a basis for interpreting the meaning of the action. This has been particularly true of small peasants. Exchange may well be a part of the process of budgetary management where it is a matter of acquiring consumption goods by exchange and of disposing of surpluses. On the other hand, the budgetary economy of a prince or a landed lord may include profit-making enterprises in the sense of the following discussion. This has been true on a large scale in earlier times.

---

[21] Weber here refers to his definition of property in *Economy and Society* as the right to economic opportunities from which others are excluded (p. 44) (RS).

Whole industries have developed out of the heterocephalous[22] and heteronomous auxiliary enterprises which seigneurial landowners, monasteries, princes, etc., have established to exploit the products of their lands and forests. All sorts of profit-making enterprises today are part of the economy of such budgetary units as local authorities or even states. In these cases it is legitimate to include in the "income" of the budgetary units, if they are rationally administered, only the net profits of these enterprises. Conversely, it is possible for profit-making enterprises to establish various types of heteronomous budgetary units under their direction for such purposes as providing subsistence for slaves or wage workers—among them are "welfare" organizations, housing and eating facilities. Net profits in the sense of point (2) of this section are money surpluses after the deduction of all money costs.

6. It has been possible here to give only the most elementary starting points for analysing the significance of economic calculations in kind for general social development.

11. The Concept and Types of Profit-Making. The Role of Capital

"Profit-making" (*Erwerben*) is activity which is oriented to opportunities for seeking new powers of control over goods on a single occasion, repeatedly, or continuously. "Profit-making activity" is activity which is oriented at least in part to opportunities of profit-making. Profit-making is "economic" if it is oriented to acquisition by peaceful methods. It may be oriented to the exploitation of market situations. "Means of profit-making" are those goods and other economic advantages which are used in the interests of economic profit-making. "Exchange for profit" is that which is oriented to market situations in order to increase control over goods rather than to secure means for consumption (budgetary exchange). "Business credit" is that credit which is extended or taken up as a means of increasing control over the requisites of profit-making activity.

There is a form of monetary accounting which is peculiar to rational economic profit-making; namely, "capital accounting." Capital accounting is the valuation and verification of opportunities for profit and of the success of profit-making activity by means of a valuation of the total assets (goods and money) of the enterprise at the beginning of a profit-making venture, and the comparison of this with a similar valuation of the assets still present and newly acquired, at the end of the process; in the case of a profit-making organization operating continuously, the same is done for an accounting period. In either case a balance is drawn between the initial and final states of the assets. "Capital" is the money value of the means of profit-making available to the enterprise at the balancing of the books; "profit" (*Gewinn*) and correspondingly "loss" (*Verlust*), the differ-

[22] See note 15.

ence between the initial balance and that drawn at the conclusion of the period. "Capital risk" is the estimated probability of a loss in this balance. An economic "enterprise" (*Unternehmen*) is autonomous action capable of orientation to capital accounting. This orientation takes place by means of "calculation": *ex-ante* calculation of the probable risks and chances of profit, *ex-post* calculation for the verification of the actual profit or loss resulting. "Profitability" means, in the rational case, one of two things: (1) the profit estimated as possible by *ex-ante* calculations, the attainment of which is made an objective of the entrepreneur's activity; or (2) that which the *ex-post* calculation shows actually to have been earned in a given period, and which is available for the consumption uses of the entrepreneur without prejudice to his chances of future profitability. In both cases it is usually expressed in ratios—today, percentages—in relation to the capital of the initial balance.

Enterprises based on capital accounting may be oriented to the exploitation of opportunities of acquisition afforded by the market, or they may be oriented toward other opportunities of acquisition, such as those based on power relations, as in the case of tax farming or the sale of offices.

Each individual operation undertaken by a rational profit-making enterprise is oriented to estimated profitability by means of calculation. In the case of profit-making activities on the market, capital accounting requires: (1) that there exist, subject to estimate beforehand, adequately extensive and assured opportunities for sale of the goods which the enterprise procures; that is, normally, a high degree of marketability; (2) that the means of carrying on the enterprise, such as the potential means of production and the services of labor, are also available in the market at costs which can be estimated with an adequate degree of certainty; and finally, (3) that the technical and legal conditions, to which the process from the acquisition of the means of production to final sale, including transport, manufacturing operations, storage, etc., is subjected, give rise to money costs which in principle are calculable.

The extraordinary importance of the highest possible degree of calculability as the basis for efficient capital accounting will be noted time and again throughout the discussion of the sociological conditions of economic activity. It is far from the case that only economic factors are important to it. On the contrary, it will be shown that the most varied sorts of external and subjective barriers account for the fact that capital accounting has arisen as a basic form of economic calculation only in the Western World.

As distinguished from the calculations appropriate to a budgetary unit, the capital accounting and calculation of the market entrepreneur are oriented not to marginal utility, but to profitability. To be sure, the opportunities of profit are in the last analysis dependent on the income of consumption units and, through this, on the marginal utility structure of the disposable money incomes of the final consumers of consumption goods. As it is usually put, it depends on their "purchasing power" for the relevant commodities. But from a technical point of view, the accounting calculations of a profit-making enterprise and of a consumption unit differ as fundamentally as do the ends of want satisfaction and of

CATEGORIES OF ECONOMIC ACTION

profit-making which they serve. For purposes of economic theory, it is the marginal *consumer* who determines the direction of production. In actual fact, given the actual distribution of power, this is only true in a limited sense for the modern situation. To a large degree, even though the consumer has to be in a position to buy, his wants are "awakened" and "directed" by the entrepreneur.

In a market economy every form of rational calculation, especially of capital accounting, is oriented to expectations of prices (*Preischancen*) and their changes as they are determined by the conflicts of interests in bargaining and competition and the resolution of these conflicts. In profitability-accounting this is made particularly clear in that system of bookkeeping which is (up to now) the most highly developed one from a technical point of view, in the so-called double-entry bookkeeping. Through a system of individual accounts the fiction is here created that different departments within an enterprise, or individual accounts, conduct exchange operations with each other, thus permitting a check in the technically most perfect manner on the profitability of each individual step or measure.

Capital accounting in its formally most rational shape thus presupposes the *battle of man with man*. And this in turn involves a further very specific condition. No economy can directly translate subjective "feeling of need" into effective demand, that is, into demand which needs to be taken into account and satisfied through the production of goods. For whether or not a subjective want can be satisfied depends, on the one hand, on its place in the scale of relative urgency; on the other hand, on the goods which are estimated to be actually or potentially available for its satisfaction. Satisfaction does not take place if the utilities needed for it are applied to other more urgent uses, or if they either cannot be procured at all, or only by such sacrifices of labor and goods that future wants, which are still, from a present point of view, adjudged more urgent, could not be satisfied. This is true of consumption in every kind of economy including a communist one.

In an economy which makes use of capital accounting and which is thus characterized by the appropriation of the means of production by individual units, that is by "property" (see chapter 1, section 10),[23] profitability depends on the prices which the "consumers," according to the marginal utility of money in relation to their income, can and will pay. It is possible to produce profitably only for those consumers who, in these terms, have sufficient income. A need may fail to be satisfied not only when an individual's own demand for other goods takes precedence, but also when the greater purchasing power of others for *all* types of goods prevails. Thus the fact that the battle of man against man on the market is an essential condition for the existence of rational money-accounting further implies that the outcome of the economic process is decisively influenced by the ability of persons who are more plentifully supplied with money to outbid the others, and of those more favorably situated for production to un-

<hr>

[23] Weber here refers to his definition of property in *Economy and Society* as the right to economic opportunities from which others are excluded (p. 44) (RS).

derbid their rivals on the selling side. The latter are particularly those well supplied with goods essential to production or with money. In particular, rational money-accounting presupposes the existence of effective prices and not merely of fictitious prices conventionally employed for technical accounting purposes. This, in turn, presupposes money functioning as an effective medium of exchange, which is in demand as such, not mere tokens used as purely technical accounting units. Thus the orientation of action to money prices and to profit has the following consequences: (1) that the differences in the distribution of money or marketable goods between the individual parties in the market is decisive in determining the direction taken by the production of goods, so far as it is carried on by profit-making enterprises, in that it is only demand made effective through the possession of purchasing power which is and can be satisfied. Further, (2) the question, what type of demand is to be satisfied by the production of goods, becomes in turn dependent on the profitability of production itself. Profitability is indeed *formally* a rational category, but for that very reason it is indifferent with respect to *substantive* postulates unless these can make themselves felt in the market in the form of sufficient purchasing power.

"Capital goods," as distinguished from mere possessions or parts of wealth of a budgetary unit, are all such goods as are administered on the basis of capital accounting. "Capital interest," as distinct from various other possible kinds of interest on loans, is: (1) what is estimated to be the minimum normal profitability of the use of material means of profit-making; (2) the rate of interest at which profit-making enterprises can obtain money or capital goods.

This exposition only repeats generally known things in a somewhat more precise form. For the technical aspects of capital accounting, compare the standard textbooks of accountancy, which are, in part, excellent. E.g. those of Leitner, Schär, etc.[24]

1. The concept of capital has been defined strictly with reference to the individual private enterprise and in accordance with private business-accounting practice, which was, indeed, the most convenient method for present purposes. This usage is much less in conflict with everyday speech than with the usage which in the past was frequently found in the social sciences and which has by no means been consistent. In order to test the usefulness of the present business-accounting term, which is now being increasingly employed in scientific writings again, it is necessary only to ask the following questions: (1) What does it mean when we say that a corporation has a "basic capital" (net worth) of one million marks? And (2), what when we say that capital is "written down"? What, (3), when corporation law prescribes what objects may be "brought in" as capital and in what manner? The first statement means that only that part of a surplus of assets over liabilities, as shown on the balance-sheet after proper inventory control and

---

[24] See e.g. Friedrich Leitner, *Die doppelte kaufmännische Buchhaltung* (Berlin: Reimer, 1919) and Johann Friedrich Schär, *Buchhaltung und Bilanz* (Berlin: Julius Springer, 1919). Leitner (1874–1945) contributed to Weber's *Grundriss der Sozialökonomik* (RS).

verification, which *exceeds* one million marks can be accounted as "profit" and distributed to the share-holders to do with as they please (or, in the case of a one-man enterprise, that only this excess can be consumed in the household). The second statement concerns a situation where there have been heavy business losses, and means that the distribution of profit need not be postponed until perhaps after many years a surplus exceeding one million marks has again been accumulated, but that the distribution of "profits" may begin at a lower surplus. But in order to do this, it is necessary to "write down" the capital, and this is the purpose of the operation. Finally, the purpose of prescriptions as to how basic capital (net worth, or ownership) can be "covered" through the bringing into the company of material assets, and how it may be "written up" or "written down," is to give creditors and purchasers of shares the guarantee that the distribution of profits will be carried out "correctly" in accordance with the rules of rational-business accounting, i.e., in such a way that (a) long-run profitability is maintained and, (b), that the security of creditors is not impaired. The rules about "bringing in" are all concerned with the admissability and valuation of objects as paid-in capital. (4) What does it mean when we say that as a result of unprofitability capital "seeks different investments"? Either we are talking about "wealth," for "investment" (*Anlegen*) is a category of the administration of wealth, not of profit-making enterprise. Or else, more rarely, it may mean that real capital *goods* on the one hand have ceased to be such by being sold, for instance as scrap or junk, and on the other have regained that quality in other uses. (5) What is meant when we speak of the "power of capital"? We mean that the possessors of control over the means of production and over economic advantages which can be used as capital *goods* in a profit-making enterprise enjoy, by virtue of this control and of the orientation of economic action to the principles of capitalistic business calculation, a specific position of power in relation to others.

In the earliest beginnings of rational profit-making activity capital appears, though not under this name, and only as a sum of money used in accounting. Thus in the *commenda* relationship various types of goods were entrusted to a travelling merchant to sell in a foreign market and at times for the purchase of other goods wanted for sale at home. The profit or loss was then divided in a particular proportion between the travelling merchant and the entrepreneur who had advanced the capital. For this to take place it was necessary to value the goods in money; that is, to strike balances at the beginning and the conclusion of the venture. The "capital" of the *commenda* or the *societas maris* was simply this money valuation, which served only the purpose of settling accounts between the parties and no other.

What do we mean by the term "capital market"? We mean that certain "goods," including in particular money, are in demand in order to be used as capital goods, and that there exist profit-making enterprises, especially certain types of "banks," which derive their profit from the business of providing these goods. In the case of so-called "loan capital," which consists in handing over money against a promise to return the same amount at a later time with or without the addition of interest, the term "capital" will be used only if lending is the object of a profit-making enterprise. Otherwise, the term "money loans" will be used. Everyday speech tends to talk about "capital" whenever "interest" is paid, because the latter is usually expressed as a percentage of the basic sum; only because of this calculatory function is the amount of a loan or a deposit called a "capital." It is true, of course, that this was the origin of the term: *capitale* was the principal sum of a loan; the term is said, though it cannot be proved, to derive from the heads counted in a loan of cattle. But this is irrelevant. Even in very early times a loan of real goods was reckoned in money terms, on which basic interest was then calculated, so that already here capital goods and capital accounting are typically related, as has been true in later times. In the case of an ordinary loan, which is made simply as a phase in the administration of budgetary wealth and so far as it is employed for the needs of a budgetary unit, the term "loan capital" will not be used. The same, of course, applies to the recipient of the loan.

The concept of an "enterprise" is in accord with the ordinary usage, except for the fact that the orientation to capital accounting, which is usually taken for granted, is made explicit. This is done in order to emphasize that not every case of search for profit as such constitutes an "enterprise," but only when it is capable of orientation to capital accounting, regardless of whether it is on a large or a small scale. At the same time it is indifferent whether this capital accounting is in fact rationally carried out according to rational principles. Similarly the terms "profit" and "loss" will be used only as applying to enterprises oriented to capital accounting. The money earned without the use of capital by such persons as authors, physicians, lawyers, civil servants, professors, clerks, technicians, or workers, naturally is also "acquisition" (*Erwerb*), but shall here not be called "profit." Even everyday usage would not call it profit. "Profitability" is a concept which is applicable to every discrete act which can be individually evaluated in terms of business accounting technique with respect to profit and loss, such as the employment of a particular worker, the purchase of a new machine, the determination of rest periods in the working day, etc.

It is not expedient in defining the concept of interest on capital to start with contracted interest returns on any type of loan. If somebody helps out a peasant by giving him seed and demands an increment on its return, or if the same is done in the case of money loaned to a household to be returned with interest, we would hardly want to call this a "capitalistic" process. It is possible, where action is rational, for the lender to secure an additional amount because his creditor is in a position to expect benefits from the use of the loan greater than the amount of the interest he pays; when, that is, the situation is seen in terms of what it would be if he had to do without the loan. Similarly, the lender, being aware of the situation, is in a position to exploit it, in that for him the marginal utility of his present control over the goods he lends is exceeded by the marginal utility at the relevant future time of the repayment with the addition of the interest. These are essentially categories of the administration of budgetary units and their wealth, not of capital accounting. Even a person who secures an emergency loan for his urgent personal needs from a "Shylock" is not for purposes of the present discussion said to be paying interest on capital, nor does the lender receive such interest. It is rather a case of return for the loan. The person who makes a business of lending charges *himself* interest on his business capital if he acts rationally, and must consider that he has suffered a "loss" if the returns from loans do not cover this rate of profitability. *This* interest we will consider "interest on capital"; the former is simply "interest." Thus for the present terminological purposes, interest on capital is always that which is calculated *on* capital, not that which is a payment *for* capital. It is always oriented to money valuations, and thus to the sociological fact that disposal over profit-making means, whether through the market or not, is in private hands; that is, appropriated. Without this, capital accounting, and thus calculation of interest, would be unthinkable.

In a rational profit-making enterprise, the interest, which is charged on the books to a capital sum, is the minimum of profitability. It is in terms of whether or not this minimum is reached that a judgment of the advisability of this particular mode of use of capital goods is arrived at. Advisability in this context is naturally conceived from the point of view of profitability. The rate for this minimum profitability is, it is well known, only approximately that which it is possible to obtain by giving credit on the capital market at the time. But nevertheless, the existence of the capital market is the reason why calculations are made on this basis, just as the existence of market exchange is the basis for making entries against the different accounts. It is one of the fundamental phenomena of a capitalistic economy that entrepreneurs are permanently willing to pay interest for loan capital. This phenomenon can only be explained by understanding how it is that the average entrepreneur may hope in the long run to earn a profit, or that entrepreneurs on the average in fact do earn it, over and above what they have to pay as interest on loan capital—that is, under what conditions it is, on the average, rational to exchange 100 at the present against 100 *plus* X in the future.

Economic theory approaches this problem in terms of the relative marginal utilities of goods under present and under future control. So far, so good. But the sociologist would then like to know in what human *actions* this supposed relation is reflected in such a manner that the actors can take the consequences of this differential valuation [of present and future goods], in the form of an "interest rate," as a criterion for their own operations. For it is by no means obvious that this should happen at all times and places. It does indeed happen, as we know, in profit-making economic units. But here the primary cause is the economic power distribution between profit-making enterprises and budgetary units (households), both those consuming the goods offered and those offering certain means of production (mainly labor). Profit-making enterprises will be founded and operated continuously (capitalistically) *only if* it is expected that the minimum rate of interest on capital can be earned. Economic theory—which could, however, also be developed along very different lines—might then very well say that this exploitation of the power distribution (which itself is a consequence of the institution of private property in goods and the means of production) permits it only to this particular class of economic actors to conduct their operations in accordance with the "interest" criterion.

2. The administration of budgetary "wealth" and profit-making enterprises may be outwardly so similar as to appear identical. They are in fact in the analysis only distinguishable in terms of the difference in *meaningful* orientation of the corresponding economic activities. In the one case, it is oriented to maintaining and improving profitability and the market position of the enterprise; in the other, to the security and increase of wealth and income. It is, however, by no means necessary that this fundamental orientation should always, in a concrete case, be turned exclusively in one direction or the other; sometimes, indeed, this is impossible. In cases where the private wealth of an entrepreneur is identical with this business control over the means of production of his firm and his private income is identical with the profit of the business, the two things seem to go entirely hand in hand. But all manner of personal considerations may in such a case cause the entrepreneur to enter upon business policies which, in terms of the rationality of the conduct of enterprise, are irrational. Yet very generally private wealth and control of the business are not identical. Furthermore, such factors as personal indebtedness of the proprietor, his personal demand for a higher present income, division of an inheritance, and the like, often exert what is, in terms of business considerations, a highly irrational influence on the business. Such situations often lead to measures intended to eliminate these influences altogether, as in the incorporation of family businesses.

The tendency to separate the sphere of private affairs from the business is thus not fortuitous. It is a consequence of the fact that, from the point of view of business interest, the interest in maintaining the private wealth of the owner is often irrational, as is his interest in income receipts at any given time from the point of view of the profitability of the enterprise. Considerations relevant to the profitability of a business are also not identical with those governing the private interests of persons who are related to it as workers or as consumers. Conversely, the interests growing out of the private fortunes and income of persons or organizations having powers of control over an enterprise do not necessarily lie in the same direction as the long-run considerations of optimizing its profitability and its market power position. This is definitely, even especially, also true when a profit-making enterprise is controlled by a producers' co-operative association. The objective interests of rational management of a business enterprise and the personal interest of the individuals who control it are by no means identical and are often opposed. This fact implies the separation as a matter of principle of the budgetary unit and the enterprise, even where both, with respect to powers of control and the objects controlled, are identical.

The sharp distinction between the budgetary unit and the profit-making enterprise should also be clearly brought out in the terminology. The purchase of securities on the part of a private investor who wishes to consume the proceeds is not a "*capital*-investment," but a "*wealth*-investment." A money loan made by a private individual for obtaining the interest is, when regarded from the standpoint of the lender, entirely different from one made by a bank to the same borrower. On the other hand, a loan made to a consumer and one to an entrepreneur for business purposes are quite different from the point of view of the borrower. The bank is investing *capital* and the entrepreneur is borrowing *capital;* but in the first case, it may be for the borrower a matter simply of borrowing for purposes of budgetary management; in the second it may be, for the lender, a case of investment of private *wealth*. This distinction between private wealth and capital, between the budgetary unit and the profit-making enterprise, is of far-reaching importance. In particular, without it it is impossible to understand the economic development of the ancient world and the limitations on the development of the capitalism of those times. (The well-known articles of Rodbertus are, in spite of their errors and incompleteness, still important in this context, but should be supplemented by the excellent discussion of Karl Bücher.)[25]

3. By no means all profit-making enterprises with capital accounting are doubly oriented to the market in that they both purchase means of production on the market and sell their product or final services there. Tax farming and all sorts of financial operations have been carried on with capital accounting, but without selling any products. The very important consequences of this will be discussed later. It is a case of capitalistic profit-making which is not oriented to the market.

4. For reasons of convenience, acquisitive activity (*Erwerbstätigkeit*) and profit-making enterprise (*Erwerbsbetrieb*) have been distinguished. Anyone is engaged in acquisitive activity so far as he seeks, among other things, in given ways to acquire goods—money or others—which he does not yet possess. This includes the civil servant and the worker, no less than the entrepreneur. But the term "profit-making enterprise" will be confined to those types of acquisitive activity which are continually oriented to market advantages, using goods as means to secure profit, either (a) through the production and sale of goods in demand, or (b) through the offer of services in demand in exchange for money, be it through free exchange or through the exploitation of appropriated advantages, as has been pointed out above under (3). The person who is a mere rentier or investor of private wealth is, in the present terminology, not engaged in profit-making, no matter how rationally he administers his resources.

5. It goes without saying that in terms of *economic* theory the direction in which goods can be profitably produced by profit-making enterprises is determined by the marginal utilities for the last consumers in conjunction with the latter's incomes. But from a *sociological* point of view it should not be forgotten that, to a large extent, in a capitalistic economy (a) new wants are created and others allowed to disappear and (b) capitalistic enterprises, through their aggressive advertising policies, exercise an important influence on the demand functions of consumers. Indeed, these are essential traits of a capitalistic economy. It is true that this applies primarily to wants which are not of the highest

---

[25] The articles by Karl Rodbertus can be found in vols. 2, 4, 5, and 6 (1864–67) of *Jahrbücher für Nationalökonomie und Statistik*. See also Karl Bücher, *Industrial Evolution* (New York: Holt, 1901), pp. 89–90, 143–44. Karl Rodbertus (1805–1875) was a German economist and economic historian (RS).

degree of necessity, but even types of food provision and housing are importantly determined by the producers in a capitalistic economy. . . .

. . .

13. SUBSTANTIVE CONDITIONS OF FORMAL RATIONALITY IN A MONEY ECONOMY

It is thus clear that the formal rationality of money calculation is dependent on certain quite specific substantive conditions. Those which are of a particular sociological importance for present purposes are the following: (1) Market struggle of economic units which are at least relatively autonomous. Money prices are the product of conflicts of interest and of compromises; they thus result from power constellations. Money is not a mere "voucher for unspecified utilities," which could be altered at will without any fundamental effect on the character of the price system as a struggle of man against man. "Money" is, rather, primarily a weapon in this struggle, and prices are expressions of the struggle; they are instruments of calculation only as estimated quantifications of relative chances in this struggle of interests. (2) Money accounting attains the highest level of rationality, as an instrument of calculatory orientation of economic action, when it is applied in the form of capital accounting. The substantive precondition here is a thorough market freedom, that is, the absence of monopolies, both of the imposed and economically irrational and of the voluntary and economically rational (i.e., market-oriented) varieties. The competitive struggle for customers, which is associated with this state, gives rise to a great volume of expenditures, especially with regard to the organization of sales and advertising, which in the absence of competition—in a planned economy or under complete monopolization—would not have to be incurred. Strict capital accounting is further associated with the social phenomena of "shop discipline" and appropriation of the means of production, and that means: with the existence of a "system of domination" (*Herrschaftsverhältniss*).[26] (3) It is not "demand" (wants) as such, but "effective demand" for utilities which, in a substantive respect, regulates the production of goods by profit-making enterprises through the intermediary of capital accounting. What is to be produced is thus determined, given the distribution of wealth, by the structure of marginal utilities in the income group which has both the inclination and the resources to purchase a given utility. In combination with the complete indifference of even the formally most perfect rationality of capital accounting towards all substantive postulates, an indifference which is absolute if the market is perfectly free, the above statement permits us to see the ultimate limitation, inherent in its very structure, of the rationality of monetary economic calculation. It is, after all, of a purely formal char-

---

[26] Domination ("*Herrschaft*") is a central category in Weber's sociology, defined in *Economy and Society* as "the probability that a command with a given specific content will be obeyed by a given group of persons" (p. 53) (RS).

acter. Formal and substantive rationality, no matter by what standard the latter is measured, are always in principle separate things, no matter that in many (and under certain very artificial assumptions even in all) cases they may coincide empirically. For the formal rationality of money accounting does not reveal anything about the actual distribution of goods. This must always be considered separately. Yet, if the standard used is that of the provision of a certain minimum of subsistence for the maximum size of population, the experience of the last few decades would seem to show that formal and substantive rationality coincide to a relatively high degree. The reasons lie in the nature of the incentives which are set into motion by the type of economically oriented social action which alone is adequate to money calculations. But it nevertheless holds true under all circumstances that formal rationality itself does not tell us anything about real want satisfaction unless it is combined with an analysis of the distribution of income.

14. Market Economies and Planned Economies

Want satisfaction will be said to take place through a "market economy" so far as it results from action oriented to opportunities in exchange on the basis of self-interest and where co-operation takes place only through the exchange process. It results, on the other hand, from a "planned economy"[27] so far as economic action is oriented systematically to an established substantive order, whether agreed or imposed, which is valid within an organization.

Want satisfaction through a market economy normally, and in proportion to the degree of rationality, presupposes money calculation. Where capital accounting is used it presupposes the economic separation of the budgetary unit (household) and the enterprise. Want satisfaction by means of a planned economy is dependent, in ways which vary in kind and degree according to its extensiveness, on calculation in kind as the ultimate basis of the *substantive* orientation of economic action. Formally, however, the action of the producing individual is oriented to the instructions of an administrative staff, the existence of which is indispensable. In a market economy the individual units are autocephalous and their action is autonomously oriented. In the administration of budgetary units (households), the basis of orientation is the marginal utility of money holdings and of anticipated money income; in the case of intermittent entrepreneurship, the probabilities of market gain, and in the case of profit-making enterprises, capital accounting are the basis of orientation. In a planned economy, all economic action, so far as "planning" is really carried through, is oriented heteronomously and in a strictly "budgetary" manner, to rules which enjoin certain modes of action and forbid others, and which establish a system of rewards and punishments. When, in a planned economy, the prospect of additional individual income is used as a means of stimulating self-interest, the type

[27] Socialist states fall under the category of "planned economy." Most economies, however, have elements of both planning and market within them (RS).

and direction of the action thus rewarded is substantively heteronomously determined. It is possible for the same thing to be true of a market economy, though in a formally voluntary way. This is true wherever the unequal distribution of wealth, and particularly of capital goods, forces the non-owning group to comply with the authority of others in order to obtain any return at all for the utilities they can offer on the market—either with the authority of a wealthy householder, or with the decisions, oriented to capital accounting, of the owners of capital or of their agents. In a purely capitalistic organization of production, this is the fate of the entire working class.

The following are decisive as elements of the motivation of economic activity under the conditions of a market economy: (1) For those without substantial property: (a) the fact that they run the risk of going entirely without provisions, both for themselves and for those personal dependents, such as children, wives, sometimes parents, whom the individual typically maintains on his own account; (b) that, in varying degrees subjectively they value economically productive work as a mode of life. (2) For those who enjoy a privileged position by virtue of wealth or the education which is usually in turn dependent on wealth: (a) opportunities for large income from profitable undertakings; (b) ambition; (c) the valuation as a "calling"[28] of types of work enjoying high prestige, such as intellectual work, artistic performance, and work involving high technical competence. (3) For those sharing in the fortunes of profit-making enterprises: (a) the risk to the individual's own capital, and his own opportunities for profit, combined with (b) the valuation of rational acquisitive activity as a "calling." The latter may be significant as a proof of the individual's own achievement or as a symbol and a means of autonomous control over the individuals subject to his authority, or of control over economic advantages which are culturally or materially important to an indefinite plurality of persons—in a word, power.

A planned economy oriented to want satisfaction must, in proportion as it is radically carried through, weaken the incentive to labor so far as the risk of lack of support is involved. For it would, at least so far as there is a rational system of provision for wants, be impossible to allow a worker's dependents to suffer the full consequences of his lack of efficiency in production. Furthermore, autonomy in the direction of organized productive units would have to be greatly reduced or, in the extreme case, eliminated. Hence it would be impossible to retain capital risk and proof of merit by a formally autonomous achievement. The same would be true of autonomous power over other individuals and important features of the economic situation. Along with opportunities for special material rewards, a planned economy may have command over certain ideal motives of

[28] In the most general sense employed below (see section 24 [not reproduced here; see *Economy and Society*, pp. 140–44—RS]) *Beruf* may be translated as occupation. In the present context, however, Weber has a more specific meaning in mind, that of an occupational role which embodies an especially strong element of ethical valuation. It is this type of attitude toward an occupational role which Weber found exemplified in the Protestant ethic, especially in the use of the term "calling", in Puritan literature. It has hence seemed to be the most appropriate translation in this passage. (Note by Parsons).

what is in the broadest sense an altruistic type, which can be used to stimulate a level of achievement in economic production comparable to that which autonomous orientation to opportunities for profit, by producing for the satisfaction of effective demand, has empirically been able to achieve in a market economy. Where a planned economy is radically carried out, it must further accept the inevitable reduction in formal, calculatory rationality which would result from the elimination of money and capital accounting. Substantive and formal (in the sense of exact *calculation*) rationality are, it should be stated again, after all largely distinct problems. This fundamental and, in the last analysis, unavoidable element of irrationality in economies is one of the important sources of all "social" problems, and above all, of the problems of socialism.

The following remarks apply to both sections 13 and 14.

1. The above exposition obviously formulates only things which are generally known, in a somewhat more precise form. The market economy is by far the most important case of typical widespread social action predominantly oriented to "self-interest." The process by which this type of action results in the satisfaction of wants is the subject matter of economic theory, knowledge of which in general terms is here presupposed. The use of the term "planned economy" (*Planwirtschaft*) naturally does not imply acceptance of the well-known proposals of the former German Minister of Economic Affairs.[29] The term has been chosen because, while it does not do violence to general usage, it has, since it was used officially, been widely accepted. This fact makes it preferable to the term used by Otto Neurath, "administered economy" (*Verwaltungswirtschaft*), which would otherwise be suitable.

2. So far as it is oriented to profit-making, the economic activity of organizations, or that regulated by organizations, is not included in the concept of "planned economy," whether the organization be a guild, a cartel, or a trust. "Planned economy" includes the economic activity of organizations only so far as it is oriented to the provision for needs. Any economy oriented to profit-making, no matter how strictly it is regulated or how stringently controlled by an administrative staff, presupposes effective prices, and thus capital accounting as a basis of action; this includes the limiting case of total cartellization, in which prices would be determined by negotiation between the cartel groups and by negotiated wage agreements with labor organizations. In spite of the identity of their objectives, *complete* socialization in the sense of a planned economy administered purely as a budgetary unit and *partial* socialization of various branches of production with the retention of capital accounting are technically examples of quite different types. A preliminary step in the direction of the budgetary planned economy is to be found wherever consumption is rationed or wherever measures are taken to effect the direct "in-kind" distribution of goods. A planned direction of *production*, whether it is undertaken by voluntary or au-

[29] Weber is here referring to a proposal for the introduction of a planned economy made by Economic Affairs Minister Rudolf Wissel in the summer of 1919. The proposal was rejected (RS).

thoritatively imposed cartels, or by agencies of the government, is primarily concerned with a rational organization of the use of means of production and labor resources and cannot, on its own terms, do without prices—or at least, not yet. It is thus by no means fortuitous that the "rationing-type" of socialism gets along quite well with the "works councils" (*Betriebsräte*) type of socialism which, against the will of its leading personalities (who are in favor of a rationalistic solution), must pursue the income interest of the workers.

3. It will not be possible to enter at this point into a detailed discussion of the formation of such economic organizations as cartels, corporations or guilds. Their general tendency is orientation to the regulation or monopolistic exploitation of opportunities for profit. They may arise by voluntary agreement, but are more generally imposed even where formally voluntary. Compare in the most general terms [the discussion of open and closed relationships in—RS] chapter 1, section 10[30], and also the discussion of the appropriation of economic advantages, section 19ff. of the present chapter.

The conflict between two rival forms of socialism has not died down since the publication of Marx's *The Poverty of Philosophy* [1847—RS]. On the one hand, there is the type, which includes especially the Marxist, which is evolutionary and oriented to the problem of production; on the other, the type which takes the problem of distribution as its starting point and advocates a rational planned economy. The latter is again today coming to be called "communism." The conflict within the Russian socialist movement, especially as exemplified in the passionate disputes between Plekhanov and Lenin, was, after all, also concerned with this issue. While the internal divisions of present-day socialism are very largely concerned with competition for leadership and for "benefices," along with these issues goes the same set of problems. In particular, the economic experience of the war has given impetus to the idea of a planned economy, but at the same time to the development of interests in appropriation.

The question of whether a planned economy, in whatever meaning or extent, *should* be introduced, is naturally not in this form a scientific problem. On scientific grounds it is possible only to inquire, what would be the probable results of any given specific proposal, and thus what consequences would have to be accepted if the attempt were made. Honesty requires that all parties should admit that, while some of the factors are known, many of those which would be important are only very partially understood. In the present discussion, it is not possible to enter into the details of the problem in such a way as to arrive at concretely conclusive results. The points which will be taken up can be dealt with only in a fragmentary way in connection with forms of organizations, particularly the state. It was possible above only to introduce an unavoidably brief discussion of the most elementary aspects of the technical problem. The phenomenon of a *regulated* market economy has, for the reasons noted above, not yet been taken up.

---

[30] Weber defines a closed social relationship in *Economy and Society* as follows: "A relationship will . . . be called 'closed' against outsiders so far as, according to its subjective meaning and its binding rules, participation of certain persons is excluded, or subjected to conditions" (p. 43) (RS).

4. The organization of economic activity on the basis of a market economy presupposes the appropriation of the material sources of utilities on the one hand, and market freedom on the other. The effectiveness of market freedom increases with the degree to which these sources of utility, particularly the means of transport and production, are appropriated. For, the higher the degree of marketability, the more will economic action be oriented to market situations. But the effectiveness of market freedom also increases with the degree to which appropriation is limited to *material* sources of utility. Every case of the appropriation of human beings through slavery or serfdom, or of economic advantages through market monopolies, restricts the range of human action which can be market-oriented. Fichte, in his *Der geschlossene Handelsstaat* (Tübingen, 1800), was right in treating this limitation of the concept of "property" to material goods, along with the increased autonomy of control over the objects which do fall under this concept, as characteristic of the modern market-oriented system. All parties to market relations have had an interest in this expansion of property rights because it increased the area within which they could orient their action to the opportunities of profit offered by the market situation. The development of this type of property is hence attributable to their influence.

5. For reasons of accuracy of expression, we have avoided the term "communal economy" (*Gemeinwirtschaft*), which others have frequently used [in the German discussions of 1918–1920], because it pretends the existence of a "common interest" or of a "feeling of community" as the normal thing, which conceptually is not required; the economic organization of a feudal lord exacting *corvée* labor or that of rulers like the Pharaohs of the New Kingdom belongs to the same category as a family household. Both are equally to be distinguished from a market economy.

6. For the purposes of the definition of a "market economy," it is indifferent whether or to what extent economic action is "capitalistic," that is, is oriented to capital accounting. This applies also to the normal case of a market economy, that in which the satisfaction of wants is effected in a monetary economy. It would be a mistake to assume that the development of capitalistic enterprises must occur proportionally to the growth of want satisfaction in the monetary economy, and an even larger mistake to believe that this development must take the form it has assumed in the Western world. In fact, the contrary is true. The extension of money economy might well go hand in hand with the increasing monopolization of the larger sources of profit by the *oikos* economy of a prince. Ptolemaic Egypt is an outstanding example. According to the evidence of the accounts which have survived, it was a highly developed money economy, but its accounting remained budgetary accounting and did not develop into capital accounting. It is also possible that with the extension of a money economy could go a process of turning fiscal advantages into benefices,[31] resulting in a traditionalistic stabilization of the economic system. This happened in China, as will

---

[31] A benefice is a lifelong, nonhereditary remuneration in exchange for services, and constitutes the income of an administrator. See Weber, *Economy and Society,* p. 1073 (RS).

have to be shown elsewhere.[32] Finally, the capitalistic utilization of money resources could take place through investment in sources of potential profit which
were not oriented to opportunities of exchange in a free commodity market and
thus not to the production of goods. For reasons which will be discussed below,[33]
this has been almost universally true outside the area of the modern Western
economic order. . . .

. . .

30. The Conditions of Maximum Formal Rationality of Capital Accounting

The following are the principal conditions necessary for obtaining a maximum
of formal rationality of capital accounting in production enterprises: (1) complete appropriation of all material means of production by owners and the complete absence of all formal appropriation of opportunities for profit in the
market; that is, market freedom; (2) complete autonomy in the selection of management by the owners, thus complete absence of formal appropriation of rights
to managerial functions; (3) complete absence of appropriation of jobs and of
opportunities for earning by workers and, conversely, the absence of appropriation of workers by owners. This implies free labor, freedom of the labor market,
and freedom in the selection of workers; (4) complete absence of substantive
regulation of consumption, production, and prices, or of other forms of regulation which limit freedom of contract or specify conditions of exchange. This may
be called substantive freedom of contract; (5) complete calculability of the technical conditions of the production process; that is, a mechanically rational technology; (6) complete calculability of the functioning of public administration and
the legal order and a reliable purely formal guarantee of all contracts by the political authority. This is a formally rational administration and law; (7) the most
complete separation possible of the enterprise and its conditions of success and
failure from the household or private budgetary unit and its property interests.
It is particularly important that the capital at the disposal of the enterprise should
be clearly distinguished from the private wealth of the owners, and should not
be subject to division or dispersion through inheritance. For large-scale enterprises, this condition tends to approach an optimum from a formal point of view:
in the fields of transport, manufacture, and mining, if they are organized in corporate form with freely transferrable shares and limited liability, and in the
field of agriculture, if there are relatively long-term leases for large-scale production units; (8) a monetary system with the highest possible degree of formal
rationality.

[32] Weber is probably referring to an unwritten section of *Economy and Society* (see, however, pp.
1031–38) (RS).

[33] See, e.g., the discussion of the different modes of capitalist profit-making in section 31, below
(RS).

Only a few points are in need of comment, though even these have already been touched on.

1. With respect to the freedom of labor and of jobs from appropriation, it is true that certain types of unfree labor, particularly full-fledged slavery, have guaranteed what is formally a more complete power of disposal over the worker than is the case with employment for wages. But there are various reasons why this is less favorable to rationality and efficiency than the employment of free labor: (a) The amount of capital which it was necessary to invest in human resources through the purchase and maintenance of slaves has been much greater than that required by the employment of free labor; (b) the capital risk attendant on slave ownership has not only been greater but specifically irrational in that slave labor has been exposed to all manner of non-economic influences, particularly to political influence in a very high degree; (c) the slave market and correspondingly the prices of slaves have been particularly subject to fluctuation, which has made a balancing of profit and loss on a rational basis exceedingly difficult; (d) for similar reasons, particularly involving the political situation, there has been a difficult problem of recruitment of slave labor forces; (e) when slaves have been permitted to enjoy family relationships, this has made the use of slave labor more expensive in that the owner has had to bear the cost of maintaining the women and of rearing children. Very often, he has had no way in which he could make rational economic use of these elements as part of his labor force; (f) hence the most complete exploitation of slave labor has been possible only when they were separated from family relationships and subjected to a ruthless discipline. Where this has happened it has greatly accentuated the difficulties of the problem of recruitment; (g) it has in general been impossible to use slave labor in the operation of tools and apparatus, the efficiency of which required a high level of responsibility and of involvement of the operator's self-interest; (h) perhaps most important of all has been the impossibility of selection, of employment only after trying out in the job, and of dismissal in accordance with fluctuations of the business situation or when personal efficiency declined.

Hence the employment of slave labor has only been possible in general under the following conditions: (a) Where it has been possible to maintain slaves very cheaply; (b) where there has been an opportunity for regular recruitment through a well-supplied slave market; (c) in agricultural production on a large scale of the plantation type, or in very simple industrial processes. The most important examples of this type of relatively successful use of slaves are the Carthaginian and Roman plantations, those of colonial areas and of the Southern United States, and the Russian "factories." The drying up of the slave market, which resulted from the pacification of the Empire, led to the decay of the plantations of Antiquity.[34] In North America, the same situation led to a continual search for cheap new land, since it was impossible to meet the costs of slaves

[34] This theme is developed in Weber's "The Social Causes of the Decay of Ancient Civilization" (reading 10 in this anthology) (RS).

and pay a land rent at the same time. In Russia, the serf "factories" were barely able to meet the competition of the *kustar* type of household industry and were totally unable to compete with free factory labor. Even before the emancipation of the serfs, petitions for permission to dismiss workers were common, and the factories decayed with the introduction of shops using free labor.

When workers are employed for wages, the following advantages to industrial profitability and efficiency are conspicuous: (a) Capital risk and the necessary capital investment are smaller; (b) the costs of reproduction and of bringing up children fall entirely on the worker. His wife and children must seek employment on their own account; (c) largely for this reason, the risk of dismissal is an important incentive to the maximization of production; (d) it is possible to select the labor force according to ability and willingness to work.

2. The following comment may be made on the separation of enterprise and household. The separation in England of the producing farm *enterprise,* leasing the land and operating with capital accounting, from the entailed *ownership* of the land is by no means fortuitous, but is the outcome of an undisturbed development over centuries which was characterized by the absence of an effective protection of the status of peasants. This in turn was a consequence of the country's insular position. Every joining of the *ownership* of land with the *cultivation* of the land turns the land into a capital good for the economic unit, thus increasing the capital requirements and the capital risks of this unit. It impedes the separation of the household from the economic establishment; the settlements paid out at inheritance, for instance, burden the resources of the enterprise. It reduces the liquidity of the entrepreneur's capital and introduces a number of irrational factors into his capital accounting. Hence the separation of landownership from the organization of agricultural production is, from a formal point of view, a step which promotes the rationality of capital accounting. It goes without saying, however, that any substantive evaluation of this phenomenon is quite another matter, and its conclusions may be quite different depending on the values underlying the judgment.

31. THE PRINCIPAL MODES OF CAPITALISTIC ORIENTATION OF PROFIT-MAKING

The "capitalistic" orientation of profit-making activity (in the case of rationality, this means: the orientation to capital accounting) can take a number of qualitatively different forms, each of which represents a definite type:

(1) It may be orientation to the profit possibilities in continuous buying and selling on the market ("trade") with free exchange—that is, absence of formal and at least relative absence of substantive compulsion to effect any given exchange; or it may be orientation to the profit possibilities in continuous production of goods in enterprises with capital accounting.

(2) It may be orientation to the profit possibilities in trade and speculation in different currencies, in the taking over of payment functions of all sorts and in

the creation of means of payment; the same with respect to the professional extension of credit, either for consumption or for profit-making purposes.

(3) It may be orientation to opportunities for predatory profit from political organizations or persons connected with politics. This includes the financing of wars or revolutions and the financing of party leaders by loans and supplies.

(4) It may be orientation to the profit opportunities in continuous business activity which arise by virtue of domination by force or of a position of power guaranteed by the political authority. There are two main sub-types: colonial profits, either through the operation of plantations with compulsory deliveries or compulsory labor or through monopolistic and compulsory trade, and fiscal profits, through the farming of taxes and of offices, whether at home or in colonies.

(5) It may be orientation to profit opportunities in unusual transactions with political bodies.

(6) It may be orientation to profit opportunities of the following types: (a) in purely speculative transactions in standardized commodities or in the securities of enterprises; (b) in the execution of the continuous financial operations of political bodies; (c) in the promotional financing of new enterprises in the form of sale of securities to investors; (d) in the speculative financing of capitalistic enterprises and of various other types of economic organization with the purpose of a profitable regulation of market situations or of attaining power.

Types (1) and (6) are to a large extent peculiar to the modern Western World. The other types have been common all over the world for thousands of years wherever the possibilities of exchange and money economy (for type 2) and money financing (for types 3–5) have been present. In the Western World they have not had such a dominant importance as modes of profit-making as they had in Antiquity, except in restricted areas and for relatively brief periods, particularly in times of war. Where large areas have been pacified for a long period, as in the Chinese and later Roman Empire, these types have tended to decline, leaving only trade, money changing, and lending as forms of capitalistic acquisition. For the capitalistic financing of political activities was everywhere the product of the competition of states with one another for power, and of the corresponding competition for capital which moved freely between them. All this ended only with the establishment of the unified empires.

(The point of view here stated has, if the author's memory is accurate, been previously put forward in the clearest form by J. Plenge in his *Von der Diskontpolitik zur Herrschaft über den Geldmarkt* [Berlin 1913].[35] Before that a similar position seems to have been taken only in the author's article, "Agrarverhältnisse im Altertum," 1909.[36])

It is only in the modern Western World that rational capitalistic enterprises

---

[35] Johann Plenge (1874–1963), German economist and sociologist (RS).

[36] What Weber here refers to as a lengthy article was originally part of a huge handbook entitled *Handwörterbuch der Staatswissenschaften* but has been published as a separate book in English, under the title *The Agrarian Sociology of Ancient Civilizations* (London: New Left Books, 1976) (RS).

with fixed capital, free labor, the rational specialization and combination of tasks, and the allocation of productive tasks on the basis of capitalistic enterprises, bound together in a market economy, are to be found. In other words, we find the capitalistic type of organization of labor, which in formal terms is purely voluntary, as the typical and dominant mode of providing for the wants of the masses of the population, with expropriation of the workers from the means of production and appropriation of the enterprises by security owners. It is also only here that we find public credit in the form of issues of government securities, the "going public" of business enterprises, the floating of security issues and financing carried on as the specialized function of rational business enterprises, trade in commodities and securities on organized exchanges, money and capital markets, monopolistic organizations as a form of rational business organization of the entrepreneurial *production* of goods, and not only of the trade in them.

This difference calls for an explanation and the explanation cannot be given on economic grounds alone. Types (3) to (5) inclusive will be treated here together as "politically oriented capitalism." The whole of the later discussion will be devoted particularly to the problem of explaining the difference.[37] In general terms, it is possible only to make the following statements:

(1) It is clear from the very beginning that the politically oriented events and processes which open up these profit opportunities exploited by political capitalism are irrational from an economic point of view—that is, from the point of view of orientation to market opportunities and thus to the consumption needs of budgetary units.

(2) It is further clear that purely speculative profit opportunities and pure consumption credit are irrational from the point of view both of want satisfaction and of the production of goods, because they are determined by the fortuitous distribution of ownership and of market opportunities. The same may also be true of opportunities for promotion and financing, under certain circumstances; but this is not necessarily always the case. . . .

· · ·

41. THE MAINSPRING OF ECONOMIC ACTIVITY

All economic activity in a market economy is undertaken and carried through by individuals acting to provide for their own ideal or material interests. This is naturally just as true when economic activity is oriented to the patterns of order of organizations, whether they themselves are partly engaged in economic activity, are primarily economic in character, or merely regulate economic activity. Strangely enough, this fact is often not taken account of.

In an economy organized on a socialist basis, there would be no fundamental difference in this respect. The decision-making, of course, would lie in the hands

---

[37] The reference is probably to planned but unwritten parts of *Economy and Society*. See, however, part 2 of *Economy and Society* (RS).

of the central authority, and the functions of the individual engaged in the production of goods would be limited to the performance of "technical" services;
that is, to "labor" in the sense of the term employed here. This would be true so
long as the individuals were being administered "dictatorially," that is, by autocratic determination from above in which they had no voice. But once any right
of "co-determination" were granted to the population, this would immediately
make possible, also in a formal sense, the fighting out of interest conflicts cen-
tering on the manner of decision-making and, above all, on the question of how
much should be saved (i.e., put aside from current production). But this is not
the decisive point. What is decisive is that in socialism, too, the individual will
under these conditions ask first whether to him, personally, the rations allotted
and the work assigned, as compared with other possibilities, appear to conform
with his own interests. This is the criterion by which he would orient his behavior, and violent power struggles would be the normal result: struggles over the
alteration or maintenance of rations once allotted—as, for instance, over ration
supplements for heavy labor; appropriations or expropriations of particular jobs,
sought after because of extra remuneration or pleasant working conditions; work
cessations, such as in strikes or lock-outs; restrictions of production to enforce
changes in the conditions of work in particular branches; boycotts and the
forcible dismissal of unpopular supervisors—in short, appropriation processes
of all kinds and interest struggles would also then be the normal phenomena of
life. The fact that they would for the most part be fought out through organized
groups, and that advantages would be enjoyed on the one hand by the workers
engaged in the most essential services, on the other hand by those who were
physically strongest, would simply reflect the existing situation. But however that
might be, it would be the interests of the individual, possibly organized in terms
of the similar interests of many individuals as opposed to those of others, which
would underlie all action. The *structure* of interests and the relevant situation
would be different, and there would be other *means* of pursuing interests, but
this fundamental factor would remain just as relevant as before. It is of course
true that economic action which is oriented on purely ideological grounds to the
interests of others does exist. But it is even more certain that the mass of men
do not act in this way, and it is an induction from experience that they cannot do
so and never will.

In a completely socialized planned economy there would be scope only for
the following: (a) the distribution of real goods on the basis of planned rationed
needs; (b) the production of these goods according to a plan of production. "Income" as a category of the money economy would necessarily disappear, but rationed "receipts" would be possible.

In a market economy the striving for *income* (*Einkommen*) is necessarily the
ultimate driving force of all economic activity. For every disposition, insofar as
it makes a claim on goods or utilities which are not available to the actor in a
form fully ready for whatever use he intends, presupposes the acquisition of and
disposition over future income, and practically every existing power of control
over goods and services presupposes previous income. All business profits of en-

terprises will at some stage and in some form be turned into the income of economically acting individuals. In a "regulated economy" the principal aim of the regulations is generally to affect in some manner the distribution of income. (In a "natural economy" we find no "income" in the usage of the present terminology; instead there are "receipts" in the form of goods and services which cannot be valued in terms of a unitary means of exchange.)

Income and receipts may, from a sociological point of view, take the following principal forms and be derived from the following principal sources:

A.—Incomes and receipts from personal services derived from specialized or specified tasks:

(1) Wages: (a) Freely determined wage incomes or receipts contracted at fixed rates per time period; (b) the same, determined on some established scale (salaries or in-kind remuneration of public officials and civil servants); (c) the labor return of hired workers on contracted piece rates; (d) entirely open labor returns.

(2) Gains: (a) Free exchange profits deriving from the procurement of goods and services on an entrepreneurial basis; (b) the same, but regulated. In cases (a) and (b), "incomes" are calculated as net returns after the deduction of costs. (c) Predatory gains; (d) Gains derived from positions of political authority, fee incomes of an office, bribes, tax farming, etc., obtained by the appropriation of power. In cases (c) and (d), costs will be deducted to calculate "income" only if the activity is conducted as a continuous organized mode of acquisition; otherwise the gross revenue is usually considered "income."

B.—Income and receipts from property, derived from the exploitation of control over important means of production:

(1) Those in which "income" is normally calculated as "net rent" after the deduction of costs. (a) Rent obtained from the ownership of human beings, as in the case of slaves, serfs or freedmen. These may be receipts in money or in kind; they may be fixed in amount or consist in shares of the source's earnings after the deduction of costs of maintenance. (b) Appropriated revenues derived from positions of political authority (after the deduction of the costs of administration). (c) Rental revenues derived from the ownership of land (*métayage* payments or fixed rents per unit of time, either in kind or in money, seigneurial rent revenues—after deduction of land taxes and costs of maintenance). (d) House rents after deduction of expenses. (e) Rent receipts from appropriated monopolies (feudal *banalités,* patent royalties after the deduction of fees).

(2) Property income and receipts normally not requiring deduction of costs from gross revenues: (a) Investment income (interest paid to households or profit-making enterprises in return for the right to utilize their resources or capital—see above, section 11. (b) "Interest" from cattle loans. (c) "Interest" from other loans of concrete objects, and contracted "annuities in kind." (d) Interest on money loans. (e) Money interest on mortgages. (f) Money returns from securities, which may consist in fixed interest or in dividends varying with profitability. (g) Other shares in profits, such as shares in the proceeds of "occasional"

in the main, interest us only in *this* respect. This will be the case regularly (but not exclusively) when institutions are involved which were *deliberately* created or used for economic ends. Such objects of our knowledge we may call "economic" events (or institutions, as the case may be). There are other phenomena, for instance, religious ones, which do not interest us, or at least do not primarily interest us with respect to their economic significance but which, however, under certain circumstances do acquire significance in this regard because they have consequences which are of interest from the economic point of view. These we shall call "economically relevant" phenomena. Finally there are phenomena which are *not* "economic" in our sense and the economic effects of which are of no, or at best slight, interest to us (e.g., the developments of the artistic taste of a period) but which in individual instances are in their turn more or less strongly influenced in certain important aspects by economic factors such as, for instance, the social stratification of the artistically interested public. We shall call these "economically *conditioned* phenomena." The constellation of human relationships, norms, and normatively determined conduct which we call the "state" is for example in its fiscal aspects, an "economic" phenomenon; insofar as it influences economic life through legislation or otherwise (and even where other than economic considerations deliberately guide its behavior), it is "economically relevant." To the extent that its behavior in non-"economic" affairs is partly influenced by economic motives, it is "economically conditioned." After what has been said, it is self-evident that: firstly, the boundary lines of "economic" phenomena are vague and not easily defined; secondly, the "economic" aspect of a phenomenon is by no means *only* "economically conditioned" or *only* "economically relevant"; thirdly, a phenomenon is "economic" only insofar as and *only* as long as our *interest* is exclusively focused on its constitutive significance in the material struggle for existence.

Like the science of social-economics (*die sozialökonomische Wissenschaft*) since Marx and Roscher, our journal is concerned not only with economic phenomena but also with those which are "economically relevant" and "economically conditioned." The domain of such subjects extends naturally—and varyingly in accordance with the focus of our interest at the moment—through the totality of cultural life. Specifically economic motives—i.e., motives which, in their aspect most significant to us, are rooted in the above-mentioned fundamental fact—operate wherever the satisfaction of even the most immaterial need or desire is bound up with the application of *scarce* material means. Their force has everywhere on that account conditioned and transformed not only the mode in which cultural wants or preferences are satisfied, but their content as well, even in their most subjective aspects. The indirect influence of social relations, institutions and groups governed by "material interests" extends (often unconsciously) into all spheres of culture without exception, even into the finest nuances of aesthetic and religious feeling. The events of everyday life no less than the "historical" events of the higher reaches of political life, collective and mass phenomena as well as the "individuated" conduct of statesmen and individual literary and artistic achievements are influenced by it. They are "economically conditioned." On the other hand, all the activities and situations constituting an historically given culture affect the formation of the material wants, the mode of their satisfaction, the integration of interest-groups and the types of power which they exercise. They thereby affect the course of "economic development" and are accordingly "economically relevant." To the extent that our science imputes particular causes—be they economic or non-economic—to *economic* cultural phenomena, it seeks "historical" knowledge. Insofar as it traces a specific element of cultural life (the economic element in its cultural significance) through the most diverse cultural contexts, it is making an historical interpretation from a specific point of view, and offering a partial picture, a *preliminary* contribution to a more complete historical knowledge of culture. . . .

.   .   .

ECONOMIC THEORY AND THE IDEAL TYPE

Economics was originally—as we have already seen—a "technique," at least in the central focus of its attention. By this we mean that it viewed reality from an at least ostensibly unambiguous and stable practical evaluative standpoint: namely, the increase of the "wealth" of the population. It was on the other hand, from the very beginning, more than a "technique" since it was integrated into the great scheme of the natural law and rationalistic worldview (*Weltanschauung*) of the eighteenth century. The nature of that worldview with its optimistic faith in the theoretical and practical rationalizability of reality had an important consequence insofar as it *obstructed* the discovery of the *problematic* character of that standpoint which had been assumed as self-evident. As the rational analysis of society arose in close connection with the modern development of natural science, so it remained related to it in its whole method of approach. In the natural sciences, the practical evaluative attitude toward what was immediately and technically useful was closely associated from the very first with the hope, taken over as a heritage of antiquity and further elaborated, of attaining a purely "objective" (i.e., independent of all individual contingencies) monistic knowledge of the totality of reality in a *conceptual* system of metaphysical *validity* and mathematical *form*. It was thought that this hope could be realized by the method of generalizing abstraction and the formulation of laws based on empirical analysis. The natural sciences which were bound to evaluative standpoints, such as clinical medicine and even more what is conventionally called "technology" became purely practical "arts." The values for which they strove, e.g., the health of the patient, the technical perfection of a concrete productive process, etc., were fixed for the time being for all of them. The methods which they used could only consist in the application of the laws formulated by the theoretical disciplines. Every theoretical advance in the construction of these laws was or could also be an advance for the practical disciplines. With the end given, the progressive reduction of concrete practical questions (e.g., a case of illness, a technical problem, etc.) to special cases of generally valid laws, meant that extension of theoretical knowledge was closely associated and identical with the extension of technical-practical possibilities.

When modern biology subsumed those aspects of reality which interest us *historically*, i.e., in all their concreteness, under a universally valid evolutionary principle, which at least had the appearance—but not the actuality—of embracing everything essential about the subject in a scheme of universally valid laws, this seemed to be the final twilight of all evaluative standpoints in all the sciences. For since the so-called historical event was a segment of the totality of reality, since the principle of causality which was the presupposition of all scientific work, seemed to require the analysis of all events into generally valid "laws," and in view of the overwhelming success of the natural sciences which took this idea seriously, it appeared as if there was in general no conceivable meaning of scientific work other than the discovery of the *laws* of events. Only those aspects of phenomena which were involved in the "laws" could be essential from the scientific point of view, and concrete "individual" events could be considered only as "types," i.e., as representative illustrations of laws. An interest in such events in themselves did not seem to be a "scientific" interest.

It is impossible to trace here the important repercussions of this will-to-believe of naturalistic monism in economics. When socialist criticism and the work of the historians were beginning to transform the original evaluative standpoints, the vigorous development of zoological research on one hand and the influence of Hegelian panlogism on the other prevented economics from attaining a clear and full understanding of the relationship between concept and reality. The result, to the extent that we are interested in it, is that despite the powerful resistance to the infiltration of naturalistic dogma due to German idealism since Fichte and the achievement of the German Historical School in law and economics and partly because of the very work of the Historical School, the naturalistic viewpoint in certain decisive problems has not yet been overcome. Among these problems we find the relationship between "theory" and "history," which is still problematic in our discipline.

The "abstract"-theoretical method even today shows unmediated and ostensibly irreconcilable cleavage from empirical-historical research. The proponents of this method recognize in a thoroughly correct way the methodological impossibility of supplanting the historical knowledge of reality by the formulation of laws or, vice versa, of constructing "laws" in the rigorous sense through the mere juxtaposition of historical observations. Now in order to arrive at these laws—for they are certain that science should be directed towards these as its highest goal—they take it to be a fact that we always have a direct awareness of the structure of human actions in all their reality. Hence—so they think—science can make human behavior directly intelligible with axiomatic certainty and accordingly reveal its laws. The only exact form of knowledge—the formulation of immediately and intuitively *evident* laws—is however at the same time the only one which offers access to events which have not been directly observed. Hence, at least as regards the fundamental phenomena of economic life, the construction of a system of abstract and therefore purely formal propositions analogous to those of the exact natural sciences, is the only means of analyzing and intellectually mastering the complexity of social life. In spite of the fundamental methodological distinction between historical knowledge and the knowledge of "laws" which the creator of the theory drew as the *first* and *only* one, he now claims empirical *validity*, in the sense of the *deducibility* of reality from "laws," for the propositions of abstract theory. It is true that this is not meant in the sense of empirical validity of the abstract economic laws as such, but in the sense that when equally "exact" theories have been constructed for all the other relevant factors, all these abstract theories together must contain the true reality of the object—i.e., whatever is worthwhile knowing about it. Exact economic theory deals with the operation of *one* psychic motive, the other theories have as their task the formulation of the behavior of all the other motives into similar sorts of propositions enjoying hypothetical validity. Accordingly, the fantastic claim has occasionally been made for economic theories—e.g., the abstract theories of price, interest, rent, etc.,—that they can, by ostensibly following the analogy of physical science propositions, be validly applied to the derivation of quantitatively stated conclusions from given real premises, since given the ends, economic behavior with respect to means is unambiguously "determined." This claim fails to observe that in order to be able to reach this result even in the simplest case, the totality of the existing historical reality including every one of its causal relationships must be assumed as "given" and presupposed as known. But if *this* type of knowledge were accessible to the finite mind of man, abstract theory would have no cognitive value whatsoever.

The naturalistic prejudice that every concept in the cultural sciences should be similar to those in the exact natural sciences has led in consequence to the misunderstanding of the meaning of this theoretical construction (*theoretische Gedankengebilde*). It has been believed that is it a matter of the psychological isolation of a specific "impulse," the acquisitive impulse, or of the isolated study of a specific maxim of human conduct, the so-called economic principle. Abstract theory purported to be based on psychological *axioms*, and as a result historians have called for an *empirical* psychology in order to show the invalidity of those axioms and to derive the course of economic events from psychological principles. We do not wish at this point to enter into a detailed criticism of the belief in the significance of a—still to be created—systematic science of "social psychology" as the future foundation of the cultural sciences, and particularly of social economics. Indeed, the partly brilliant attempts which have been made hitherto to interpret economic phenomena psychologically, show in any case that the procedure does not begin with the analysis of psychological qualities, moving then to the analysis of social institutions, but that, on the contrary, insight into the psychological preconditions and consequences of institutions presupposes a precise knowledge of the latter and the scientific analysis of their structure. In concrete cases, psychological analysis can contribute then an extremely valuable deepening of the knowledge of the historical cultural *conditioning* and cultural *significance* of institutions. The interesting aspect of the psychic attitude of a person in a social situation is specifically particularized in each case, according to the special cultural significance of the situation in question. It is a question of an extremely heterogeneous and highly concrete structure of psychic motives and influences. Social-psychological research involves the study of various very disparate *individual* types of cultural elements with reference to their interpretability by our empathic understanding. Through social-psychological research, with the knowledge of individual institutions as a point of departure, we will learn increasingly how to understand institutions in a psychological way. We will not however deduce the institutions from psychological laws or explain them by elementary psychological phenomena.

Thus, the far-flung polemic, which centered on the question of the psychological justification of abstract theoretical propositions, on the scope of the "acquisitive impulse" and the "economic principle," etc., turns out to have been fruitless.

In the establishment of the propositions of abstract theory, it is only apparently a matter of "deductions" from fundamental psychological motives. Actually, the former are a special case of a kind of concept-construction which is peculiar and to a certain extent, indispensable, to the cultural sciences. It is worthwhile at this point to describe it in further detail since we can thereby approach more closely the fundamental question of the significance of theory in the social sciences. Therewith we leave undiscussed, once and for all, whether the particular analytical concepts which we cite or to which we allude as illustrations, correspond to the purposes they are to serve, i.e., whether in fact they are well-adapted. The question as to how far, for example, contemporary "abstract theory" should be further elaborated, is ultimately also a question of the strategy of science, which must, however concern itself with other problems as well. Even the "theory of marginal utility" is subsumable under a "law of marginal utility."

We have in abstract economic theory an illustration of those synthetic constructs which have been designated as *"ideas"* of historical phenomena. It offers us an ideal picture of events on the commodity-market under conditions of a society organized on the principles of an exchange economy, free competition and rigorously rational conduct. This conceptual pattern brings together certain relationships and events of historical life into a complex, which is conceived as a cosmos without contradictions. Substantively, this construct in itself is like a *utopia* which has been arrived at by the analytical accentuation of certain elements of reality. Its relationship to the empirical data consists solely in the fact that where market-conditioned relationships of the type referred to by the abstract construct are discovered or suspected to exist in reality to some extent, we can make the *characteristic* features of this relationship pragmatically *clear* and *understandable* by reference to an *ideal type*.

This procedure can be indispensable for heuristic as well as expository purposes. The ideal-typical concept will help to develop our skill in analytical judgment in *research*: it *is* no "hypothesis" but it offers guidance to the construction of hypotheses. It is not a *description* of reality but it aims to give unambiguous means of expression to such a description. It is thus the "idea" of the *historically* given modern society, based on an exchange economy, which is developed for us by quite the same logical principles as are used in constructing the idea of the medieval "city economy" as a "genetic" concept. When we do this, we construct the concept "city economy" not as an average of the economic structures actually existing in all the cities observed but as an *ideal type*.

An ideal type is formed by the one-sided *accentuation* of one or more points of view and by the synthesis of a great many diffuse, discrete, more or less present and occasionally absent *concrete individual* phenomena, which are arranged according to those one-sidedly emphasized viewpoints into a unified *analytical* construct (*Gedankenbild*). In its conceptual purity, this mental construct cannot be found empirically anywhere in reality. It is a *utopia*. Historical research faces the task of determining in each individual case, the extent to which this ideal construct approximates to or diverges from reality, to what extent for example, the economic structure of a certain city is to be classified as a "city economy." When carefully applied, those concepts are particularly useful in research and exposition. In very much the same way one can work the "idea" of "handicraft" into a utopia by arranging certain traits, actually found in an unclear, confused state in the industrial enterprises of the most diverse epochs and countries, into a consistent ideal construct by an accentuation of their essential tendencies. This ideal type is then related to the idea which one finds expressed there. One can further delineate a society in which all branches of economic and even intellectual activity are governed by maxims which appear to be applications of the same principle which characterizes the ideal-typical "handicraft" system. Furthermore, one can juxtapose alongside the ideal-typical "handicraft" system the antithesis of a correspondingly ideal-typical capitalistic productive system, which has been abstracted out of certain features of modern large scale industry. On the basis of this, one can delineate the utopia of a "capitalistic" culture, i.e., one in which the governing principle is the investment of private capital. This procedure would accentuate certain individual concretely diverse traits of modern material and intellectual culture in its unique aspects into an ideal construct which from our point of view would be completely self-consistent. This would then be the delineation of an *"idea" of capitalistic culture*.

We must disregard for the moment whether and how this procedure could be carried out. It is possible, or rather, it must be accepted as certain that numerous, indeed a very great many, utopias of this sort can be worked out, of which *none* is like another, and *none* of which can be observed in empirical reality as an actually existing economic system, but *each* of which however claims that it is a representation of the "idea" of capitalistic culture. *Each* of these can claim to be a representation of the "idea" of capitalistic culture to the extent that it has really taken certain traits, meaningful in their essential features, from the empirical reality of our culture and brought them together into a unified ideal construct. For those phenomena which interest us as cultural phenomena are interesting to us with respect to very different kinds of evaluative ideas to which we relate them. Inasmuch as the "points of view" from which they can become significant for us are very diverse, the most varied criteria can be applied to the selection of the traits which are to enter into the construction of an ideal-typical view of a particular culture.

Marginal Utility Analysis and "The Fundamental Law of Psychophysics"

THE TREATISE under review[1] is a partly synoptic, partly critical exposition of the results to which the investigations concerning the development of value theory since Aristotle have led. Stimulated by Brentano, these investigations were initially undertaken by his student Ludwig Fick, only to be cut short by Fick's premature death. They were then quite independently resumed and concluded by another of Brentano's students, Dr. R. Kaulla.[2] Out of the multitude of provocative ideas which this treatise—like any of Brentano's works—offers, reference will here be made only to the discussion regarding the relationship of the concepts of "utilizability" and "use value" (p. 42f.). This discussion probably affords the clearest, most concise exposition on this subject to date.

We shall here address ourselves to the sole point in Brentano's exposition that invites *contradiction*. The point concerns the supposed relations of "marginal utility theory"—indeed, of any "subjective" value theory—to certain general propositions of experimental psychology, especially to the so-called Weber-Fechner law.[3] The attempt to understand economic value theory as a special case of application of this law is by no means herewith made for the first time, as Brentano himself stresses. A clear attempt at such an analysis appears in the second edition of F. A. Lange's *The Worker Question (Arbeiterfrage)*. Relevant approaches, indeed, are even to be found in the first edition of Fechner's *Psychophysics (Psychophysik)* of 1860, and since then the matter has come up with extraordinary frequency.

Like Brentano, Lange had looked upon the famed Weber-Fechner law as a confirmation and generalization of theses which Bernoulli had proposed for the

Reprinted by permission of the University of Texas Press from *Social Science Quarterly* 56 (1975): pp. 24–36. Translated by Louis Schneider. Copyright 1975 by the University of Texas Press. Originally published in 1908; see *Gesammelte Aufsätze zur Wissenschaftslehre* (1922) (Tübingen: J. C. B. Mohr, 1988), pp. 384–99.

[1] In this article Weber discusses a work by the economist Lujo Brentano (1844–1931) on "the development of value theory." See Lujo Brentano, *Die Entwicklung der Wertlehre* (Munich: Verlag der Akademie, 1908) (RS).

[2] R. Kaulla, *Die geschichtliche Entwicklung der modernen Werttheorien* (Tübingen, 1906). Compare also O. Kraus, "Die aristotelische Werttheorie in ihrer Beziehung zu den Lehren der modernen Psychologenschule", *Zeitschrift für Staatswissenschaft*, vol. 61 (1905), pp. 573 ff.

[3] The Weber-Fechner law, named after Ernst Heinrich Weber (1795–1878) and Gustav Theodor Fechner (1801–1878), represents a famous attempt to quantify the relationship between stimulus and sensation. The law asserts that a just noticeable difference in the intensity of a sensation corresponds to an increase or decrease in the intensity of a stimulus by a constant fraction of its original intensity (RS).

connection between the relative (personal) evaluation of a sum of money and the absolute level of the wealth of its owner or receiver or user. Moreover, Lange had sought to adduce instances for the still more universal significance of the law from the sphere of political life (in terms of sensitivities to political pressure, and so on). The assertion that the value theory of the so-called "Austrian School" is "psychologically based" has in any case been made repeatedly. At the same time, in the opposing camp, the most outstanding representatives of the "historical school" claim to have helped "psychology" to achieve its proper status, in contrast to the abstract handling of value theory characteristic of "natural law." Given the ambiguity of the word "psychological," it serves no useful purpose to bicker with the two groups about which has the legitimate claim to the word. Depending on the point of view, it could be both or neither. Here we are rather concerned with Brentano's much more pointed assertion that "the fundamental law of psychophysics" is the foundation of "marginal utility theory" and that the latter accordingly is an application of the former. The thesis to be expounded here is simply that *this* view is in error.

As Brentano himself mentions, the fundamental law of psychophysics has gone through changes as regards its formulation, its (presumptive) range of validity, and its interpretation. Brentano himself summarizes the content of the law, initially (p. 66) in very general terms, in this way: Fechner showed "that in all spheres of sensation *the same* law of the dependence of sensation on stimulus asserts itself—the same law which Bernoulli had set up for the dependence of the sensation of *happiness* (which increase of a sum of money brings) on the amount of the wealth of the one who experiences the sensation." Although the reference to Bernoulli comes up in quite the same way in Fechner, it is nevertheless misleading. Surely Fechner among others was stimulated by Bernoulli's method. But the question of how far particular, related concepts have enriched two generically different sciences in the course of their formative development is a purely textual and historical one. It has nothing to do with our problem. That problem is whether the Weber-Fechner law provides the *theoretical* foundation of marginal utility theory. Thus, Darwin was influenced by Malthus, but the Malthusian theory is not the same as Darwin's, nor is either theory a special case of the other, nor are both theories special cases of a yet more general law. The situation is similar in what confronts us now.

"Happiness" is not a psychophysically apprehensible concept. Certainly it is no qualitatively unitary concept—as there was a disposition to think it was in the age of utilitarian ethics. The psychologists would no doubt refrain from identifying this concept with that of "pleasure." (They have serious internal disputes about the coverage of the latter.) But aside from this, even as a vague analogy, even regarded as mere image or comparison, the parallel proposed by Brentano and Fechner would be defective. For it is cogent only in a formal way and for a portion of the problem.

Fechner's stimulus (always an "external," that is, bodily event[4]) is, at least in principle, if not in actuality, directly quantitatively measurable. This stimulus is

---

[4] Hereby of course one also means to take in events emanating from the "inside" of one's body.

associated with specific conscious "sensations" which are its "effects" or constitute "parallels" to it. Bernoulli's increase of a sum of money (for it, too, is an "external" event) would have to correspond to this stimulus and—quite formally regarded—might indeed correspond to it. But then, what is there in connection with the fundamental psychophysical law which corresponds to the "wealth" that he who (in Bernoulli's view) obtains an increment of wealth already has?

At least formally, this too seems easy to answer. Given the well known Weberian experiments on differential individual sensitivity to *increase* in weight, we may think of a burden of weight already sustained as corresponding to wealth already present in the form of money. Then, if we accept this, according to the Weberian observations that constitute the grounds for the fundamental psychophysical law, the following simple propositions should hold: If someone is already sustaining a weight of three ounces (say on the palm of his hand) and feels an increase of one-thirtieth (or one-tenth of an ounce) of this weight, then this same person, sustaining a weight of six ounces, will experience an increase of one-thirtieth (now two-tenths of an ounce) as an increase which is equivalent to the first. In the case of other "sense-stimulations" the situation will be one that corresponds to what we have here in the case of the "sensations of feeling." If in each of two cases the relationship of stimulus-increase to basic stimulus is objectively the same, then the two increases of stimulus are consciously experienced as the same. To put it in other terms: The strength of a stimulus must increase in geometric ratio if the perceived strength of sensation is to increase in arithmetic ratio.

We here leave quite aside the question of the extent to which the "law" thus formulated has been empirically confirmed. The concepts of "stimulus threshold" and "stimulus level," of "subobservable" and "superobservable" stimuli have been added and a whole slew of special laws (for example, that of Merkel) has been grouped about the general law. Should we now apply the simple old Weberian formula to economic events and, with Brentano—risky as this is—assume that increase in wealth is equal to enhancement of *"stimulus,"* then (as with Bernoulli) we would get this result: If an individual who possesses a thousand marks experiences a sensation of increased "happiness" of a certain intensity upon obtaining a hundred-mark increase of what he possesses, then be it noted, *this same individual,* if he should possess a million marks, would experience an increase of a hundred thousand marks with the *same* intensity of feeling of happiness. Let us assume this would be the case and that the concepts of "stimulus threshold" and "stimulus level," and particularly the curve indicating the Weber law, can somehow be analogously made applicable in the case of acquisition of money. Then does all this bear on the questions which economic theory seeks to answer? And is the validity of the logarithmic line of the psychophysicists the foundation for the propositions of economic theory, lacking which they would not be comprehensible?

Without doubt, it is worth while to analyze the various large sets of economically relevant "needs" in terms of how they react according to the degree to which they are satisfied. But further, and above all, it is worth while to analyze them in terms of *how* they are satisfied. And at this point the fundamental law of psychophysics no longer accomplishes anything. Not a few discussions, for instance on the significance of money economy for the qualitative expansion of needs, belong to this sphere, as well as perhaps investigations of nutritional changes under the pressure of economic transformations; and so on. But obviously the consideration of such matters would in no way be concerned with the supposedly fundamental Weber-Fechner theory.

Further, if one were to analyze particular sets of needs—say, needs relating to nutrition, housing, sex, alcohol, "spirit," beauty, and so on, taking them as they intensify and subside, according to the *quantity* of supply of "means of satisfaction"—then one would occasionally find more or less far-reaching analogies to the logarithmic curve of the Weber-Fechner rule. But, on the other hand, he would occasionally find only quite trivial analogies or even none at all. Indeed, he would find, not infrequently, that the rule was stood on its head. (See below.) Sometimes the curves would break off suddenly. Sometimes they would become negative; sometimes not. Sometimes they would run their course proportionally to "satisfaction"; sometimes they would run asymptotically toward the zero point. For each kind of "need" they would present a different picture. Yet, still, one could at least find analogies here and there. Let us assume, without investigating the matter, that such—always rather vague and accidental—analogies should be found also for the so important possibility of changing the *mode* (hence, the means) of "satisfaction" of the needs.

But now, let us consider again: In the economic theory of marginal utility and in every "subjective" value theory—particularly if we refer back to the "psychic" appurtenances of the individual—there is, to begin with, *not* an external "stimulus" but a "need." This is of course the reverse of the situation we have in the case of the fundamental law of psychophysics. Accordingly, if we wish to express ourselves in "psychological" terms, we deal with a complex of "sensations," "feeling-states," states of "tension," "discomfort," "expectation," and the like, which may at any time be of most intricate character. And these, moreover, combine with "memory images," "purposes," and perhaps conflicting "motives" of the most various kinds. Also, while the fundamental law of psychophysics instructs us about how an *external* stimulus evokes psychic conditions ("sensations"), economics, rather, is concerned with the fact that in virtue of such "psychic" conditions a specifically oriented *external* behavior (action) is evoked. This external conduct then, to be sure, has its proper return effect on the "need" out of which it arose, as it obviates or at any rate seeks to obviate this need through "satisfaction." Psychologically speaking, again, we have here a most complex and far from unambiguous process, that could in any event only quite exceptionally be equated with a simple "sensation" in the psychological sense. In psychological terms, the mode of *"reaction,"* not that of "sensation," would then constitute the problem.

Thus, we have in these (here deliberately quite crudely sketched) elementary processes of "action" a course of events that, on the most favorable assumptions, are in some small part—the least relevant part—of their development possibly "analogous" to what we get when we consider the matters investigated in the

Weberian weight-experiments. But obviously, as a whole, we now deal with phenomena that have a quite different structure from the objects dealt with in the Weberian weight experiments or anything like them.

It must, however, be added that these elementary processes here depicted, even in the form in which we have depicted them, obviously could not now or ever bring about or make possible the emergence of economics as a science. Properly, they represent at most *one* component of the events with which our discipline must deal. For, as Brentano's own further exposition also presupposes, economics has to investigate how human action is shaped. How is it shaped in consequence of (1) the competition of *different* "needs" seeking their "satisfaction?" (2) the *limitations* placed on not only—let us say—"need-capacity" but above all on the "goods" and "labor powers" that are objectively utilizable for the gratification of the needs referred to? (3) finally, a quite specific kind of co-existence of *different* men? These men, be it noted, have the same or similar needs, but at the same time they are equipped with different supplies of goods for their satisfaction and are engaged in competition with one another for the means of satisfaction.

The *problems* that arise here *cannot* be regarded as special cases or complications of "the fundamental psychophysical law." Moreover, the *methods* appropriate to the solution of these problems are *not* within the range of applied psychophysics or psychology. Applied psychophysics and psychology, on the contrary, have nothing to do with such a solution. The propositions of marginal utility theory are, as the simplest reflection shows, absolutely independent of the extent to which Weber's law is valid or of whether it is applicable at all or of whether *any* general statement on the relation of "stimulus" and "sensation" can be propounded.

For marginal utility theory to be feasible, it is quite sufficient if these provisos be true: (1) Common experience is justified in the view that men in their conduct are, *among other things*, motivated also by "needs" such as can be satisfied only by consumption of commodities that at any time are available only in limited supply—or by outputs of labor or the products thereof. Further, (2) common experience does not deceive us on the point that, for most needs—and particularly for such as are most urgently felt subjectively—it will be the case that, with increasing consumption of the commodities and labor outputs referred to, an increasing measure of "satisfaction" is attained. (Moreover, once this occurs, *other,* "unsatisfied" needs appear to be more urgent.) Finally, (3) men—be it in ever so varying degree—are able to act "expediently", that is, in the light of "experience" and of "prior calculation." This means to act in such fashion that they allocate the quantitatively limited "goods" and "labor powers," which they can dispose of or obtain, to the particular "needs" of the present and of the foreseeable future according to the *importance* they attach to this present and future. This "importance" obviously is not identical with—shall we say—a "sensation" produced through physical "stimulus."

Whether, further, the "satisfaction" of "needs" *ever* occurs in a progression which has *any* kind of similarity to that which the Weber-Fechner law affirms for the intensity of "sensations" evoked by "stimuli"—this question may be allowed to remain open. But *once* we reflect about the progression of "satisfaction" with Tiffany vases, toilet paper, sausage, editions of classical writers or the services of prostitutes, doctors or priests, then the logarithmic curve of the "fundamental law of psychophysics," as an analogy, appears to be exceedingly problematic. And if someone shows his "need"—even, for instance, at the cost of sacrificing food—to satisfy his "psychic requirements" by buying books and expending money for education while his hunger remains unappeased, this does not in any case become more "understandable" than it would otherwise be by a psychophysical "analogy." It quite *suffices* for economic theory if we can *theoretically conceive* of a relatively large number of people (on the basis of the previously alluded to, entirely trivial, but indisputable facts of everyday experience) each of whom disposes of the available "supplies of commodities" and "labor powers" (available to him simply as a matter of fact or in virtue of the protection given by a "legal order") for the sole and exclusive purpose of peaceably achieving an "optimum" of satisfaction of his *various* competing needs.

Every "psychologist" must surely turn up his nose at such "everyday experiences" as a foundation for a scientific theory. Take the very concept of "need." What a crude category of "vulgar psychology"! What vastly different physiological and psychological causal chains "need" can start up! Consider first that a consciously perceptible, rather complex psycho-physical situation may lie at the basis of the very "need" to eat. And this situation itself may be essentially conditioned by *various* effective circumstances operating as "stimuli"—for example, a physically empty stomach or even merely habituation to eating at particular hours of the day. Second, however, any subjective disposition of consciousness may be lacking, and the "need" to eat may be conditioned by an implanted "idea," arising, say, from obedience to doctor's orders. The "need for alcohol" may rest upon "habituation" to "external" stimuli, which in their turn create an "inner" "stimulus-condition"; and the need can be *intensified* by actually supplying alcohol—in defiance of the Weberian logarithmic curve. Finally, "need" for "reading" of a certain kind is determined by processes which—even if the psychophysicist, for his purpose, "reinterprets" them in terms of functional alterations of certain events occurring in the brain—can in any case scarcely be illuminated by mere reference to the Weber-Fechner law.

The "psychologist" here sees an entire series of the most difficult puzzlers in point of the inquiries that interest *him*—and economic "theory" wholly fails to look into these things, and with the easiest scientific conscience at that! Now, finally, think of "purposive action," "experiencing," "prior calculation," which are most complex from a psychological point of view, and in some degree perhaps even incomprehensible, but in any case most difficult to analyze—think of these and similar concepts as "foundations" of a discipline! And at that, there is no recasting of these concepts to make them susceptible to the psychologist's usual work with revolving drums or other laboratory apparatus! Yet this is the situation. The discipline, further, even claims—it actually presumes, I say—to obtain *mathematical* formulations for its theoretically conceived course of economically relevant action. It does this without concerning itself in the least whether materialism, vitalism, psychophysical parallelism, any of the theories of reciprocal effect, the "unconscious" of Lipps or of Freud or some other "unconscious," and so on, afford usable foundations for *psychological* disciplines. For its purposes, indeed, it operates with the explicitly stated assurance that all this sort of thing is *simply a matter of indifference.*

Still more important, the discipline really brings all this off. The significance of its results may be ever so much disputed, on the most various grounds in the field of its *own* methods. Nevertheless, in point of "correctness" they are still just as unqualifiedly independent of the greatest conceivable transformations of basic biological and psychological hypotheses as it is a matter of indifference for them whether, for example, Copernicus or Ptolemy was right. Nor is it of any significance for them how matters stand with theological hypotheses or, say, with the "tricky" perspectives of the second law of thermodynamics. Changes, no matter how extensive, in such basic theories of natural science simply cannot bring into question even a single *"properly"* construed proposition of the economic theory of price or income.

Of course, within the sphere of *empirical* analysis of economic life, the *facts* established by the natural sciences referred to (and by any number of others) may at particular junctures become quite important. Nothing that has been said above denies this. Nor—for a second point—is it denied that the mode of *conceptualization* which has proven useful for these disciplines would occasionally serve well as a model for certain problems of economic analysis.

As regards the first of these two points, I hope shortly to have the opportunity to investigate what use can possibly be made of certain works in experimental psychology, for instance, in the area of particular conditions of factory work. And as regards the second point, not only mathematical modes of thought (as has long been the case) but also, by way of example, certain biological modes of thought have a legitimate place in our discipline. At every step and on countless particular points of interest to our discipline, we economists are and must be involved in fruitful interchange of findings and viewpoints with workers in other fields. This is something to be taken for granted as common to all economists. But the matter of just how this interchange is to take place, and in which direction, in the sphere of *our* concerns—this depends unequivocally on the questions *we* pose. And every effort to decide a priori which theories from other disciplines must be "fundamental" for economics is futile—like all efforts to obtain a "hierarchy" of the sciences according to the Comtean model.

It is not only that, at least by and large, the most general hypotheses and assumptions of the "natural sciences" (in the usual sense of this term) are the most irrelevant ones for our discipline. But further, and above all, precisely as regards the point which is decisive for the peculiar quality of the questions proper to our discipline: In economic theory ("value theory") we stand entirely on our own feet. The "everyday experience" from which our theory takes its departure (see above) is of course the common point of departure of *all* particular empirical disciplines. Each of them aspires beyond everyday experience and must so aspire,

for thereon rests its right to existence as a "science." But each of them in its as-
pirations "goes beyond" or "sublimates" everyday experience in a different way
and in a different direction. Marginal utility theory and economic "theory" generally do this not, say, in the manner and with the orientation of psychology but
rather pretty much in opposite ways. Economic theory does not, one may say,
break down *internal* experimental correlates of everyday experience into psy-
chical or psychophysical "elements" ("stimuli," "sensations," "reactions," "au-
tomatisms," "feelings," and so on). Instead, it seeks to "understand" certain
"adaptations" of man's *external* behavior to conditions of existence of a quite specific sort that are *outside* man himself.

This outside world which is relevant for economic theory may in the particular case be "nature" (in the sense of ordinary language) or it may be "social environment." But in either case, the effort is always made to render "adaptation"
(to this world) understandable on the ad hoc, heuristic assumption that that action with which the theory is concerned runs its course on strictly "rational"
terms (in the sense discussed above).

Marginal utility theory, in order to attain specific objects of knowledge, treats
human action as if it ran its course from beginning to end under the control of
commercial calculation—a calculation set up on the basis of *all* conditions that
need to be considered. It treats individual "needs" and the goods available (or
to be produced or to be exchanged) for their satisfaction as mathematically calculable "sums" and "amounts" in a continuous process of bookkeeping. It treats
man as an agent who constantly carries on "economic enterprise," and it treats
his life as the object of his "enterprise" controlled according to calculation. The
outlook involved in commercial bookkeeping is, if anything, the starting point of
the constructions of marginal utility theory. Now, does its procedure rest upon
the Weberian law? Is it an application of any propositions concerning the relationship of "stimulus" and "sensation"? For its purposes, marginal utility theory
treats the "psyche" of all men (conceived of as isolated entities and regardless of
whether they are involved in buying and selling) as a *merchant's soul,* which can
assess quantitatively the "intensity" of its needs as well as the available means of
their satisfaction. It is in this way that the theory attains to its theoretical constructions. But all this is certainly *opposite* to the procedure of any "psychology"!

Nevertheless, the theory that has grown up on the basis indicated hardly creates its presuppositions out of nothing, although it is quite true that they are "unreal." The "value" of goods in the "isolated economy" constructed by the theory
would be precisely like the *book value* which they would necessarily show in an
ideally perfect bookkeeping of an isolated household.[5] This book value has about
it as much and as little of what is "unreal" as any actual commercial bookkeeping activity. If in some balance-sheet the "stock-capital" is shown, for example,
as a million marks under "liabilities," or if a building is "valued at" a hundred
thousand marks—does that million or that hundred thousand lie in some drawer

---

[5] This of course does not mean that the "technique" of the book entries should be conceived to
be quite the same as that of a present-day isolated economic enterprise.

or other? And yet the recording of these sums makes very good sense!—quite the same sense (necessary things being changed) as the "value" in the isolated economy of marginal utility theory. One simply must not seek to ascertain the character of this value by "psychological" means!

The theoretical "values" with which marginal utility theory works should in principle make understandable to us the circumstances of economic life, in a manner like that in which commercial book values render information to the businessman about the state of his enterprise and the conditions for its continued profitability. And the general theorems which economic theory sets up are simply constructions that state what consequences the action of the individual man in its intertwining with the action of all others would *have to* produce, *on the assumption that* everyone were to shape his conduct toward his environment exclusively according to the principles of commercial bookkeeping—and, in *this* sense, "rationally." As we all know, the assumption does not hold—and the empirical course of those proceedings for the understanding of which the theory was formulated accordingly shows only an "approximation" (varying considerably according to the particular case) to the theoretically constructed course of strictly rational action. Yet, the historical peculiarity of the capitalistic epoch, and thereby also the significance of marginal utility theory (as of every economic theory of value) for the understanding of this epoch, rests on the circumstances that—while the economic history of some epochs of the past has not without reason been designated as "history of non-economic conditions"—under today's conditions of existence the approximation of reality to the theoretical propositions of economics has been a *constantly increasing* one. It is an approximation to reality that has implicated the destiny of ever-wider layers of humanity. And it will hold more and more broadly, as far as our horizons allow us to see.

The heuristic significance of marginal utility theory rests on this *cultural-historical* fact, but not on its supposed foundation in the Weber-Fechner law. It is, for example, no accident that an especially striking degree of approximation to the theoretical propositions of price formation (as Böhm-Bawerk, connecting his work with that of Menger, developed them) has been represented by the fixing of the Berlin market-rate under the system of the so-called uniform quotation. This Berlin situation could serve directly as a paradigm for the theoretical propositions.[6] But this is certainly not because those who come to the stock exchange are in special and specific degree (with reference to the relation between "stimulus" and "sensation") subject to the fundamental law of psychophysics. Rather it is because action on the stock exchange is economically rational in especially high degree—or *can* be so.

The rational *theory* of price formation not only has nothing to do with the concepts of experimental psychology. More generally, it has nothing to do with any

---

[6] I do not really see the justification for the disparaging treatment of the "Austrians" by Brentano. Carl Menger proposed excellent views even if they were not methodologically finished. And as regards the question of "style", which is today usually overvalued at the expense of pertinent content of thought, even in this Böhm-Bawerk, if perhaps not Menger, is a master.

"psychology" of any kind which aspires to be a "science" going beyond everyday experience. Anyone who, let us say, stresses the necessity to consider a specific "stock exchange psychology," *besides* purely abstract price theory, fancies the object of such theory to be precisely the influence of economically *irrational* factors, of "disturbances" of the laws of price formation that are to be postulated *theoretically*. Marginal utility theory and, more broadly, any subjective theory of value are not psychologically, but—if a methodological term be desired—"pragmatically" founded, that is, on the use of the categories "ends" and "means." Something more will be said about this later.

Now the tenets which constitute specifically economic *theory* do *not* represent (as everyone knows and as was first mentioned) "the whole" of our science. These tenets afford but a single means (often, to be sure, an underestimated means) for the analysis of the causal connections of empirical reality. As soon as we take hold of this reality itself, in its culturally significant components, and seek to explain it causally, economic history is immediately revealed as a sum of "ideal-typical" concepts. This means that its theorems represent a series of *conceptually* constructed events, which, in "ideal purity," are seldom, or even not at all, to be found in the historical reality of any particular time. But on the other hand, these theorems—since in fact their elements are derived from experience and *intensified* to the point of pure rationality only in a process of thought—are useful both as heuristic instrumentalities of analysis and as constructive means for the representation of the empirical manifold.

In concluding, let us go back to Brentano once more. He sets out the Weber-Fechner law (p. 67) more finely in the form in which in his opinion it also lies at the foundation of economics. Then it has this sense: In order to evoke a sensation at all, it is necessary to go beyond the stimulus threshold. (See above.) When this has been achieved, every additional stimulation intensifies sensation at least proportionally—until, after attainment of the (individually variant) optimum, the intensity of sensation still indeed increases in absolute terms, but less than in proportion to stimulus-increase. This goes on until finally, with ever greater intensification of stimulus, the point is reached at which sensation decreases even in absolute terms. At last sensation disappears entirely in virtue of nerve-deadening.

Brentano now continues: "This law was recognized in economics . . . as the law of *decreasing yield of land*, for it governs the growth of plants." One's first reaction is to ask in astonishment: Do arable land and plants operate according to *psychological* laws? But, on page 67, Brentano had said somewhat more generally that, according to a general *physiological* law, every "life process" decreases in intensity with increase of the conditions favorable to it beyond a specific optimum; and obviously the example of decreasing yield of land relates to this proposition, not to the immediately preceding one. But in any event we may say that he conceives the Weber-Fechner law as a special case of the general principle of the *optimum* and, once again, marginal utility theory as a sub-case of that special case. The theory thereby seems to be directly tied up with a fundamental law of all "life."

Now the concept of the "optimum" is in fact one which economic theory has in common with the physiological and psychophysical approach; and to refer *illustratively* to *this* analogy may (according to the concrete educational purpose one entertains) very well have *pedagogical* value. But such "optima" are by no means restricted to "life processes." Thus, every machine is likely to have an optimum of productivity for specific purposes. An administration of fuel beyond this point, an excess supplying of raw material, and so on, will diminish performance, first relatively and then absolutely. And, in the case of the machine, a "heating threshold" corresponds to the psychophysical "stimulus threshold." The concept of the "optimum" is thus (as are the other concepts adduced by Brentano which are connected with it) one that has a still larger field of application and does *not* merely go together with the principles of "life processes."

On the other hand, there is involved in the concept of the optimum, as inspection of the meaning of the word at once indicates, a teleological "function-value." ("Optimum," one says—optimum for what?) It is easy to see that this comes up especially where we operate explicitly or by implication with the category of "purpose" (and we are not interested in whether it might come up more generally). This occurs as we conceive a given manifold as a *unity,* relate this *unity* to a *determinate* outcome, and then *evaluate* the unity with respect to this concrete outcome as "means" for the attainment of the outcome. (We herewith consider the outcome in terms of whether it is attained, not attained, incompletely attained, and attained through use of few or many means.) For example, a given manifold of diversely shaped pieces of iron and steel is referred by us to the purpose of making a "woven fabric" out of "yarn." This manifold presents itself to us as a "machine" of a specific kind. We look upon it from the point of view of *how much* woven fabric of a particular sort it "can" produce in the unit time needed for consumption of determinate quantities of coal and labor capacities.

One may say the same kind of thing occurs where we test structures consisting of "nerve cells" to the end of ascertaining what their "function" (which, however, means their "performance" for a "purpose") may be, as parts of a living organism, by way of mediating specific sensations. Or where we look upon cosmic and meteorological constellations from the standpoint of the question where and when, say, an astronomical observation we intend to make will have the "optimum" chance of success. Or where we see the economic man treat his environment from the standpoint of "satisfaction" of his needs.

This discussion need not be further spun out, since I shall on another occasion return to these conceptual problems insofar as they are to be found in *our* area of science—for "biological" questions are better left to the biologists. On these matters, Gottl and O. Spann, for example, have recently said some good things, but also—particularly in Gottl's case—other things with which I could not agree. By way of reassurance, let it be further noted that the problems of "absolute" values or of "universal cultural values" (the subjects of so much controversy), or indeed the supposed "opposition" of "cause and purpose" that has been set up in such badly confusing fashion by Stammler—that such problems have nothing whatever to do with the purely *technical* questions of concept construction with which we are here concerned. The connection is about as slight as that between commercial bookkeeping—a process doubtless to be "interpreted" in "teleological-rational" terms—and the teleology of a divine overlordship of the world.

It has been our intention here to show only this: Even the concept of an "optimum," which Brentano appears to regard as important for his thesis, is neither specifically psychological nor psychophysical nor physiological nor biological. Rather, the concept is common to a whole set of problems which otherwise differ from one another greatly. Consequently, it tells nothing about what the foundations of economic theory are and certainly does not mark out marginal utility theory as a special case of the application of the Weber-Fechner law or of any basic physiological law.

GLOSSARY

THIS GLOSSARY has a very simple purpose, namely to assist the reader when studying Weber's texts in this volume or his economic sociology more generally. The most important concepts in Weber's economic sociology are to be found in "Sociological Categories of Economic Action," the second chapter of *Economy and Society* (for an excerpt, see reading 16 in this anthology), and whenever a term is defined there, this fact has been noted.[1] In general, preference has been given to works from Weber's last decade since it was during these years that he decided to develop an economic sociology. This means that most definitions are taken from *Economy and Society*, though a few also come from *The Protestant Ethic*. Weber never had the time to personally inspect the text of the *General Economic History*, so references to this work have been kept to a minimum.

Concepts of several different kinds have been included in this glossary. Among these are new terms that Weber invented, such as "political capitalism" and "open and closed economic relationships." Another category covers terms that are commonly used but which Weber defined in his own way, such as "property" and "class." There are also some terms pertaining to matters where it may simply be of interest to the reader to know Weber's stance, such as "income distribution" and "prices and price theory." Since this glossary is intended for English-speaking readers, the concepts are listed under their English names, with the original German names given in parentheses. Further information on many of the concepts in this glossary can also be found in the author's *Max Weber and the Idea of Economic Sociology*.[2] Weber himself was much concerned with the exact meaning of concepts, and one can agree with the assessment of Peter Ghosh that it is the "classical and philological training of Weber which lies at the root of Weber's pertinacity over exact terminology."[3] The best-known example of Weber's philological skill is no doubt to be found in his discussion of the term "calling" (*Beruf*) in *The Protestant Ethic*.[4] In addition, Weber was impressed by G. F. Knapp's attempt to introduce a totally new terminology in the analysis of

---

[1] When references are made in the glossary to specific texts by Weber, the following standard editions have been used: *Economy and Society* (1922) (Berkeley: University of California Press, 1978); Max Weber, *From Max Weber*, ed. Hans Gerth and C. Wright Mills (New York: Oxford University Press, 1946); *The Methodology of the Social Sciences* (New York: The Free Press, 1949); and *The Protestant Ethic and the Spirit of Capitalism* (London: Allen & Unwin, 1930).

[2] Richard Swedberg, *Max Weber and the Idea of Economic Sociology* (Princeton, N.J.: Princeton University Press, 1998).

[3] Peter Ghosh, "Some Problems with Talcott Parsons' Version of 'The Protestant Ethic,'" *Archives européénnes de sociologie* 35 (1994): 116.

[4] See especially Weber, *The Protestant Ethic and the Spirit of Capitalism* (London: Allen & Unwin, 1930), pp. 204–11, notes 1–3, or "Die protestantische Ethik," *Gesammelte Aufsätze zur Religionssoziologie*, vol. 1 (Tübingen: J. C. B. Mohr, 1988), pp. 63–69.

money, declaring that this lessened the risk of the kind of misunderstandings that are common when concepts from everyday life are used for scientific purposes.[5] Not many of Knapp's other contemporaries appreciated his efforts, and Weber's use of Knapp's terminology makes the reading of certain parts of "Sociological Categories of Economic Action" (sections 32–36, not reproduced in this volume), contrary to Weber's intentions, additionally difficult.

It may finally be noted that very few of the concepts that Weber himself tried to introduce through his economic sociology in "Sociological Categories of Economic Action" have become part of social science terminology. This is a pity since many of these seem extremely useful, such as "appropriation," "open and closed economic relationships," "political capitalism," and "rational capitalism." One of the reasons for this, however, may simply be that Weber's economic sociology has so far not been very well known.

accounting. See calculation

acquisitive instinct (Erwerbstrieb) — Weber is very critical of this concept, especially of the attempt to explain the emergence of modern capitalism as somehow the result of an inborn instinct of acquisition (see especially *The Protestant Ethic*, p. 17). The concept of acquisitive instinct, Weber says, is "wholly imprecise and better not used at all" (*Economy and Society*, pp. 1190–91).

adventurers' capitalism (Abenteuerkapitalismus) — This term covers a type of capitalism which Weber describes as having always existed and as being characterized by ruthlessness; it is either speculative-irrational or violent in nature—but never rational. The term "adventurers' capitalism" is used in Weber's sociology of religion, but not in the important discussion of the principal modes of capitalist profit-making in "Sociological Categories of Economic Action" (section 31, pp. 236–38 above). In *The Protestant Ethic* the term is mainly used as a contrast to the novel and much more ethical type of capitalism advocated by the ascetic Protestants. *See also* capitalism; economic superman; politically oriented capitalism; speculation

agrarian constitution. See constitution

appropriation (Appropriation) — This concept plays an important role in Weber's general sociology as well as in his economic sociology. It is defined in chapter 1 of *Economy and Society* as a situation where in a closed social relationship opportunities are monopolized on a permanent basis and have become more or less alienable (p. 44). Weber states that "appropriated opportunities will be called 'rights'" (*Economy and Society*, p. 44). To own something (property), to sell something, and to inherit something, all presuppose different forms of rights in this sense. "Sociological Categories of

---

[5] Weber, "Antikritisches zum 'Geist' des Kapitalismus," in *Die protestantische Ethik, vol. 2: Kritiken und Antikritiken* (Gütersloh: Gütersloher Verlagshaus Mohn, 1978), pp. 155, 176, note 5. In chapter 2 of *Economy and Society* Weber also refers to Knapp's "able and valuable attempt to systematize terminology and concepts" (p. 78).

Economic Action" contains elaborate typologies of different forms of appropriation of labor, managerial functions, and the means of production (sections 19–22, not reproduced in this volume). *See also* open and closed economic relationships; economic relationships; property; stereotyping of the economy

authority. See domination

autocephalous (autokephal) — In his discussion of the concept of organization in *Economy and Society*, Weber writes: "Autocephaly means that the chief and his staff are selected according to the autonomous order of the organization itself, not as in the case of heterocephaly, that they are appointed by outsiders" (p. 50). The term "autocephalous" comes from the Greek *autokephalos* ("self-headed") and was used in medieval Byzantine law to indicate that a church organization was independent.

availability. See economic availability

benefice (Pfründe) — According to *Economy and Society*, "The benefice is a life-long, not a hereditary, remuneration for its holder in exchange for his real or presumed services; the remuneration is an attribute of the office, not of the incumbent" (p. 1073). Benefices can consist of fees or of land, or be in kind. There is usually an attempt by the administrator to make the benefice hereditary. Benefices can help to block the emergence of rational capitalism by preventing rationalization of the state machinery. The term "prebend" is sometimes used instead of "benefice."

budgetary management (Haushalt) — Following the classical distinction between the management of a household and moneymaking, Weber contrasts what he calls "budgetary management" (sometimes also translated as "householding") with profit-making. According to Weber's definition in "Sociological Categories of Economic Action," "the continual utilization and procurement of goods, whether through production or exchange, by an economic unit for purposes of its own *consumption* will be called 'budgetary management'" (section 10, pp. 215–19 above). "Wealth" is related to budgetary management and is used to produce "rent"; in profit-making, "capital" is the equivalent term. "Income" is the amount of goods, valued in money, which is available to a household during a particular time period. In budgetary management calculations are oriented to marginal utility, while in profit-making they are oriented to profitability. Calculations in budgetary management can be rational and are in that case carried out in accordance with a budget. A problem with calculations in a household is that they often have to be carried out without the assistance of effective market prices. Units with budgetary management include the family, the *oikos* (the household of a lord), and the planned state economy. *See also* capital; capital accounting; firm; planned economy; profit-making

bureaucracy (Bürokratie) — Bureaucracies are portrayed as efficient machines in Weber's sociology, and there exist economic as well as political and religious bureaucracies. Large-scale capitalistic enterprises are usually organized as bureaucracies. As a rule, only small organizations can avoid bureaucracy. The tendency in a bureaucracy to treat everybody without regard to the person goes very well with capitalism; and this is also true for the tendency in bureaucracies to separate the means of administration from those who work in them. In general, rational capitalism can only exist on condition that enterprises and the state are organized as dependable bureaucracies. Historically, bureaucratization has been furthered by capitalist interests, especially through the alliance between capital and absolutist rulers. Further bureaucratization of capitalism is to be expected in the future, according to Weber. *See also* economic organization; firm

calculation *(Kalkulation, Rechnung)* — Weber uses the concept of calculation in a broad sense, and when he says that "the modern capitalist enterprise rests primarily on *calculation,*" he includes not only economic calculation but also a predictable political and legal administration (*Economy and Society,* p. 1394). Economic calculation is very old; and it is intimately connected to the nature as well as the existence of money. Economic calculation can exhibit different degrees of rationality; it is clear, for example, that errors of calculation are still made today and that economic calculation is often of a conventional and traditional kind. Unpredictable elements cannot be totally eliminated from calculation (*see* speculation). In capital accounting, calculations are made before as well as after business has been transacted (*Vorkalkulation* and *Nachkalkulation*). Accounting has played a crucial role in the development of rational capitalism, according to Weber, especially double-entry bookkeeping which constitutes its technically most advanced form. Calculation in kind, as in planned economies, poses special problems. *See also* capital accounting; money; planned economy; rational economic action

calling *(Beruf)* — In *The Protestant Ethic* Weber discusses how the notion of "calling" or "vocation" emerged in Protestantism, and how in ascetic Protestantism it came to mean the ethical duty to perform one's work well and in a methodical manner. The concept of *Beruf* has its origin in religious tasks set by God, and was extended by Luther to secular work. In "Sociological Categories of Economic Action" Weber also uses *Beruf* in a different and more modern sense, namely as "occupation." "The term 'occupation' (*Beruf*) will be applied to the mode of specialization, specification and combination of the functions of an individual so far as it constitutes for him the basis of a continuous opportunity for income or earnings" (section 24, not reproduced here). *See also* work

capital *(Kapital)* — Capital is connected to profit-making, just as wealth is connected to householding or budgetary management. According to "Sociological Categories of Economic Action," "'Capital' is the money value of the means of profit-making available to the enterprise at the balancing of the books" (section 11, pp. 219–20 above). *See also* budgetary management (especially the concept of wealth); profit-making

capital accounting *(Kapitalrechnung)* — Weber speaks of calculations in kind (*Naturalrechnung*), calculations made with the help of money (*Geldrechnung*), and calculations using capital or capital accounting (*Kapitalrechnung*).

The last form of accounting is central to rational capitalism, and it is defined in "Sociological Categories of Economic Action" as follows: "Capital accounting is the valuation and verification of opportunities for profit and of the success of profit-making activity by means of a valuation of the total assets (goods and money) of the enterprise at the beginning of a profit-making venture, and the comparison of this with a similar valuation of the assets still present and newly acquired, at the end of the process; in the case of a profit-making organization operating continuously, the same is done for an accounting period" (section 11, p. 219 above). Capital acounting can be used for market activities but also for economic activities based on political power. Capital accounting has only emerged in the West, and certain institutional conditions are necessary for its existence (for an enumeration of these, see section 30, pp. 234–36 above). *See also* calculation; firm; profit-making

capitalism *(Kapitalismus)* — Even though Weber was fascinated by capitalism all his life and regarded it as "the most fateful force in our modern life" (*The Protestant Ethic*, p. 17), it is difficult to find a straightforward definition of capitalism in his work. On the whole, Weber seems to have been more interested in mapping out different types of capitalism than in defining capitalism in general. The closest one can get to a definition of capitalism as such may well be the following statement, which can be found in his sociology of religion: "We will define a capitalist economic action as one which rests on the expectation of profit by the utilization of opportunities for exchange, that is on (formally) peaceful chances of profit" (*The Protestant Ethic*, p. 17; for a good introductory discussion of different types of capitalism, see ibid., pp. 17–27). In "Sociological Categories of Economic Action," where a more stringent terminology is used, one very important paragraph is devoted to capitalism (section 31, pp. 236–38 above). Here, however, Weber does not speak of capitalism in general but of half a dozen qualitatively different forms of "'capitalist' orientation of profit-making activity." These six forms of orientation, he says, can be divided into two categories: (a) one that is unique to the West, and (b) a few others that have existed for several thousand years. The latter category is further divided into "politically oriented capitalism" and profit-making activity centered around commodity trade and dealings in money. The modern, specifically Western type of capitalism is characterized as a "rational, market-oriented form of capitalism," and is described as having the following traits: rational enterprises in a market economy, labor that is formally free, and sophisticated forms of financing (cf. also section 39, not reproduced in this volume). Weber, however, also makes clear that modern capitalism has its irrational elements and a distinct dynamic of its own. When profit-making is replaced by rent in modern capitalism, the whole economic system is transformed in a nondynamic direction. Weber refers to many other types of capitalism in his writings besides those that have been mentioned here, and the most important of these are discussed in separate entries. *See also* adventurers' capitalism; capital; capital accounting; capitalist spirit; class; economic traditionalism (for traditional capitalism); imperialism (for imperialist capitalism); pariah capitalism; politically oriented capitalism; profit-making; rational capitalism; speculation; traditional commercial capitalism

capitalist adventurer. See adventurers' capitalism

capitalist spirit. See spirit of capitalism

chance. See economic opportunities

chartal. See money

class (Klasse) — Weber speaks of three different types of classes in Part I of *Economy and Society*: "property classes," "commercial classes," and "social classes" (pp. 302–7; see also reading 5). The first type can be found in a society where property is decisive, and the second in a society where profit-making is decisive. The term "social classes" has less to do with the economy and refers instead to classes as (potential) communities. Weber contrasts class with status, and argues that while the former typically deals with the way that "life chances" are connected to the market, and entails little sense of honor, status is primarily connected to consumption, entails a very distinct sense of honor, and has to do with people's lifestyles. A class rarely constitutes a community, as opposed to status groups. Change favors class over status, while stability has the opposite effect. See also the entry for status.

closure. See open and closed economic relationships

commercialization (Kommerzialisierung) — This concept is described in "Sociological Categories of Economic Action" as "the transformation of rights to appropriated profit opportunities into securities or other negotiable instruments" (section 29a, not reproduced in this volume). Commercialization represents one of the presuppositions of present-day capitalism.

communism (Kommunismus) — Weber mentions three major forms of communism in "Sociological Categories of Economic Action": household communism (within a family), military communism (between comrades in arms), and religious communism (in communities based on love and charity) (section 26, not reproduced in this volume). These types of communism are indifferent to calculation and based on noneconomic considerations. Modern communism represents a new historical phenomenon, especially since it is rational in spirit. *See also* planned economy

competition (Konkurrenz) — Competition can be of a noneconomic as well as an economic nature, and is defined in *Economy and Society* as follows: "a peaceful conflict is 'competition' insofar as it consists in a formally peaceful attempt to attain control over opportunities and advantages which are also desired by others" (p. 38). Within the economy this type of behavior mainly takes the form of competition for economic opportunities in exchange relationships. Economic actors become interested in curbing competition when the number of competitors, in relation to the profit span, grows (*Economy and Society*, pp. 341–42). Political competition, as opposed to economic competition, may affect the economy, for example, if the ruler has to compete with other rulers for economic resources. *See also* exchange; market; open and closed economic relationships

constitution (Verfassung, as in Agrarverfassung, Arbeitsverfassung, Sozialverfassung, and so on) — Following the custom in German social science around the turn of the century, Weber used the term "constitution" in a variety of contexts. The term is hard to translate and means, among other things, "organization." In his early work Weber was innovative in his use of the term "agrarian constitution," according to some commentators, especially in that he included a social or sociological dimension.

consumption. See budgetary management

contract (Kontrakt) — A contract is defined in *Economy and Society* as "a voluntary agreement constituting the foundation of claims and obligations" (p. 671). Weber's sociology of law contains an extensive discussion of different types of contracts and their historical emergence. An important distinction is drawn between "the status contract" (*"Status"-Kontrakt*) and "the instrumental contract" (*Zweck-Kontrakt*). The former "involves a change in what may be called the total legal situation (the universal position) and the social status of the person involved" (p. 672); while the latter "aims solely . . . at some specific (especially economic) performance or result" (p. 673). When an individual, for example, becomes somebody's slave or master, a status contract is involved; while barter is an early example of a purposive contract. Formal freedom of contract is crucial to modern capitalism.

depersonalization (Versachlichung) — Modern or rational capitalism entails a certain "depersonalization" of economic life, and this makes it difficult to regulate economic activities in accordance with some ethical doctrine. In feudalism, for example, it was possible for the church to identify specific powerful persons and demand that these change their behavior in some specified way, but this is not possible in capitalism, since all capitalists have to obey the impersonal "laws" of the market or go under. The difficulty of intervening ethically in rational capitalism sets it on a collison course with religions and ethical doctrines. Depersonalization is characteristic for the economic ethic of rational capitalism. *See also* economic ethic

discipline (Disziplin) — This concept is defined in *Economy and Society* as follows: "'Discipline' is the probability that by virtue of habituation a command will receive prompt and automatic obedience in stereotyped forms, on the part of a given group of persons" (p. 53; compare the definition of domination). The disciplining of the workers represents an important step in the history of capitalism. Discipline is easier to create, Weber notes, if the workers have been separated from the means of production and if there is free labor.

division of labor (Leistungsverteilung) — In "Sociological Categories of Economic Action" the concept of division of labor is discussed in close connection with the concept of the combination of labor (*Leistungsverbindung*). Long sections are devoted to what Weber calls types of economic division of labor, types of the technical division of labor, and social aspects of the division of labor (sections 15–21, not reproduced in this volume). These sections are difficult to penetrate and mostly of interest to economic historians. While Weber pays attention to the division of labor between the sexes in his various writings, this topic is not singled out in a separate section in "Sociological Categories of Economic Action." The technical divison of labor is centered around the fact that work has to be divided up and united in order to solve technical problems. The economic division of labor has to do with the fact that work is carried out within a unit that is oriented either to profit-making or to household needs (more precisely, to budgetary management). Social aspects of the division of labor include, for example, whether the unit within which the work is carried out is autonomous or not, and whether it is autocephalous or not (the latter meaning that the chief and the staff are appointed from within rather than from outside the organization). *See also* utility; work

domination (Herrschaft) — Domination affects the economy in two ways: (1) each economy is part of a political system characterized by some kind of domination (legal, charismatic, and/or traditional domination), and (2) certain parts of the economy operate via domination. The exact definition of domination in Part I of *Economy and Society* is the following: "'Domination' is the probability that a command with a given specific content will be obeyed by a given group of persons" (p. 53; cf. p. 946). It should be noted that the market does not operate according to the principle of domination, and when a worker enters a labor contract, he or she is not in a situation of domination. Once the contract has been signed, however, the worker is expected to obey. In an early version of *Economy and Society* Weber used a somewhat different terminology and applied the notion of domination also to what goes on in the market. Weber then distinguished between "domination by virtue of a constellation of [economic] interests" as well as "domination by virtue of authority." As an example of the former he mentions "monopolistic domination" and the ability of an economic actor who has economic power over another to direct the latter's actions without giving explicit orders (*Economy and Society*, pp. 943–44). In the final version of *Economy and Society*, however, this terminology is explicitly rejected (p. 214). *Herrschaft*, it may finally be mentioned, has been translated in many other ways than "domination," including "authority," "leadership," and "rulership." *See also* discipline; power of control and disposal

dualistic (economic) ethic (doppelte (Wirtschafts)Ethik) — During most of history human communities have had an in-group morality, which differed radically from out-group morality. For economic life this meant that there was an obligation to help members of one's own community who were in distress, while outsiders could be mercilessly cheated. One of the results of ascetic Protestantism was to introduce a uniform treatment in economic affairs of members of one's own community as well as people from the outside. In modern capitalism there is typically no distinction between in-group morality and out-group morality in economic questions. *See also* economic ethic; norms in the economy

economic action (Wirtschaften) — Economic (social) action constitutes the basic unit in Weber's economic sociology. It is defined in section 1 of "Sociological Categories of Economic Action" as "any peaceful exercise of an actor's control over resources which is in its main impulse oriented towards economic ends" (above, p. 199). Economic action, as defined here, is social in that it is oriented to the behavior of others; and it is economic in that it is concerned with what is subjectively perceived as a choice between ends, in a situation of scarcity. More precisely, economic action is concerned with "the satisfaction of a desire for 'utilities'"; and this desire can be based on material as well as on ideal needs. Desire for utilities comes from the need for want satisfaction as well as profit-making. Economic actions may be rational, traditional, or affectual (e.g. inspired by loyalty). What Weber calls "economically oriented action" differs from economic action in that it is either primarily oriented to noneconomic goals or that violence is used. Throughout history economically oriented action has been more important than economic action (even though the opposite is now the case); and "Sociological Categories of Economic Action" starts out by defining economically oriented action rather than economic action. *See also* ideal and material interests; power of control and disposal; rational economic action; technology; utility

economic availability (ökonomische Abkömmlichkeit) — Someone is economically available who can afford to engage in politics without giving up his or her ordinary job or status position. An industrial worker is typically not available in this sense, while a rentier is. Unless some way is found to pay those who are not economically available to participate in politics, power will drift into the hands of those who are economically available.

economic calculation. See calculation

economic closure. See open and closed economic relationships

economic domination. See domination

economic ethic (Wirtschaftsethik) — In each society economic activities are evaluated negatively or positively, and the sum of these evaluations (or norms) makes up its economic ethic. Manual labor, making profit through trade, and so on can be either approved of or looked down upon. There often exists one ethic regarding people from one's own community and another regarding people from outside. The economic ethic of capitalism entails a certain depersonalization. Just as one can speak of the economic ethic of a society, Weber notes, one can also speak of the economic ethic of a religion. What counts in the latter case is not the official religious doctrine but rather "the practical impulses for action which are founded in the psychological and pragmatic contexts of religions" (Max Weber, *From Max Weber,* p. 267). *See also* depersonalization; dualistic (economic) ethic; norms in the economy

economic form. See spirit of capitalism

economic history — Weber had a very broad concept of economic science ("social economics"), which was to include not only economic theory and economic sociology but also economic history. While sociology deals with type concepts and generalized uniformities, history aims at "the causal explanation of individual actions, structures, and personalities possessing cultural significance" (*Economy and Society,* p. 29). *See also* social economics

economic laws — According to Weber, it is "a naturalistic prejudice" to believe that the goal of the social sciences should be to produce laws (*The Methodology of the Social Sciences,* p. 101, cf. pp. 72–73). Many of the so-called laws of the social sciences—e.g., Gresham's Law, the law of marginal utility or the alleged laws of Marxism—should be seen as heuristic tools. At most, these laws constitute "sociological generalizations," (*Economy and Society,* p. 18).

economic motivation, willingness to work (Triebfeder des Wirtschaftens, Arbeitswilligkeit) — People are motivated in their economic activities by the need to provide for their ideal and material interests. According to "Sociological Categories of Economic Action," "In a market economy the striving for *income* is necessarily the ultimate driving force of all economic activity" (section 41, p. 239 above). Those in a privileged position are primarily motivated by large incomes, ambition, and/or a sense of calling. Those without property, such as workers, are motivated by the fact that they and their families would starve if they did not work; they also view productive work as something positive in itself. A planned economy would weaken the incentive to work since it is oriented to a substantive order. Willingness to work can be traditional, affectual, inspired by absolute values, or of a more egoistic nature (ibid., section 25, not reproduced in this volume). See also the entry for ideal and material interests.

economic norms. See norms in the economy

economic opportunities (ökonomische Chancen) — The term *Chance* is used in many different meanings in *Economy and Society,* such as "chance," "probability," and "opportunity." *Chance* in the last of these three senses is usually translated as "advantage," which causes confusion; hence, the translation "opportunity" has been adopted in this volume. The notion of "economic opportunities" is defined in "Sociological Categories of Economic Action" as "the opportunities . . . which are made available by custom, by the constellation of interest, or by a conventional or legal order for the purposes of an economic unit" (section 2, p. 205 above). Weber also speaks of a variety of different types of economic opportunities (e.g. profit opportunities (*Erwerbschancen*), market opportunities (*Marktchancen*), and so on). *See also* appropriation; class (life chances); speculation; utility

economic order (Wirtschaftsordnung) — This concept is defined in *Economy and Society* as follows: "We shall apply the term *economic order* to the distribution of the actual control over goods and services, the distribution arising in each case from the particular mode of balancing interests consensually; moreover, the term shall apply to the manner in which goods and services are indeed used by virtue of these powers of disposition, which are based on *de facto* recognition" (p. 312). Weber contrasts the economic order to the "legal order," which portrays reality as it should be according to the law, rather than as it actually is.

economic organization (Wirtschaftsverband) — An economic organization is defined in "Sociological Categories of Economic Action" as an organization characterized by "*primarily* autocephalous economic action of a given kind" (section 5, p. 210 above). To this may be added that Weber defines an organization as a social relationship that is closed or limited and which is enforced by a staff; that "autocephalous" means that the chief and the staff are appointed from inside the organization and not by outsiders. Examples of economic organizations include business corporations, cooperatives, and workshops for artisans. There also exist "economically active organizations" and "economically regulative organizations." The former are primarily noneconomic in nature but carry out some economic activity as well, such as states and churches. The latter regulate economic activity, for example trade unions and employers' associations. The term "economic organization" is close but not identical to some other terms in Weber's economic sociology. *See* bureaucracy; establishment; firm

economic phenomena ("wirtschaftliche" Erscheinungen) — This term is used in Weber's essay of 1904 on objectivity, where it is defined as "events and constellations of norms, institutions, etc., the economic aspect of which constitutes their primary cultural significance for us" (see reading 17, p. 242 above). *See also* economically conditioned phenomena; economically relevant phenomena; economy

economic power. See power of control and disposal

economic rationality. See rationality in the economy

economic sociology (Wirtschaftssoziologie) — The conceptual foundation for this type of analysis, developed by Weber in his last years (1918–20), can primarily be found in "Sociological Categories of Economic Action." The basic idea is that the focus should be on economic actions that are oriented to the behavior of others, not on economic actions per se, as in economic theory. On a more general level, Weber's economic sociology can be described as an attempt to unite an interest-driven type of analysis with a social one. Like all sociology, economic sociology "seeks to formulate type concepts and generalized uniformities of empirical process" (*Economy and Society*, p. 19). It naturally falls under Weber's general definition of sociology: "Sociology . . . is a science concerning itself with the interpretive understanding of social action and thereby with a causal explanation of its course and consequences" (ibid., p. 4). Economic sociology is finally also part of the much broader science of economics or social economics, as Weber called it. *See also* economic action; interest; social economics

economic sphere (ökonomische Sphäre and similar expressions) — According to Weber, the life of the individual as well as society itself can be conceptualized as consisting of separate spheres or orders, which tend to become more autonomous over time. These spheres are often in conflict with one another; they are also governed by a certain autonomy and have an inner logic of their own (*Eigengesetzlichkeit*—translated by Robert K. Merton as "limited autonomy"). The economic sphere is largely autonomous today, but it would nonetheless be incorrect to state that economic actions are exclusively governed by economic factors. For a discussion of the concept of economic sphere, see especially Weber, *From Max Weber,* pp. 331–33; for the other spheres, see pp. 323–30, 333–57.

economic spirit. See spirit of capitalism

economic stereotyping. See stereotyping of the economy

economic struggle. See struggle in the economy

economic superman (ökonomischer Übermensch) — This category covers extremely successful businessmen, who have existed in all periods and who consider themselves "beyond good and evil." Weber especially uses this term in *The Protestant Ethic* and in his contributions to the debate over this work, probably to point a contrast to the new type of businessman ushered in by ascetic Protestantism.

economic system. See economy

economic theory — Together with economic history and economic sociology, economic theory is part of the science of economics ("social economics"). The insights of economic theory, Weber says in "Sociological Categories of Economic Action," provide "the basis for economic sociology" (section 1, p. 204 above). The way that Weber constructs "economic action" (the basic concept in economic theory) and "economic social action" (the basic concept in economic sociology) illustrates this fact; they are identical, except that economic social action is also oriented to the behavior of other actors. Economic sociology and economic theory are furthermore similar in that they both use ideal types and that the analysis starts with the assumption of rational action. Weber seems to have equated economic theory more or less with the marginal utility theory of the Austrian type that existed around the turn of the century. In a few places in "Sociological Categories of Economic Action," it should be noted, Weber indicates where economic sociology diverges from economic theory. He also introduces some concepts that it would be difficult to accommodate in economic theory, such as struggle and power of control and disposal. In certain cases involving historical developments of the economy, Weber warns, "the explanatory methods of *pure* economics are as tempting as they are misleading" (section 15, not reproduced in this volume). *See also* marginal utility; prices and price theory; social economics

economic traditionalism (ökonomischer Traditionalismus) — Even though this concept is not singled out and defined in *Economy and Society,* economic traditionalism and how it was overcome in the West constitutes one of the great themes in Weber's economic sociology. In *The Protestant Ethic* Weber also discusses a form of traditional capitalism, which is contrasted to the modern, more systematic and rational type of capitalism (pp. 65–68). Today also, it should be added, traditionalism plays a considerable role in the economy. *See also* entrepreneur; stereotyping of the economy; traditional commercial capitalism

economically conditioned phenomena ("ökonomisch bedingte" Erscheinungen)— This term is used in Weber's essay of 1904 on objectivity, where it is defined as "phenomena which are *not* 'economic' in our sense and the economic effects of which are of no, or at best slight, interest to us . . . but which in individual instances are in their turn influenced in certain important aspects by economic factors" (see reading 17, p. 243 above). Weber's definition, it can be argued, was later expanded to include phenomena influenced by the economy more generally. *See also* economic phenomena; economically relevant phenomena; economy

economically oriented action. See economic action

economically relevant phenomena ("ökonomisch relevante" Erscheinungen) — This term is used in Weber's 1904 essay on objectivity, where it is defined as "phenomena . . . which do not interest us, or at least do not primarily interest us with respect to their economic significance but which, however, under certain circumstances do acquire significance in this regard because they have consequences which are of interest from the economic point of view" (see reading 17, p. 243 above). *See also* economic phenomena; economically conditioned phenomena; economy

economics. See economic theory; social economics

economy (Wirtschaft) — In section 1 (p. 200 above) of "Sociological Categories of Economic Action" the following definition is given: "We will call autocephalous economic action an 'economy.'" ("Autocephalous" means in this context that the economy is independent.) In his 1904 essay on objectivity Weber approaches the concept of the economy from a different angle, and argues that it can be conceptualized as consisting of the following three categories: "economic phenomena" (economic events or institutions); "economically relevant phenomena" (noneconomic phenomena whose consequences are of interest from the economic point of view); and "economically conditioned phenomena" (noneconomic phenomena which are to some degree influenced by economic factors). (See reading 17, pp. 242–43 above.) *See also* economic action; economic phenomena; economically conditioned phenomena; economically relevant phenomena; market economy

Eigengesetzlichkeit. See economic sphere

England Problem — According to a widely held interpretation of Weber's sociology of law, there exists a contradiction between Weber's argument that rational capitalism demands the existence of rational law, and the fact that England did not have such a legal system at the time when capitalism made its breakthrough. It is this that constitutes the so-called England Problem. See especially David Trubek, "Max Weber on Law and the Rise of Capitalism," *Wisconsin Law Review* (1972): 720–53; for a critique of this argument, see, e.g., chapter 4 in Richard Swedberg, *Max Weber and the Idea of Economic Sociology*.

enterprise. See firm

entrepreneur (Unternehmer) — This concept is not defined in "Sociological Categories of Economic Action," but Weber touches on entrepreneurship now and then in his economic sociology as well as in his writings on the economy more generally. As opposed to Schumpeter, Weber does not focus on the creativity of the individual entrepreneur but on the capitalist enterprise, as directed by the entrepreneur. According to Weber, the average entrepreneur hopes to make more profit than the existing rate of interest and draws on his or her "business imagination" in this effort. The modern entrepreneur is not part of the bureaucracy and is the only person who knows more than the bureaucrats; he or she is also "the 'directing mind' [and] the 'moving spirit'" in the enterprise (*Economy and Society*, p. 1403). In his various writings Weber often points out that entrepreneurship has been looked down upon by certain groups and in certain societies. In *The Protestant Ethic* Weber also contrasts "the new entrepreneur," who saw money-making as a calling and who wanted to reform things, with the traditional kind of entrepreneur, who was satisfied with the way things were. *See also* capitalism; firm; profit-making; work (for managerial work, as opposed to entrepreneurship)

establishment (Betrieb) — "Establishment" is defined in "Sociological Categories of Economic Action" as "a *technical* category which designates the continuity of the combination of certain types of services with each other and with material means of production" (section 15, not reproduced in this volume). It should furthermore be noted that in *Economy and Society* the term *Betrieb* is also translated as "(noneconomic) enterprise" when the contrast to the firm is not at issue; and in this case *Betrieb* simply means "continuous rational activity" (p. 52). When this continuous action is entrepreneurial in nature, Weber uses the term "profit-making enterprise" (*Erwerbsbetrieb*). *See also* economic organization; firm (for the distinction between the firm or enterprise, the establishment, and discontinuous economic activity)

exchange (Tausch) — This concept is defined in "Sociological Categories of Economic Action" as "a compromise of interests on the parts of the parties in the course of which goods or other advantages are passed in reciprocal compensation" (section 4, p. 208 above—which also contains a broader definition). The essence of exchange or "the struggle over exchange," as Weber also calls it, is the resolution of two conflicts of interest: one with the exchange partner, decided through bargaining ("the struggle over the price"); and the other with potential rivals, decided through competition ("the struggle between competitors"). An exchange is formally voluntary; and it can be occasional, traditional, or rational. It is made for profit or for consumption; and it always means that one type of utility is given up for another. *See also* competition; market; struggle in the economy

firm (Unternehmung, Unternehmen) — In "Sociological Categories of Economic Action," the firm or enterprise is defined as follows: "An economic 'enterprise' is autonomous action capable of orientation to capital accounting" (section 11, p. 220 above). Weber emphasizes that it is sometimes important to make a distinction between "firm" (Ger. *Unternehmung*) and "establishment" (Ger. *Betrieb*). While the firm is primarily an economic term, establishment is primarily a technical term. The antithesis of a firm is a budgetary unit (Ger. *Haushalt*), while the antithesis of an establishment is discontinuous activity, as found in any household. *See also* economic organization; establishment.

formal rationality. See rational economic action

goods. See utility

heterocephalous. See autocephalous

household. See budgetary management

ideal and material interests (ideelle und materielle Interessen) — While Marx emphasizes the driving role of material interests throughout history, Weber also speaks of ideal interests. "All economic activity in a market economy," he writes in "Sociological Categories of Economic Action," "is undertaken and carried through by individuals acting to provide for their own ideal and material interests" (section 41, p. 238 above). In a famous formulation of the relationship between ideas and interests, Weber also says that "not ideas, but ideal and material interests, directly govern men's conduct"—but he immediately adds that certain ideas may operate like "tracks," along which the interests are pushed by their own dynamic (Weber, *From Max Weber*, p. 280). *See also* interest; self-interest; struggle in the economy

imperialism (Imperialismus) — No definition is given in *Economy and Society* but Weber tends to see imperialism as basically a political phenomenon. Weber discusses the economic foundations of imperialism at some length in *Economy and Society* (pp. 913–21). This discussion does not contain a full theory of imperialism but some interesting reflections on the relationship between politics and economic interests. Weber, for example, looks at the relationship between trade and political expansion, and finds that trade is not the decisive factor in political expansion. As opposed to trade, the general economic structure of a society determines imperialism—but only to some extent. If the state provides capitalist opportunities, as in Rome, there will be a tendency towards "imperialist capitalism." But just as there are industries that profit from war, there also exist industries that profit from peace. *See* politically oriented capitalism

impersonality. See depersonalization

incentives. See economic motivation

income. See budgetary management

income distribution (Einkommensverteilung) — This concept is not defined in *Economy and Society* but plays a key role in Weber's analysis. The distribution of income affects, for example, effective demand and also the process of price formation via the interest struggle that precedes it. There is a struggle in the economy between formal and substantive rationality, and the existing distribution of income typically represents a source of substantive irrationality. *See also* rational economic action (with discussion of formal and substantive rationality)

instrumentally rational social action. See rational economic action

interest (Interesse) — This category is absolutely central to Weber's whole sociology and in particular to his economic sociology. Indeed, the latter can be characterized as an attempt to unite an interest-driven type of analysis with a social one. In Weber's scheme, action is mainly driven by interest but also by tradition and sentiments (*Economy and Society*, pp. 24–26). Interests can be ideal as well as material; there also exist empirical uniformities, determined by self-interest. For more details, *see* ideal and material interests; self-interest

iron cage (stahlhartes Gehäuse) — This metaphor plays a central role in *The Protestant Ethic* and denotes the harsh and stultifying conditions under which the individual is forced to live in capitalist-industrial society.

labor. See work

life chances. See class

liturgy (Leiturgie) — This concept is defined as follows in *Economy and Society*: "want satisfaction through negative privileges is called *liturgy*" (p. 350). Liturgies were typically used to make privileged groups help finance the state, and they also represent the most important way of financing the state, apart from taxation. Liturgies can be in kind or in money. Weber distinguishes between "class liturgies" and "status liturgies"; the former are attached to property and the latter to a monopolistic group for which individuals are collectively responsible. The system of liturgies was carried through with the greatest consistency in ancient Egypt.

marginal utility — Weber refers often to marginal utility in "Sociological Categories of Economic Action," but he uses it as an economic concept (mainly inspired by its use in Austrian economics) and not as a sociological concept. Reasoning in accordance with marginal utility theory follows a distinct logic, as in jurisprudence or mathematics, but what sociology focuses on is what happens in reality, and to understand this, other factors as well have to be taken into account. Weber also indicates a few cases where the way that economists use marginal utility goes directly counter to the way in which sociology analyzes things. The notion of marginal utility, as used in economic theory, Weber explains, is not based on psychology but on common experiences in everyday life of three kinds: (1) people are motivated by needs which can be satisfied through scarce material means; (2) the more that is consumed, the more a need is usually satisfied; and (3) people allocate scarce goods according to the importance they attach to different needs ("Marginal Utility Theory and 'The Fundamental Law of Psychophysics'" (1908); reading 18 in this anthology). The more capitalist reality advances, Weber also notes in this article, the more applicable the theory of marginal utility will be. *See also* economic theory

market (Markt, Marktvergemeinschaftung) — Weber's fullest definition of this concept can be found in a fragment that has been included in *Economy and Society*, where it is suggested that a market is made up of two different types of economic (social) action: competition in relation to rivals ("competitive struggle"); and struggle over price with the exchange partner ("price struggle"). "A market," to cite Weber's definition, "may be said to exist wherever there is competition, even if only unilateral, for opportunities of exchange among a plurality of potential actors. Their physical assemblage in one place, as in the local market square, the fair (the long distance market), or the exchange (the merchants' market), only constitutes the most consistent kind of market formation" (p. 635). Weber also notes that exchange in the market represents "the archetype of all rational social action" (p. 635). For terms such as "market situation," "market freedom," and "marketability," see section 8 in "Sociological Categories of Economic Action" (above, pp. 211–12). The concept of equilibrium is not part of Weber's analysis of the market, nor is it discussed in his economic sociology. *See also* competition; exchange; market economy

market economy (Verkehrswirtschaft) — According to "Sociological Categories of Economic Action," "Want satisfaction will be said to take place through a 'market economy' so far as it results from [economic] action oriented to advantages in exchange on the basis of self-interest and where co-operation takes place only through the exchange process" (section 14, p. 229 above). This definition, Weber points out, does not address the issue of whether, and to what extent, an economy is capitalistic. In a market economy individual economic units are independent, and calculations are made in money. As a contrast to this type of economy Weber describes the "planned economy," where economic action is oriented to a substantive order, where individual economic units are not independent, and where a budget is used and calculations are made in kind. The incentive to work is stronger in a market economy than in a planned economy since no substantive order is involved. *See also* planned economy

means of production (Beschaffungsmittel) — The expropriation of the workers from the means of production is discussed in "Sociological Categories of Economic Action" (sections 22–23, not reproduced in this volume). A similar process has also taken place in other areas of society, such as the army and the bureaucracy (see, e.g., Weber, *From Max Weber,* pp. 221–24). Separation of workers from the means of production, of employees from the means of administration, and so on, tends to increase formal rationality.

methodological individualism — This concept goes back to the ideas of John Stuart Mill and Carl Menger but was coined by Joseph Schumpeter around the turn of the century. It means, in all brevity, that the analysis of social phenomena starts from the individual—which is exactly what Weber advocates in the first chapter of *Economy and Society.* Sociology, Weber here says, focuses on those aspects of an individual's action which takes the behavior of others into account (*Economy and Society,* p. 4). Weber's version of methodological individualism can be characterized as social rather than atomistic in nature.

money (Geld) — The following definition is given in "Sociological Categories of Economic Action": "'Money' we call a chartal means of payment which is also a means of exchange" (section 6, not reproduced in this volume). The term "chartal" means that an authority has validated the material which is used for money, by marking it. Weber says that he will not develop a theory of money in "Sociological Categories of Economic Action," but only look at the sociological consequences of its use. The most important of these is clearly the way in which money is used as a tool for economic calculation. Money, according to Weber, is the most abstract and impersonal element in human life. It is, however, neither neutral nor innocent; it is rather a "weapon" in "a struggle of man against man" (section 13, p. 228 above). This last statement is probably not to be seen as a refutation of conventional monetary theory, but rather as meaning that in any discussion of how actual money prices are determined, interest conflicts and power struggles must be included in the analysis. "Sociological Categories of Economic Action" (sections 32–36, not reproduced here) also contains a very long (and partly outmoded) discussion of monetary politics which is much indebted to G. F. Knapp's *The State Theory of Money* (1905). *See also* calculation; prices and price theory

monopoly. See domination; open and closed economic relationships; status

needs. See wants

norms in the economy — The term "norm" (*Norm*) is occasionally used in *Economy and Society,* but not defined in its first chapter on basic sociological categories or anywhere else in this work. Weber, however, comes very close to the current concept of norms in his discussion in chapter 1 of "legitimate order," which is defined as "a social relationship . . . oriented toward determinable 'maxims' [for behavior]" (*Economy and Society*, p. 31). For the order to be valid or legitimate, these maxims must also be experienced by the actor as "obligatory or exemplary." Weber stresses that an order is always more than mere uniformity of behavior, caused by custom or by self-interest. If the maxims are backed up by a significant reaction of disapproval, you have a "convention" in Weber's terminology; and if they are backed up by coercion, administered by a staff, you have a "law" (p. 34). There are, for example, conventions in the market; they also play a key role in Weber's concept of economic ethic. *See also* dualistic (economic) ethic; economic ethic

occupation. See calling

open and closed economic relationships ("offene" und 'geschlossene' Wirtschaftsbeziehungen) — It is a fundamental quality of all social relationships, according to *Economy and Society*, that they can be either open or closed to outsiders (pp. 43–46). Certain relationships *within* a group may also be closed to those on the inside. When it is favorable to some actors' ideal or material interests to keep certain relationships open, they will typically be kept open, and when it is favorable to keep them closed, they will typically be closed. Economic relationships may similarly be open or closed, and this is true for relationships in markets, guilds, economic organizations, and many other economic phenomena (pp. 342–43). One reason for the closure of economic relationships is that the number of competitors in relation to the possibilities for profit-making has increased. Weber calls this "scope of economic resources in relation to acquisition" (*Erwerbsspielraum*); he also speaks of "scope of economic resources in relation to consumption needs" (*Nährungsspielraum*). When competition is curbed and some people excluded, a pretext for this is usually advanced; and this pretext can attach to anything, including the religion, race, or language of those who have been excluded (*Economy and Society*, p. 342). When someone succeeds in excluding others from an opportunity, Weber speaks of appropriation. Property is consequently a form of appropriation. *See also* appropriation; economic organization; property

opportunities. See economic opportunities

pariah capitalism (Paria-Kapitalismus) — Although this is a general category, Weber only applies it to the kind of capitalism created by the Jewish people. Here it includes profit-making activities involving moneylending, and those of a political character—but not those of an industrial nature. The term "pariah" refers to the ritual segregation of the Jews as well as to their negative status in the eyes of those who surround them. The Jews did not invent rational, industrial capitalism, according to Weber, who criticizes Sombart for arguing this. Weber's use of the term "pariah" in connection with the Jewish people has been criticized. *See also* capitalism (with a discussion of rational capitalism); politically oriented capitalism *planned economy (Planwirtschaft)* — According to "Sociological Categories of Economic Action," "want satisfaction . . . results . . . from a 'planned economy' so far as economic action is oriented systematically to an established substantive order, whether agreed or imposed, which is valid within an organization" (section 14, p. 229 above). Individual economic units in a planned economy are not independent; and calculations in kind are used as well as a budget. Weber's notion of market economy can be used as a contrast to that of planned economy: in the former, economic action is oriented to exchange, individual units are independent, and money is used for calculation. The incentive to work in a market economy is in principle stronger than in a planned economy since the market is the ultimate judge of how much, if anything, a person will earn. A key problem in a planned economy is how to formulate effective prices since market prices cannot be used. *See also* budgetary management; calculation; market economy; prices and price theory

political capitalism. See politically oriented capitalism

politically oriented capitalism (politisch orientierter Kapitalismus) — Politically oriented capitalism—or just political capitalism, as it is often referred to in the secondary literature—represents an irrational form of capitalism, which typically lives in some kind of symbiosis with political power. No formal definition can be found in "Sociological Categories of Economic Action," where Weber nevertheless describes the three principal modes of capitalist orientation that together constitute this type of capitalism: (1) "opportunities for predatory profit from political organizations or persons connected with politics," (2) "profit opportunities in continuous business activity which arise by virtue of domination by force or of a position of power guaranteed by the political authority," and (3) "profit opportunities in unusual transactions with political bodies" (section 31, p. 237 above). The kind of capitalism that existed in antiquity was primarily of this type. Politically oriented capitalism has a tendency to emerge in connection with war, and this applies to modern times as well. *See also* adventurers' capitalism; capitalism; economic superman; rational capitalism; traditional commercial capitalism

power of control and disposal (Verfügungsgewalt) — This concept can roughly be characterized as Weber's version of economic power; it differs in principle from political power in that violence is not directly used. No formal definition is given of this important concept, which according to "Sociological Categories of Economic Action" is part of the concept of economic action (section 1, pp. 203–04 above). Weber also includes power of control and disposal in his definitions of such central concepts as competition, credit, the market, profit-making, and class. In his discussion of economic action, Weber says that it is imperative to include power of control and disposal in the sociological concept of economic action since the economy consists of a network of exchanges of this type of power. Power of control and disposal can exist independently of legal guarantees; if it has the support of law, however, it becomes stronger. A slave lacks power of control and disposal over himself or herself (*Eigenverfügung*), as opposed to a modern worker. *See also* domination; economic action

prebend. See benefice

prices and price theory (Preise, Preistheorie) — Weber does not discuss the
technical formation of prices in "Sociological Categories of Economic Action."
He does, however, make two major points about prices from a sociological
viewpoint. First, prices exemplify the kind of uniformity that is associated with
self-interested action (*see* self-interest). And second, while price formation on
a theoretical level is to be conceptualized in accordance with marginal utility
theory, in actual life prices are also determined by struggle: "Prices are expressions of the struggle [of man against man]; they are instruments of calculation only as estimated quantifications of relative chances in this struggle of
interests" (section 13, p. 228 above). In *Economy and Society* one can also find
observations on usury, the just price, and effective versus fictitious (or accounting) prices. According to Weber, there exist specific problems for the
formulation of effective prices in socialism; on this issue, *see* planned economy. *See also* exchange; marginal utility; struggle in the economy

profit. See budgetary management

profit-making (Erwerben) — Following the classical distinction between money-
making and the management of a household, Weber contrasts what he calls
profit-making with budgetary management. According to Weber's definition
in "Sociological Categories of Economic Action," "'Profit-making' is activity
which is oriented to opportunities for seeking new powers of control over
goods on a single occasion, repeatedly, or continuously" (section 11, p. 219
above). "Capital" is related to profit-making, while "wealth" is the equivalent
in budgetary management; and while the former aims at "profit," the latter
aims at "rent." In profit-making, calculations are oriented to profitability,
while in budgetary management they are based on marginal utility. Rational
profit-making entails capital accounting. Profit-making is indifferent to substantive postulates; it is furthermore central to the concept of enterprise. *See
also* budgetary management; capital accounting; capitalism; enterprise

property (Eigentum) — This concept is defined in chapter 1 of *Economy and
Society* as a form of monopolized and appropriated opportunity, in connection with the discussion of open and closed relationships: "Appropriated rights
which are enjoyed by individuals through inheritance or by hereditary groups,
whether communal or associative, will be called 'property' of the individual or
of groups in question; and, insofar as they are alienable, 'free' property"
(p. 44). (A "right" is defined as an appropriated opportunity.) *See also* appropriation; economic opportunities; open and closed economic opportunities;
stereotyping of the economy

rational capitalism — Weber rarely uses the expression "rational capitalism" in
his scientific writings. In section 31 (pp. 236–37 above) of "Sociological Categories of Economic Action," which is very important for an understanding of
Weber's view of capitalism, he nonetheless mentions one type of capitalism
that is unique to the West and which can be described as rational capitalism.
It has the following traits: rational enterprises in a market economy; labor that
is formally free; and sophisticated forms of financing (see also section 39, not

reproduced in this volume; *Economy and Society*, p. 240). Rational capitalism has only emerged in the West; elsewhere it was blocked, mainly by religious but also by political and social forces. Many different factors were important to the emergence of rational capitalism, and Weber rejects all one-factor theories (see especially *General Economic History*, pp. 352–54). *See also* capital accounting; capitalism; politically oriented capitalism; traditional commercial capitalism

rational economic action (rationales Wirtschaften) — According to "Sociological Categories of Economic Action," rational economic action is defined as economic action which has "instrumental rationality in [its] orientation, that is, deliberate planning" (section 1, p. 199 above). All action which is instrumentally rational (*zweckrational*) is, however, not economic action. There also always remains a considerable element of traditionalism in economic action. Economic action which is not instrumentally rational but value rational (*wertrational*) has no specific name in Weber's scheme. The distinction between instrumental rationality and value rationality can, however, be found in a similar conceptual pair in chapter 2 of *Economy and Society*, namely that of "formal rationality of economic action" versus "substantive rationality of economic action" (*formale und materielle Rationalität der Wirtschaft*). The former is easy to handle, Weber says, and has to do with quantitative calculation or accounting; the latter is notoriously difficult and has to do with the provisioning of people under the impact of ultimate values. Formal rationality and substantive rationality may coincide, but they may also diverge. Formal rationality can only exist under specific substantive conditions. *See also* calculation; rationality as a heuristic tool; rationalization of the economy; technology

rationality — This important topic is discussed in three separate entries in this glossary. *See* rational economic action; rationalization of the economy; rationality as a heuristic tool

rationality as a heuristic tool — According to chapter 1 of *Economy and Society*, it is convenient to start the analysis in sociology by assuming rational behavior (pp. 6–7). Irrational behavior should according to this approach be treated as a deviation to be explained. Weber emphasizes, however, that the rational approach of sociology must not be confused with a belief that empirical social life is rational. *See also* rational economic action; rationalization of the economy

rationalization of the economy (Rationalisierung der Wirtschaft and similar expressions) — Rationality can be used as a methodological tool, according to Weber; social phenomena, however, can also be more or less rational. The different areas of society are typically rational in different ways. Rationality in the economy means first and foremost calculability, but also that things are done in a methodical manner; in rational capitalism capital accounting is used and there is a great measure of depersonalization in economic life. Whether something is regarded as rational or not, Weber stresses, always depends on the viewpoint; furthermore, what is formally rational may also be substantively irrational. For a long time there has existed a general tendency toward rationalization in the West, and in this process the economy has played a fundamental role. *See also* depersonalization; rational economic action; rationality as a heuristic tool

rent (Rente) — This concept is not formally defined in "Sociological Categories of Economic Action," but nonetheless plays an important role in Weber's economic sociology. While profit is associated with capital and the enterprise, rent is associated with wealth and the budgetary unit or the household. Rent is economically "conservative," while profit is economically "revolutionary" (section 41, p. 241 above). In a society where the economy is centered on rent, there are property classes; and in a society centered on profit, there are commercial classes. *See also* budgetary management; class

scope of economic resources. See open and closed economic relationships

selection (Auslese) — This concept, which is important for an understanding of Weber's view on Social Darwinism, is defined in *Economy and Society* as follows: "The struggle, often latent, which takes place between human individuals or social types, for advantages and for survival, but without a meaningful orientation in terms of struggle, will be called 'selection.' Insofar as it is a matter of the relative opportunities of individuals during their own lifetime, it is 'social selection'; insofar as it concerns differential chances for the survival of hereditary characteristics, 'biological selection'" (p. 38).

self-interest — There are three different kinds of empirical uniformities, according to the first chapter of *Economy and Society*: usage, custom, and action "determined by self-interest" (*interessenbedingt; bedingt durch Interessenlage*) (p. 29). This last type of behavior represents a more stable form than behavior that is oriented to tradition or to norms. Action which is determined by self-interest is very common in the economy and explains the stability of prices. *See also* interest; ideal and material interests

services. See utility

social economics (Sozialökonomik) — Weber uses this term as synonymous with the science of economics, and it roughly includes theoretical economics, economic history, and economic sociology. The term *Sozialökonomik* emerged in Germany toward the end of the nineteenth century and was used by a small number of economists besides Weber, such as Wagner, Dietzel, and Schumpeter, as an alternative to political economy, economics, and so on. The term, however, never caught on and became rare after the 1920s. It figures prominently in Weber's essay on objectivity of 1904 and in the encyclopedia of economics that he edited, *Grundriss der Sozialökonomik* (1914–20). The term "social economics" is invested with a special content by Weber. It covers a very large area: in Weber's formulation, both economic phenomena, economically relevant phenomena, and economically conditioned phenomena. Several sciences, Weber argues, are needed for a full study of these phenomena, according to Weber—especially theoretical economics, economic history, and economic sociology. *See also* economic history; economic sociology; economic theory; economy

socialist economy. See planned economy

sociology. See economic sociology

speculation (Spekulation) — In "Sociological Categories of Economic Action"
the following definition is provided: "The calculations underlying trading activity will be called 'speculative' to the extent to which they are oriented to opportunities, the realization of which is regarded as fortuitous and is in this
sense uncalculable" (section 29, not reproduced in this volume). "Rational calculation" stands at the opposite end of "speculative calculation," but there is
no sharp divide between the two and both contain elements of unpredictability. The three major forms of capitalism that are discussed in "Sociological Categories of Economic Action"—rational capitalism, political capitalism, and traditional commercial capitalism (section 31, pp. 236–38
above)—all draw on speculation to some extent. *See also* adventurers' capitalism; economic opportunity; economic superman

spheres of life. See economic sphere

spirit of capitalism (Geist des Kapitalismus) — This concept comes from
Weber's famous study *The Protestant Ethic and the Spirit of Capitalism* and
denotes the kind of methodical approach to work and profit-making that
emerged in the West during the late sixteenth and seventeenth centuries,
under the impact of ascetic Protestantism. The spirit of capitalism is described
as a new lifestyle, and it is contrasted to the traditional spirit of capitalism
which preceded it. Weber differentiates between economic spirit or economic
mentality, on the one hand, and economic form or economic organization, on
the other. The economic spirit may, for example, change while the economic
form remains the same. The spirit of modern capitalism in the West is predominantly rational, but it also has some charismatic-speculative elements.
See also calling; capitalism

status (Stand) — The following definition can be found in Part 1 of *Economy
and Society*: "'Status' shall mean an effective claim to social esteem in terms
of positive or negative privileges; it is typically founded on a) style of life,
hence, b) formal education, . . . c) hereditary or occupational prestige" (p. 305;
cf. reading 5). Weber contrasts status with class, and argues that status is connected to consumption, entails a very distinct sense of honor, and has to do
with people's lifestyles. Class, on the other hand, deals with the way one's
"life chances" are connected to the market, and entails no specific sense of
honor. A class rarely constitutes a community, as opposed to status groups.
Changes disturb the status order, while stability operates in the opposite direction and favors status over class. There is an affinity between status and
monopoly, and Weber speaks of "status monopolies." Furthermore, one of the
typical ways in which status gains expression is through "the monopolistic appropriation of privileged modes of acquisition or as the abhorrence of certain
kinds of acquisition" (*Economy and Society*, p. 306). It should finally be mentioned that some commentators find *Stand* very hard to translate and argue
that it rather means "estate." *See also* class

stereotyping of the economy (Stereotypisierung der Ökonomik) — In Weber's
days to "stereotype" meant to fix something according to a predetermined

pattern; and stereotyping of the economy consequently means opposition to inventions, innovations, and competitive profit-making. Magic, religion, the caste system, and political capitalism may all entail stereotyping. Also: "every opportunity which is appropriated . . . *may* have the effect of stereotyping existing forms of social action" (*Economy and Society*, p. 202). Among the economic items and activities that may be stereotyped, Weber mentions tools, crafts, rents, and ways of conducting trade. *See also* discipline; economic traditionalism

struggle in the economy (ökonomischer Kampf) — Weber sees the economy as pervaded by struggle (or by "conflict," as *Kampf* is often translated). In *Economy and Society* the following definition of struggle is given: "A social relationship will be referred to as 'struggle' insofar as action is oriented intentionally to carrying out the actor's own will against the resistance of the other party or parties" (p. 38; the translation has been changed). In "Sociological Categories of Economic Action" Weber speaks of a number of different struggles in the economy, such as struggle over prices (*Preiskampf*), struggle between competitors (*Konkurrenzkampf*), and so on. In every market there is in addition a "struggle of man against man" (*Kampf des Menschen mit dem Menschen*). *See also* exchange; prices and price theory; selection

substantive rationality. See rational economic action

technology (Technik) — In "Sociological Categories of Economic Action" Weber contrasts economic action to "technical action" in the following manner: "Economic action is primarily oriented to the problem of choosing the *end* to which a thing should be applied; technology, to the problem, given the end, of choosing the appropriate *means*" (section 1, p. 203 above). But even if Weber makes a sharp conceptual distinction between economic and technical action, in reality economic concerns are nearly always taken into account when technical problems are solved. Weber argues against the tendency to see human history or the economy as driven by technology. The causality between technology and the economy can go both ways; no technological advances, however, can spread through the economy unless the social structure is ready for this. *See also* rational economic action

theodicy of good fortune (Theodizee des Glückes) — This concept is used in Weber's sociology of religion and indicates the need of successful and wealthy people for an ideology that justifies their position in life and explains why those who are unsuccessful and poor deserve to be unsuccessful and poor: "Good fortune thus wants to be 'legitimate' fortune" (Weber, *From Max Weber*, p. 271). There also exists an equivalent need among the unsuccessful for an ideology that explains and justifies their position, and Weber calls this "theodicy of suffering" (*Theodizee des Leidens*).

traditional commercial capitalism — In the important section 31 in "Sociological Categories of Economic Action" Weber enumerates a number of different types of capitalist activities. One of these can be called "traditional commercial capitalism," and it covers trade in commodities and different types of money business, such as extension of credit, speculation in currencies, and the like.

traditionalism. See economic traditionalism
uniformity determined by self-interest. See self-interest
utility (Nutzleistung) — This concept is part of Weber's definition of economic
   action, and is defined in "Sociological Categories of Economic Action" as follows: "By 'utilities' will always be meant the specific and concrete, real or
   imagined, opportunities *(Chancen)* for present or future use as they are estimated and made an object of specific provision by one or more economically
   acting individuals" (section 2, p. 204 above). Utilities can either be "goods" or
   "services." A "good," Weber specifies, does not so much refer to the object in
   question as to its potential use. What drives people is what Weber calls a desire for utilities, and this means a desire for want satisfaction as well as for
   profit-making. The term "services" is also translated as "work" in *Economy
   and Society. See also* economic action; economic theory; work
value-rational social action. See rational economic action
vocation. See calling
wants (Bedürfnisse) — Economic action is not only defined in Weber's economic sociology as an effort to satisfy wants or needs in a situation of scarcity,
   but also as an effort to satisfy "a desire for 'utilities'" ("Sociological Categories
   of Economic Action," section 1, p. 199 above). The reason for this is not that
   Weber underestimates the role of needs—provision for these always has to be
   made, he emphasizes—but that it is absolutely essential to have a concept of
   economic action that also includes profit-making. Needs, Weber says, can be
   ideal as well as material. Want satisfaction can also be organized in different
   ways. In a planned economy, want satisfaction is part of the substantive order,
   toward which economic actions are oriented. In a market economy, on the
   other hand, want satisfaction takes place through the market. *See also* utility
wealth. See budgetary management
work (Leistungen) — The word *Leistungen* is sometimes translated as "work"
   and sometimes as "services" in "Sociological Categories of Economic Action"
   (for a discussion of services, *see* utility). A distinction is made by Weber between managerial work and other kinds of work, called "labor" *(Arbeit)* (section 15, not reproduced in this volume). Weber also distinguishes between
   three different aspects of work: technical, economic, and social. Technical aspects have to do with the fact that work has to be divided up and united in
   order to solve technical problems; economic aspects, with the fact that work
   is carried out within the context of a unit that is oriented either to profit-
   making or to household needs (more precisely, to budgetary management).
   Social aspects, finally, have to do with the question whether the unit within
   which the work is carried out is autonomous or not, and whether it is autocephalous or not (meaning that the chief and the staff are appointed from
   within rather than by outsiders). *See also* calling; division of labor; economic
   motivation; willingness to work

THIS BRIEF BIBLIOGRAPHY has been assembled for those who are interested in doing research on Max Weber's economic sociology (for a much more extensive bibliography, see Swedberg 1998b). The introduction, which is intended as a general guide to the literature, consists of three parts: a discussion of which works of Weber are relevant in this context; comments on the secondary literature on Weber's economic sociology; and remarks on other secondary literature that can be helpful in situating Weber's work in this field in relation to economics in general. Most of the works listed in the bibliography itself are in English. When a work by Weber does not exist in English, however, the German original has been cited. It may also be mentioned that useful summaries of most of Weber's works can be found in Reinhard Bendix, *Max Weber: An Intellectual Portrait* (1960) and Dirk Käsler, *Max Weber: An Introduction to His Life and Work* (1988).

WEBER'S WORK IN ECONOMIC SOCIOLOGY

To determine exactly which works by Weber should be classified as studies in economic sociology is difficult since Weber, from early on, always included a social dimension in his writings on economic topics. This is true, for example, of his well-known study of the rural workers east of the Elbe and also of his two dissertations on medieval trading companies and agrarian legislation in Rome (Weber 1986 [1891], 1988 [1889]). Weber's Freiburg inaugural address (1980 [1895]) and his contributions to the discussion of the stock exchange are also relevant in this context (Weber 1895, 1895–96, 1897, 1988 [1894–96]. A translation of "The Stock Exchange" is scheduled to appear in 1999; in the meantime, see the excerpt in Weber 1978 [1894]).

That *The Protestant Ethic and the Spirit of Capitalism* has much to offer for those who are interested in economic sociology is clear (see Weber 1930 [1904–5] for the standard English translation; Weber 1988 [1920] for the current German text, and Weber 1993b for a comparison of the first and second editions). Much of interest to economic sociology is also to be found in Weber's book-length study of antiquity and in his work in what we today call industrial sociology (Weber 1976 [1909]), 1995 [1909], 1995). The reader may furthermore want to look at Weber's contribution to the debate over *The Protestant Ethic* (Weber 1978 [1907–10]; the only translation into English being Weber 1978 [1910]). A few of Weber's methodological essays are also of great importance for a full understanding of his economic sociology, especially "'Objectivity' in Social Science and Social Policy" and "Marginal Utility Theory and the 'Fundamental Law of Psychophysics'" (Weber 1949 [1904], 1949 [1917], 1975 [1908]; and Nau 1996 for a complete collection of the contributions to the debate over value freedom in the *Verein für Sozialpolitik* in 1913).

Weber himself only used the term "economic sociology" (*Wirtschaftssoziologie*) in two of his writings: *Economy and Society* (Weber 1978 [1922]) and *The Economic Ethics of the World Religions*. In the former there is especially "Sociological Categories of Economic Action" part 1, chapter 2, but the reader may also want to take a close look at part 2, chapters 1 and 2 ("The Economy and Social Norms" and "The Economic Relationships of Organized Groups"). It is furthermore clear, as I show in *Max Weber and the Idea of Economic Sociology* (Swedberg 1998a), that *Economy and Society* contains an attempt to map out, in sociological terms, the relationship of the economy to politics as well as to the legal system and to religion. The volumes that make up *The Economic Ethics of the World Religions* fall, according to Weber himself, primarily in the sociology of religion, but also make a contribution to economic sociology (see Weber 1946a [1920], 1951 [1920], 1952 [1921], 1958 [1921]). *General Economic History*, finally, represents an attempt on Weber's part to trace the emergence of the modern economy and can perhaps best be characterized as a work in economic history. Many of the categories that Weber uses, however, come straight out of his sociology (Weber 1981 [1923]).

SECONDARY LITERATURE ON WEBER'S ECONOMIC SOCIOLOGY

The number of studies that directly focus on Weber's economic sociology is small, especially if we leave aside the contributions to the debate over *The Protestant Ethic and the Spirit of Capitalism*. Only a few major studies have actually been carried out (e.g., Holton and Turner 1989, Swedberg 1998a; Swedberg 1998a as well as Bruhns 1996 also attempt to briefly discuss *all* works on the economy by Weber, including those that can be characterized as studies in economic history and economics). A few good texts on Weber's notion of capitalism exist (see, e.g., Durtschi 1966, Mommsen 1974; see also Swedberg 1999). Very little, however, has been written on what is the absolute key text in this context, namely "Sociological Categories of Economic Action" (however, see, e.g., Parsons 1947; Bader, Berger, Ganssmann, and Jost 1987 [1976]). More work is also needed on specific concepts in Weber's economic sociology (see, e.g., Murphy 1988; see also Dahrendorf 1979).

Several writers have commented on Weber's dissertations, his study of the rural workers east of the Elbe, and his inaugural address (see, e.g., Tribe 1989; Love 1986a, 1986b, 1991; Winkelmann 1963; also the introduction to Weber 1986 [1891]). There also exist some analyses of Weber's work in industrial sociology (see, e.g., Oberschall 1965, Schmidt 1976).

An enormous literature has been devoted to *The Protestant Ethic*, but no up-to-date bibliography exists (see, however, the huge number of studies cited in Richard F. Hamilton 1996). Many items in this literature, though by no means all, are of much interest to economic sociology (see especially the studies by

Gordon Marshall 1979, 1980, 1981, 1982, but also Eisenstadt 1968 and Lehmann-Roth 1993). Weber's contribution to the social capital debate in "The Protestant Sects and the Spirit of Capitalism" (Weber 1946b [1920]) is discussed by Fukuyama in *Trust* (1995). For the more general debate among sociologists about the work ethic, see, e.g., Lipset 1992. Economists, as opposed to economic historians, have not paid much attention to *The Protestant Ethic* (for some exceptions, see again Richard Hamilton 1996). Weber's study of antiquity has, for obvious reasons, mainly attracted comments from historians (see, e.g., Momigliani 1977).

Little attempt has up to now been made to extract the contributions to economic sociology that Weber makes in *The Economic Ethics of the World Religions*. A starting point for an attempt in this direction can, however, be found in the many conference volumes devoted to this work that have been edited by Wolfgang Schluchter (1983, 1984, 1985, 1987, 1988; see also, e.g., Gellner 1982, Elvin 1984). The introductions to the separate volumes of *The Economic Ethics of the World Religions,* which have been published in Weber's collected works, also contain much valuable material. In general, the volume introductions in the collected works are of great help to the student of Weber's work, including his economic sociology. Some of these volumes also contain new and useful material by Weber himself (see, e.g., Weber 1993a).

There exist special topics in Weber's economic sociology that deserve to be highlighted, especially how he viewed the relationship of the economy to politics, to law, and to religion (for a lengthy discussion, see Swedberg 1998a). Some of the literature on *The Protestant Ethic* is relevant for the last of these three topics, although most discussions of this work do not address what Weber has to say on the relationship of the economy to religion in *Economy and Society*. The economic dimension of politics has been commented upon in some of the secondary literature, and the reader may wish to consult such standard works as Beetham 1992 and Mommsen 1984. A thorough study of how Weber viewed economic social policy still remains to be written. For law and economy, there is the debate on the so-called England Problem, initiated by Trubek in 1972. It should, however, be pointed out that Weber's view of law and economy went far beyond the issue of whether English law "fitted" rational capitalism or not.

LITERATURE PERTAINING TO WEBER'S ECONOMIC SOCIOLOGY AND ECONOMICS

In order to place Weber's economic sociology within its proper intellectual context, it is useful to know something about his relationship to economics as well as to other economists. The best information on Weber as an economist can be found in the introductions to the various volumes of the collected works (see, e.g., Mommsen and Aldenhoff 1993; for the mercantile tradition of the Weber family, see Roth 1993). Lists of the literature that Weber wanted his first-year students of economics to consult have recently been made available in Germany

(Weber 1990 [1898]). A number of studies of his relationship to other economists also exist (for Weber and Marx, see, e.g., Löwith 1982 [1932], Mommsen
1974; for Knies, Hennis 1987; for Schumpeter, Osterhammel 1987; for Pareto,
Eisermann 1989, Sica 1992; and for Schmoller, Schön 1987). For Weber and
Austrian economics, see Holton-Turner 1989 and also Prendergast 1986; and for
Weber and the other economists in the *Verein für Sozialpolitik* (including his
brother Alfred), Krüger 1987 and Demm 1987; see also, e.g., Schluchter 1995
for Max and Alfred Weber). The history of how *Economy and Society* was written has been best told by Winkelmann (1986) and Schluchter (1989, 1998). The
history of the *Grundriss der Sozialökonomik* has, on the other hand, only attracted a preliminary study (Swedberg 1997, which also contains a full list of all
the individual contributions to the handbook).

A good starting point for the history of German economics is to be found in
the works by Winkel (1977) and Tribe (1988, 1995). A small number of works by
German economists which have been translated into English have also been included in the bibliography (see, e.g., Roscher 1895 [1843], Menger 1985 [1883]).
The reader will also find a few items on German economists who were Weber's
contemporaries (e.g., Hayek 1968 on Menger; Schumpeter 1926 on G. F.
Knapp, and Schumpeter 1951 [1927] on von Wieser; Bruno Lasker et al. 1940
on Lederer; Backhaus 1996 on Sombart). Finally, for the general economic situation of Germany in the nineteenth and early twentieth centuries, the works of
Barkin (1970) and Stolper (1940) are recommended.

Antonio, Robert J., and Ronald M. Glassman, eds. 1985. *A Weber-Marx Dialogue*. Lawrence: University Press of Kansas.

Aron, Raymond. 1970 [1967]. "Max Weber." Pp. 219–317 in vol. 2 of *Main Currents in Sociological Thought*. Trans. Richard Howard and Helen Weaver. New York: Doubleday.

Backhaus, Jürgen, ed. 1996. *Werner Sombart (1863–1941), Social Scientist*. Marburg: Metropolis-Verlag.

Bader, Veit Michael, Johannes Berger, Heiner Ganssmann, and Jost v. d. Knesebeck. 1987 [1976]. *Einführung in die Gesellschaftstheorie: Gesellschaft, Wirtschaft und Staat bei Marx und Weber*. 4th ed. Frankfurt: Campus Verlag. (On chapter 2 of *Economy and Society*).

Barkin, Kenneth D. 1970. *The Controversy over German Industrialization 1890–1902*. Chicago: University of Chicago Press.

Beetham, David. 1992. *Max Weber and the Theory of Modern Politics*. 2d ed. Cambridge: Polity Press.

Bell, Daniel. 1976. *The Cultural Contradictions of Capitalism*. New York: Harper & Row.

Bellah, Robert. 1957. *Tokugawa Religion: The Cultural Roots of Modern Japan*. Glencoe, Ill.: The Free Press.

———. 1963. "Reflections on the Protestant Ethic Analogy in Asia." *Journal of Social Issues* 19:52–60.

Bendix, Reinhard. 1960. *Max Weber: An Intellectual Portrait*. New York: Doubleday.

Berger, Stephen D. 1971. "The Sects and the Breakthrough into the Modern World: On the Centrality of the Sects in Weber's Protestant Ethic Thesis." *Sociological Quarterly* 12 (Autumn): 486–99.

Biggart, Nicole Woolsey. 1990. *Charismatic Capitalism: Direct Selling Organizations in America*. Chicago: University of Chicago Press.

Böröcz, József. 1997. "*Stand* Reconstructed: Contingent Closure and Institutional Change." *Sociological Theory* 15:215–48.

Boese, Franz. 1939. *Geschichte des Vereins für Sozialpolitik 1872–1932*. Schriften des Vereins für Sozialpolitik, vol. 188. Berlin: Duncker & Humblot.

Boudon, Raymond. 1987. "The Individualistic Tradition in Sociology." Pp. 45–70 in Jeffrey Alexander et al., eds., *The Micro-Macro Link*. Berkeley: University of California Press.

Brubaker, Rogers. 1984. *The Limits of Rationality: An Essay on the Social and Moral Thought of Max Weber*. London: George Allen & Unwin.

Bruhns, Hinnerk. 1996. "Max Weber, l'économie et l'histoire." *Annales: Histoire, Sciences Sociales* 51:1259–87.

Campbell, Colin. 1987. *The Protestant Ethic and the Spirit of Modern Consumerism*. Oxford: Basil Blackwell.

Carlin, Edward A. 1956. "Schumpeter's Constructed Type—The Entrepreneur (A Comparison between Weber and Schumpeter)." *Kyklos* 9:27–42.

Carruthers, Bruce, and Wendy Nelson Espeland. 1991. "Accounting for Rationality: Double-Entry Bookkeeping and the Rhetoric of Economic Rationality." *American Journal of Sociology* 97:31–69.

Clarke, Simon. 1982. *Marx, Marginalism and Modern Sociology: From Adam Smith to Max Weber*. London: Macmillan.

Coleman, James S. 1990. *Foundations of Social Theory*. Cambridge, Mass.: Harvard University Press.

Collins, Randall. 1980. "Weber's Last Theory of Capitalism." *American Sociological Review* 45:925–42. (Reprinted with modifications in Collins 1986).

Collins, Randall. 1986. *Weberian Sociological Theory*. Cambridge: Cambridge University Press.

Dahrendorf, Ralf. 1979. *Life Chances: Approaches to Social and Political Theory*. Chicago: University of Chicago Press.

Demm, Eberhard. 1987. "Max and Alfred Weber in the Verein für Sozialpolitik." Pp. 88–98 in Wolfgang J. Mommsen and Jürgen Osterhammel, eds., *Max Weber and His Contemporaries*. London: Unwin Hyman.

DiMaggio, Paul, and Walter Powell. 1991. "The Iron Cage Revisited: Institutional Isomorphism and Collective Rationality." Pp. 63–82 in Walter Powell and Paul DiMaggio, eds., *The New Institutionalism in Organizational Analysis*. Chicago: University of Chicago Press. This is a revised version of a 1983 article.

Durtschi, Georges. 1966. "Der Begriff des Kapitalismus bei Max Weber." Ph.D. diss., University of Zürich.

Eisenstadt, S. N., ed. 1968. *The Protestant Ethic and Modernization: A Comparative View*. New York: Basic Books.

Eisermann, Gottfried. 1989. *Max Weber und Vilfredo Pareto: Dialog und Konfrontation*. Tübingen: J. C. B. Mohr.

———. 1993. *Max Weber und die Nationalökonomie*. Marburg: Metropoliş-Verlag.

Elvin, Mark. 1984. "Why China Failed to Create an Endogenous Industrial Capitalism: A Critique of Max Weber's Explanation." *Theory and Society* 13:379–91.

Ewing, Sally. 1987. "Formal Justice and the Spirit of Capitalism: Max Weber's Sociology of Law." *Law and Society Review* 21:487–512.

Factor, Regis. 1988. *Guide to the* Archiv für Sozialwissenschaft und Sozialpolitik *Group, 1904–1933: A History and Comprehensive Bibliography*. New York: Greenwood Press.

Finley, M. I. 1977. "The Ancient City: From Fustel de Coulanges to Max Weber and Beyond." *Comparative Studies in Societies and History* 19:305–27.

Freund, Julien. 1972 [1966]. *The Sociology of Max Weber*. Trans. Mary Ilford. Harmondsworth: Penguin Books.

Frisby, David. 1992. "Some Economic Aspects of [Georg Simmel's] *Philosophy of Money*." Pp. 80–97 in *Simmel and Since*. London: Routledge.

Frommer, Sabine. 1994. "Bezüge zu experimenteller Psychologie, Psychiatrie und Psychopathologie in Max Webers methodologischen Schriften." Pp. 239–58 in Gerhard Wagner and Heinz Zipprian, eds., *Max Webers Wissenschaftslehre*. Frankfurt am Main: Suhrkamp.

Fukuyama, Francis. 1995. *Trust: The Social Virtues and the Creation of Prosperity*. London: Penguin Books.

Gellner, David. 1982. "Max Weber, Capitalism and The Religion of India." *Sociology* 16:526–43.

Gerschenkron, Alexander. 1989 [1943]. *Bread and Democracy in Germany*. With a foreword by Charles Maier. Ithaca, N.Y.: Cornell University Press.

Ghosh, Peter. 1994. "Some Problems with Talcott Parsons' Version of 'The Protestant Ethic.'" *Archives européennes de sociologie* 30:104–23.

Giddens, Anthony. 1971. *Capitalism and Modern Social Theory: An Analysis of the Writings of Marx, Durkheim and Max Weber*. Cambridge: Cambridge University Press.

Goldschmidt, Levin. 1891. *Universalgeschichte des Handelsrechts*. 3d ed. Stuttgart: Verlag von Ferdinand Enke.

Gouldner, Alvin. 1954. *Patterns of Industrial Bureaucracy*. New York: The Free Press.

Green, Robert W., ed. 1973. *Protestantism, Capitalism, and Social Science: The Weber Thesis Controversy*. 2d ed. Lexington, Mass.: D. C. Heath and Company.

Hamilton, Gary. 1984. "Patriarchalism in Imperial China and Western Europe: A Revision of Weber's Sociology of Domination." *Theory and Society* (13):393–425.

―――. 1985. "Why No Capitalism in China? Negative Questions in Historical Comparative Research?" *Journal of Developing Societies* 1:187–211.

Hamilton, Gary, and Cheng-shu Kao. 1987. "Max Weber and the Analysis of East Asian Industrialization." *International Sociology* 2:289–300.

Hamilton, Gary, and Nicole Woolsey Biggart. 1988. "Market, Culture, and Authority: A Comparative Analysis of Management and Organization in the Far East." *American Journal of Sociology* 94:S52–S94.

Hamilton, Richard F. 1996. "Max Weber and the Protestant Ethic." Pp. 32–106 in *The Social Misconstruction of Reality*. New Haven, Conn.: Yale University Press.

Hayek, Friedrich von. 1948 [1935–40]. "Socialist Calculation, I–III." Pp. 119–208 in *Individualism and Economic Order*. Chicago: University of Chicago Press.

―――. 1968. "Menger, Carl." *International Encyclopaedia of the Social Sciences,* 10:124–27. New York: The Macmillan Company and The Free Press.

―――. 1994. *Hayek on Hayek*. Ed. Stephen Kresge and Leif Wenar. London: Routledge.

Hennis, Wilhelm. 1987. "A Science of Man: Max Weber and the Political Economy of the German Historical School." Pp. 25–58 in Wolfgang J. Mommsen and Jürgen Osterhammel, eds., *Max Weber and His Contemporaries*. London: Unwin Hyman.

―――. 1991. "The Pitiless 'Sobriety of Judgment': Max Weber between Carl Menger and Gustav von Schmoller—The Academic Politics of Value Freedom." *History of the Human Sciences,* 4:27–59.

Hernes, Gudmund. 1989. "The Logic of *The Protestant Ethic*." *Rationality and Society* 1, no. 1:123–62.

Heyman, Ernst. 1931. "Goldschmidt, Levin (1829–97)." *Encyclopaedia of the Social Sciences,* 6:694–95. New York: Macmillan.

Hill, Christopher. 1961. "Protestantism and the Rise of Capitalism." Pp. 15–39 in F. J. Fisher, ed., *Essays in the Economic and Social History of Tudor and Stuart England*. Cambridge: Cambridge University Press.

Hintze, Otto. 1982 [1926]. "Max Webers Soziologie." (Review of *Wirtschaft und Gesellschaft*.) Pp. 135–47 in *Gesammelte Abhandlungen zur Soziologie, Politik und Theorie der Geschichte*, vol. 2: *Soziologie und Geschichte*. 3d ed. Göttingen: Vandenhoeck & Ruprecht.

Holton, Robert J., and Bryan S. Turner. 1989. *Max Weber on Economy and Society*. Routledge: London and New York. See especially "Max Weber, Austrian Economics, and Liberalism," pp. 30–67.

Hoselitz, Bert. 1960. "Theories of Stages of Economic Growth." Pp. 193–238 in Bert F. Hoselitz et al., *Theories of Economic Growth*. Glencoe, Ill.: The Free Press.

Iggers, Georg G. 1983. *The German Conception of History: The National Tradition of Historical Thought from Herder to the Present*. Rev. ed. Middletown, Conn.: Wesleyan University Press.

Jones, Bryn. 1977. "Economic Action and Rational Organization in the Sociology of Weber." Pp. 28–65 in Barry Hindess, ed., *Sociological Theory of the Economy*. London: Macmillan.

Käsler, Dirk. 1983. "In Search of Respectability: The Controversy over the Destination of Sociology during the Conventions of the German Sociological Society." *Knowledge and Society* 4:227–72.

―――. 1988. *Max Weber: An Introduction to His Life and Work*. Trans. Philippa Hurd. Cambridge: Polity Press. See especially "Economic Sociology," pp. 156–61.

Kalberg, Stephen. 1983. "Max Weber's Universal-Historical Architectonic of Economically-Oriented Action: A Preliminary Reconstruction." *Current Perspectives in Social Theory* 4:253–88.

Kantowsky, Detlef, ed. 1986. *Recent Research on Max Weber's Studies of Hinduism*. Munich: Weltforum Verlag.

Kent, Stephen A. 1983. "The Quaker Ethic and the Fixed Price Policy." *Sociological Inquiry* 53 (Winter): 16–32.

Kisch, Herbert. 1968. "Knies, Karl." *International Encyclopaedia of the Social Sciences*, 8:422–24. New York: Macmillan.

Knapp, G. F. 1924 [1923]. *The State Theory of Money*. Abridged trans. by H. M. Lucas and J. Bonar of the 4th ed. London: Macmillan. (The first edition appeared in 1905.)

Knight, Frank H. 1956 [1928]. "Historical and Theoretical Issues in the Problem of Modern Capitalism." Pp. 89–103 in *On the History and Method of Economics*. Chicago: University of Chicago Press.

Kocka, Jürgen. 1981. "Capitalism and Bureaucracy in German Industrialization before 1914," *Economic History Review* 34:453–68.

Krüger, Dieter. 1983. *Nationalökonomen im wilhelminischen Deutschland*. Göttingen: Vandenhoeck & Ruprecht.

———. 1987. "Max Weber and the 'Younger' Generation in the Verein für Sozialpolitik." Pp. 71–87 in Wolfgang J. Mommsen and Jürgen Osterhammel, eds., *Max Weber and His Contemporaries*. London: Unwin Hyman.

Kruse, Volker. 1990. "Von der historischen Nationalökonomie zur historischen Soziologie: Ein Paradigmenwechsel in den deutschen Sozialwissenschaften um 1900." *Zeitschrift für Soziologie* 19:149–65.

Lachmann, Ludwig M. 1970. *The Legacy of Max Weber*. London: Heinemann.

———. 1992. "Socialism and the Market: A Theme of Economic Sociology Viewed from a Weberian Perspective." *South African Journal of Economics* 60 (March): 24–43.

Lasker, Bruno et al. 1940. "Emil Lederer, 1882–1939. I. The Sociologist." *Social Research* 7:337–58. (See Marshak et al. 1941 for "Emil Lederer, 1882–1939. II. The Economist.")

Lazarsfeld, Paul F., and Anthony R. Oberschall. 1965. "Max Weber and Empirical Social Research." *American Sociological Review* 30:185–99.

Lehmann, Hartmut, and Guenther Roth, eds. 1993. *Weber's Protestant Ethic: Origin, Evidence, Contexts*. Cambridge: Cambridge University Press.

Lindenlaub, Dieter. 1967. *Richtungskämpfe im Verein für Sozialpolitik*. Wiesbaden: Franz Steiner Verlag.

Lipset, S. M. 1992. "The Work Ethic, Then and Now." *Journal of Labor Research* 13:45–54.

Löwith, Karl. 1982 [1932]. *Max Weber and Karl Marx*. Trans. Hans Fantel. London: George Allen & Unwin.

Love, John R. 1986a. "The Character of the Roman Agricultural Estate in the Light of Max Weber's Economic Sociology." *Chiron* 16:99–146.

———. 1986b. "Max Weber and the Theory of Ancient Capitalism." *History and Theory* 25:152–72.

———. 1991. *Antiquity and Capitalism: Max Weber and the Sociological Foundations of Roman Civilization*. London: Routledge.

McClelland, David. 1961. *The Achieving Society*. Princeton, N.J.: Van Nostrand.

Macdonald, Ronald. 1965. "Schumpeter and Max Weber—Central Visions and Social Theories." *Quarterly Journal of Economics* 79:373–96.

Machlup, Fritz. 1978. "The Ideal Type: A Bad Name for a Good Construct." Pp. 211–21 in *Methodology of Economics and the Other Social Sciences*. New York: Academic Press.

Manasse, Ernst Moritz. 1947. "Max Weber on Race." *Social Research* 14:191–221.

Marcuse, Herbert. 1971 [1964]. "Industrialism and Capitalism." Pp. 133–51 in Otto Stammer, ed., *Max Weber and Sociology Today*. Trans. Kathleen Morris. New York: Harper Torchbooks.

Marshak, Jakob, et al. 1941. "Emil Lederer, 1882–1939. II. The Economist." *Social Research* 8:79–105. (See also Lasker et al. 1940 for "Emil Lederer, 1882–1939. I. The Sociologist.")

Marshall, Gordon. 1979. "The Weber Thesis and the Development of Capitalism in Scotland." *Scottish Journal of Sociology* 3, no. 2:173–211.

———. 1980. "The Dark Side of the Weber Thesis: The Case of England." *British Journal of Sociology* 31:419–40.

———. 1981. *Presbyteries and Profits: Calvinism and the Development of Capitalism in Scotland, 1560–1707*. Oxford: Oxford University Press.

———. 1982. *In Search of the Spirit of Capitalism: An Essay on Max Weber's Protestant Ethic Thesis*. London: Hutchinson.

Menger, Carl. 1985 [1883]. *Investigations into the Method of the Social Sciences with Special Reference to Economics*. Trans. Francis Y. Nock. New York: New York University Press.

Merton, Robert K. 1968 [1940]. "Bureaucratic Structure and Personality." Pp. 249–60 in *Social Theory and Social Structure*. Enlarged ed. New York: The Free Press.

———. 1968. *Social Theory and Social Structure*. Enlarged ed. New York: The Free Press. See especially the chapters on Puritanism, the economy, and science.

Meyer, Marshall. 1990. "The Weberian Tradition in Organizational Research." Pp. 191–215 in Craig Calhoun et al., eds., *Structures of Power and Constraint*. Cambridge: Cambridge University Press.

Mises, Ludwig von. 1960 [1929]. "Sociology and History." Pp. 68–129 in *Epistemological Problems of Economics*. Trans. George Reisman. Princeton: Van Nostrand.

———. 1977 [1929]. "Max Weber and the Socialists of the Chair." Pp. 102–4 in *A Critique of Interventionism*. New Rochelle: Arlington House.

———. 1935 [1920]. "Economic Calculation in the Socialist Commonwealth." Pp. 87–130 in Friedrich von Hayek, ed., *Collectivistic Economic Planning*. London: George Routledge & Sons.

Momigliani, Arnaldo. 1977. "The Instruments of Decline" (review of Max Weber, *The Agrarian Sociology of Ancient Civilizations*). *Times Literary Supplement* 3917 (April 8): 435–36.

Mommsen, Wolfgang J. 1974. *The Age of Bureaucracy: Perspectives on the Political Sociology of Max Weber*. Oxford: Basil Blackwell. See especially "The Alternative to Marx: Dynamic Capitalism instead of Bureaucratic Socialism," pp. 47–71.

———. 1981. "Max Weber and Roberto Michels: An Asymmetrical Partnership." *Archives européennes de sociologie* 22:100–116.

———. 1984. *Max Weber and German Politics 1890–1920*. Trans. Michael S. Steinberg. Chicago: University of Chicago Press.

———. 1989. "Capitalism and Socialism: Weber's Dialogue with Marx." Pp. 53–73 in *The Political and Social Theory of Max Weber*. Cambridge: Polity Press.

Mommsen, Wolfgang J., and Rita Aldenhoff. 1993. "Einleitung." Pp. 1–68 in vol. 1 of Max Weber, *Landarbeiterfrage, Nationalstaat und Volkswirtschaftspolitik: Schriften und Reden 1892–1899. Max Weber Gesamtausgabe* I/4. Tübingen: J. C. B. Mohr.

Murphy, Raymond. 1986. "Weberian Closure Theory: A Contribution to the Ongoing Assessment." *British Journal of Sociology* 37:21–41.

———. 1988. *Social Closure: The Theory of Monopolization and Exclusion.* Oxford: Clarendon Press.

Nau, Heino Heinrich. 1997. *Eine "Wissenschaft vom Menschen." Max Weber und die Gründung der Sozialökonomik in der deutschsprachigen Ökonomie 1871 bis 1914.* Berlin: Duncker & Humblot.

———, ed. 1996. *Der Werturteilsstreit: Die Äusserungen zur Werturteilsdiskussion im Ausschuß des Vereins für Sozialpolitik (1913).* Marburg: Metropolis-Verlag.

Nelson, Benjamin. 1969 [1949]. *The Idea of Usury: From Tribal Brotherhood to Universal Otherhood.* 2d ed., enlarged. Chicago: University of Chicago Press.

Nevaskar, Balwant. 1971. *Capitalists without Capitalism: The Jains of India and the Quakers of the West.* Westport, Conn.: Greenwood.

Oberschall, Anthony. 1965. *Empirical Social Research in Germany 1848–1914.* New York: Basic Books.

Osterhammel, Jürgen. 1987. "Varieties of Social Economics: Joseph A. Schumpeter and Max Weber." Pp. 106–20 in Wolfgang J. Mommsen and Jürgen Osterhammel, eds., *Max Weber and His Contemporaries.* London: Unwin Hyman.

Parkin, Frank. 1974. "Strategies of Social Closure in Class Formation." Pp. 1–18 in Frank Parkin, ed., *The Social Analysis of Class Structure.* London: Tavistock Publications.

Parsons, Talcott. 1928–29. "'Capitalism' in Recent German Literature: Sombart and Weber, I–II," *Journal of Political Economy* 36 (1928): 641–61; 37 (1929): 31–51.

———. 1935. "H. M. Robertson on Max Weber and His School." *Journal of Political Economy* 43:688–96.

———. 1947. "Weber's 'Economic Sociology.'" Pp. 30–55 in Max Weber, *The Theory of Social and Economic Organization.* Trans. A. M. Henderson and Talcott Parsons. New York: Oxford University Press. (This is part of Parsons's introduction, pp. 3–86.)

———. 1948. "Max Weber's Sociological Analysis of Capitalism and Modern Institutions." Pp. 287–308 in Harry Elmer Barnes, ed., *An Introduction to the History of Sociology.* Chicago: University of Chicago Press.

———. 1968 [1937]. *The Structure of Social Action: A Study in Social Theory with Special Reference to a Group of Recent European Writers.* 2 vols. New York: The Free Press.

Poggi, Gianfranco. 1983. *Calvinism and the Capitalist Spirit.* Amherst: University of Massachusetts Press.

Prendergast, Christopher. 1986. "Alfred Schutz and the Austrian School of Economics." *American Journal of Sociology* 92:1–26.

Ray, Larry J., and Michael Reed, eds. 1994. *Organizing Modernity: New Weberian Perspectives on Work, Organization and Society.* London: Routledge.

Redding, S. Gordon. 1990. *The Spirit of Chinese Capitalism.* Berlin: Walter de Gruyter.

Rehmann, Jan. 1997. "Max Weber: Modernisierung als Antizipation des Fordismus." *Das Argument* 222:613–29.

Robertson, H. M. 1935. *Aspects of the Rise of Economic Individualism: A Criticism of Max Weber and His School.* Cambridge: Cambridge University Press.

Roscher, Wilhelm. 1895 [1843]. "Roscher's Program of 1843 (trans. W. J. Ashley)." *Quarterly Journal of Economics* 9:99–105.

Roth, Guenther. 1979. "Duration and Rationalization: Fernand Braudel and Max Weber." Pp. 166–93 in Guenther Roth and Wolfgang Schluchter, *Max Weber's Vision of History: Ethics and Methods.* Berkeley: University of California Press.

———. 1993. "Between Cosmopolitanism and Ethnocentrism: Max Weber in the

Nineties" (review of Max Weber, *Landarbeiterfrage, Nationalstaat und Volkswirt-schaftspolitik*). *Telos* 96:148–62.

Ryan, Alan. 1987. "Mill and Weber on History, Freedom and Reason." Pp. 170–81 in Wolfgang J. Mommsen and Jürgen Osterhammel, eds., *Max Weber and His Contemporaries*. London: Unwin Hyman.

Samuelsson, Kurt. 1961. *Religion and Economic Action*. Trans. E. Geoffrey French, ed. D. C. Coleman. London: Heinemann.

Schefold, Bertram, et al. 1992. *Max Weber und seine "Protestantische Ethik."* Düsseldorf: Verlag Wirtschaft und Finanzen.

Schluchter, Wolfgang. 1989. *Rationalism, Religion and Domination: A Weberian Perspective*. Trans. Neil Salomon. Berkeley: University of California Press. See especially "Economy and Society: The End of A Myth," pp. 433–63, which constitutes an excellent history of the coming into being of *Economy and Society*.

———. 1995. "Max Weber und Alfred Weber. Zwei Wege von der Nationalökonomie zur Kultursoziologie." Pp. 199–221 in Hans G. Nutzinger, ed., *Zwischen Nationalökonomie und Universalgeschichte: Alfred Webers Entwurf einer umfassenden Sozialwissenschaft in heutiger Sicht*. Marburg: Metropolis-Verlag.

———. 1998. "Max Webers Beitrag zum 'Grundriss der Sozialökonomik,'" *Kölner Zeitschrift für Soziologie und Sozialpsychologie* 50:327–43.

———, ed. 1981. *Max Webers Studie über das antike Judentum: Interpretation und Kritik*. Frankfurt am Main: Suhrkamp.

———, ed. 1983. *Max Webers Studie über Konfuzianismus und Taoismus: Interpretation und Kritik*. Frankfurt am Main: Suhrkamp.

———, ed. 1984. *Max Webers Studie über Hinduismus und Buddhismus: Interpretation und Kritik*. Frankfurt am Main: Suhrkamp.

———, ed. 1985. *Max Webers Sicht des antiken Christentums: Interpretation und Kritik*. Frankfurt am Main: Suhrkamp.

———, ed. 1987. *Max Webers Sicht des Islams: Interpretation und Kritik*. Frankfurt am Main: Suhrkamp.

———, ed. 1988. *Max Webers Sicht des okzidentalen Christentums: Interpretation und Kritik*. Frankfurt am Main: Suhrkamp.

Schmidt, Gert. 1976. "Max Weber and Modern Industrial Sociology: A Comment on Some Recent Anglo-Saxon Interpretations." *Sociological Analysis and Theory* 6: 47–73.

Schön, Manfred. 1987. "Gustav Schmoller and Max Weber." Pp. 59–70 in Wolfgang J. Mommsen and Jürgen Osterhammel, eds., *Max Weber and His Contemporaries*. London: Unwin Hyman.

Schumpeter, Joseph A. 1926. "G. F. Knapp." *Economic Journal* 36:512–14.

———. 1951 [1927]. "Friedrich von Wieser, 1851–1926." Pp. 298–301 in *Ten Great Economists*. New York: Oxford University Press.

———. 1954. *History of Economic Analysis*. London: George Allen & Unwin.

———. 1991 [1920]. "Max Weber's Work." Pp. 220–29 in Joseph Schumpeter, *The Economics and Sociology of Capitalism*. Princeton, N.J.: Princeton University Press.

Shils, Edward S. 1948. "Some Remarks on [Max Weber's] 'The Theory of Social and Economic Organization,'" *Economica*, n.s. 15:36–50.

Sica, Alan. 1992. *Weber, Irrationality and Social Order*. Berkeley: University of California Press. (One chapter is on Pareto.)

Stigler, George J. 1950. "The Development of Utility Theory. II." *Journal of Political Economy* 58:373–96.

Stinchcombe, Arthur. 1986. "Max Weber's *Economy and Society.*" Pp. 282–89 in *Stratification and Organization: Selected Papers*. Cambridge: Cambridge University Press.

Stolper, Gustav. 1940. *German Economy 1870–1940: Issues and Trends*. New York: Reynal & Hitschcock.

Swedberg, Richard. 1987. "Economic Sociology: Past and Present." *Current Sociology* 35 (Spring): 1–221.

———. 1991. *Schumpeter—A Biography*. Princeton, N.J.: Princeton University Press.

———. 1997. "Max Weber's Handbook in Economic Sociology: *Grundriss der Sozialökonomik.*" Stockholm University, Department of Sociology, Working Papers (Work—Organization—Economy), no. 51.

———. 1998a. *Max Weber and the Idea of Economic Sociology*. Princeton, N.J.: Princeton University Press.

———. 1998b. "Max Weber's Economic Sociology: A Bibliography." Stockholm University, Department of Sociology, Working Papers (Work—Organization—Economy), no. 61.

———. 1999. "Max Weber's Sociology of Capitalism." Stockholm University, Department of Sociology, Working Papers (Work—Organization—Economy), no. 70.

Tawney, R. H. 1954 [1926]. *Religion and the Rise of Capitalism*. New York: New American Library.

Tribe, Keith. 1988. *Governing Economy: The Reformation of Economic Discourse 1750–1840*. Cambridge: Cambridge University Press.

———. 1995. *Strategies of Economic Order: German Economic Discourse, 1750–1950*. Cambridge: Cambridge University Press. (See especially chap. 4, "Historical Economics, the *Methodenstreit*, and the Economics of Max Weber.")

———, ed. 1989. *Reading Weber*. London: Routledge.

Trubek, David M. 1972. "Max Weber on Law and the Rise of Capitalism." *Wisconsin Law Review* 1972:720–53.

Waltzer, Michael. 1964. "Puritanism as a Revolutionary Ideology." *History and Theory* 3:59–90.

Waszek, Norbert, ed., *Die Institutionalisierung der Nationalökonomie an deutschen Universitäten*. St. Katharinen: Scripta Mercaturae Verlag.

Weber, Marianne. 1975 [1926]. *Max Weber: A Biography*. Trans. Harry Zohn. New York: John Wiley & Sons.

Weber, Max. 1895. "Börsenwesen (Die Vorschläge der Börsenenquetekommission)." Pp. 241–52 in suppl. vol. 1 of J. Conrad et al., eds., *Handwörterbuch der Staatswissenschaften*. Jena: Gustav Fischer.

———. 1895–96. "Die Ergebnisse der deutschen Börsenenquete, I–II, III–IV." *Zeitschrift für das gesamte Handelsrecht* 43 (1895): 83–219, 457–514; 44 (1896): 29–74, 69–156.

———. 1896. "Die technische Funktion des Terminhandels." *Deutsche Juristen-Zeitung* 11 (June 1): 207–10; 13 (July 1): 248–50.

———. 1897. "Börsengesetz." Pp. 222–46 in suppl. vol. 2 of J. Conrad et al., eds., *Handwörterbuch der Staatswissenschaften*. Jena: Gustav Fischer.

———. 1902. Review of Philipp Lotmar, *Der Arbeitsvertrag*. *Archiv für Sozialwissenschaft und Sozialpolitik* 17:723–34.

———. 1906a. Participation in the Debate at the Meeting of the *Verein für Sozialpolitik* in 1905. Pp. 213–17, 382–90, 432–35 in vol. 116 of *Verhandlungen des Vereins für Sozialpolitik*. Leipzig: Duncker und Humblot.

———. 1906b. "Die Stellung der Frau im modernen Erwerbsleben" (review of Marie

Baum, *Drei Klassen von Lohnarbeiterinnen in Industrie und Handel der Stadt Karlsruhe*). *Frankfurter Zeitung*, August 13, p. 1.

————. 1908. Participation in the Debate at the Meeting of the *Verein für Sozialpolitik* in 1907. Pp. 294–301 in vol. 125 of *Verhandlungen des Vereins für Sozialpolitik*. Leipzig: Duncker und Humblot.

————. 1909. Review of Adolf Weber, *Die Aufgaben der Volkswirtschaftslehre als Wissenschaft*. *Archiv für Sozialwissenschaft und Sozialpolitik* 29:615–20.

————. 1910. Participation in the Debate at the Meeting of the *Verein für Sozialpolitik* in 1909. Pp. 580–85, 603–7 in vol. 132 of *Verhandlungen des Vereins für Sozialpolitik*. Leipzig: Duncker und Humblot.

————. 1911a. Contribution to the Discussion of Andreas Voigt's Lecture, *Wirtschaft und Recht*. Pp. 265–70 in *Verhandlungen des Ersten Deutschen Soziologentages vom 19.–22. Oktober 1910 in Frankfurt a. M.* Tübingen: J. C. B. Mohr.

————. 1911b. "Geschäftsbericht." Pp. 39–62 in *Verhandlungen des Ersten Deutschen Soziologentages vom 19.–22. Oktober 1910 in Frankfurt a. M.* Tübingen: J. C. B. Mohr.

————. 1914. "Vorwort." Pp. vii–ix in *Wirtschaft und Wirtschaftswissenschaft: Grundriss der Sozialökonomik, Abt. I.* Tübingen: J. C. B. Mohr. (Signed "Schriftleitung und Verlag," but Weber is generally considered the author.)

————. 1922. *Wirtschaft und Gesellschaft*. Tübingen: J. C. B. Mohr. (Part I of this work actually appeared in 1921. This is, however, the first edition of Part I and Part II together, as edited by Marianne Weber and revised for a second edition in 1925. The third edition (1947) is identical to the second edition. The fourth edition, edited by Johannes Winkelmann, appeared in 1956. The fifth, revised edition, likewise edited by Winkelmann, appeared in 1972 and is the one currently in use in Germany.)

————. 1927 [1923]. *General Economic History*. Trans. Frank H. Knight. New York: Greenberg Publishers.

————. 1930 [1904–5]. *The Protestant Ethic and the Spirit of Capitalism*. Trans. Talcott Parsons. London: Allen & Unwin. (The first version of this work was published in 1904–5 though this translation is based on the revised version of 1920. Most later editions in English are reprints of this edition.)

————. 1946a [1920]. "The Social Psychology of the World Religions." Pp. 267–301 in *From Max Weber: Essays in Sociology*. Ed. and trans. H. H. Gerth and C. Wright Mills. New York: Oxford University Press. (This constitutes the "Einleitung" to the studies of economic ethics; the "Zwischenbetrachtung" can be found on pp. 323–59.)

————. 1946b [1920]. "The Protestant Sects and the Spirit of Capitalism." Pp. 302–22 in *From Max Weber: Essays in Sociology*. Ed. and trans. H. H. Gerth and C. Wright Mills. New York: Oxford University Press.

————. 1949a [1904]. "'Objectivity' in Social Science and Social Policy." Pp. 49–112 in Max Weber, *The Methodology of the Social Sciences*. Ed. and trans. Edward A. Shils and Henry A. Finch. New York: The Free Press.

————. 1949b [1917]. "The Meaning of 'Ethical Neutrality' in Sociology and Economics." Pp. 1–47 in Max Weber, *The Methodology of the Social Sciences*. Ed. and trans. Edward A. Shils and Henry A. Finch. New York: The Free Press.

————. 1949–51 [1896]. "The Social Causes of the Decay of Ancient Civilization." *Journal of General Education* 4–5:75–88. Trans. Christian Mackauer. Reprinted in this volume.

————. 1951 [1920]. *The Religion of China*. Ed. and trans. H. H. Gerth. Glencoe, Ill.: The Free Press.

Weber, Max. 1952 [1921]. *Ancient Judaism*. Ed. and trans. H. H. Gerth and D. Martin-dale. New York: The Free Press.

———. 1958 [1921]. *The Religion of India*. Ed. and trans. H. H. Gerth and D. Martin-dale. New York: The Free Press.

———. 1964 [1913]. "Gutachten zur Werturteilsdiskussion im Ausschuss des Vereins für Sozialpolitik." Pp. 102–39 in Eduard Baumgarten, *Max Weber: Werk und Person*. Tübingen: J. C. B. Mohr.

———. 1969 [1922]. "The Three Types of Legitimate Rule." Trans. Hans Gerth. Pp. 6–15 in Amitai Etzioni, ed., *A Sociological Reader on Complex Organizations*. New York: Holt, Rinehart and Winston. Reprinted (in its complete version) in this volume.

———. 1971a [1908]. "Methodological Introduction for the Survey of the Society for So-cial Policy Concerning Selection and Adaptation (Choice and Source of Occupation) for the Workers of Major Industrial Enterprises." Trans. D. Hytch. Pp. 103–55 in Max Weber, *The Interpretation of Social Reality*. Ed. J. E. T. Eldridge. London: Nelson.

———. 1971b [1910]. "Max Weber on Race and Society." Trans. Jerome Gittleman. *So-cial Research* 38:30–41.

———. 1972a [1908]. "Georg Simmel as Sociologist." *Social Research* 39:156–63. Intro. and trans. Donald N. Levine. (The original German title is "Georg Simmel als Soziolog und Theoretiker der Geldwirtschaft.")

———. 1972b [1922]. *Wirtschaft und Gesellschaft: Grundriss der verstehenden Sozi-ologie*. 5th rev. ed. Studienausgabe. Tübingen: J. C. B. Mohr. (For the different edi-tions of this work, see the 1922 entry.)

———. 1973a [1910]. "Max Weber on Church, Sect, and Mysticism." *Sociological Analy-sis* 34:140–49. (Discussion by Weber and others of a lecture by Ernst Troeltsch at the 1910 meeting of the German Sociological Society.)

———. 1973b [1910]. "Max Weber, Dr. Alfred Ploetz, and W. E. B. DuBois (Max Weber on Race and Society II)." Trans. Jerome Gittleman. *Sociological Analysis* 34:308–12.

———. 1975a [1903–6]. *Roscher and Knies: The Logical Problems of Historical Eco-nomics*. Trans. Guy Oakes. New York: The Free Press.

———. 1975b [1908]. "Marginal Utility Theory and 'The Fundamental Law of Psy-chophysics.'" *Social Science Quarterly* 56:21–36. Trans. Louis Schneider. Reprinted in this volume.

———. 1976a [1909]. *The Agrarian Sociology of Ancient Civilizations*. Trans R. I. Frank. London: New Left Books.

———. 1976b [1911]. "The Schools of Economics [Die Handelshochschulen: Eine Ent-gegnung]." Pp. 36–39 in Max Weber, ed., *Max Weber on Universities*. Ed. Edward Shils. Chicago: University of Chicago Press.

———. 1977 [1907]. *Critique of Stammler*. Trans. Guy Oakes. New York: The Free Press.

———. 1978a [1894]. "The Stock Exchange." Pp. 374–77 in Max Weber, *Max Weber: Selections in Translation*. Ed. W. G. Runciman. Trans. Eric Matthews. Cambridge: Cambridge University Press.

———. 1978b [1907–10]. *Die protestantische Ethik, II: Kritiken und Antikritiken*. Ed. Johannes Winkelmann. Gütersloh: Gütersloher Verlagshaus Mohn.

———. 1978c [1910]. "Anticritical Last Word on *The Spirit of Capitalism*." *American Journal of Sociology* 83:1105–31.

———. 1978d [1922]. *Economy and Society: An Outline of Interpretive Sociology*. Ed. Guenther Roth and Claus Wittich. Trans. of the 4th German ed. (1956), ed. Ephraim Fischoff et al. 2 vols. Berkeley: University of California Press.

———. 1979 [1894]. "Development Tendencies in the Situation of East Elbian Rural Workers." Trans. Keith Tribe. *Economy and Society* 8:177–205.

———. 1980 [1895]. "The National State and Economic Policy (Freiburg Address)." Trans. Ben Fowkes. *Economy and Society* 9:29–50.

———. 1981a [1913]. "Some Categories of Interpretive Sociology." Trans. Edith E. Graber. *Sociological Quarterly* 22 (Spring): 151–80.

———. 1981b [1923]. *General Economic History*. Trans. Frank H. Knight. New Brunswick, N.J.: Transaction Books.

———. 1984a [1892]. *Die Lage der Landarbeiter im ostelbischen Deutschland, 1892. Max Weber Gesamtausgabe* I/3. Ed. Martin Riesebrodt. 2 vols. Tübingen: J. C. B. Mohr.

———. 1984b [1909]. "'Energetic' Theories of Culture." Trans. Jon Mark Mikkelsen. *Mid-American Review of Sociology* 9, no. 2:27–58.

———. 1985a [1895]. "'Roman' and 'Germanic' Law." Trans. Piers Beirne. *International Journal of the Sociology of Law* 13:237–46.

———. 1985b [1906]. "'Churches' and 'Sects' in North America: An Ecclesiastical Sociopolitical Sketch." Trans. Colin Loader. *Sociological Theory* 3:7–13.

———. 1986 [1891]. *Die römische Agrargeschichte in ihrer Bedeutung für das Staats- und Privatrecht, 1891. Max Weber Gesamtausgabe* I/2. Ed. Jürgen Deininger. Tübingen: J. C. B. Mohr.

———. 1988a [1889]. "Zur Geschichte der Handelsgesellschaften im Mittelalter." Pp. 312–443 in *Gesammelte Aufsätze zur Sozial- und Wirtschaftsgeschichte*. Tübingen: J. C. B. Mohr.

———. 1988b [1894–96]. "Die Börse." Pp. 256–88 in *Gesammelte Aufsätze zur Soziologie und Sozialpolitik*. Tübingen: J. C. B. Mohr.

———. 1988c [1909]. "Debattereden auf der Tagung des Vereins für Sozialpolitik in Wien 1909 zu den Verhandlungen über die Produktivität der Volkswirtschaft." Pp. 416–23 in *Gesammelte Aufsätze zur Soziologie und Sozialpolitik*. Tübingen: J. C. B. Mohr.

———. 1988d [1910]. "Diskussionsrede zu W. Sombarts Vortrag über Technik und Kultur. Erster Soziologentag." Pp. 449–56 in *Gesammelte Aufsätze zur Soziologie und Sozialpolitik*. Tübingen: J. C. B. Mohr.

———. 1988e [1920]. *Gesammelte Aufsätze zur Religionssoziologie*. Ed. Marianne Weber. Vol. 1. Tübingen: J. C. B. Mohr.

———. 1988f [1921]. *Gesammelte Aufsätze zur Religionssoziologie*. Vols. 2–3. Ed. Marianne Weber. Tübingen: J. C. B. Mohr.

———. 1988g [1924]. *Gesammelte Aufsätze zur Sozial- und Wirtschaftsgeschichte*. Ed. Marianne Weber. 2d ed. Tübingen: J. C. B. Mohr.

———. 1988h [1924]. *Gesammelte Aufsätze zur Soziologie und Sozialpolitik*. Ed. Marianne Weber. 2d ed. Tübingen: J. C. B. Mohr.

———. 1989 [1897]. "Germany as an Industrial Nation." Trans. Keith Tribe. Pp. 210–20 in Max Weber, *Reading Weber*. Ed. Keith Tribe. London: Routledge.

———. 1990 [1898]. *Grundriss zu den Vorlesungen über allgemeine ("theoretische") Nationalökonomie (1898)*. Tübingen: J. C. B. Mohr.

———. 1993a. *Landarbeiterfrage, Nationalstaat und Volkswirtschaftspolitik: Schriften und Reden 1892–1899. Max Weber Gesamtausgabe* I/4. Ed. Wolfgang J. Mommsen with Rita Aldenhoff. 2 vols. Tübingen: J. C. B. Mohr.

———. 1993b. *Die protestantische Ethik und der "Geist" des Kapitalismus*. Hain: Neue Wissenschaftliche Bibliotek Athenäum. (Marks changes that Weber made for the second edition of *The Protestant Ethic*.)

Weber, Max. 1994 [1919]. "Socialism." Pp. 272–303 in Max Weber, *Political Writings*. Ed. and trans. Peter Lassman and Ronald Speirs. Cambridge: Cambridge University Press.

———. 1995a. *Zur Psychophysik der industriellen Arbeit: Schriften und Reden 1908– 1912. Max Weber Gesamtausgabe I/11*. Ed. Wolfgang Schluchter with Sabine Frommer. Tübingen: J. C. B. Mohr.

———. 1995b [1909]. "On the Method of Social-Psychological Inquiry and Its Treatment" (reviews of works by Adolf Levinstein). Trans. Thomas W. Segady. *Sociological Theory* 13:102–6.

———. 1998. *Wirtschaft, Staat und Sozialpolitik. Max Weber Gesamtausgabe I/8*. Tübingen: J. C. B. Mohr.

Weiss, Johannes. 1981. *Das Werk Max Webers in der marxistischen Rezeption und Kritik*. Opladen: Westdeutscher Verlag.

Wieser, Friedrich von. [1914] 1927. *Social Economics*. Trans. A. Ford Hinrichs. London: George Allen & Unwin.

Wiley, Norbert. 1983. "The Congruence of Weber and Keynes." Pp. 30–57 in Randall Collins, ed., *Sociological Theory, 1983*. San Francisco: Jossey-Bass.

Winkel, Harald. 1977. *Die deutsche Nationalökonomie im 19. Jahrhundert*. Darmstadt: Wissenschaftliche Buchgesellschaft.

Winkelmann, Johannes. 1976. *Wirtschaft und Gesellschaft. Erläuterungsband*. Tübingen: J. C. B. Mohr.

———. 1986. *Max Webers hinterlassenes Hauptwerk: Die Wirtschaft und die gesellschaftlichen Ordnungen und Mächte*. Tübingen: J. C. B. Mohr.

Milton Keynes UK
Ingram Content Group UK Ltd.
UKHW022148131123
432504UK00001B/17/J